The Gateless Barrier

THE GATELESS BARRIER

Zen Comments on the Mumonkan

Zenkei Shibayama

Translated into English by
SUMIKO KUDO

SHAMBHALA
Boston
2000

Shambhala Publications, Inc.
Horticultural Hall
300 Massachusetts Avenue
Boston, Massachusetts 02115
www.shambhala.com

Previously published as *Zen Comments on the Mumonkan*.
Published by arrangement with HarperCollins Publishers, New York, New York.

Printed in the United States of America

♻ This edition is printed on acid-free paper that meets
the American National Standards Institute Z39.48 Standard.
Distributed in the United States by Random House, Inc.,
and in Canada by Random House of Canada Ltd

The Library of Congress Cataloging-in-Publication Data:
Shibayama, Zenkei, 1894–1974.
[Zen comments on the Mumonkan]
Gateless barrier: Zen comments on the Mumonkan / Zenkei Shibayama.
p. cm.
Originally published: Zen comments on the Mumonkan.
New York: Harper & Row, 1974.
Includes index.
ISBN 0-06-067279-X (cloth)
ISBN 1-57062-726-6 (pbk.)
1. Hui-k'ai, 1183–1260. Wu men kuan. 2. Koan
I. Title: Zen comments on the Mumonkan. II. Hui-k'ai, 1183-1260.
Wu men kuan. English. III. Title.
BQ9289.H843 S513   2000
294.3'443—dc21   00-041015

BVG 01

Contents

APPENDIX

Note on Calligraphy

Calligraphy is by Shibayama Roshi

Title page:	Bright Gem Is in Your Hand
Following page 15:	Purity: Clear Like a Cloud
Following page 163:	Mu: Orchids Have Elegance; Chrysanthemums Have Fragrance
Following page 267:	Serenity: Quietly Sitting, I Listen to the Pine Breeze

Preface

For more than seven centuries the *Mumonkan* has been used in Zen monasteries to train monks, and by lay Buddhists as a means of refining their religious experience. The *Mumonkan* is a thirteenth-century collection of the sayings and doings of Zen Masters in which they freely and directly express their Zen experience, together with commentary by Master Mumon. As guideposts to students in training, a Zen Master will often make his own comments, or teisho, on the *Mumonkan*.

After Shibayama Roshi, the Zen Master of Nanzenji Monastery in Kyoto, gave his teisho on passages from the *Mumonkan* to American college students, he was asked to supervise the translation of the *Mumonkan* into English and to write his comments based on the teisho he had been giving for a quarter-century to Zen students in training in his monastery.

These comments give an authentic introduction to Rinzai Zen for those who, when they study religious beliefs and practices other than their own, want to see the religious path as presented by its perceptive followers rather than as described by outsiders.

Zenkei Shibayama was born in 1894, ordained a Zen monk in 1908, entered Nanzenji Zen Monastery in 1916, and remained there in training for over ten years. He was finally given the Dharma Sanction by Abbot Bukai Kono of Nanzenji. He served as professor at Hanazono University and at Otani University for eight years. From 1948 to 1967 he was Zen Master (Roshi) of Nanzenji Zen Monastery. After 1959 he was head of the Nanzenji Organization of some five hundred Rinzai Zen temples in Japan.

This book would not have been possible in English without the skill and insight of Miss Sumiko Kudo, the translator. She was a lay disciple of Shibayama

Roshi, participating regularly in the monthly sesshin at Nanzenji and serving as his interpreter when he lectured in the United States.

John Moffitt has also helped by his critical reading of the manuscript.

There are no footnotes; explanations are included when they seem to be needed, as they would be in a spoken commentary. There is a glossary designed to identify names, places, and writings, and to clarify the Zen meaning of terms which might be unfamiliar to some readers.

It was an arduous task for Shibayama Roshi, then in his late seventies and burdened with his duties as head of the Nanzenji Organization, to write his teisho on the forty-eight koan of the *Mumonkan*. We are grateful to him for doing his part to "create refreshing Zen breezes in the world."

KENNETH W. MORGAN

Colgate University

Introduction

It was said of old that "silence is more suitable to Zen than eloquence." This is still true today. Zen is always based on the fact of religious experience which belongs to a dimension different from the various forms of culture and philosophy derived from it. This religious experience, which is of primary importance in Zen, must be personally had by each individual after hard and sincere searching and discipline, in either a natural or an artificially created situation. This is why intellectual explanations and interpretations, which are apt to be dualistically conceptualized, are flatly negated in Zen, and why actual training is considered to be a vital necessity.

In the long course of history, there grew up naturally a means of training designed to help students carry on their discipline correctly and effectively. This is Zen training by koan studies, which is called "Kanna-Zen" in Japanese. Koan are Zen Masters' sayings and doings in which they freely and directly express their Zen experience. The primary role of the koan in Zen is to help in the actual training of Zen monks. The philosophical or dogmatic studies of koan are of secondary significance because the standpoint of such studies is fundamentally different from that of *true* Zen training, in which the only aim is to experience and live the *real* working spirit of Zen.

In Japan today, the koan is widely and actively used at authentic Zen monasteries where training is carried on. In studying a koan two approaches are possible: one is for the student to take it up as the subject of scholastic or philosophical research, and another is to do zazen with it as a means of training. At a monastery, doing zazen with a koan is considered the authentic way to study it, and in order to help students with their koan studies, teisho is given by the Master.

Zazen is a most important Zen practice for a monk or student in training. When doing zazen the student sits in full lotus posture and tries to eradicate all of his discriminating consciousness in order to awaken to his True Self.

Teisho is the occasion for a Master to present directly and concretely his own Zen experience or spirituality to his disciples, using a specific koan. He may also give his comment on the koan from the fundamental Zen standpoint. The purpose of teisho is to give direction to the experiences of the monks in their search and their discipline, and to encourage and stimulate them. On the other hand, the purpose of a lecture is to explain Zen philosophically and dogmatically so that students may have an intellectual understanding of it. A lecture is therefore a kind of cultural activity and is not directly related to actual training.

Recently Zen has attracted general attention as a unique religion or religious philosophy which has greatly influenced various phases of Asian culture. Even though people in Europe and America have long been brought up in a quite different culture, they have now begun to show great interest in Zen. However, as everybody realizes, there are several obstacles to mutual understanding and exchange between Asian and non-Asian cultures: the language difficulty is one of the main hindrances, plus the difference in ways of thinking, in value systems, and in the patterns of their long traditions.

Our predecessors have untiringly tried to overcome these barriers to cultural exchange, but although much has been accomplished, thanks to their efforts, we cannot deny that the difficulties still definitely exist. In Zen, which insists that experience rather than speculative thought or philosophy is of primary importance, these difficulties in intercultural understanding are felt even more keenly.

It is for the purpose of contributing to intercultural understanding that I have decided to make these *Mumonkan* teisho available in English, and have worked hard together with my collaborators, sparing no efforts.

The book *Mumonkan* was originally published in China toward the end of the southern Sung dynasty (thirteenth century A.D.), and has ever since been famous in Zen circles as a representative koan collection. It is a handy volume with forty-eight koan. The commentary on each by Master Mumon, the compiler, is extremely direct and to the point, and the book is well suited to encourage the seeking and the training of monks. Because of the forty-eight outstanding koan, together with Mumon's incisive commentaries, *Mumonkan* has been widely used as a standard text in Zen circles in modern times, valued as equal to *Hekigan-roku* ("The Blue Rock Records"), another koan collection which is called "the first text of Zen." *Mumonkan* has naturally been the subject of a variety of teisho, lectures, talks, or commentaries, both good and bad. The few books written in English seem to require further study and revision.

This *Mumonkan* teisho translated into English is intended for those non-Asians who are interested in studying Zen. It presents the original text of the *Mumonkan* in English, and my teisho follows each original koan and commentary to illustrate their traditional significance. It also points out the direction of training for students. The book does not aim at making analytical or literary studies, and I have not gone into these details at all.

As is well known, Zen was most creative and vital in the T'ang dynasty (618–906 A.D.); then it began to develop cultural and artistic aspects and gradually took on a reminiscent, traditional character in the northern Sung dynasty. Finally, toward the end of the southern Sung dynasty, training in Zen by koan studies was established, and the *Mumonkan* appeared in response to the requirements of the time. It fulfilled this historical mission.

Although the *Mumonkan* and the *Hekigan-roku* are both koan collections, their historical background and the significance of their appearance are naturally different. These differences are reflected in the characteristics of the books: while the *Hekigan-roku* is poetic and spiritual with literary splendor, the *Mumonkan* is direct, straightforward, with a stimulating and disciplinary tone, and is apparently designed to encourage the actual training of monks.

Because of these characteristic differences, it is often commented that the *Mumonkan* is stiff and argumentative, and compared to the *Hekigan-roku* less elegant, lacking poetic refinement. This may of course be due to Master Mumon's personal disposition. We have also to remember that the *Mumonkan* came into the world with the historical task of establishing Zen by koan studies, and the character of the book may have been the natural result of attempting to meet such a requirement. In other words, the *Mumonkan* serves to shatter the intellectual understanding and reasoning of the monks, and in this respect can be used as a textbook in actual Zen training. The *Hekigan-roku,* on the other hand, is a highly refined and literary Zen text which shows the noble, lofty, and profound spirituality of Zen.

When the different characteristics of these two Zen texts are considered, I think it most opportune that the *Mumonkan* has been translated first. Just when Zen is being introduced to the world as a universal approach to Truth, it is in good order that these *Mumonkan* teisho should be made available in English prior to the *Hekigan-roku.*

Although I use the term, ''teisho'' in English for European and American students is naturally different in its significance and purpose from the traditional teisho I give to the monks in my monastery in Japan. It is significant that I first felt the necessity for publishing this book in English when I participated in the course of Zen study in the January Special Studies Program at Colgate University in the United States a few years ago. In that course I used some koan from the *Mumonkan* to give my teisho to the students, and my experience there led me to undertake this work.

I am thankful to those who have helped me complete this book. My special appreciation and respect go to Professor Kenneth W. Morgan of Colgate University, who assumed the most difficult and unrewarding task of checking the English translation and editing the manuscript.

I am happy that the book may be a pioneer in helping those who want to study Zen seriously as a guide to actual training, and I am grateful for the historical and cultural role it may play at the time when Zen is beginning to be studied throughout the world.

ZENKEI SHIBAYAMA

Nanzenji, Kyoto
May 1974

ZEN COMMENTS ON THE MUMONKAN

Shuan's Preface to the *Mumonkan*

If it is explained as "no-gate," everybody on earth will enter through it. If it is explained that there is a gate, our dear Master did not have to choose such a title in the first place. He dared to add notes and commentaries, which is very much like putting one more hat on top of another. I, old Shu, was urged to write complimentary words about the book. This is like squeezing the sap out of a dried-up bamboo and putting it on a children's book. Throw it away without waiting for me to do so. Let no drop of it fall into the world. Even Usui, the finest horse, which gallops a thousand miles, would never be able to pursue it.

End of July, first year of Jotei [1228]
Written by Shuan Chin Ken

TEISHO ON SHUAN'S PREFACE

Shuan, whose real name was Ken, was remarkably brilliant from his childhood and passed the civil service examination of the government at an early age. Later he was promoted to a high government position. He is said to have been an unusually bright and refined man of taste and culture. Although the details of his life are not known, as far as we can see from the preface he must have had a considerable understanding and interest in Zen, too. Or it may have been a general requirement of the time that any first-class gentleman who might be asked to write a preface to a book like the *Mumonkan* would certainly have an understanding of Zen.

On the surface Shuan reviles the *Mumonkan* from beginning to end. Because of his derogatory expressions there are some who conclude that he is denouncing it as a good-for-nothing book. The fact is just the opposite. Shuan is praising it highly by freely using abusive language. This contradictory, ironic way of writing, which recurs frequently among the old Masters, makes his preface very interesting.

First he takes up the name of the book, *Mumonkan,* "The Gateless Barrier." With paradoxical expressions he tries to make the true significance of "Mumon" (no-gate, or gateless) clear. "If there is actually no gate, everybody on earth must be able to go through it. If, on the contrary, there is a gate, you must not choose the name 'Mumon' [no-gate] to begin with." Shuan's remark is quite scathing, and with these cutting words he tries to illustrate "it"—that which transcends both yes and no, affirmation and negation.

Shuan goes on to say in the second sentence, "If there is actually no gate, one can go freely in and out, and there is no need for any explanation; yet you made all sorts of commentaries on the forty-eight koan, wrote poems and added notes on them. It is all so unnecessary and even foolish, just like putting another hat on the one that is already on your head." From earliest times Zen has insisted on "not relying on letters," stressing that "it" has to be attained by oneself personally, has to be experienced as one's own actual fact. From that standpoint, Shuan is right in making such a criticism. We must not, however, overlook his real intention to try to clarify the characteristics of Zen.

In the third sentence Shuan says, "Nevertheless, Mumon has asked me to write a preface to the book. Yet how can such a book be praised? Besides, I am not by nature very smart, so even if I wrote something, it would be as if I should try to squeeze the sap out of a dried-up bamboo and put it on this childish book. It is all useless and of no avail." Essentially, the Great Tao, Truth, has no gate; it can neither be affirmed nor denied. All attempts in the world of words and letters are of no avail. Here again Shuan is praising Zen in his unique paradoxical way.

"A book like this had better be thrown away immediately. Do not wait for me to do it. Never let it circulate in the world even a little." Thus Shuan flatly negates the book in the next sentence. Did not Master Daie burn up the *Hekigan-roku,* a book written by his teacher Master Engo? Why does Zen, which does not rely on letters and is transmitted outside scriptures, need a book? With these high words Shuan is in fact expressing his wholehearted appreciation and is also displaying characteristics of Zen.

He ends his preface with "Even Usui, the finest horse, which gallops a thousand miles, would never be able to pursue it." "The black horse that gallops a thousand miles" figuratively means the fastest possible speed. Once upon a time, it was said, the famous brave Chinese general Kou had a fine black horse named Usui which could gallop a thousand miles a day. Today it might be compared to a supersonic airplane. Even such a swift steed will never be able to catch up with it. In other words, if once a foolish slip is made, it is forever irreparable however much you may regret it.

By way of emphatic paradox, Shuan tries to give a true picture of Zen experience, which transcends all discriminations and reasoning. This is indeed an interesting and significant preface, in which Shuan admires the *Mumonkan* in his own unique manner.

Dedication to the Throne

On the fifth of January, the second year of Jotei, I celebrate the anniversary of Your Majesty. I, Monk Ekai, on the fifth of November of last year, published a commentary on forty-eight koan that the Buddhas and Patriarchs had given on various occasions. I dedicate this book to Your Majesty's eternal prosperity.

I respectfully express my wish that your imperial virtue may be as bright as the sun and the moon. May your royal life be as long as that of the universe. May people in the eight directions praise your virtue, and of the four seas enjoy your supremely blessed reign.

Respectfully written by
Monk Ekai,
The Dharma Transmitter,
Former Abbot of Hoinyuji,
The Zen Temple dedicated to Empress Jii

Master Mumon's Preface

Zen-shu Mumonkan
"The Gateless Barrier of Zen"

The Buddha Mind is the basis, and gateless is the Dharma Gate. If it is gateless, how can you pass through it? Have you not heard that "nothing that enters by the gate can be a family treasure—whatever is causally gained is always subject to change"? These talks would serve to stir up waves where there is no wind, or to gash a wound in a healthy skin. Even more foolish is one who clings to words and phrases and thus tries to achieve understanding. It is like trying to strike the moon with a stick, or scratching a shoe because there is an itchy spot on the foot. It has nothing to do with the Truth.

In the summer of the first year of Jotei [1228], I, Ekai, was the head of the monks at Ryusho in Toka. The monks begged me for instruction. Finally I took up the koan of ancient Masters and used them as brickbats to knock at the gate in guiding the monks in accordance with their capabilities and types. I have noted down these koan and they have now unwittingly become quite a collection. There are now forty-eight of them, which I have not arranged in any order. I will call the collection the *Mumonkan,* "The Gateless Barrier."

If a fellow is brave, he will plunge straight in with no regard to any danger. The eight-armed Nata may try to stop him, but in vain. Even the twenty-eight Patriarchs of India and the six Patriarchs of China would cower at his bravery and have to beg for their lives. If he hesitates, however, he will be like a man watching a horse gallop past the window. In the twinkling of an eye it is already gone.

MUMON'S POEM

> Gateless is the Great Tao,
> There are thousands of ways to it.
> If you pass through this barrier,
> You may walk freely in the universe.

TEISHO ON MUMON'S PREFACE

The compiler of the *Mumonkan*, Master Mumon, was born in 1183 in the southern Sung dynasty, at Sento of Koshu, and died on April 7, 1260, in his seventy-eighth year. He was born when the hour of the doom of the southern Sung dynasty was at hand because of the increasing pressures of neighboring nations.

Master Mumon was first ordained as a Buddhist monk under Master Tenryu Ko and later moved to Master Getsurin Shikan. He studied very hard with the koan "Has a Dog the Buddha Nature?" under Master Getsurin for six long years, going through most assiduous training, and one day when he heard the drumbeat he was suddenly enlightened. The poem he made on that occasion is:

> A thunderclap under a clear blue sky!
> All beings on earth have opened their eyes.
> Everything under the sun has bowed at once.
> Mount Sumeru jumps up and dances.

The next day Mumon presented his attainment to Master Getsurin, who verified his satori. Finally he succeeded the Master. It was in Mumon's forty-sixth year that he published the *Mumonkan*, a collection of forty-eight koan with his commentaries which he had given at Ryushoji in Toka.

By imperial order, Master Mumon founded Gokoku Ninnoji when he was in his sixty-fourth year. Later he wanted to lead a quiet retired life by Lake Seiko, but was not able to do so because there were always truth-seekers calling on him one after another.

Mumon is described in this poem:

> The Master looked thin and holy,
> His words were simple but profound.
> Long and dark his hair and beard;
> He was clothed in tattered rags.

He was nicknamed Lay Monk Ekai.

Master Mumon wrote a preface to this collection, and a commentary on each koan. His writing is in the direct and exclamatory Zen style popular among Zen Masters in those days; he never tried to explain or preach.

From of old it has been a point at issue whether the first phrase, "Zen-shu Mumonkan," is the title of the book or the first sentence, meaning "There is no gate in Zen." I have followed the traditional, generally accepted interpretation here that it is the title.

At the very beginning of the Preface Master Mumon clarifies the basic characteristics of Zen and his attitude toward expression in words and letters. "The Buddha Mind is the basis, and gateless is the Dharma Gate"—these words, first used by Master Baso in his teisho to his disciples, were quoted originally from *Ryoga-kyo* (the Lankavatara Sutra). With these first two lines Master Mumon concisely defines Zen. He may have used the term "Mumon" ("gateless" or "no-gate") with reference to the title of his own book, too.

"Zen is based on the mind or the spirit of Buddha's sayings. In other words, the formless Reality, which is called the Buddha Mind, True Mind, Original Nature, etc., is its basis. Zen therefore never establishes or provides creeds or dogmas of any sort, any forms at all. No definition, no limitation: that is, no-gate is the only invaluable Dharma Gate to Zen." Thus at the beginning Master Mumon clarifies the primary standpoint of Zen.

He then goes on to give teisho-commentary on "Mumon" (no-gate), which he has just emphasized as the foundation of Zen. "Since there is no gate from the beginning, there can be no question of passing or not passing through it. Now, how do you pass through this no-gate? Those who can really pass through it, do so and show it to me," Mumon challenges. Here is, however, an important experiential question to be answered in actual training by each individual, that is, whether to regard Mumon as no-gate and not to concern oneself about it, or to take no-gate as a barrier and break through it. Each student has to take it up as a concrete question of his self-realization.

Mumon then quotes an old saw to show what the real no-gate is: "Nothing that enters by the gate can be a family treasure. Whatever is causally gained is always subject to change." The real, invaluable treasure is that which has always been kept in the family and not something that has been brought in from outside. Anything gained by chance will finally be lost by change. "It," which is essentially in oneself, is eternally unchanging. This noncoming, nongoing "it" does definitely pass through no-gate, and freely works everywhere with no-form.

"Nothing that enters by the gate can be a family treasure" is an old popular saying in China which means "Nothing given by others can be really good."

Anything received from others will not have sufficient value to deserve being treasured as an heirloom. What is basically in oneself is the real treasure with eternal value.

This saying may have reference to the following mondo between Master Ganto and his disciple Seppo. Once long ago, when Master Seppo was studying under Master Ganto, the latter rebuked him for searching outwardly, outside himself, and said, "Have you not heard that 'nothing that enters by the gate can be a family treasure'?" Seppo asked in return, "How should I carry on with my training then?" Ganto replied, "If you want to get and spread the Great Truth, grasp 'it' that flows out of your own mind, and present it here for me!"

Do not seek outwardly, but get hold of "it," which gushes out of your own mind. If you foolishly look after others' treasures saying that it is so written in this holy book, or it is thus explained by that wise man, you can never pass through this gate of no-gate. Mumon thus warns us.

He goes on to say, "These talks would serve to stir up waves where there is no wind, or to gash a wound in a healthy skin." "These talks" refers to the forty-eight koan compiled in this book and the commentaries on them. From the primary standpoint of Zen the forty-eight talks are all unnecessary waste. To give them is just like raising waves on a windless quiet sea, or performing an operation on a beautiful natural skin and leaving an ugly scar. It is unnecessary meddling. And being unnecessary it does much harm. Mumon thus denounces the whole book as a meaningless effort.

"To gash a wound in a healthy skin" means, metaphorically, to do something unnecessary and useless. The expression may have been taken from Master Unmon's saying, "Even if you were capable of clarifying the whole universe by twisting a single hair, it would be as meaningless as gashing a wound in the skin."

Mumon further disparages the foolishness of the person who "clings to words and phrases and thus tries to achieve understanding."

To introduce a lot of talk is already uncalled-for meddling. The foolishness of the person who clings to words and phrases, interprets them intellectually, and thus tries to understand is preposterous and beyond description. Such people may be compared to the man who tries to strike the moon with a stick and scratches his shoe because he has an itchy spot on his foot. "It has nothing to do with the Truth." Mumon emphatically speaks of the foolishness of such a letter-bound student.

From the fundamental standpoint of Zen, which declares no-gate to be its Dharma Gate, it is meaningless and useless to introduce these forty-eight koan and give teisho on them. It is as foolish as trying to strike the moon or as scratching a shoe when one has an itchy foot. Such meddling has nothing to do with the gate of no-gate. Mumon harshly criticizes his own book as an altogether unnecessary effort. What is Mumon's real intention in ending the first part of his own preface with these strong words? Using such abusive language, based on the fundamental standpoint of Zen, Mumon wants us to open our eyes to the Truth of Zen, the Absolute. In other words, he urges us to pass firmly and directly through no-gate.

In the second part, changing his tone, Mumon explains how this book was made. "In the summer of the first year of Jotei [1228], I, Ekai, was the head of the monks at Ryusho in Toka. The monks begged me for instruction. Finally I took up the koan of ancient Masters and used them as brickbats to knock at the gate in guiding the monks in accordance with their capabilities and types."

Mumon says, "When I was the head monk at the Ryushoji Monastery of Mount Koshin in the summer of 1228, the monks begged me to give them some instruction that might be useful for them in their training. Being unable to turn down their earnest request, I finally told them old Zen Masters' mondo and sayings which have been studied as koan, as a means of instructing the monks in accordance with their abilities and inclinations. From the fundamental standpoint of Zen "it" can never be taught or shown by others, yet I hoped these koan might serve as brickbats to knock at the door, or as a finger pointing to the moon until no-gate might be opened. The notes and records of these koan and commentaries have in the course of time become considerable and I now have forty-eight koan. I have not arranged them in any order, but gave them one at a time. I have now compiled this collection, and will name it *Mumonkan.*"

In the first year of Jotei (1228) Master Mumon was forty-six years old. The power of the southern Sung dynasty had begun to wane. Toward the end of the dynasty the nation was in a state of confusion. Zen, too, was gradually declining, without the lively spirit it used to have in its heyday. A book like the *Mumonkan,* to be used as a good manual for monks in training, was much needed then. It was at such a time that Master Mumon appeared in the world and met the current needs of the students of Zen. In short, the *Mumonkan* may be characterized as a standard Zen text designed to point out the direction for students in their training.

In concluding his own preface, Master Mumon raises his voice and addresses his disciples: "A truly brave man will plunge straight into the Reality of no-gate, staking his own life. He will never hesitate, no matter what danger may be involved. Then even a demon with supernatural power like Nata will be unable to interfere with the training of such a brave truth-seeker. Before such a courageous monk, even the twenty-eight Patriarchs of India and the succeeding six Chinese Patriarchs will cower in wonder at his sincere searching and will have to beg for their lives." With much emphasis Mumon encourages the students to give their hearts and souls to their discipline.

He goes on to say, "If, on the contrary, you hesitate to stake your life on your training, you will miss it in an instant, just as if you were to catch a glimpse of a horse galloping past the window. You will immediately lose sight of the Zen mind and will never be able even to approach the gate of no-gate." Mumon ends his preface with these stimulating words with which he tells us how difficult it is to attain Zen Truth, as well as stirring up in us a strong will and intrepid spirit.

TEISHO ON MUMON'S POEM

> Gateless is the Great Tao,
> There are thousands of ways to it.
> If you pass through this barrier,
> You may walk freely in the universe.

"The Great Tao" is the "Ultimate Way," "Supreme Truth," and the essence of Zen. It may be called by various names, but the fundamental Truth is one and ever unchanging. Therefore the Great Tao has no gate. Because it is gateless, it is now in front of you and suddenly you see it behind you. It pervades the universe.

The Japanese word for Tao is "michi," which means "abounding." It is abundant everywhere.

Long ago in China a monk asked Master Gensha, "I am a novice just arrived at this monastery. From where can I enter into Zen?" Gensha said, "Can you hear the murmuring of the mountain stream?" "Yes, I can," replied the monk. "Enter Zen from there," was Master Gensha's answer.

Enter from anywhere freely. It is all open in every direction and is gateless. Rather, I should say, because it is gateless it is the Great Tao. There is no argument about passing through or not passing through. It is therefore said, "There are thousands of ways to it." The fact that it is gateless means that everything as it is is "it." Also it means there are infinitely different ways to it. An old Zen Master said, "Look under your feet!" If you stand, the very place where you stand is Tao. If you sit down, the very place you sit on is Tao. In fact, to say the Great Tao is gateless is only a partial truth. To say there are thousands of ways to it is also a half-truth. Apart from the principle of fundamental equality, there can never be phenomena of differentiation. Apart from the phenomena of differentiation, there can never be the principle of fundamental equality. Equality is at once differentiation; differentiation is at once equality—this is how the Great Tao is. This is the Reality of no-gate, which transcends both yes and no, affirmation and negation.

An old proverb says, "Fish do not know of water while they are in water." However true it may be that everyone lives in the Great Tao, if he does not realize the fact then we have to say that there definitely is the gate of no-gate for him. Zen Masters then have to insist on his breaking through the gateless barrier. From this secondary point of view Master Mumon declares,

> If you pass through this barrier,
> You may walk freely in the universe.

As repeatedly stressed, Zen is not something to be philosophically thought about or intellectually understood. It has to be the concrete fact personally attained by one's realization experience. Thus in Zen the religious experience of breaking through the gateless barrier is the absolute requisite for every student. When he has actually broken through the barrier, he can for the first time declare as an actual fact that it is gateless. He is then wholly free, and there will be nothing in the universe that interferes with his creative working. Until one has this experience, his no-gate remains an idea and a concept.

Master Rinzai says, in describing this absolute freedom of striding through the universe, "Once you are the Absolute Master [subjectively], wherever you may be, everything is true for you. Circumstances may change but they cannot affect you."

This is the new vista of Zen that will be opened to you when you have actually broken through the Great Tao that has no gate. This is the Zen life which you will freely develop. Master Mumon presents the true picture of the Great Tao in a poem, and asks for the renewed determination of his monks to carry on with their training.

KOAN

1

Joshu's "Mu"

A monk once asked Master Joshu, "Has a dog the Buddha Nature or not?" Joshu said, "Mu!"

In studying Zen, one must pass the barriers set up by ancient Zen Masters. For the attainment of incomparable satori, one has to cast away his discriminating mind. Those who have not passed the barrier and have not cast away the discriminating mind are all phantoms haunting trees and plants.

Now, tell me, what is the barrier of the Zen Masters? Just this "Mu"— it is the barrier of Zen. It is thus called "the gateless barrier of Zen." Those who have passed the barrier will not only see Joshu clearly, but will go hand in hand with all the Masters of the past, see them face to face. You will see with the same eye that they see with and hear with the same ear. Wouldn't it be wonderful? Don't you want to pass the barrier? Then concentrate yourself into this "Mu," with your 360 bones and 84,000 pores, making your whole body one great inquiry. Day and night work intently at it. Do not attempt nihilistic or dualistic interpretations. It is like having bolted a red hot iron ball. You try to vomit it but cannot.

Cast away your illusory discriminating knowledge and consciousness accumulated up to now, and keep on working harder. After a while, when your efforts come to fruition, all the oppositions (such as in and out) will naturally be identified. You will then be like a dumb person who has had a wonderful dream: he only knows it personally, within himself. Suddenly you break through the barrier; you will astonish heaven and shake the earth.

It is as if you have snatched the great sword of General Kan. You kill the Buddha if you meet him; you kill the ancient Masters if you meet them. On the brink of life and death you are utterly free, and in the six realms and the four modes of life you live, with great joy, a genuine life in complete freedom.

Now, how should one strive? With might and main work at this "Mu," and *be* "Mu." If you do not stop or waver in your striving, then behold, when the Dharma candle is lighted, darkness is at once enlightened.

MUMON'S POEM

> The dog! The Buddha Nature!
> The Truth is manifested in full.
> A moment of yes-and-no:
> Lost are your body and soul.

TEISHO ON THE KOAN

This koan is extremely short and simple. Because of this simplicity, it is uniquely valuable and is an excellent koan.

Joshu is the name of a place in northern China, and Master Junen (778–897) who lived in Kannon-in Temple at Joshu, is now generally known as Master Joshu. He was an exceptionally long-lived Zen Master who died at the age of one hundred and twenty years.

Joshu was fifty-seven years old when his teacher Nansen died. The great persecution of Buddhism by Emperor Bu-so (845) took place in Joshu's sixty-seventh year, Master Rinzai Gigen died (867) in Joshu's ninetieth year, and Master Gyozan died when he was in his one hundred and fifteenth year. This means that Joshu lived toward the end of the T'ang dynasty when Zen with its creative spirits flourished in China. At that time Joshu was one of the leading figures in Zen circles. People who described his Zen said, "His lips give off light," and greatly respected him.

Joshu was born in a village near Soshufu in the southwestern part of Santosho and entered a Buddhist temple when he was a young boy. Later, while he was still young, he came to Chishu to study under Master Nansen.

When he first met Nansen, the latter was resting in bed. Nansen asked him, "Where have you been recently?" "At Zuizo [literally "auspicious image"], Master," replied Joshu. "Did you then see the Auspicious Image?" the Master asked. Joshu said, "I did not see the Image, but I have seen a reclining Tathagata." Nansen then got up and asked, "Do you already have a Master to study under or not?" Joshu replied, "I have." Nansen asked, "Who is he?" At this, Joshu came closer to Nansen and, bowing to him, said, "I am glad to see you so well in spite of such a severe cold." Nansen recognized in him unusual character and allowed him to be his disciple. After that, Joshu steadily carried on his Zen studies under Nansen.

When Joshu was fifty-seven years old, his Master Nansen died, and four years later Joshu started on a pilgrimage with the determination: "Even a seven-year-old child, if he is greater than I am, I'll ask him to teach me. Even a hundred-year-old man, if I am greater than he is, I'll teach him." He continued on the pilgrimage to deepen and refine his Zen spirituality until he reached his eightieth year. Later he stayed at Kannon-in Temple, in Joshu, and was active as a leading Zen Master of the time in northern China, together with Rinzai.

In the biography of Joshu a series of mondo are recorded, from which this koan is extracted. There have been many attempts to interpret these mondo and to explain the koan in relation to them. We do not have to worry about such attempts here but should directly grip the koan itself. Knowing well its context, Master Mumon presents a simple, direct, and clear koan. Its simplicity plays an important role.

"A monk once asked Master Joshu, 'Has a dog the Buddha Nature or not?' " This monk was well aware that all sentient beings have the Buddha Nature without exception. This is therefore a piercingly effective and unapproachable question which would not be answered if the Master were to say Yes or No. The monk is demanding that Joshu show him the real Buddha Nature, and he is not asking for its interpretation or conceptual understanding. What a cutting question!

Joshu, like the genuine capable Master that he was, answered "Mu!" without the least hesitation. He threw himself—the whole universe—out as "Mu" in front of the questioner. Here is no Joshu, no world, but just "Mu." This is the koan of Joshu's "Mu."

The experience of the Buddha Nature itself is creatively expressed here by "Mu." Although literally "Mu" means No, in this case it points to the incomparable satori which transcends both yes and no, to the religious experience of the Truth one can attain when he casts away his discriminating mind. It has nothing to do with the dualistic interpretation of yes and no, being and nonbeing. It is Truth itself, the Absolute itself.

Joshu, the questioning monk, and the dog are however only incidental to the story, and they do not have any vital significance in themselves. Unless one grasps the koan within himself as he lives here and now, it ceases to be a real koan. We should not read it as an old story; you yourself have to *be* directly "Mu" and make not only the monk, but Joshu as well, show the white feather. Then the Buddha Nature is "Mu"; Joshu is "Mu." Not only that, you yourself and the whole universe are nothing but "Mu." Further, "Mu" itself falls far short, it is ever the unnamable "it."

Master Daie says, "Joshu's 'Mu'—work directly at it. Be just it." He is telling us to be straightforwardly no-self, be "Mu," and present it right here. This is a very inviting instruction indeed.

Once my own teacher, Master Bukai, threw his nyoi (a stick about fifty centimeters long which a Zen Master always carries with him) in front of me and demanded, "Now, transcend the yes-and-no of this nyoi!" and he did not allow me even a moment's hesitation. Training in Zen aims at the direct experience of breaking through to concrete Reality. That breaking through to Reality has to be personally attained by oneself. Zen can never be an idea or knowledge, which are only shadows of Reality. You may reason out that "Mu" transcends both yes and no, that it is the Absolute Oneness where all dualistic discrimination is exhausted. While you are thus conceptualizing, real "Mu" is lost forever.

My teacher also asked me once, "Show me the form of 'Mu'!" When I said, "It has no form whatsoever," he pressed me, saying "I want to see that form which has no-form." How cutting and drastic! Unless one can freely and clearly present the form of "Mu," it turns out to be a meaningless corpse.

In the biography of Master Hakuin we read the following moving story of his first encounter with his teacher, Master Shoju. Shoju asked Hakuin, "Tell me, what is Joshu's 'Mu'?" Hakuin elatedly replied, "Pervading the universe! Not a spot whatsoever to take hold of!" As soon as he had given that answer, Shoju took hold of Hakuin's nose and gave it a twist. "I am quite at ease to take hold of it," said Shoju, laughing aloud. The next moment he released it and abused Hakuin, "You! Dead monk in a cave! Are you self-satisfied with such 'Mu'?" This completely put Hakuin out of countenance.

We have to realize that this one word "Mu" has such exhaustive depth and lucidity that once one has really grasped it as his own he has the ability to penetrate all Zen koans.

Often people remark that "Mu" is an initial koan for beginners, which is a great mistake. A koan in Zen is fundamentally different from questions and problems in general. Etymologically the term *koan* means "the place where the truth is." In actual training its role is to smash up our dualistic consciousness and open our inner spiritual eye to a new vista. In actual cases there may be differences in the depth of the spirituality and ability of Zen students who break through a koan. This is inevitable for human beings living in this world. For any koan, however, there should be no such discrimination or gradation as an initial koan for beginners or difficult ones for the advanced. An old Zen Master said, "If you break through one koan, hundreds and thousands of koan have all been penetrated at once." Another Master said, "It is like cutting a reel of thread: one cut, and all is cut."

The use of a koan in Zen training developed spontaneously in the southern Sung dynasty in China when a reminiscent, traditionalist tendency began to prevail in Zen circles. In the early period of the southern Sung, Joshu's "Mu" was already being used widely as a koan. Mumon himself was driven into the abyss of Great Doubt by this koan and finally had the experience of breaking through it. Out of his own training and experience, he must have extracted the most essential part from several mondo and presented it to his disciples as a simple, direct koan.

This koan is taken from a mondo between Joshu and a monk, and *Joshu Zenji Goroku* ("Sayings of Master Joshu") and a few other books record similar mondo. In the chapter "Joshu Junen" in *Goto Egen*, volume 4, we read, "A monk asked Joshu, 'Has a dog the Buddha Nature or not?' The Master said, 'Mu.' The monk asked, 'From Buddhas above down to creeping creatures like ants, all have the Buddha Nature. Why is it that a dog has not?' 'Because he has ignorance and attachment,' the Master replied."

Joshu Zenji Goroku has the following mondo: "A monk asked, 'Has a dog the Buddha Nature or not?' The Master said, 'Mu.' Monk: 'Even creeping creatures all have the Buddha Nature. Why is it that the dog has not?' Master: 'Because he has ignorance and attachment.' "

Another monk asked Joshu, "Has a dog the Buddha Nature or not?" The Master said, "U" (Yes). The monk asked, "Having the Buddha Nature, why is he in such a dog-body?" Master: "Knowingly he dared to be so."

Although generally Joshu is supposed to have originated this mondo on the Buddha Nature, we read the following mondo in the biography of Master Ikan (755–817) of Kozenji at Keicho: Monk: "Has a dog the Buddha Nature or not?" Master: "Yes" (U). Monk: "Have you, O Master, the Buddha Nature or not?" Master: "I have not." Monk: "All sentient beings have the Buddha Nature. Why is it that you alone, Master, have not?" Master: "I am not among all sentient beings." Monk: "If you are not among sentient beings, are you then a Buddha or not?" Master: "I am not a Buddha." Monk: "What kind of thing are you after all?" Master: "I am not a thing either." Monk: "Can it be seen and thought of?" Master: "Even if you try to think about it and know it, you are unable to do so. It is therefore called 'unknowable.' " (*Keitoku Dento-roku*, volume 7)

Let us put aside for the time being historical studies of the koan. "Mu" as a koan is to open our spiritual eye to Reality, to "Mu," that is, to Joshu's Zen —this is the sole task of this koan, and everything else is just complementary and not of primary importance. We may simply read about it for our information.

All sentient beings without exception have the Buddha Nature. This is the fundamental Truth of nondualism and equality. On the other hand, this actual world of ours is dualistic and full of discriminations. The above mondo presents to us the basic contradiction between the fundamental Truth of nondualism and actual phenomena. The ancient Masters made us face the fact that we human beings from the very beginning have been living in this fundamental contradiction. It was the compassion of the Masters that led them to try thus to intensify their disciples' Great Doubt, their spiritual quest, and finally lead them to satori by breaking through it. If here one really breaks through this koan, which uniquely presents before him the core of human contradiction, he can clearly see for himself with his genuine Zen eye what these mondo are trying to tell us.

TEISHO ON MUMON'S COMMENTARY

Mumon comments: "In studying Zen, one must pass the barriers set up by ancient Zen Masters. For the attainment of incomparable satori, one has to cast away his discriminating mind. Those who have not passed the barrier and have not cast away the discriminating mind are all phantoms haunting trees and plants.

"Now, tell me, what is the barrier of the Zen Masters? Just this 'Mu'— it is the barrier of Zen. It is thus called 'the gateless barrier of Zen.' Those who have passed the barrier will not only see Joshu clearly, but will go hand in hand with all the Masters of the past, see them face to face. You will see with the same eye that they see with and hear with the same ear. Wouldn't it be wonderful? Don't you want to pass the barrier? Then concentrate yourself into this 'Mu,' with your 360 bones and 84,000 pores, making your whole body one great inquiry. Day and night work intently at it. Do not attempt nihilistic or dualistic interpretations. It is like having bolted a red hot iron ball. You try to vomit it but cannot.

"Cast away your illusory discriminating knowledge and consciousness accumulated up to now, and keep on working harder. After a while, when your efforts come to fruition, all the oppositions (such as in and out) will naturally be identified. You will then be like a dumb person who has had a wonderful dream: he only knows it personally, within himself. Suddenly you break through the barrier; you will astonish heaven and shake the earth.

"It is as if you have snatched the great sword of General Kan. You kill the Buddha if you meet him; you kill the ancient Masters if you meet them. On the brink of life and death you are utterly free, and in the six realms and the four modes of life you live, with great joy, a genuine life in complete freedom.

"Now, how should one strive? With might and main work at this 'Mu,' and be 'Mu.' If you do not stop or waver in your striving, then behold, when the Dharma candle is lighted, darkness is at once enlightened."

According to Master Mumon's biography, he stayed in a cave in a mountain where he practiced zazen and disciplined himself for six long years. In spite of such hard training he could not fundamentally satisfy his spiritual quest. It was this koan of "Joshu's 'Mu' " that made him plunge into the abyss of Great Doubt and finally attain satori, breaking through it as if the bottom had fallen out of a barrel. His commentary on this koan is therefore especially kind and detailed. He tells us most frankly of the hard training he himself went through and tries to guide Zen students on the basis of his own experiences.

"In studying Zen, one must pass the barriers set up by the ancient Zen Masters. For the attainment of incomparable satori, one has to cast away his discriminating mind."

First Mumon tells us what must be the right attitude for a Zen student, that is, what is fundamentally required of him in studying Zen. As Master Daiye says, "Satori is the fundamental experience in Zen." One has to cast his ordinary self away and be reborn as a new Self in a different dimension. In other words, the student must personally have the inner experience called satori, by which he is reborn as the True Self. This fundamental experience of awakening is essential in Zen. Although various different expressions are used when talking about the fact of this religious awakening, it cannot be real Zen without it. Mumon therefore declares at the very beginning that "in studying Zen one must pass the barriers set up by the ancient Zen Masters." The barrier of the ancient Zen Masters is the barrier to Zen, and the obstacle to transcend is the dualism of yes and no, subject and object. Practically, the sayings of ancient Masters, which are called koan, are such barriers.

The phrase "incomparable satori" indicates the eternal emancipation or absolute freedom that is attained by directly breaking through the Zen barrier. In order to break through it, Mumon stresses that one must once and for all cast away his discriminating mind completely. "Discriminating mind" is our ordinary consciousness, which is dualistic, discriminating, and the cause of all sorts of illusions. Mumon asks us to cast this away. To get rid of it requires that one's whole being must be the koan. There should be nothing left, and the secret of Zen lies in this really throwing oneself away. One does not have to ask what would be likely to happen after that; whatever happens would naturally and automatically come about without any seeking for it. What is important here is for him to actually do it himself.

"Those who have not passed the barrier and have not cast away the discriminating mind are all phantoms haunting trees and plants."

There is a superstition that the phantoms of those who after death are not in peace haunt trees and plants and cast evil spells on people. Here it means those people who do not have a fundamental spiritual basis, those who cling to words and logic and are enslaved by dualistic views, without grasping the subjective point of view.

Mumon says that anyone who is unable to pass the barrier of the old Masters or to wipe out his discriminating mind—that is, if his Zen mind is not awakened—is like a phantom, without reality. There is no significance in such an existence. Thus, by using extreme and abusive language Mumon tries to make us ashamed of our unenlightened existence and to arouse in us the great spiritual quest.

"Now, tell me," Mumon demands, "what is the barrier of the Zen Masters?" Having aroused our interest, he answers himself that this "Mu" is the ultimate barrier of Zen. If once one has broken through it, he is the master of all the barriers and the forty-eight koan and commentaries of the *Mumonkan* are all his tools. This is therefore called "The Gateless Barrier of Zen," Mumon remarks. We should remember however that it is not only the first koan, but that any of the forty-eight koan of the *Mumonkan* is the barrier of Zen.

"Those who have passed the barrier will not only see Joshu clearly, but will go hand in hand with all the Masters in the past, see them face to face. You will see with the same eye that they see with and hear with the same ear. Wouldn't it be wonderful?"

Mumon tells us how wonderful it is to experience breaking through the barrier and to live the life of satori. Once the Gate is broken through, ultimate peace is attained. You can get hold of old Joshu alive. Further, you will live in the same spirituality with all the Zen Masters, see them face to face, and enjoy the Truth of Oneness. How wonderful, how splendid! He praises the life of satori in the highest terms. There are no ages in satori; no distinctions of I and you, space and time. Wherever it may be and whenever it may be, just here and now you see and you hear—it is Joshu, it is your Self, and "Mu." There can be no greater joy. To experience this is to attain eternal peace.

"Don't you want to pass the barrier? Then concentrate yourself into this 'Mu' with your 360 bones and 84,000 pores, making your whole body one great inquiry."

Having described the great joy of satori, Mumon now turns to his disciples and speaks directly to them, "Are there any among you who want to pass this barrier of the ancient Masters?" He then goes on to give practical instructions as to how they should carry on their training in order to break through the barrier—how to attain satori. He tells them to inquire, with their heart and soul, what it is to transcend yes and no, you and I. They are to cast their whole being, from head to foot, into this inquiry and carry on with it. There will be no world, no self, but just one Great Doubt. This is "Mu." "Just be 'Mu'!" Mumon urges the disciples.

"To concentrate" is to be unified and identified. "To concentrate oneself into 'Mu' " is for "Mu" and the self to be one—to be one and then to transcend both "Mu" and the self.

"Day and night work intently at it; do not attempt nihilistic or dualistic interpretations."

Mumon's instructions continue: never be negligent, even for a short while, but do zazen and devote yourself to the koan day and night. An old Master described this training process, saying, "Work like a mother hen trying to hatch her eggs." Do not misunderstand "Mu" as nihilistic emptiness. Never in the world take it as a dualistic No in opposition to Yes. Needless to say, it has nothing to do with intellectual discrimination or dualistic reasoning. It is utterly beyond all description.

"It is like having bolted a red hot iron ball; you try to vomit it but cannot. Cast away your illusory discriminating knowledge and consciousness accumulated up to now, and keep on working harder. After a while, when your efforts come to fruition, all the oppositions (such as in and out) will naturally be identified. You will then be like a dumb person who has had a wonderful dream: he only knows it personally, within himself."

"Like having bolted a red hot iron ball" describes the one who, with his whole being, body and soul, has plunged into the Great Doubt, the spiritual quest. All the emotions are exhausted, all the intellect has come to its extremity; there is not an inch for the discrimination to enter. This is the state of utmost spiritual intensification. When it is hot, the whole universe is nothing but the heat; when you see, it is just one pure act of seeing—there is no room there for any thought to come in. In such a state, Mumon warns us, never give up but straightforwardly carry on with your striving. In such a state no thought of discrimination can be present. "Illusory discriminating knowledge and consciousness accumulated up to now" refers to our dualistically working mind we have had before. No trace of it is now left. You are thoroughly lucid and transparent like a crystal. Subject and object, in and out, being and nonbeing are just one, and this very one ceases to be one any longer. Rinzai said, describing this state, "The whole universe is sheer darkness." Hakuin said, "It was like sitting in an ice cave a million miles thick." This is the moment when the I and the world are both altogether gone. This is exactly the moment when one's discriminating mind is emptied and cast away. When one is in the abyss of absolute "Mu" in actual training, the inexpressible moment comes upon him—the moment when "Mu" is awakened to "Mu," that is, when he is revived as the self of no-self. At this mysterious moment, he is like a dumb person who has had a wonderful dream, for he is fully aware of it, but is unable to use words to express it. The Absolute Nothingness ("Mu") is awakened to itself. This is the moment of realization when subject-object opposition is altogether transcended. To describe it we have to use such words as inexpressible or mysterious. "You will then be like a dumb person who has had a wonderful dream: he only knows it personally, within himself."

Then Mumon tries again to describe the experience of the one who has just broken through the barrier: "Suddenly you break through the barrier; you will astonish heaven and shake the earth." I myself, however, should like to reverse the order of these two sentences and say, "Suddenly you break through the barrier; you will astonish heaven and shake the earth. You will then be like a dumb person who has had a wonderful dream: he only knows it personally, within himself." This would be more faithful to actual experience. Zen calls this experience "incomparable satori," or "to die a Great Death once and to revive from death." Mumon described his experience of attaining satori by saying that "all beings on earth have opened their eyes." This is the most important and essential process one has to go through in Zen training.

"It is as if you have snatched the great sword of General Kan. You kill the Buddha if you meet him; you kill the ancient Masters if you meet them. On the brink of life and death, you are utterly free, and in the six realms and the four modes of life you live, with great joy, a genuine life in complete freedom."

General Kan was a brave general famous in ancient China. With his great sword he used to freely cut and conquer his enemies. Once one attains the satori of this "Mu," his absolute inner freedom can be compared to the man who has the great sword of that famous strong general in his own hand.

Having experienced this exquisite moment of breaking through the barrier, one's self, the world, and everything change. It is just like one who was born blind getting his sight. Here Mumon tells us how absolutely free he now is. He sees, he hears, and everything, as it is, is given new life. Mumon in his own poem speaks of this wonder, "Mount Sumeru jumps up and dances." Only those who have actually experienced it themselves can really appreciate what Mumon sings here.

"You kill the Buddha if you meet him; you kill the ancient Masters if you meet them."

This expression is often misunderstood. Zen postulates absolute freedom in which all attachments and restraints are completely wiped away. The Buddha therefore is to be cast away and so are the Patriarchs. Any restraints whatsoever in the mind are to be cast away. For the one who has passed through the abyss of Great Doubt, transcending subject and object, you and I, and has been revived as the True Self, can there be anything to disturb him? The term "to kill" should not be interpreted in our ordinary ethical sense. "To kill" is to transcend names and ideas. If you meet the Buddha, the Buddha is "Mu." If you meet ancient Masters, they are "Mu." Therefore he says that if you pass the barrier you will "not only see Joshu clearly, but go hand in hand with all the Masters in the past, see them face to face. You will see with the same eye that they see with and hear with the same ear."

To live is an aspect of "Mu"; to die is also an aspect of "Mu." If you stand, your standing is "Mu." If you sit, your sitting is "Mu." The six realms refer to the six different stages of existence, i.e., the celestial world, human world, fighting world, beasts, hungry beings, and hell. The four modes are four different forms of life, i.e., viviparous, oviparous, from moisture, and metamorphic. Originally the phrase referred to various stages of life in transmigration, depending on the law of causation. The reference to the six realms and the four modes of life means, "under whatever circumstances you may live, in whatever situation you may find yourself." Both favorable conditions and adverse situations are "Mu," working differently as you live, at any time, at any place. How wonderful it is to live such a serene life with perfect freedom, the spiritual freedom of the one who has attained religious peace!

"Now, how should one strive? With might and main work at this 'Mu,' and *be* 'Mu.'"

Mumon once again gives his direct instruction on how one should carry out his Zen training in order to break through the barrier of the Zen Masters to attain incomparable satori and his Zen personality. How should he work at "Mu"? All that can be said is: "Be just 'Mu' with might and main." To be "Mu" is to cast everything—yourself and the universe—into it.

"If you do not stop or waver in your striving, then behold, when the Dharma candle is lighted, the darkness is at once enlightened."

This can be simply taken as a candle on the altar. Once one's mind bursts open to the truth of "Mu," the ignorance is at once enlightened, just as all darkness is gone when a candle is lighted.

Mumon warns his disciples that they should not stop or waver in their striving. In other words, he says that with might and main you must be "Mu" through and through, and never stop striving to attain that. An old Japanese Zen Master has a waka poem:

> When your bow is broken and your arrows are exhausted,
> There, shoot!
> Shoot with your whole being!

A Western philosopher has said, "Man's extremity is God's opportunity." When man is at his very extremity and still goes on striving with his whole being, without stopping, the moment to break through suddenly comes to him. This is the moment of fundamental change when one is reborn as a True Self. It is as if a candle were lighted in darkness. Darkness is at once illumined.

Master Engo has a poem in the *Hekigan-roku:*

> It is like cutting a reel of thread:
> One cut, and all is cut.
> It is like dyeing a reel of thread:
> One dip and all is dyed.

I join Mumon in saying, "Wouldn't it be wonderful!" In his commentary Mumon has tried his best to tell us how exquisite and wonderful true Zen attainment is, and pointed out the way to experience it.

TEISHO ON MUMON'S POEM

> The dog! the Buddha Nature!
> The Truth is manifested in full.

A moment of yes-and-no:
Lost are your body and soul.

Following his detailed commentary on Joshu's "Mu," Mumon wrote this poem to comment on it once more, so that he might clearly and simply present the essence of satori.

He first presents the koan itself directly to us: "The dog! the Buddha Nature!" What else is needed here? As it is, it is "Mu." As they are, they are "Mu." Those who really know it will fully understand it all by this.

The second line says, "The Truth is manifested in full." The original Chinese term used for Truth literally means "True Law," that is, the Buddha's fundamental command. It is nothing but "Mu" itself. Look, it is right in front of you, Mumon says. A blind person fails to see the sunlight, but it is not the fault of the sun.

"A moment of yes-and-no: lost are your body and soul." Out of his compassion Mumon adds the last two lines, which say that if even a thought of discrimination comes, the truth of "Mu" is altogether gone. When one is really "Mu" through and through, to call it "Mu" is already incorrect, for that belongs to the dualistic world of letters. "Mu" here is just temporarily used in order to transcend U (yes) and Mu (no). If one is afraid of losing his body and soul, what can be accomplished? The secret here can be communicated only to those who have once died the Great Death.

2

Hyakujo and a Fox

KOAN

Whenever Master Hyakujo gave teisho on Zen, an old man sat with the monks to listen and always withdrew when they did. One day, however, he remained behind, and the Master asked, "Who are you standing here before me?" The old man replied, "I am not a human being. In the past, in the time of the Kasho Buddha, I was the head of this monastery. Once a monk asked me, 'Does an enlightened man also fall into causation or not?' I replied, 'He does not.' Because of this answer, I was made to live as a fox for five hundred lives. Now I beg you, please say the turning words on my behalf and release me from the fox body." The old man then asked Hyakujo, "Does an enlightened man also fall into causation or not?" The Master said, "He does not ignore causation." Hearing this the old man was at once enlightened. Making a bow to Hyakujo he said, "I have now been released from the fox body, which will be found behind the mountain. I dare to make a request of the Master. Please bury it as you would a deceased monk."

The Master had the Ino strike the gavel and announce to the monks that there would be a funeral for a deceased monk after the midday meal. The monks wondered, saying, "We are all in good health. There is no sick monk in the Nirvana Hall. What is it all about?"

After the meal the Master led the monks to a rock behind the mountain, poked out a dead fox with his staff, and cremated it.

In the evening the Master ascended the rostrum in the hall and told the monks the whole story. Obaku thereupon asked, "The old man failed to give the correct turning words and was made to live as a fox for five hundred lives, you say; if, however, his answer had not been incorrect each time, what would he have become?" The Master said, "Come closer to me, I'll tell you." Obaku then stepped forward to Hyakujo and slapped him. The Master laughed aloud, clapping his hands, and said, "I thought a foreigner's beard is red, but I see that it is a foreigner with a red beard."

MUMON'S COMMENTARY

"Not falling into causation." Why was he turned into a fox? "Not ignoring causation." Why was he released from the fox body? If you have an eye to see through this, then you will know that the former head of the monastery did enjoy his five hundred happy blessed lives as a fox.

MUMON'S POEM

> Not falling, not ignoring:
> Odd and even are on one die.
> Not ignoring, not falling:
> Hundreds and thousands of regrets!

TEISHO ON THE KOAN

This is a so-called nanto koan, a koan used for refining students' spirituality after satori. While there is no such distinction as an easy or a difficult koan, it is possible for a Zen Master, as a means of guiding monks, to use a koan in different ways. For instance, some koan can be used to stress Oneness, others to show the working aspects of Oneness in differentiation, and still others to illustrate that Oneness is differentiation and differentiation is Oneness. In the case of this koan, the fundamental Truth and its working aspects are so intricately interwoven that only students with their Zen eye clearly opened can get the significance of it. In this nanto koan the spirituality of a real Zen man is clarified in connection with causality, in this case the causality of transmigration, which had been a popular folk belief in India. The point of the koan is to make Zen students realize what real emancipation is, and the superficial ghost story is just a means to illustrate the point. We should not, therefore, stick to the story itself—which is nothing more than a means—and get entangled in it.

The ancient Indians had a religious view that we, beings living in ignorance, are subject to transmigration determined by our good and evil karma. Buddhism, adopting this view based on the chain of causation, teaches that we should therefore follow the Buddha's teachings and be awakened to the Truth, for only in this way can we leave ignorance and achieve eternal peace.

The fact of cause and effect is so clear and undeniable! In all ages and places there can be nothing on this earth that does not exist through the action of cause and effect. Every moment, every existence is causation itself. Outside it there is neither I nor the world. This being the case, the man of real freedom would be the one who lives in peace in whatever circumstances cause and effect bring about. Whether the situation be favorable or adverse, he lives it as the absolute situation with his whole being—that is, he is causation itself. He never dualistically discriminates different aspects of the situation; his heart is never disturbed by any outside elements. When he lives like this, he is the master of cause and effect and everything is blessed as it is. The eternal peace is established here. This is the indescribable spiritual happiness a Zen man enjoys. We can just say, like an old Zen Master, "Those who know it do not talk. Those who talk about it are far from it."

What is the old man? What is Hyakujo? Neither is a man; neither is a fox. Anything is just "it." Anything is just causation. What else could we say?

It is therefore said in the *Monju Shosetsu-kyo,* "A miscreant monk does not fall into hell." This very place is the absolute place; there is no hell to fall into. It further says, "A holy saint does not go to heaven." This very place is the absolute place; there is no heaven to ascend to. When the whole universe is causation itself, how can there be "falling" or "not falling"? You may therefore correctly call it "not falling," or just as correctly "not ignoring." If even a thought of knowledge moves there, both "not falling" and "not ignoring" are in error. An infinitesimal discrepancy is at once a vital difference, poles apart, and you are turned into a fox and fall into hell.

You may say, "not ignoring causation," yet if discriminating consciousness moves there and if you become attached to "not ignoring," you are turned into a fox. You may say, "not falling into causation," and if you do not become attached to it, you are released from the fox body. The essence of this koan can really be appreciated when one experiences the fact of no-mind. He then does not make such dualistic discriminations as "not falling" and "not ignoring," or whether the one is good and the other not; falling and ignoring are both broken through and transcended.

Perhaps I have said enough to make the point clear. Now let us turn to some of the details of the koan.

The reference to Kasho Buddha in the story of Hyakujo and a fox indicates that it happened a long time in the past. Buddhist legend has a genealogical table of transmission (which is different from the fact of Dharma transmission), according to which there were seven Buddhas in the past, of whom Kasho Buddha was the sixth and Sakyamuni Buddha the seventh. "Once upon a time" the old man was the head of this monastery.

Master Ekai (720–814) is generally known as Hyakujo, the name of the mountain where his monastery, Daichi-in, was located in Nanshofu, Koshu. He lived for ninety-five years in the T'ang dynasty when the lively spirit of Zen flourished in the rising T'ang culture. It was at this time, when the role of Zen was gradually being established in society, that a need was felt for rules and regulations for Zen monasteries, and it is well known in Zen history that Hyakujo enacted the first formal monastery rules, later called the Hyakujo Rules. He led an active, working Zen life, joined in manual labor with the monks even in his old age, and is famous for his saying, "A day of no work is a day of no eating."

Ekai was born into the Oh family in Choraku, Fukushu. He entered the priesthood when he was a child and in his early years received training in scholastic Buddhist studies. Some years later he heard of Baso, who was teaching Zen at Kosei, and joined him there to devote himself to Zen studies. Nansen Fugan and Seido Chizo, both of whom became noted Zen Masters later, were also among Baso's disciples in those days, and they worked hard together in their training.

One day Hyakujo was walking with his teacher Baso. Seeing a wild goose flying in the sky, Baso asked Hyakujo, "What is it?" "A wild goose, Master," replied Hyakujo. Baso asked, "Where is it flying to?" Hyakujo replied, "It is already gone." Thereupon Baso clutched Hyakujo's nose and wrenched it. Hyakujo cried in pain. Baso demanded, "Do you say that it has flown away?" This at once awakened Hyakujo.

Some years later Hyakujo came to have a Zen interview with Baso, and after exchanging mondo on the subject of a hossu hanging in the alcove, Baso uttered a great KWATZ! cry which completely crushed everything in Hyakujo, and he was thoroughly enlightened.

These two stories are famous in Zen history. People gradually came to study under Master Ekai, and finally he was asked to be the abbot of a monastery at Mount Daiyu in Koshu. As this mountain was very rugged and precipitous, people called it Hyakujo (one hundred feet high). Many monks came to study under him; Isan Reiyu and Obaku Kiun were two of his senior disciples. He died on January 17, 814, in his ninety-fifth year.

Master Obaku Kiun, the other Master in this koan, was born in Binken,

Fukushu, but his date of birth is unknown. When he was a boy he was ordained in a Zen temple in Fukusei-ken, Fukushu, called Obaku-san Kempuku-ji. (Obaku is the name of a plant used for making dye which grew profusely near the Zen temple.) Later, Governor Haikyu became a disciple of Master Kiun and built a monastery for him in Koshu. Kiun, who loved his home countryside very much, called this new monastery Obaku-san, and he himself came to be known as Obaku. He wrote a book, *Denshin Hoyo,* in which we can see the characteristics of Obaku's Zen.

When he was a student on pilgrimage to continue his scholastic studies of Buddhism, he heard of the reputation of Hyakujo and came to study under him. It is recorded that once Obaku visited his friend Nansen, and when he was taking leave Nansen, who came to the gate to see him off, lifted up Obaku's hat and said, "Your body is big, but your hat is quite small, isn't it?" Obaku replied, "Yet the whole universe is under it." "I am under it too, am I not?" retorted Nansen. Obaku then briskly walked away without turning around even once. He is said to have been a man of magnificent physique.

One day Hyakujo asked Obaku, "Where have you been?" "I have been to the foot of Mount Daiyu to gather mushrooms," replied Obaku. "Then didn't you come across a tiger?" At this question from Hyakujo, Obaku instantly roared at him, himself becoming a tiger. Hyakujo swung up his axe to strike him but Obaku gripped his teacher's arm, slapped him, and left him, laughing heartily. Later, at the time of teisho, Hyakujo ascended the dais and said to the monks, "At the foot of Mount Daiyu there is a tiger. You monks should have a good look at him. I myself was bitten by him today."

It is apparent from such recorded stories that Obaku's Zen was characteristically direct, ardent, and glowing. Obaku, with his grand, strict, and thoroughgoing personality greatly influenced Zen circles in his time. He died in 850, five years after the great persecution of Buddhism by Emperor Bu-so of the T'ang dynasty.

An "enlightened man" is one who has completed his training and has been fully enlightened, he is the man of satori who has accomplished his emancipation and attained eternal peace. He is not subject to retribution and transmigration. To be free from the chain of causation is the ultimate aim of the discipline in Mahayana Buddhism. This is such an obvious fact among Buddhists that there is no room for any further discussion of it. Now, the former head of the monastery, the old man, gave this clear and matter-of-fact reply when he said, "An enlightened man does not fall into causation." Why then did he, as the result of this answer, have to live as a fox for five hundred lives? What is it to be free from retribution? The Truth of Zen lies here. The teaching of "not falling into causation" will surely result in turning one into a fox, unless he clearly knows what that Truth actually is.

When the old man asked, "Now I beg you, please say the turning words on my behalf and release me from the fox body," Hyakujo immediately replied, "He does not ignore causation." (The turning words are the real words that will turn one's mind to the Truth and awaken it to satori; one ultimate utterance expressing the Truth.)

Literally interpreted, Hyakujo's reply means that "an enlightened man does not ignore the fact of cause and effect, but lives according to it." It is diametrically opposed to "He does not fall into causation." Why did Hyakujo dare to give such a contradictory reply, which stands over against the Mahayana teaching of emancipation from transmigration and almost sounds like affirming continuing reincarnations? Again, the inexpressibly deep significance should be found here.

My teacher once commented on "not ignoring causation." "What a pity!" he said. "If I had been asked, I should have raised my voice and replied, 'He does not fall into causation!' " From what standpoint did my teacher comment in this way? I should like to say: "not falling into causation" and "not ignoring causation"—how are they different? Such a logical contradiction makes this a good and interesting koan.

"Hearing this the old man was at once enlightened." The old man was enlightened when he heard Hyakujo say, "He does not ignore causation." One has made an irreparably fatal mistake if he thinks that "not falling into causation" is an incorrect reply while "not ignoring causation" is correct, and that the old man then realized that the enlightened man "does not ignore causation."

At his words, the old man lost his self; the whole universe crumbled away. There was neither the old man nor the fox. "Not falling" and "not ignoring" were both wiped away and there was not a cloud in his mind. He had his satori. If one becomes attached to it, "not ignoring" turns out to be the same as "not falling." And "not falling into causation," if one does not become attached to it, is the same as "not ignoring causation."

Listen to an old Zen Master who dared to say:

> "Not falling into causation"
> And he was turned into a fox—the first mistake.
> "Not ignoring causation"
> And he was released from the fox body—the second mistake!

When "not falling" and "not ignoring" are both transcended and wiped away, you can for the first time yourself see Hyakujo and Mumon and get hold of the real significance of this koan. What kind of experience is it, then, to transcend both "not falling" and "not ignoring"? Zen studies should be concentrated on this point.

Often people say that the old man had to be turned into a fox because "not falling into causation" denies the fact of cause and effect and thus forms a one-sided, mistaken view of equality that is not real equality. He was released from the fox body because "not ignoring causation" acknowledges the reality of cause and effect and knows the acceptance of differentiation. But the essence of this koan can never be found in such a common-sense interpretation. Neither am I saying that Zen denies causality. What I want you to know is that Zen is alive and active in quite another sphere where it makes free use of both "not falling" and "not ignoring."

"Making a bow to Hyakujo he said, 'I have now been released from the fox body, which will be found behind the mountain. I dare to make a request of the Master. Please bury it as you would a deceased monk."

When a fox is really a fox, and not a thought of discriminating consciousness moves there, he is truly "a former head of a monastery." When an old man cannot be an old man and goes astray with his dualistic thinking, he is a fox. Master Dogen said, "Once you have attained satori, if you were to transmigrate through the six realms and the four modes of life, your transmigration would be nothing but the work of your compassionate life of satori."

The fox behind the mountain is enjoying its life as it is, regardless of whether it is released from the fox body or not. The unique Zen life is developed here.

Hyakujo led the monks of the monastery to a rock at the back of the mountain, poked out a dead fox, and cremated it in accordance with the rituals for a deceased monk. Hyakujo here had no such discrimination as that of a deceased monk and a fox. This also shows characteristic Zen spirituality. The story has been thus satisfactorily ended.

Now the second part of the koan develops. For the evening teisho, Hyakujo told the monks the whole story of the old man and wanted to test the Zen ability of his disciples.

"Obaku thereupon asked, 'The old man failed to give the correct turning words and was made to live as a fox for five hundred lives, you say; if, however, his answer had not been incorrect each time, what would he have become?"

Obaku stepped out of the assembled monks and asked a cutting question: "The old man [the former head of the monastery] was made to live as a fox for five hundred lives because his reply was not correct. If his answer had been correct for every question, what would he have been turned into each time?" Obaku's question implies that "sentient and nonsentient beings all have the Buddha Nature. The tall one is a tall Buddha, the short one is a short Buddha. Each as it is is enlightened. Everything, as it is, is the Truth. It is impossible to go astray or to be in error."

"The question is in the answer; the answer is in the question," is an old saying. Obaku challenged Hyakujo, fully realizing the point of the story.

"The Master said, 'Come closer to me. I'll tell you.' Obaku then stepped forward to Hyakujo and slapped him."

Hyakujo, the teacher, was an old campaigner and well aware of what was in Obaku's mind. He did not expect that a mushy answer would satisfy him. "Come closer and I'll tell you," said Hyakujo. Obaku, however, knew too well that no words could reach "it." Approaching Hyakujo, Obaku gave his teacher a slap in the face. Did he mean, "Your reply—I'll give it to you?" Wonderful indeed is the greatness of Hyakujo. Splendid indeed is the freedom of Obaku. The Master and the disciple are living in the same spirituality, and the great working of Zen is here naturally developed. The point of the koan should be clearly grasped here.

"The Master laughed aloud, clapping his hands, and said, 'I thought a foreigner's beard is red, but I see that it is a foreigner with a red beard!' "

Hyakujo smiled with joy at Obaku's great action which showed that he did not yield even a step to his teacher. The Master clapped his hands and said, laughing heartily, "I thought a foreigner's beard is red, but I see that it is a foreigner with a red beard." Expressions can be different, but the fact remains the same. "I was ready to slap you, but you slapped me instead"—this is what Hyakujo meant. Hyakujo's spirituality and the spirituality of Obaku—they are like two mirrors reflecting each other. A genius clearly understands another genius. Here is real understanding and appreciation. They are both equally great champions, spots of the same ink. By such a comment, Hyakujo is acknowledging Obaku's attainment.

Let me ask you again here: "If his answer had not been incorrect each time, what would he have become?"

TEISHO ON MUMON'S COMMENTARY

Mumon commented, " 'Not falling into causation.' Why was he turned into a fox? 'Not ignoring causation.' Why was he released from the fox body?

If you have an eye to see through this, then you will know that the former head of the monastery did enjoy his five hundred happy blessed lives as a fox."

With his clear and direct comment, Mumon beautifully summed up the essence of this rather long koan consisting of two parts. He is remarkably clever in presenting the key point for Zen students.

First he pointedly asks why the former head of the monastery was turned into a fox as the result of his reply that an enlightened man does not fall into causation. Then his cross-examination continues: "Why was he released from the fox body as the result of Hyakujo's answer that an enlightened man 'does not ignore causation'?" It has been said from olden times that the essence of Zen is in this one word "Why?" How could it be so, I want to ask. Actually, there is no falling, no releasing. Based on this absolute standpoint, what really is it to be released from the fox body? And what could it be to live as a fox? We have to inquire closely into this point. Mumon asks us to wipe away completely such obstructions as "to be turned into a fox" or "to be released from the fox body." I should like to quote again the Master's poem, since it may point out the right direction for your study:

> "Not falling into causation"
> And he was turned into a fox—the first mistake.
> "Not ignoring causation"
> And he was released from the fox body—the second mistake!

Mumon says "if you have an eye . . ."—that is, the spiritual eye to see that fundamentally the Buddha and ignorant beings are one, purity and defilement are one. From the Absolute standpoint, therefore, dualism has been transcended. This is the third eye in the forehead. If you have that eye, the Zen eye of satori, then you will know that the five hundred fox lives, just as they were, were happy, blessed lives for the former head of the monastery. When the old man is truly an old man through and through, that life is happy and blessed. When the fox has transcended "falling and releasing" and is truly a fox through and through, that life is happy and blessed. It is not limited only to five hundred lives, but eternal happiness through all ages and places will develop thus. Needless to say, Mumon's comment answers well Obaku's question: "If his answer had not been incorrect each time, what would he have become?"

TEISHO ON MUMON'S POEM

> Not falling, not ignoring:
> Odd and even are on one die.
> Not ignoring, not falling:
> Hundreds and thousands of regrets!

Mumon in this short poem sums up once more his comments on the koan of "Hyakujo and a Fox."

From the standpoint of Zen, "not falling" or "not ignoring" is just "it" (the essence of Zen). Wherever it may be, whenever it may be, it is always causation itself. Nothing can ever be outside causation. Odd and even are on one and the same die. They are after all two faces of the same coin. Nay, if I say that they are one and the same, people may attach to this oneness and be caught in the net of sameness. "Not ignoring" or "not falling"—whatever one may say, it is "hundreds and thousands of regrets."

Let me ask you at the end: What kind of life is it, this life of "hundreds and thousands of regrets"? I should like to point out that the essence of this koan is in the last line. The key of the five hundred happy, blessed lives is hidden here.

3

Gutei Raises a Finger

Master Gutei, whenever he was questioned, just stuck up one finger.

At one time he had a young attendant, whom a visitor asked, "What is the Zen your Master is teaching?" The boy also stuck up one finger. Hearing of this, Gutei cut off the boy's finger with a knife. As the boy ran out screaming with pain, Gutei called to him. When the boy turned his head, Gutei stuck up his finger. The boy was suddenly enlightened.

When Gutei was about to die, he said to the assembled monks, "I attained Tenryu's Zen of One Finger. I used it all through my life, but could not exhaust it." When he had finished saying this, he died.

MUMON'S COMMENTARY

The satori of Gutei and of the boy attendant are not in the finger. If you really see through this, Tenryu, Gutei, the boy, and you yourself are all run through with one skewer.

MUMON'S POEM

Gutei made a fool of old Tenryu,
With a sharp knife he chastised the boy.
Korei raised his hand with no effort,
And lo! the great ridge of Mount Ka was split in two!

TEISHO ON THE KOAN

This koan has three parts. The first part is the first sentence: "Master Gutei, whenever he was questioned, just stuck up one finger." The second paragraph, starting with "At one time he had a young attendant" and ending with "The boy was suddenly enlightened," makes the second part, which tells us how Gutei's young attendant was enlightened. The last paragraph, from "When Gutei was about to die" to the end is the third part of the koan.

The most important, however, is the first part. The essence of this koan is in the first sentence. The second part gives a remarkable example of Gutei's Zen ability, and the third tells of the infinite and limitless working of the "Zen of One Finger."

"Master Gutei, whenever he was questioned, just stuck up one finger." Gutei was certainly an unusual Zen Master. He just stuck up his finger, whenever and whatever he was asked by anybody at all. For instance, someone might ask: "What is the essence of Buddhism?" and he stuck up one finger. "What is Joshu's 'Mu'?" he might be asked, and he stuck up one finger. "Bring out your mind and show it to me," he was asked, and he stuck up one finger. In reply to "When your body is all decomposed, where do you go?" he stuck up one finger. Throughout his life he gave no talks. What a hearty Master he was! The fact was, he could never put it in words even if he wished to do so. Or I might say he expressed it fully.

One is all. There is nothing to add. True it may be, but tell me, "What is the finger?" Is there anybody who does not have a finger? Or Truth, or the Buddha Nature, or whatever you may call it? Pitiful indeed are those who are not aware of the foolishness of seeking after water while they are in the midst of it. Yet if you stick to the finger, you are thousands of miles away from the Truth.

Mumon also simply says to his disciples, "Whenever he was questioned, Gutei just stuck up one finger," and adds no further comment. "I stick up my finger." True teisho is complete with this act. Those who know, should know it by this, and those who cannot understand it will just have to strive further until they become able to get it. There are no other means or devices to get the Truth of Zen.

However, perhaps I should not end my teisho by sticking up my finger. So I will come down a step and add some words, though from a less absolute standpoint.

Gutei was a Zen Master in China in the ninth century. According to his biography, when he was young Gutei lived alone on a mountain doing zazen. One day a nun happened to come by. According to the custom in China, when two people meet they take off their hats and exchange greetings. This nun, however, did not follow the proper etiquette. She was impolite enough to walk around Gutei three times without taking off her head-covering, stood right in front of him, and said, "If you can tell me the word that satisfies me, I will take off my head-covering." Gutei, whose spiritual eye was unfortunately not yet open, could say nothing in reply. The nun immediately turned to leave. Gutei called out, "It is getting dark. Why don't you stay here overnight and start your trip tomorrow morning?" The nun turned back and demanded again, "I will stay if you can give me the word." Once again Gutei was unable to say anything, and the nun simply left him.

Let me ask you: if you were to talk to the nun in place of Gutei, how would you answer?"

Gutei was now greatly ashamed of himself for having been unable to give an answer to the nun. He made up his mind to leave his mountain hut to visit various great Zen Masters and have further training to open his Zen eye. According to the legend, that night he had a dream in which a foreigner told him that a great Master who would be his teacher would soon come to the hut. In accordance with the dream, Gutei decided to remain on the mountain. Sure enough, ten days later an old monk came by. He was Master Tenryu, the successor to Master Taibai Hojo. Gutei was convinced that this must be the Master the dream had foretold, and he welcomed him with reverence. He told Tenryu of his encounter with the nun and asked him what the "fundamental word of Zen" could be. Tenryu, without saying anything, just stuck up his finger. At this Gutei was enlightened. The darkness in his mind was all dispersed, and his spiritual eye was opened to a new vista.

His biography just tells us, "Tenryu stuck up one finger. At this Gutei had satori." No detailed account is given of his inner struggle before getting satori. Yet those who themselves have gone through hard training and searching will appreciate behind this short sentence the painful searching and striving Gutei must have gone through before this moment of breakthrough was given to him.

What is important here is not the lifted finger, but the intensity of the inner struggle Gutei went through. In Zen training one has to strive with soul and body to transcend his dualistic discriminating consciousness. One has to come to the ultimate extremity where any slightest touch may effect a great change in his personality, so fundamental as to be described by saying that "the earth splits and the mountains collapse." He has to plunge into the abyss of "sheer darkness altogether," as an old Master expressed it.

When Master Tenryu stuck up his finger, Gutei must have been at his ultimate extremity. He had spent years on the mountain doing zazen, but somehow his discipline could not go beyond the dualistic limitations. The incident of his encounter with the nun made him ashamed of his training and intensified his spiritual quest to somehow break through the barrier. He was finally driven to the abyss of his ultimate extremity. He was in a spiritual state that made him ready to explode at the slightest touch. Tenryu's finger was an arrow shot at the right moment. It served to effect the breakthrough. The intensification of Gutei's searching and the presentation by Tenryu were like a chicken ready to break open the eggshell and its mother hen pecking at it to help the chicken out. Gutei's satori was a happy result of both of them hitting the right moment. If one starts asking what this one finger might mean and tries to find some significance in sticking up the finger, apart from the actual inner struggle Gutei went through, he is a complete stranger to Zen. If one's spritual quest—or Great Doubt—is intensified to the ultimate extremity and his striving has come to the breaking point, a bird's singing, the sound of a stone hitting bamboo, the Master's slapping, his holding up one finger, or anything will do.

Tenryu's finger effected this breaking through the barrier—the fact of having actually, personally, transcended the dualism of yes and no, having really cast away the dichotomy of subject and object, is here. If I dare to explain it philosophically, one finger held up here is not a finger any longer; it is Gutei himself, I-myself, the universe itself—but if one clings to such an explanation, Zen is no longer there.

On my recent trip to the United States, an artist in Kyoto asked me to bring to an American friend of his a painting of a plum branch, and also asked me to write an aphorism on his painting. Often a painter in Japan will ask a Zen Master to write a Zen saying on his painting so that people will recognize the Zen spirit in his work. On this painting of a plum branch I wrote, "Three thousand worlds [the whole universe] are fragrant." I wanted this one plum branch to symbolize Gutei's finger, or Zen itself. A single tiny plum branch is fragrant throughout the whole universe; that is, the plum branch is the Absolute and embraces the whole universe, transcending all forms of dualistic opposites. The whole universe is a plum branch; a plum branch is the whole universe. The Zen of One Finger is inexhaustible indeed.

"At one time he had a young attendant, of whom a visitor asked, 'What is the Zen your Master is teaching?' The boy also stuck up one finger. Hearing of this, Gutei cut off the boy's finger with a knife. As the boy ran out screaming with pain, Gutei called to him. When the boy turned his head, Gutei stuck up his finger. The boy was suddenly enlightened."

Mumon is kind enough to introduce another story related to Zen of One

Finger in the hope of presenting Gutei's Zen even more clearly to us. Gutei had a young lay disciple attending him, a youth who stayed in the monastery to study sutras and receive training but had not yet been ordained as a monk. The boy got the habit of imitating his teacher by sticking up one finger, and when visitors would ask him, "What kind of teaching does Gutei give?" he would stick up his finger without a word. Hearing of this, Gutei one day took drastic measures and cut off the boy's finger; that is, he cut off the boy's finger of imitation, which is no better than a corpse.

Gutei called out to him as he ran away screaming with pain. When the boy involuntarily turned his head, Gutei stuck up one finger. At this, fortunately the boy was awakened to the True One Finger. In the extreme pain penetrating the universe, he grasped the Truth of One Finger. The boy, losing his finger, attained the true finger and eternal life. This Zen of One Finger is nothing but the Truth pervading the whole universe. It can never be found in the boy's imitating finger, which is like a corpse. The marvelous capability of Gutei in cutting it off should certainly be admired.

I myself have a similar story of my own training days, which of course is not comparable with that of the boy attendant. I had already spent three years at the monastery and was in the abyss of darkness. I did not know how to proceed, where to go, or what to do. There is an occasion in the sesshin (the intensive week-long training period at a monastery) when every monk has to go to the Master's room for sanzen, which is the occasion for a monk to show his Zen ability to his teacher in private. (It is totally different from logical or philosophical discussions, or questions and answers.) I struck the bell of sanzen and stepped into the Master's room feeling like a lamb dragged to a slaughter house, for I did not have anything to say. In a fix, I instantly raised my hand and exclaimed, "The Truth pervading the whole universe!" The Master, with piercing eyes, stood up and drove me out of the room of sanzen, saying, "You good-for-nothing monk! You had better return to college!" I shall never forget the pain I had at this Master's rebuke.

Philosophically speaking, my statement that "the Absolute Truth pervades the whole universe" is certainly correct as far as content goes. But it was just an idea, a thought—that is, a carcass that merely looked alive on the surface —it was not a fact I had personally experienced. Gutei's finger and his young attendant's finger are the same finger. Still, there is a fundamental difference. While Gutei's finger was Zen itself, the universe itself, the attendant's finger was just an imitation without the fact of his own experience. It was a fake with no life, and should be cut off.

The Zen of One Finger is in the finger and yet transcends the finger. If one fails to grasp correctly the Truth of One Finger here, he is altogether out of Zen.

"When Gutei was about to die, he said to the assembled monks, 'I attained Tenryu's Zen of One Finger. I have used it all through my life, but could not exhaust it.' When he had finished saying this, he died."

Mumon generously adds this last remark to complete this koan of Zen of One Finger. Although the physical body of Gutei, a historical person called Gutei, did die, his Zen is alive here now, in my finger and your finger, transcending space and time. The whole universe is a finger; a finger is the whole universe. It should then be ever new and alive, and its creative work can never be exhausted; it exists forever together with the universe itself.

TEISHO ON MUMON'S COMMENTARY

"The satori of Gutei and of the boy attendant are not in the finger. If you really see through this, Tenryu, Gutei, the boy, and you yourself are all run through with one skewer."

Mumon first comments that the satori of Gutei and of the boy are not in the finger. Where is the satori then? We should not be misled by the word *finger*. What is it that is in front of you? What is it that is behind you? Cast yourself away, die in yourself, and be the seen when you see, be the heard when you hear. If you truly die in yourself, whether you may be standing or sitting, going or coming, it is nothing but the finger; it is nothing but Zen. Heaven and earth, Gutei and the boy, I and you, are all run through with one finger; all is in one finger. Mumon tries his best to uphold the Zen of One Finger.

It is recorded that long ago Master Gensha said, "In the past, had I witnessed Gutei sticking up one finger, I should certainly have wrenched it away!" Does this comment of Gensha praise the Zen of One Finger or abuse it?

TEISHO ON MUMON'S POEM

Gutei made a fool of old Tenryu,
With a sharp knife he chastised the boy.
Korei raised his hand with no effort,
And lo! the great ridge of Mount Ka was split in two!

Mumon made a poem to complete this koan and also to illustrate its point clearly. Originally, the Truth of Zen is clear and manifest. It is lucidly revealed everywhere. Nothing is lacking anywhere. Why is it necessary then to stick up one finger, or to cut it off? From the absolute standpoint, both Tenryu and Gutei are making fools of everybody. Furthermore, to make the boy attain satori by cutting off his finger—how absurd! Even to hear it pollutes the ear. Thus with much zeal Mumon comments on the koan.

Lastly, Mumon refers to a Chinese myth and says, "Korei raised his hand with no effort, and lo! the great ridge of Mount Ka was split in two!" Once upon a time there was a god named Korei who had supernatural mysterious powers. He split the Great Mountain Ka into two parts and let the great river run through the range of mountains. Even the supernatural powers of Korei are no match for the Zen of One Finger. In the phrase "with no effort," Mumon implies how dynamically and extraordinarily One Finger works.

When one wants to go, he goes; when he wants to sit, he sits; this is how a Zen man lives. Where does he get this Truth in Zen? We must clearly see this supernatural power, so creative and mysterious.

4

The Foreigner Has No Beard

KOAN

Wakuan said, "Why has the foreigner from the West no beard?"

MUMON'S COMMENTARY

Training in Zen has to be real training. Satori has to be real satori. You have to see this foreigner here clearly yourself; then you actually know him. If, however, you talk about "clearly seeing," you have already fallen into dichotomy.

MUMON'S POEM

> In front of a fool
> Talk of no dream.
> The foreigner has no beard:
> It is adding stupidity to clarity.

TEISHO ON THE KOAN

Master Wakuan lived from 1108 to 1179. He died about four years before Mumon was born, so they belonged to almost the same period in the southern

Sung dynasty. We know that Wakuan was the successor to Master Gokuku Keigen, but know little of the story of his life. He made the following poem on his deathbed:

> An iron tree is in bloom,
> A cook lays an egg.
> Seventy-two years.
> The cradle has fallen.

Wakuan must have been an exceptionally capable Zen Master, for otherwise he could not have made such an outstanding koan.

The foreigner from the West is Bodhidharma, who came to China from India in the sixth century. It may also be said to refer to any foreigner from the West.

"Why had Bodhidharma no beard?"—this short and simple question has the strength and sharpness of a naked dagger thrust at the throat. The word "Why?" in particular is the key to this koan. How can it be so? Bodhidharma's face is covered with a bushy beard—there is no denying this fact. A beardless face can never be identified as Bodhidharma's face. The beard is even the symbol of Bodhidharma. Referring to this heavily bearded Bodhidharma, Wakuan presses the question, "Why has he no beard?" This contradiction should be thoroughly appreciated. It is the same as demanding, "Why have you no nose?"

For something that definitely *is,* why does he say it *is not?* From what standpoint does Wakuan insist, "He has no beard," while he actually has one? What is Mumon's ultimate motive in presenting this koan? If one fails to see the real significance of the above contradiction, he is unable to grasp the essence of the koan.

Wakuan asks us to cast away all of our dualistic consciousness in this Great Doubt "Why?" In this "Why?" yes and no are to be abandoned; subject and object are to be transcended. The one who has actually gone through Zen training and transcended dualism should immediately understand where the real significance of this koan is.

Is there such a distinction of yes and no in the thing itself? Are there such distinctions as big or small, this or that, in the reality of a thing itself? Be the Reality itself. Be the beard itself through and through. At this moment the whole universe is the beard; the whole universe is no-beard. The universe, or the infinite, does not know the dichotomy of yes-and-no, this-and-that, big-and-small. Wakuan's intention should be grasped here. If there is even a thought of discriminating consciousness, it will be just an ordinary beard in the world of yes-and-no.

There is an interesting story: Once there was a gentleman with a beautiful beard so long it reached his chest. One day his friend, admiring his beard, asked, "Your beard is splendid indeed! When you go to bed, do you place such a beautiful beard outside the bed quilt, or under it?" The gentleman, who had never thought about it, was not able to answer the question. From that evening, however, all through the night he kept putting his long beard over the bed quilt, then under it, again over it and under it. He could not peacefully fall asleep any longer and finally became neurotic. What a pitiable fool he was!

Another gentleman with a beautiful long beard, when he heard the above story, said with a smile, "Sometimes I put it under the bed quilt, and sometimes over it."

"Why has the foreigner from the West no beard?" If he has the beard, just with it, as it is, he has no beard. If he has no beard, then just without it, as he is, he has a beard. Such a beard is the true beard that can even bind the whole universe. The one who has this beard is the man of eternal peace.

TEISHO ON MUMON'S COMMENTARY

"Training in Zen has to be real training. Satori has to be real satori. You have to see this foreigner here clearly yourself; then you actually know him. If, however, you talk about 'clearly seeing,' you have already fallen into dichotomy."

Mumon emphatically maintains that training in Zen has to be real training; satori has to be real satori. Needless to say, Zen is totally different from intellectual methods aiming at getting a theoretical or conceptual conclusion. It lives in quite another dimension. Zen asks us to transcend dualism, to attain no-mind. If Zen is only philosophically interpreted, it remains an idea and a concept. When one personally experiences the Truth of Zen and testifies to it, his training is real training and his satori real satori. Apart from this very person, this I, there can be no Zen.

Wakuan says, "The foreigner has no beard." To know whether he really has a beard or no beard, one has to grasp Bodhidharma alive with his whole being. To grasp Bodhidharma alive is to be, oneself, Bodhidharma. When he is truly Bodhidharma through and through, he himself is the Truth that transcends being and nonbeing. If, however, one calls it "clearly seeing him," he has already fallen into dichotomy and has missed the Absolute.

TEISHO ON MUMON'S POEM

> In front of a fool
> Talk of no dream.
> The foreigner has no beard:
> It is adding stupidity to clarity.

Mumon angrily says to Wakuan, "Don't tell an empty dream, lacking the truth, to a fool who at the very start is out of his senses." A fool is the one who clings to the discriminating thinking of yes-and-no and is enslaved by his dualistic intellect. Fundamentally speaking, both Mumon and Wakuan are just talking of a dream. Mumon goes on to say, "With a calm and fresh-looking face you make a sleeper talk and ask, 'Why has the foreigner from the West no beard?'" Mumon flatly casts away the whole koan as the fantastic dream of a fool. Having cast it away, what does he expect from us? Does he mean that "the Truth of no beard is to be seen there"? It is Mumon's compassionate attempt to revive us from the dead.

5

Kyogen's Man Up a Tree

Master Kyogen said, "It is like a man up a tree who hangs from a branch by his mouth; his hands cannot grasp a bough, his feet cannot touch the tree. Another man comes under the tree and asks him the meaning of Bodhidharma's coming from the West. If he does not answer, he does not meet the questioner's need. If he answers, he will lose his life. At such a time, how should he answer?"

MUMON'S COMMENTARY

Even though your eloquence flows like a river, it is all to no avail. Even if you can expound the Great Tripitaka, it is also of no use. If you can really answer it, you will revive the dead and kill the living. If, however, you are unable to answer, wait for Maitreya to come and ask him.

MUMON'S POEM

> Kyogen is just gibbering;
> How vicious his poison is!
> Stopping up the monks' mouths,
> He makes their devil's eyes glare!

Master Kyogen was a contemporary of Gyozan, who died in 890, so he must have lived toward the end of the T'ang dynasty.

Kyogen presents this koan out of his compassion and states it in this drastic form in an effort to smash through the restraint of human discrimination at one blow. He wants us to cast away our discriminating mind by means of the koan.

Asking "the meaning of Bodhidharma's coming from the West" may be taken as asking the meaning of "the essence of Zen."

There is an interesting story of how Kyogen attained his satori, which undoubtedly motivated him to ask this strange question here. The story is well known in Zen circles, and as it may help us to understand him as a Zen Master, I will digress and tell it here.

Kyogen was a man of erudition and strong memory, and was unusually bright and talented. From his childhood he was fond of learning. He first studied under Master Hyakujo, but as the latter died soon after he started, he continued his Zen training under Isan. Isan recognized unusual genius in him and wished somehow to open his spiritual eye. One day he called Kyogen and said, "I do not want to hear from you what you have learned from scriptures nor the result of your accumulated studies and speculations. Just give me the essential word about your Self before you were born, before you knew either east or west." At this unexpected question, Kyogen was quite at a loss and could not utter a word. He searched diligently, but each time he presented an answer to Isan he found the Master flatly rejected it. Finally, with his energy all exhausted, Kyogen came to Isan and implored him, "Please teach 'it' to me!" "Even if I might show it to you," said Isan, "it is my word and has nothing to do with your answer." And he paid no attention to Kyogen's plea.

In disappointment, Kyogen took out his books and the notes from his years of study and burned them all, saying, "Pictures of cake do not satisfy one's hunger." Driven to despair by his inability to break through the barrier, he gave up his training and left Isan's monastery in tears. He visited the grave of National Teacher Echu and decided to lead his life as a nameless grave-keeper there. Although his biography does not give us any details, his inner struggle and searching must have continued and increased day and night, even after he despaired of his ability and decided to live as a grave-keeper. His religious Great Doubt must have been intensified to the point where the slightest touch might result in an explosion. The opportunity was ripe.

One day while cleaning the yard, Kyogen threw the rubbish into the bushes. A stone hit a bamboo. He heard the crash, and at that moment, all of a sudden, he was enlightened and burst into laughter in spite of himself.

He immediately returned to his hut and changed his clothes. Burning incense, he prostrated himself in the direction of Isan and praised the virtue of his teacher. "The compassion of Isan is indeed greater than that of my parents. Had he taught 'it' to me when I asked him, I could never have had this great joy today."

As we can see from the above story, Kyogen was originally a man of intelligence and learning. Because of that, he had to go through even greater contradictions and more painful struggles to transcend his sagacity and learning. He succeeded beautifully, however, in his spiritual struggle to transcend intellectual contradictions and become a Great Master of real peace and freedom. His unique training processes and experiences gave him the background to come out with a koan such as this.

Truly, a life controlled by its dualistic intellect may be likened to the man in this strange koan proposed by Kyogen. A man up a tree who hangs from a branch by his mouth is asked by another man under the tree the essence of Zen. If he answers, he will fall from the tree and die. If he does not answer, he cannot meet the need of the questioner. How can he break through the barrier of this great dilemma? Unless one faces the inescapable crisis and has once had the experience of dying, one will not have true freedom. Master Mumon stresses this in his commentary on the first koan: "In studying Zen, one must pass the barriers set up by the ancient Zen Masters. For the attainment of incomparable satori, one has to cast away his discriminating mind." When his discriminating mind is got rid of and cast away, what kind of spirituality will he have? What kind of life will he live? Kyogen says in the koan "at such a time." This means "just as he is," with no thought working, no consciousness moving. If he hangs from a tree, just as he is hanging, the essence of Zen is alive and manifest there.

A Zen Master, commenting on this koan, said, "Now, setting aside the man up a tree, what is 'the meaning of Bodhidharma's coming from the West' when you have fallen from the tree?" This also points to "at such a time." If one has fallen from the tree, just as he has fallen, the essence of Zen should be alive and manifest there. Here and now, just as it is—this is "it." What other answer can be possible? Apart from the fact, concrete, lucid, and penetrating, there is no Zen.

What is essential in Zen is "to cast away one's discriminating mind." When this is done, for the first time one can transcend yes and no, good and evil, and can declare that everything, everywhere, is "it." One can then truly grasp Kyogen's Zen.

TEISHO ON MUMON'S COMMENTARY

Mumon comments, "Even though your eloquence flows like a river, it is all to no avail. Even if you can expound the Great Tripitaka, it is also of no use. If you can really answer it, you will revive the dead and kill the living. If, however, you are unable to answer, wait for Maitreya to come and ask him."

Kyogen demands in the koan that his disciples give the answer "at such a time." Mumon, however, commenting on it, says that "at such a time it is of no avail at all, even if you have eloquence flowing like a river and could expound the Great Tripitaka." If you can give a truly apt answer at such a time, you are then absolutely free and are capable of reviving the dead and killing the living. That is to say, you can freely take satori away from the so-called enlightened one who is attached to satori, and turn the ignorant one to enlightenment. Certainly you are capable of it, for you are now a man of absolute freedom, having fundamentally solved the contradictions in the mind.

Mumon goes on to say that those who are not yet capable of giving the truly apt answer at such a time will have to wait for the advent of Maitreya Buddha, the Buddha of the future who, it is said, will appear in this world 5,670,000,000 years after Sakyamuni Buddha's death, to save human beings. They can ask Maitreya. This is not just a sarcastic remark but a compassionate condemnation by Mumon, who thus encourages his disciples to return from the abyss of death.

TEISHO ON MUMON'S POEM

> Kyogen is just gibbering;
> How vicious his poison is!
> Stopping up the monk's mouths,
> He makes their devil's eyes glare!

"Gibbering" is a translation of *zusan*. In former times there was a man in China named Zusan who used to write eccentric poems that did not rhyme. Hence "zusan" came to mean anything without rhyme or reason. Here it means nonsense uttered at random. In the first two lines Mumon is saying, "What an absurd Master this Kyogen is! And how vicious is the poison he has presented here!" We may interpret this comment as describing how fatal his question is, which has taken the lives of so many monks. Zen, however, sometimes uses a device called "praise by means of denouncing." By heaping abuse upon him, Mumon is really admiring the extraordinary capability of Master Kyogen. Mumon finishes his poem, saying, "To such a dreadful question by Kyogen, those who regard themselves as Zen experts would be unable to utter even a word in reply. They would just have to shut their mouths with their eyes wide open, trembling in fear."

Let me add, however, that just when Kyogen has stopped up the monks' mouths and has made their devil's eyes glare, Zen—"it"—is ever alive and manifest. Mumon is clearly answering Kyogen. If you fail to get "it," so vividly presented here, Zen is completely out of your reach.

6

Sakyamuni Holds Up a Flower

KOAN

Long ago when the World-Honored One was at Mount Grdhrakuta to give a talk, he held up a flower before the assemblage. At this all remained silent. The Venerable Kasho alone broke into a smile. The World-Honored One said, "I have the all-pervading True Dharma, incomparable Nirvana, exquisite teaching of formless form. It does not rely on letters and is transmitted outside scriptures. I now hand it to Maha Kasho."

MUMON'S COMMENTARY

Yellow-faced Gotama is certainly outrageous. He turns the noble into the lowly, sells dog-flesh advertised as sheep's head. I thought there was something interesting in it. However, at that time if everyone in the assemblage had smiled, to whom would the True Dharma have been handed? Or again, if Kasho had not smiled, would the True Dharma have been transmitted? If you say that the True Dharma can be transmitted, the yellow-faced old man with his loud voice deceived simple villagers. If you say that it cannot be transmitted, then why was Kasho alone approved?

MUMON'S POEM

A flower is held up,
And the secret has been revealed.

Kasho breaks into a smile;
The whole assemblage is at a loss.

TEISHO ON THE KOAN

"The World-Honored One" is a name given to Sakyamuni Buddha. He is said to have been born in the kingdom of Magadha as Prince Siddhartha of the Sakya tribe in 565 B.C., to have renounced the world at the age of twenty-nine, attained Buddhahood at thirty-five, and entered Nirvana in 486 B.C. at the age of eighty after spending his life teaching Buddhism as its founder.

Mount Grdhrakuta is a mountain near the capital of Magadha where Sakyamuni used to give his talks. Because its shape looks like the head of an eagle, it is also called Mount Eagle.

Maha Kasho (Kashyapa in Sanskrit) was one of Sakyamuni's Ten Great Disciples. He was respected for his most assiduous discipline and after Sakyamuni's death was active as the leader of the Buddhist community, the Sangha. He is respected as the Buddha's successor. He died around 436 B.C.

Zen maintains that it directly transmits Sakyamuni Buddha's religious experience itself, and that the life of Zen lies in the fact of this transmission. How then does the Dharma transmission actually take place in Zen? This koan of "Sakyamuni Holds Up a Flower" is a very significant one as it gives us a clear and concrete example of the unique Dharma transmission in Zen. Before giving my teisho on the koan, it may be helpful to give a brief explanation of its background.

There are a number of books in China with stories more or less similar to the one in this koan. They all record this account of "Sakyamuni Holds Up a Flower" as if it were a historically traceable event. The source of the incident is *Daibontenno Monbutsu Ketsugi-kyo,* and there are no Sanskrit scriptures in India in which it can be found. Moreover, it is the general opinion of bibliographers that *Daibontenno Monbutsu Ketsugi-kyo* must be a spurious work of a later date in China, and the tale of "Sakyamuni Holds Up a Flower" is criticized as a fabrication without historical basis.

True it may be that the story cannot be supported by history, yet this does not mean that the fact of Dharma transmission in Zen from a Master to his disciple is to be denied. It is perfectly natural that someone whose experience was based on such transmission should give a Zen interpretation to the fact of Dharma transmission from a Master to his disciple as we see it here in this koan. The significance of the koan and its historical basis belong to two different orders, and the former will not be affected by the latter.

Needless to say, the life of Zen as a religion is in the fact of religious experience personally attained by each individual. From the beginning, initiation following any ritual or scripture was utterly denied in Zen. Zen transmission is always based on the actual experience of each individual, and at the same time the experience of a disciple and that of his teacher are to be one and the same. This is why Zen, while insisting on the absolute necessity of standing on one's own experience, attaches much importance to teacher-disciple transmission and takes it most seriously. If this is neglected, the light of the true, live Zen tradition will immediately go out. Thus "teacher-disciple transmission" in Zen is described as "mind-to-mind" and has come to have a unique significance and tradition.

Even though it may be mind-to-mind, the term "transmission" already implies transfer in space and time from *A* to *B*. For Zen, which is solely based on one's own religious experience and denies initiation or inheritance in any form at all, this concept of transfer is an inexcusable misapprehension. A new, creative meaning has therefore been given to the word transmission, explaining that it is "transmission of the untransmittable," or "to transmit is to be identified with." In other words, "teacher-disciple transmission" in Zen is "teacher-disciple identification," where the experience of the teacher and that of his disciple are in complete accord with each other. They fundamentally originate in one and the same Truth.

From very early times it has been said, "It is like pouring water from one vessel into another exactly like it." The disciple's experience has always to be approved by his teacher. It is a unique characteristic of Zen transmission that the teacher's verification is thus essential, for by it the genuineness of the Zen tradition has been maintained.

Whether the story of "Sakyamuni Holds Up a Flower" can be supported by history or not is a matter of historical and bibliographical interest and has nothing to do with the fact of teacher-disciple transmission of Zen. That is to say, the fact of transmission in Zen transcends historical concern, and in this sense the koan has a profound Zen significance for us even today.

This koan says that long ago Sakyamuni was at Mount Grdhrakuta and one day took his place in front of the audience. Before the people who were waiting eagerly for the talk, he held up a lotus flower and did not utter even a word. Sakyamuni held up a flower—did he really give a talk, or not? It has all been settled in this instant of holding up a flower.

I am a flower. The whole universe is a flower. If a thought of consciousness moves, it is gone altogether. Gutei stuck up one finger; Joshu cried out "Mu!" Are these the same, or are they different? Those who know will immediately know it. Those who can see will at once see it. All has been thoroughly expounded—what a wonderful talk! An old Zen Master sings:

> As I see it with my mind of no-mind,
> It is I-myself, this flower held up!

We should not, however, just draw the conceptual conclusion that I and the whole world are one.

There is a sentence in *Hoke-kyo:* "The meeting at Mount Grdhrakuta is definitely present here." This means that the talk on Mount Grdhrakuta is vividly taking place now, right before us. Does this sentence ask us, then, to listen to Sakyamuni's grand talk of holding up a flower directly here and now, transcending space and time? Does it tell us to grasp the Truth before the dawn of human consciousness?

Nobody was there, however, who could hear the grand talk of Sakyamuni with his heart and soul. All the audience remained silent and there was no response to it. Then the Venerable Kasho broke into a smile. The Venerable Kasho alone fully appreciated this "talk of no talk" and responded to it with a smile.

The "smile" created a stir in Zen circles and from earliest times has been the cause of divided opinions.

Talk of no talk, hearing without hearing. What did Kasho get from the flower held up by Sakyamuni? After all, what is the real significance of Kasho's smile? This must naturally be the core of the question; and the actual Zen experience of each individual is the key to clarify the point.

A Zen Master said, commenting on the Venerable Kasho's smile, "A child does not mind the ugliness of its mother." Why could Sakyamuni's holding up a flower be ugly? The Zen eye has to be opened to see it. Again, how did Sakyamuni dare to be ugly? It must have been his irresistible compassion toward his disciples that forced him to be so. Kasho understood Sakyamuni's ugliness and appreciated it, and in his smile the wonder of the teacher-disciple identification was accomplished. Sakyamuni, the teacher, and Kasho, the disciple, are sharing one "family shame." Tell me what this "family shame" is. Here lies the secret of "holding up a flower" and "a smile," the secret of complete teacher-disciple identification in silence.

Another Master commented, "The father stole a sheep, and the son acknowledged it." This was originally a popular saying in China to illustrate silly honesty, that "the father did evil, which his son disclosed." The comment is significantly interesting in that father and son are in admirable accord with each other while taking different standpoints. We must here, however, clearly understand what "stealing a sheep" really means.

After all, without our own transparent experience, we are unable to appreciate what the old Zen Masters said or did. Be just a flower; be just a nyoi. Be it through and through. Where is the universe then? Here give me a word. You can be silent; or you can be smiling, as you will. And here for the first time you can truly grasp this koan.

There is a mondo in connection with the story of "Sakyamuni Holds Up a Flower." One day a Governor asked Master Ungo, "It is said, 'The World-Honored One gave a secret talk of holding up a flower, and Kasho by smiling did not conceal it.' What does this mean?" Ungo called out, "Oh, Governor!" "Yes, Master," replied the Governor. "Do you understand?" asked the Master. When the Governor said, "No, I don't," Ungo told him, "If you do not understand, it shows that the World-Honored One did make the secret talk. If you do understand, it means that Kasho did not conceal it."

What an interesting mondo this is on the koan of holding up a flower! If the flower held up by Sakyamuni is fragrant throughout the universe now, the Governor's "Yes, Master" must be echoing throughout the world now. Let those who can get it, get it.

At Kasho's "breaking into a smile" Sakyamuni verified the complete accord of their spirituality and declared in front of all the people, "I have the all-pervading True Dharma, incomparable Nirvana, exquisite teaching of formless form. It does not rely on letters and is transmitted outside scriptures. I now hand it to Maha Kasho." He thus testified to the fact of Dharma transmission to Kasho.

From olden times, such transmission of the untransmittable has been called Buddha-to-Buddha "testimony." This is not the handing over from Sakyamuni to Kasho, but from Sakyamuni to Sakyamuni. It is not the succession of Kasho to Sakyamuni, but Kasho to Kasho.

The teacher-disciple transmission in Zen is possible in such a manner, and teacher-disciple accord is verified in such an identification. This is why in Zen to transmit is to be identified with, and it is defined as "the transmission of the untransmittable."

Now Dharma, to be thus transmitted by nontransmission, transcends all objectification and conceptualization. It should be the "ever unnamable 'it.' " How ridiculous it is that Sakyamuni gave this unnamable "it" such long and complex names, saying, "I have the all-pervading True Dharma, incomparable Nirvana, exquisite teaching of formless form. It does not rely on letters and is transmitted outside scriptures." The moment we are deluded by the name, its life is all gone. Here, however, we can see Sakyamuni's infinite compassion toward his fellow beings in later generations. Perhaps it would help if I should try to clarify the meaning of each word used in Sakyamuni's list of unnamable names.

"True Dharma" is the Dharma of as-it-is-ness, where not even a thought of consciousness is working. It is "it," or the Truth that transcends space and time.

"All-pervading" means it is the source of creativity and wonderful working, which is absolutely free, perfect, inexhaustible, and infinite.

"Incomparable Nirvana" is the never-born, never-dying Reality itself. It is the subjectivity that freely expresses itself and works under all different situations.

"Formless form." A form takes a shape and shows discrimination. When there is no discrimination, there is no form, and this formless form is the true form of Reality, for it is the self-manifestation of "Mu."

"Not relying on letters." The Truth itself has no room for intellection to enter, for experiential fact does not belong to the realm of logic and intellect.

"Transmission outside scriptures." A teaching once expounded, however excellent it may be, is already a conceptualized corpse. The experiential fact is the foundation that gives birth to teachings and dogmas. It can never be restricted by teachings and dogmas and is always new, alive, and creative.

These explanations about names and words, though they may be helpful, are after all no more than conceptualization and objectification of one kind or another, and we should not be deluded by them. Negatively expressed, not a particle of "it" is there. Affirmatively explained, the True Dharma pervades the universe. Therefore just as it is, "it" is here right now. If you truly cast yourself away, True Dharma is ever luminous here and now.

The Truth Sakyamuni Buddha attained under the bodhi tree is nothing but this. The Dharma that has been transmitted from Buddha to Buddha, Master to Master, is nothing but this. We should clearly understand that apart from the fact experienced and testified to by each one of us there can be no true Zen tradition, no active Zen transmission.

TEISHO ON MUMON'S COMMENTARY

Mumon said, "Yellow-faced Gotama is certainly outrageous. He turns the noble into the lowly, and sells dog-flesh advertised as sheep's head. I thought there was something interesting in it. However, at that time if everyone in the assemblage had smiled, to whom would the True Dharma have been handed? Or again, if Kasho had not smiled, would the True Dharma have been transmitted? If you say that the True Dharma can be transmitted, the yellow-faced old man with his loud voice deceived simple villagers. If you say that it cannot be transmitted, then why was Kasho alone approved?"

Master Mumon, trying to point out the true significance of the koan, gives his characteristically unique and free comment. As usual, his commentary is full of sharply ironic remarks, but if we cling to their superficial meanings the true significance is at once lost. We have to grasp his real meaning beyond the expressions used.

"Oh, you yellow-faced Gotama!" Mumon addresses Sakyamuni in a familiar and teasing tone. "You should not be so absurd and be talking such nonsense. Talking to a rich nobleman, you call him poor and lowly; crying wine you sell vinegar. Stop deceiving people like that. I thought you would be a little better, but good gracious! It was after all sheer nonsense." Mumon is addressing Sakyamuni, the Wise Man of the Sakyas, in a familiar and rather informal way by calling him "yellow-faced Gotama." Gotama is his personal name, and by yellow-faced he means golden-faced—golden because he is enlightened. Mumon goes on, "crying wine you sell vinegar": you use fine phrases like "all-pervading True Dharma" and then hold up a flower. This comment should not be taken as merely teasing words. Thus with an air of severely denouncing Sakyamuni's talk of holding up a flower, Mumon in fact highly praises him.

He is saying, "In my eyes, everybody is a rich nobleman with the Buddha Nature. Why do you regard all people as poor and lowly and treat Kasho alone as a nobleman? Besides, pretending to give a good talk, you just held up a flower in silence. Aren't you going too far in deceiving people?" With such abusive language Mumon upholds Sakyamuni's exquisite talk of no talk.

Mumon's comment becomes even more cutting: "It was fortunate for you that only the Venerable Kasho understood it and broke into a smile. Suppose all the people had smiled at it. How then would you have handed on the True Dharma? If, on the contrary, the Venerable Kasho had not smiled, could the True Dharma possibly be transmitted?" Mumon is urging our clear grasp of the "transmission of the untransmittable" from a Master to his disciple. His penetrating inquiry continues to the end, where he says that if you mean that there is Dharma transmission in Zen, you are deceiving people; and he asks, "If you say there is no transmission in Zen, then why did you declare that you had handed it to the Venerable Kasho alone?" By such pressing inquiries

Mumon tries to illustrate for his disciples the true significance of the transmission of the untransmittable in Zen and to show them how its teacher-disciple transmission is possible.

Master Hakuin gave his teisho on this koan: "Everybody, male or female, without exception, has the True Dharma. Still, Sakyamuni expressly declared that he had handed it to Kasho alone. He is certainly deceiving people. Yet I won't say that there was no transmission taking place. I now hold up my hossu like this, the truth of which no dull ordinary monks can ever grasp. Kasho grasped it, so he smiled. There will not be too many who can fully appreciate the real significance of this smile. When one gets it, there is the true transmission." We should carefully listen to what Hakuin says as well as to Mumon, and clearly comprehend what transmission in Zen is.

TEISHO ON MUMON'S POEM

> A flower is held up,
> And the secret has been revealed.
> Kasho breaks into a smile:
> The whole assemblage is at a loss.

In the second line of this poem the word translated "secret" is literally "tail," a word which sometimes implies a "hidden face under a mask." Here it means secret—the Truth that transcends words and letters. In this poem Mumon comments sharply on Sakyamuni's holding up a flower, "I have seen through your trick and I won't be deceived." By saying that he has seen through the secret of the transmission of the untransmittable, Mumon shows the depth of his own experience. "You may make a fool of everybody else, but not me," Mumon tells Sakyamuni.

Tell me what kind of flower this is, the flower Sakyamuni held up. It is the flower that will never be burned by fire, never wilt in frost. It is the flower that is neither big nor small, and in the fields and mountains it is ever bright and fresh in bloom, in the past or at present. At the same time, it is the flower that will immediately be gone if one becomes attached to words and logic and is deluded by concepts.

In the last two lines of the poem Mumon simply repeats the story: "Kasho alone broke into a smile in full appreciation, but all the rest of them were utterly at a loss." I can almost hear him tell his disciples, "It is not an old tale but your own question now!" He is in fact telling them, "You, every one of you, are holding the eternal flower in your hand, or rather, are the flower itself. Why don't you open your eye?"

An old Zen Master symbolically commented on the koan in a poem:

> The rain last night scattered the flowers;
> Fragrant is the castle surrounded by running waters.

How are we to read the essence of Zen in this beautiful poem? Does it imply that everyone, whether he smiles or not, is living in the same True Dharma? Truly there is not a spot where the sun does not shine, yet pitiable are the blind who have to live in darkness.

Permit me to make one additional comment. In one of the popular books I once read a criticism of this koan of "Sakyamuni Holds Up a Flower." It said, "Because Mumon saw the koan through cloudy binoculars, he failed to see the exchange of delicate human feelings shining at the back of the story." This is a surprising misunderstanding. What the koan illustrates for us is the Truth of Zen seen in Dharma transmission through teacher-disciple identification, and such an ethical question as the beauty of the human relation between the teacher and his disciple is not at issue. Zen points to the fundamental realization from which ethics and other human virtues originate.

7

Joshu Says "Wash Your Bowls"

Once a monk made a request of Joshu. "I have just entered the monastery," he said. "Please give me instructions, Master." Joshu said, "Have you had your breakfast?" "Yes, I have," replied the monk. "Then," said Joshu, "wash your bowls." The monk had an insight.

MUMON'S COMMENTARY

Joshu opened his mouth and showed his gallbladder, and revealed his heart and liver. If this monk, hearing it, failed to grasp the Truth, he would mistake a bell for a pot.

MUMON'S POEM

Because it is so very clear,
It takes longer to come to the realization.
If you know at once candlelight is fire,
The meal has long been cooked.

TEISHO ON THE KOAN

"Joshu's lips give off light," thus it was said of old, describing his Zen. Like Rinzai and Tokusan, Joshu was a Zen Master active in the later years of the T'ang dynasty, when Zen in China was full of a fresh and creative spirit. Unlike other famous Masters who were fond of swinging a stick or uttering a KWATZ! cry, Joshu expressed his Zen with wonderfully apt and pithy words. Its dynamic strength was vividly demonstrated in his sayings, although he did not use any physical or violent means.

This koan, in which Joshu directly presents the essence of Zen in our daily life, shows clearly the characteristics of his Zen.

One day a monk in training came to see Joshu with a request: "I am a novice in this monastery. Please instruct me in the essence of Zen." The monk spoke of himself as having just entered the monastery. I think he was a newcomer at Joshu's monastery, but may not necessarily have been a novice in Zen training, for it is presumed from the mondo in the koan that he had already gone through the hard inner searching to a considerable extent. Otherwise he could not so easily have had an insight into the Truth. Those who have gone through the actual training processes themselves will unanimously agree that real spiritual peace and happiness cannot be so easily and accidentally attained in an instant. From the mondo we can also see that the monk is very sincere in his search for the Truth.

Joshu therefore gave him a very kind and appropriate answer: "Have you had your breakfast?" He did not bring in any philosophy or concept in answering the monk. An old saw says, "Because it is so close, nobody sees it." Apart from "this person, I-myself, here now," what Truth can there be? When you see, see directly! What are you looking for, turning your eyes away from yourself? What a pity that the monk failed to grasp what Joshu really meant.

The monk therefore naïvely answered, "Yes, I have had my breakfast." That's it! That's it! Still he does not realize it. With much regret an old Zen Master comments on this questioning monk, "Being on the finest horse, he does not know how to ride it." (This is not only about the monk—let me ask, how about you?)

Joshu, realizing that his first arrow had missed the mark, immediately shot the second: "Then wash your bowls." What an excellent instruction this is! I should like to clap my hands and cry out, "There it is!" Sharp, dynamic spirituality gushes out of his words. Certainly "his lips give off light." For Joshu, to live Zen was not to lead a Zen-like life; but to live an ordinary life, just as it is, was Zen.

Referring to these words of Joshu, Hakuin said, "If you want to get the real significance of 'Then wash your bowls,' first ask yourself how you can recite the Nembutsu without opening your mouth." I would ask you to "wash your bowls without using your hands." It is nothing but asking you to live with no-mind, which can be attained only after long, sincere, and assiduous striving.

Most fortunately the questioning monk here "had an insight" at Joshu's words. His spiritual eye was opened to the fact that it is as it is—that he, as he is, is "it"; that "it" cannot be outside himself. Once having awakened, he has always been in "it." Essentially he has always been "it," the Truth. His walking, standing, or sitting are all nothing but "it." I feel like crying out, "How dull and late you are to know it only now!" Yet how many will there be who will have the happiness of knowing it at all?

Master Shido Bunan has the following poem:

> Do not let the word "Tao" delude you;
> Realize it is nothing else
> Than what you do morning and night.

Master Tendo Shogaku wrote a poem on this koan of "Joshu Says 'Wash Your Bowls' ":

> Breakfast was over and the monk was asked to wash the bowls.
> Immediately he had an insight.
> Tell me, accomplished monks at monasteries today,
> Have you satori or not?

The first line refers to Joshu's instruction given in reply to the monk's question, and the second to the monk who had an insight at Joshu's words. These two lines do not require any particular comment, but the third and fourth lines show Master Shogaku's outstanding view on this koan. He says, "At present there may be many Zen monks at various monasteries who have become advanced in their training. Let me ask them if they have satori or not." Master Shogaku is asking them, "Do you have satori or not, you monks studying Zen today? If you have any smack of satori at all, you cannot stand beside Joshu, whose Zen is so superb and indeed without comparison." He thus severely warns against Zen-savoring Zen, or Zen-monkish Zen with the stink of satori. At the same time he highly admires Joshu, whose spirituality is so immaculate and exceptionally outstanding, with no traces of superiority, yet enjoying deep and lucid Zen spirituality in an ordinary daily life.

TEISHO ON MUMON'S COMMENTARY

"Joshu opened his mouth and showed his gallbladder, and revealed his heart and liver. If this monk, hearing it, failed to grasp the Truth, he would mistake a bell for a pot."

Mumon first speaks of Joshu: "Uttering a word, he revealed all his heart." However much he may talk about revealing, the fact is Zen can never be hidden away.

One autumn day Master Maido and his lay disciple Kosan-goku took a walk together on the mountain. Maido asked Kosan-goku, "Can you smell the fragrance of the mokusei tree?" "Yes, I can," answered Kosan-goku. "I have nothing to hide from you," was the Master's reply, which greatly impressed his lay disciple.

Next Mumon severely criticizes the questioning monk, "If this monk, hearing it, failed to grasp the Truth, he would mistake a bell for a pot." Although the koan says that the monk had an insight, Mumon distinguishes his insight from true satori in Zen. He may have had an insight, but Mumon does not approve it as satori.

Mumon comments that unfortunately the monk's Zen ability was not sufficient to see through the generous instruction of Joshu, who thoroughly opened his heart to him. A bell and a pot are two completely different things although their shapes look alike. Do not swallow Joshu's instruction in hasty misunderstanding seems to be Mumon's emphatic warning to the questioning monk when it is, of course, addressed to his own disciples.

TEISHO ON MUMON'S POEM

Because it is so very clear,
It takes longer to come to the realization.
If you know at once candlelight is fire,
The meal has long been cooked.

Because it is so clear and manifest, people find it difficult to come to the realization, Mumon says. When you see, see it directly; grasp it in your seeing. When you hear, hear it directly; grasp it in your hearing. But tell me, how do you grasp it? It immediately is "it." Not only "having breakfast," "washing bowls," but every movement of your hand and foot is no other than "it."

In the entrance hall of a Japanese Zen temple one will find a small wooden board on which is written: "Look under your feet." It asks you to see clearly the very place where you stand. Alas! Because it is too close nobody bothers to see it! Aren't we living in it day and night?

The monk may have an insight, hearing Joshu say, "Wash your bowls." It is, however, nothing special to make a fuss about, for it is like realizing that candlelight is fire. He just recognized water while in the midst of water.

The meal has already been prepared. You do not have to ask Joshu anew, nor do you have to wait for Joshu to point it out for you. It is here, there, everywhere, from the beginning.

An old Zen Master sings:

> Do not think
> The moon appears when the clouds are gone.
> All the time it has been there in the sky
> So perfectly clear.

8

Keichu Makes Carts

Master Gettan said to a monk: "Keichu made a cart whose wheels had a hundred spokes. Take both front and rear parts away and remove the axle: then what will it be?"

MUMON'S COMMENTARY

If you can immediately see through this, your eye will be like a shooting star and your spirituality like lightning.

MUMON'S POEM

> When the vividly working wheel turns
> Even an expert is lost.
> Four directions, above and below:
> South, north, east, and west.

TEISHO ON THE KOAN

There are many stories about Keichu, who was an expert cart-maker in ancient China; none of them is definitely known to be true. It is said that he made the first cart to be pulled by a horse, in the days of Emperor U of the Ka dynasty, and that he made a grand cart whose wheels had a hundred spokes and amazed the people. In this koan Master Gettan, referring to the story of this extraordinary cart, tries to awaken his disciples to the Truth of Zen.

Master Gettan Zenka lived at Mount Daii in Tanshu. Although he was a Zen Master who preceded Mumon in the same line of Dharma transmission and lived comparatively close to Mumon's time, little is known about him.

One day Gettan said to a monk, "Long ago Keichu is said to have made a most splendid cart with wheels having a great number of spokes. If, however, the hubs and the body of the cart are taken away and the axle is removed, what will become of it?"

Literally this question may be interpreted as follows: "Keichu made a wonderful cart by putting together various parts. Now, if all these parts are taken away and the very shape of the cart is gone, what will become of it?" Based on such an interpretation, there are many who take it as a doctrine of sunyata, which teaches that everything is primarily empty. There is an old Japanese poem:

> Put grasses together and tie twigs one to another:
> Behold, here is a cottage!
> Dismantle it and take it to pieces:
> Behold, it is the original grass field!

Quoting this, they would say that a cart can take shape when various parts such as an axle, hubs, spokes, wheels, etc., are all put together. When it is dismantled and taken to pieces, the very form of the cart is there no more. This may be one Buddhist doctrine, but it is not Zen.

"Then what will it be?" Gettan presses you for the answer. He does not ask for a philosophical interpretation but wants you to show your dynamic Zen working. This is a very sharp and direct demand. In other words, he asks you to open your eye to the Truth of Zen, where human consciousness has not yet started to work. Gettan asks you to "take both front and rear parts away, and remove the axle," that is, to directly transcend the form of a cart. To objectively transcend the form of the cart is to subjectively cast away one's own existence. It is to transcend the dualistic distinction of I-and-you, subject-and-object, and to live and work in the transcendental and yet individualistic Oneness.

Gettan's question "What will it be?" has such direct and profound significance! It comes out of his great compassion!

With reference to "What will it be?" I should like to add a few words. In

Japan there is a famous saying to describe the secret of horsemanship: "No rider on the saddle; no horse under the saddle." To become an expert rider, one must practice diligently, undergoing long and difficult training, until finally he achieves the state of complete unity of man and horse, where there is neither the rider nor the horse to ride on. Further, he must come to the stage where he is not even conscious of the unity itself. This is the samadhi of "both transcended." When both the rider and the horse are forgotten, they can best work and exhibit their utmost skill. This sounds very much like the work of no-mind, or Oneness of subject and object in Zen. Keichu, the expert cart-maker, was in a similar samadhi. When he made a cart, he himself was a cart through and through. When such vividly working wheels turn, with both front and rear parts taken away and the axle removed, certainly even a master must be at a loss. Keichu was an unparalleled past master in cart-making.

Here, however, a very important question is involved. Can we regard an expert rider as a Zen man and look upon an expert cart-maker as a Zen Master, because of their skill and samadhi when they are at their work? The answer is definitely No. Why? When one puts his soul and body into his work, often he will be in the state of samadhi where he forgets himself and transcends the distinction of subject and object. Such unity has its own value and beauty and may justly be admired. But it is limited in most cases to a particular aspect of one's work, which is psychologically or technically separated from the rest of his life. One will be in that samadhi only while he is engaged in that particular work, and his unity may be gone once he comes out of it. The vital point is that his samadhi is not based on a fundamental awakening which will completely change his personality and life.

Zen teaches samadhi and emphatically encourages the monks in training to achieve oneness of soul and body, identity of subject and object. It requires the monks to have no-mind and to be no-self. Since this training process in Zen seems to resemble psychological or technical disciplines in art, many people are likely to confuse them.

Training in Zen aims to bring about a fundamental change in the whole personality, by which one attains realization (which is called satori) and lives a new Zen life as a new man. Zen maintains that this experience of attaining religious personality is essential. It is therefore basically different from forget-fulness of oneself in an art or skill, which covers only one special aspect of one's life. Let me repeat: the ultimate aim of Zen is to accomplish a completely new religious personality by the satori experience, and to live Zen at every moment. Without this fundamental experience, whatever special skill or psyche one may have, it is not Zen at all.

In this koan Master Gettan first speaks of Keichu's unparalleled skill in cart-making, which was the result of his long training, and ends the koan with "then what will it be?" Referring to hard and assiduous training in art, which resembles that in Zen, as a means of leading the monks to the final spiritual leap, Gettan stressed the necessity of having the fundamental realization experience that should change their whole personality. The last sentence is thus most important; without it the problem posed loses its Zen significance as a koan.

Often I come across people who just naïvely believe that samadhi in art, or no-mind in expert skill, is the same as that of Zen because of their superficial resemblance. According to them there can naturally be dancing Zen, painting Zen, piano-playing Zen, or laboring Zen. This is an extremely careless misunderstanding. They have failed to see the basic difference between Zen and psychological absorption in an art or skill.

TEISHO ON MUMON'S COMMENTARY

"If you can immediately see through this, your eye will be like a shooting star and your spirituality like lightning," comments Mumon.

His comment is direct and to the point: "If you can immediately see into the experiential truth of taking away both front and rear parts and removing the axle, your eye will be like a shooting star and your spirituality like lightning; there will be no room for even a thought of consciousness to get in."

In other words, he asks you to immediately cast away all your consciousness and be directly the cart itself. Then there is neither you nor the cart, neither moving nor not-moving. Transcend them all, then you are utterly free in heaven and on earth, to kill or to revive. Even lightning cannot interfere with your transcendental freedom. Now, what could this transcendental freedom be? It is illustrated in the poem that concludes Mumon's commentary.

TEISHO ON MUMON'S POEM

> When the vividly working wheel turns
> Even an expert is lost.
> Four directions, above and below:
> South, north, east, and west.

Mumon, referring to a cart, figuratively describes the marvelous working of Oneness. When this transcendental cart of no-form runs with all its parts cast away, it moves but is unmoving; it does not move, but is moving—this is the true moving which even a supersonic spaceship can never achieve. Even an expert will be utterly unable to use his discrimination here.

An old Zen Master sings:

> The mind turns and works
> In accordance with ten thousand situations.
> Wherever it may turn,
> It is mysteriously serene.

I raise my hand, and the sun and moon lose their light under my hand. I lift my foot, and the vastness of the earth is altogether gone under my foot. There is no room at all here for intellect.

Four directions, above and below: south, north, east, and west. Everywhere the wonderful cart of no-form turns. Everything is the work of the true Self of no-form. How then, let me ask, does it turn right here, right now? "Four directions, above and below: south, north, east, and west!"

9

Daitsu Chisho

Once a monk said to Master Seijo of Koyo, "Daitsu Chisho Buddha did zazen on a bodhi seat for ten kalpas. Buddha Dharma was not manifested, nor did he attain Buddhahood. Why was it?" Jo said, "Your question is splendid indeed." The monk persisted, "He did practice zazen on a bodhi seat. Why did he not attain Buddhahood?" Jo replied, "Because he did not attain Buddhahood."

MUMON'S COMMENTARY

The old foreigner may know it, but he cannot really grasp it. An ordinary man, if he knows it, is a sage. A sage, if he grasps it, is an ordinary man.

MUMON'S POEM

Rather than give the body relief, give relief to the mind:
When the mind is at peace, the body is not distressed.
If mind and body are both set free,
Why must the holy saint become a lord?

TEISHO ON THE KOAN

This koan was taken from a metaphorical story in *Hoke-kyo,* chapter 7. From the standpoint of Buddhist philosophy, various doctrines can be derived from this tale of Daitsu Chisho Buddha. Quoting a part of his story from *Hoke-kyo,* the koan tries to make Zen students cut off all the doctrinal tangles of religious philosophy and directly get hold of the real, live Daitsu Chisho Buddha.

Rinzai said of him in *Rinzai-roku:* "Daitsu means the one who has attained, at all places, the no-nature, no-self reality of all things. Chisho means the one who does not rely on any teaching and has no doubt whatsoever under any circumstances. Buddha is the one whose mind is pure and lucid, and whose light penetrates through the Dharma world. To do zazen on a bodhi seat for ten kalpas refers to the life of the Ten Paramitas. 'Buddha Dharma was not manifested' means that the Buddha is originally unborn, Dharma is undying. How then could it ever manifest itself? 'He did not attain Buddhahood' means that being Buddha originally he does not become Buddha again." Rinzai's explanations are, after all, literal tangles too. A Zen man has to live with a different vista.

Now let us study the koan. One day a monk put to Master Seijo of Koyo the question, "In *Hoke-kyo* it is written about Daitsu Chisho Buddha that he did zazen on a bodhi seat for ten kalpas. Buddha Dharma was not manifested, nor did he attain Buddhahood. What does this mean?" The monk is of course asking the question from the Zen standpoint, and he is not asking for philosophical explanations or doctrinal discussions.

It may be necessary for me to take a page or two to clarify the terms used by the monk.

"Ten kalpas" means a very long period of time, beyond calculation.

"He did zazen on a bodhi seat" means that true zazen is the Buddha's deed itself. If one does zazen, it is Buddha's zazen. Hakuin said, "Why is it necessary to do zazen on a bodhi seat? You sit here now, and you are, as you are, Daitsu Chisho Buddha."

"Buddha Dharma was not manifested." Buddha Dharma is the fundamental, universal Reality itself that is ever unborn and undying, undefiled and unpurified, not-increasing and not-decreasing. The true Buddha Dharma of nonmanifestation is beyond manifesting and nonmanifesting. In *Shodoka* we read, "It is ever manifest, and can never be missing. If you seek after it, you can never get it."

"He did not attain Buddhahood." Everyone is in the Buddha Dharma. He should not cry with thirst while he is himself in the water. The one who does not attain Buddhahood should be the one who really has attained Buddhahood, shouldn't he? If he tries to attain Buddhahood further, he is stupid enough to try to put another hat on top of the one he already has on his head. To be able to say, however, that he who does not attain Buddhahood is the one who has attained it, one must actually live the Buddha life of nonattainment. Apart from him-himself, or from you-yourself, there is no Zen.

Seijo was a great and capable Master, and in reply to the monk's question he said, "That's it! You are right!" Because Seijo was living Zen of nonattainment himself, he could immediately cry out the Truth. An ancient Zen Master commented on this superb answer of Seijo, "So wonderful indeed! He chases after the burglar on the burglar's own horse!" He is saying, "He certainly is Daitsu Chisho Buddha. Not to attain Buddhahood is indeed the true life of Buddha Dharma."

Unfortunately, however, this splendid answer was a pearl cast before swine for the monk. He could not appreciate it at all, and foolishly asked again, "He did practice zazen on a Bodhi seat. Why did he not attain Buddhahood?" "You have missed it," I feel like crying out to him. How foolish for him to ask where water is while he himself is in it!

"Because he did not attain Buddhahood." Seijo kindly presented the true picture of Daitsu Chisho Buddha. Why does a Buddha have to seek after a Buddha? Because he is a true Buddha, he does not attain Buddhahood. Seijo was enjoying his life of a true Buddha himself. There is a waka poem:

> Let us admire the moon and cherish the flowers—
> Thus we should like to live.
> Never try to become Buddhas
> And ruin our precious life!

Let us read the heart of the poem as well as the heart of Seijo's answer.

TEISHO ON MUMON'S COMMENTARY

"The old foreigner may know it, but he cannot really grasp it. An ordinary man, if he knows it, is a sage. A sage, if he grasps it, is an ordinary man." Thus Mumon starts his comments with the old saying that even the greatest Masters like Sakyamuni and Bodhidharma cannot say that they have grasped the truth of Daitsu Chisho Buddha. The reality of Buddha does not belong to the domain of knowing and not-knowing, of grasping and not-grasping.

He continues to say that an ordinary man, if he knows the reality of Daitsu Chisho Buddha, is already a sage. I should say that the ordinary man who does not show any refinement is the man of real refinement. The man who does not assume a look of a sage must be a real sage.

"A sage, if he grasps it, is an ordinary man," Mumon says. The Truth which is unattainable even for Buddhas and Patriarchs is beyond the question of grasping and not-grasping. An ordinary man who does not attain Buddhahood might be a real sage. By taking away such dualistic argument as knowing and not-knowing, grasping and not-grasping, Mumon tries to reveal the reality of Daitsu Chisho Buddha.

TEISHO ON MUMON'S POEM

Rather than give the body relief, give relief to the mind.
When the mind is at peace, the body is not distressed.
If mind and body are both set free,
Why must the holy saint become a lord?

In this poem Mumon again tries to depict the true picture of Daitsu Chisho Buddha. "Rather than give the body relief, give relief to the mind." If one wants to solve fundamentally the question of his existence and get eternal peace and freedom, he has both to relieve his "body" and to emancipate his "mind." Body is a typical example of all discriminations, such as Buddha and unenlightened man, sage and ordinary man, satori and ignorance, while mind is the origin of such discrimination.

"When the mind is at peace, the body is not distressed." When the self is truly transcended and is awakened to the fundamental Mind, and realizes that "the whole is just One Mind," all the discriminations and differentiations in the world will have new and creative significance, for they in fact glorify the One Mind. Each varied phenomenon of differentiation is a working aspect of the Mind, and in the midst of discrimination as it is, the mind is at peace. With a willow it is green, with a flower it is red—each, as it is, is the working of him-himself.

Mumon's comments continue: "If mind and body are both set free . . ." —in actual training, however, when one really has given relief to his body, he has given relief to his mind. For the mind to be really at peace, the body has to be set free. Body and mind are primarily one, and in this Oneness in peace we are able to see the Truth of Daitsu Chisho Buddha.

"Why must the holy saint become a lord?" A holy saint is one who has transcended all earthly, relativistic values. In this poem the holy saint is another name for Daitsu Chisho Buddha. For the holy saint who is completely free from all earthly values, any form of human honor or credit on earth, even the status of a king or a lord, means nothing. The very fact that he does not seek after Buddha is the proof that Daitsu Chisho Buddha is a real Buddha.

There is an interesting story. Once there was a Zen Master in Japan named Tosui. He did not want to be the abbot of a big temple, and for a long time enjoyed life as a beggar. One day an old Shin (Pure Land) Buddhist visited Tosui's hovel. He noticed that there was no Buddha image in the half-broken-down hut. The devout Pure Land follower thought Tosui ought to worship the Buddha, no matter how poor he might be. In his faith and friendship he brought a picture of Amitabha, hung it on the wall of the hut, and advised him to worship it every morning and evening. Tosui immediately took up a brush and wrote a poem on the Amitabha picture:

> Though my hut is so very small,
> I will let you stay here, O Amitabha.
> But please do not get the impression
> That I want you to assure my rebirth in the Pure Land.

10

Seizei, a Poor Monk

A monk once said to Master Sozan, "I am poor and destitute. I beg you, O Master, please help me and make me rich." Sozan said, "Venerable Seizei!" "Yes, Master," replied Seizei. Sozan remarked, "Having tasted three cups of the best wine of Seigen, do you still say that your lips are not yet moistened?"

MUMON'S COMMENTARY

Seizei assumed a condescending attitude. What is his intention? Sozan has a penetrating eye and has seen through Seizei's mind. Be that as it may, just tell me how the Venerable Seizei could have drunk the wine.

MUMON'S POEM

His poverty is like Hantan's,
His spirit like that of Kou.
With no way of earning a livelihood
He dares to compete with the richest of men.

TEISHO ON THE KOAN

Sozan was a successor to Tozan and together with the latter is well known as a founder of Soto Zen in China. He was born in the year 858, ordained at the age of nineteen, and died in his sixty-second year in 919. He lived between the two great persecutions of Buddhism in the T'ang dynasty (which came in 845 and 955), a period when Zen enjoyed its heyday in China. He is famous for the free and delicate display of his Zen.

Apparently the petitioning monk, Seizei, was well known in the Zen circles of his time, but no other facts are known about him. He must have thought he had some insight, otherwise he could not have said his spirituality was "poor."

One day a monk, Seizei by name, came to see Master Sozan and made the request: "I am extremely poor and destitute—please help me out of this poverty and make me rich."

In connection with the "poverty" I remember that once a British gentleman came to study Zen under Master Daigi, who used to be my fellow student in our training days. For a koan Master Daigi gave him the famous Christian saying, "Blessed are the poor in spirit." I do not know what the orthodox traditional interpretation of this passage may be in Christianity. It would be interesting to see how Master Daigi took it up from the Zen standpoint and used it as a Zen koan.

Needless to say, the "poverty" Seizei talks of does not retain its literal meaning. "I do not have either satori or ignorance, heaven or hell, subject or object. I am pure and immaculate and even a helping hand is unable to do anything for me. How would you save a poor man like me?" The monk is challenging Sozan with this searching question so he can fathom Sozan's response. In other words, thrusting his static insight of poverty at Sozan, the monk wants to see how Sozan will work.

Sozan, however, was a capable Master who could freely use his Zen. He was too great to waver at such a question. Immediately he called out, "Venerable Seizei!" When Seizei answered, "Yes, Master," Sozan remonstrated, "Having emptied three cups of the best wine of Seigen, do you say that you have not even tasted it?" What in the world is lacking in you? If you see, your eyes are full of "it"; if you hear, your ears are full of "it." If you want to go, you go; if you want to sit, you sit. Far from being poor, what a rich man you are! Sozan's reply is wonderful indeed, a reply in which question and answer are completely interfused. They are one, and at the same time they are two. Here we see a characteristic of Soto Zen.

Master Ingen has a poem on "blessed poverty":

> Do not light a lamp: in the house is no oil.
> How pitiable it is if you want a light.
> I myself have a means to bless poverty:
> I will let you feel your way along the wall.

The last two lines especially have deep significance. We should appreciate them, along with Sozan's reply. If one is poor, he feels unhappy in poverty; if one is rich, he feels uneasy about it—this is the usual pattern of human life. When he transcends rich and poor, yes and no, he can be truly free and live in real peace.

Once a lay Zen student came to see Master Bankei, a famous Zen Master in the Tokugawa period in Japan. The student said, "My wisdom is tightly confined within me and I am unable to make use of it. How can I use it?" Bankei said to him, "My friend, come closer to me, please." When the lay disciple came a few steps closer, Bankei remarked, "How wonderfully well you are using it!"

TEISHO ON MUMON'S COMMENTARY

"Seizei assumed a condescending attitude. What is his intention? Sozan has a penetrating eye and has seen through Seizei's mind. Be that as it may, just tell me how the Venerable Seizei could have drunk the wine."

Mumon first comments on Seizei's attitude: "Seizei moved an inch and assumed a humble attitude." What is his real intention in doing so? The static principle of oneness or equality of course deserves admiration in a sense. If, however, one clings to it and lacks free working in differentiation, it turns out to be an attachment and ceases to be real oneness. Mumon is warning his disciples against such relativistic, dead oneness.

Mumon then praises Sozan, "He is a capable Master. He at once saw through Seizei's Zen ability and gave a fitting answer."

Changing his tone, Mumon goes on to say, "Be that as it may, Sozan told Seizei that he had had hearty draughts of the best wine. How could Sozan say so?" Mumon is advising his monks not to leave the koan just as an old story, but to take it as their own question and to open their religious eye to see through its real significance. Mumon's comment is a compassionate instruction for us today, too.

Zen negates everything and at the same time affirms everything. Without this absolute affirmation working in every different situation, negation is just a corpse to be cast away.

A Japanese folk song sings:

> I'm tipsy, tipsy indeed, with one glass of wine,
> Tipsy I am with a glass of wine I have not drunk.

To be tipsy with undrunk wine refers to talking with no-mind and acting with no-mind. In the light of Mumon's comment we should grasp the heart of the song.

TEISHO ON MUMON'S POEM

> His poverty is like Hantan's,
> His spirit like that of Kou.
> With no way of earning a livelihood
> He dares to compete with the richest of men.

In his poem Mumon remarks that Seizei is utterly poor, even more so than Hantan, a Chinese gentleman of the second century A.D. who lived in extreme poverty and never looked worried at all. Being confident of his poverty, Seizei came to Sozan to make a challenging request. He is certainly brave to do so, and his courage can be likened to that of Kou, a brilliantly courageous Chinese general in the third century B.C., of whom it is recorded: "His power was so great as to move a mountain; his spirit was so high as to cover the whole world."

Living in extreme poverty and destitution, still he answered, "Yes, Master" out of nothingness when Sozan addressed him. He showed no hesitation, no diffidence in answering—certainly he was rich enough to compete in wealth with Sozan, a Croesus. Though Seizei came out upholding his poverty, he was completely defeated by Sozan's wonderful working in differentiation.

11

Joshu Sees the True Nature
of Two Hermits

Joshu came to a hermit and asked, "Are you in? Are you in?" The hermit held up his fist. "The water is too shallow to anchor a vessel," said Joshu, and went away. He then came to another hermit and called out, "Are you in? Are you in?" This hermit also held up his fist. "You are free either to give or to take away, either to kill or to give life," said Joshu, bowing to him.

MUMON'S COMMENTARY

Both held up their fists. Why did he approve the one and disapprove the other? Tell me, where is the core of the complication? If you can give a turning word on the point, you will see that Joshu is unrestrained in saying what he wants to say and utterly free either to help the one rise up or to push the other down. Be that as it may, do you know that it was Joshu, on the contrary, whose true nature was seen by the two hermits? If you say the one hermit is superior to the other, you have not yet got the Zen eye. Or if you say there is no difference between the two, you have not yet got the Zen eye, either.

MUMON'S POEM

His eye is a shooting star,
His spirit is lightning.

A sword to kill,
A sword to give life.

TEISHO ON THE KOAN

In this koan the famous Joshu is again the central figure. I have already noted his well-known saying, recorded in his biography: "Even if he is a small child seven years old, if he is superior to me in any sense I will beg him to teach me. Even if he is an old man a hundred years old, if he is inferior to me I will teach him." With this motto Joshu continued on his training journey until he was eighty years old. The incident here would have taken place while he was on that pilgrimage. Zen men are not too particular about the environmental situations of the koan, which are of secondary importance from the Zen standpoint, and they do not inquire into them too closely. The primary significance of a koan exists in its role as a means of training.

One day Joshu came to a hermit and asked, "Are you in?" Often in the exchange of ordinary daily greetings Zen men train each other and try to refine their spirituality. In this koan, too, an ordinary question at once started a Zen mondo.

The hermit in reply to Joshu's question held up his fist in silence. A fist held up, just that—splendid indeed! A fist is a fist through and through. Here is no room for discrimination.

Seeing it, however, Joshu said, "The water is too shallow to anchor a vessel here," and immediately walked away. Superficially it may be interpreted: "He is not much of a Zen monk. It is not worth having a mondo with him," and Joshu immediately turned away.

Joshu used and displayed his Zen as he wished. Could there be such a distinction as superiority or inferiority in the fist held up by itself? An old Zen Master commented on the fist:

> Whether to call it crazy or rude
> I leave it to someone else to judge.
> Peach blossoms are by nature pink;
> Pear blossoms by nature white.

How did he see the fist to make such a poem? What does the fist signify? Clear understanding is required on this crucial point.

Again Joshu went to another hermit, and asked in the same manner, "Are you in?" The hermit in silence held up his fist. A fist held up, just that—

splendid indeed! A fist is a fist through and through. Here is no room for discrimination. Seeing it, however, Joshu immediately made a profound bow to him, saying, "You are free either to give or to take away, either to kill or to give life." Here again Joshu used and displayed his Zen as he wished. Let us allow him to do just as he wills.

Let me ask: "Is there any discrimination in the fist itself?" It is after all just a fist—that is all. How could Joshu see the true nature of the two hermits who held up their fists alike? Where is the key to know Joshu's mind? This is the vital point of this koan.

First of all you should have your eye on the fist itself. When you can really see through this fist, then Joshu's remarks, and his Zen, will naturally be clear to you. A Zen Master has a poem on it:

> The spring breeze in a tree
> Has two different faces:
> A southward branch looks warm,
> A northward branch looks cool.

What kind of Zen life does he live to make such a comment on this koan? One is all; all is one. Equality is at once differentiation. We have to have our own penetrating experience to be able really to agree with him.

TEISHO ON MUMON'S COMMENTARY

Mumon comments: "Both held up their fists. Why did he approve the one and disapprove the other? Tell me, where is the core of the complication? If you can give a turning word on the point, you will see that Joshu is unrestrained in saying what he wants to say and utterly free either to help the one rise up or to push the other down. Be that as it may, do you know that it was Joshu, on the contrary, whose true nature was seen by the two hermits? If you say the one hermit is superior to the other, you have not yet got the Zen eye. Or if you say there is no difference between the two, you have not yet got the Zen eye, either."

Mumon's commentary consists of three parts. In the first part he asks why Joshu approved of one hermit and disapproved of the other when they both held up their fists alike. Where is the core of this complication? Thus Mumon points out the heart of the question and says, "If you can give an apt answer on this point, you can then see into the heart of Joshu and will understand how absolutely free he was in doing whatever he liked, giving or taking away."

Joshu's superficially contradictory and haphazard remarks in fact issued from his utterly free and creative Zen life. This first part of Mumon's commentary expresses his own position and his approval of Joshu, who approved of one hermit and disapproved of the other.

In the second part Mumon changes his tone and says, "Be that as it may, in my eye it was Joshu whose true nature was seen by the two hermits, although he thinks he has seen theirs."

Now, tell me how the two hermits saw Joshu's true nature. Each one in silence held up his fist—they too must have been Zen Masters with their Zen eye opened. In other words, they demonstrated the truth that "Everything returns to One."

Lastly, Mumon ends his commentary with very fine and opportune remarks, "If you say, like Joshu, that one hermit is superior to the other, you have not yet opened your Zen eye. If, however, you say there is no difference between them, your Zen eye has not yet been opened, either."

Mumon warns us that as far as the fists are concerned, we should not judge that there is a difference between their abilities, nor should we conclude that there is no difference. Why does he say so? Transcend such dualistic distinctions as superiority and inferiority, is and is not, and be the fist itself through and through. When you cast away such discrimination, the key to make free use of both yes and no, is and is not, is yours.

Master Hakuin remarked on Mumon's commentary: "Mumon says he will not approve saying there *is* a difference, or there *is not* a difference. Although this is a good comment, I would not give such a clumsy explanation if I were doing it, because he may explain it, but you cannot understand it; he may teach it, but you cannot learn it. One has to experience it personally himself, otherwise any knowledge about it will be to no avail."

Equality has differentiation in it, and differentiation is based on equality. There are neither one, nor two. But one has to grasp this secret oneself as a fact of one's own experience. It should never be a conceptual conclusion. Hakuin compassionately pointed this out.

TEISHO ON MUMON'S POEM

His eye is a shooting star,
His spirit is lightning.
A sword to kill,
A sword to give life.

Mumon highly praises the capability of Joshu, who saw the true nature of the two hermits who held up their fists alike, and describes him as one whose eye is as quick as a shooting star and whose spirit is as lofty and dynamic as lightning.

The fist held up is indeed wonderful; it freely works either to give life or to kill. Mumon admires both the wonderful work of Joshu's Zen and the exquisite mystery of one fist as well.

Unless one can fully appreciate each of Mumon's comments and clearly see the point he raises, one has not yet understood the significance of this koan or the essence of Zen.

12

Zuigan Calls "Master"

Every day Master Zuigan Shigen used to call out to himself, "Oh, Master!" and would answer himself, "Yes?" "Are you awake?" he would ask, and would answer, "Yes, I am." "Never be deceived by others, any day, any time." "No, I will not."

MUMON'S COMMENTARY

Old Zuigan himself sells and himself buys. He has a lot of masks of goblins and demons to play with. Why? Nii! A calling one, an answering one, an awake one, and one who will not be deceived by others. If you take these different appearances as really existing, you are altogether mistaken. If, however, you would imitate Zuigan, your understanding is that of a fox.

MUMON'S POEM

Those who search for the Way do not realize the Truth,
They only know their old discriminating consciousness.
This is the cause of the endless cycle of birth and death,
Yet ignorant people take it for the Original Man.

TEISHO ON THE KOAN

Master Shigen of Zuigan, Taishu, was born in Binetsu, ordained early in life, and was the successor of Master Ganto Zenkatsu (828–887). When he first met Ganto he asked, "What is the Eternal Truth?" Ganto replied, "You have missed it!" "What is it when I miss it?" asked Zuigan. "It is no longer Eternal Truth," said Ganto. Zuigan had to work very hard at this and finally was enlightened. Later Ganto moved to Tankyu, where he sat like a rock all day long, like a fool. All the people loved Master Shigan and respected him, his biography tells us, and they invited him to the Zuigan Monastery as the abbot. He was strict and precise in guiding the monks and was much admired by everyone.

Because of its unusual and novel form, this koan is very famous. In spite of its popularity, however, there are unexpectedly few who have a correct Zen understanding of its true significance.

Needless to say, koan are sayings and doings that have come out of the old Zen Masters' deep Zen experiences. Behind their superficial expressions through words and actions there is the Truth of Zen, which really transcends such expressions. The primary significance of koan can be truly appreciated only when students personally plunge into the Truth of Zen behind such sayings and doings. Those who have not yet attained Zen experience can open their spiritual eye with the koan, and those who have broken through the barrier should refine and deepen their spiritual insight with it.

The ethical teachings or guidance on human conduct one may draw out of a certain koan are all of secondary importance. If one looks only at such accompanying merits of koan, he altogether misses their primary significance in Zen. Zen of course does not deny ethical life or moral and humanistic teachings, but these have to be the direct outcome of the Zen Truth that underlies them.

Often people interpret this koan of "Master" simply as an ethical teaching and take it to mean that Master Zuigan entered into a life of self-examination and introspection. If it remains just that, it ceases to be a Zen koan. If it had been only good ethical advice, Master Zuigan would never have been respected and looked upon as a great Zen Master.

Needless to say, Master Mumon did not take up this particular story of Zuigan from his biography for ethical instruction, but gave his teisho on it so that his disciples would get in touch with Zuigan's Zen and apply themselves to deepen their Zen mind and to truly live Zen.

The koan says that Master Zuigan every day called out to himself "Oh, Master," and himself answered "Yes?"

Prior to this, Zuigan had had long and most assiduous training under Master Ganto, had opened his Zen eye, and had become an accomplished Zen Master. Whatever he said or did, it was the work of his Zen. For Zuigan, the real Master is manifest and alive in his calling out and in his answering. If we fail to grasp this vividly manifested Master, the essence of the koan is altogether missed.

Let me digress here a little to give some explanation of the use of the word "Master." Commonly speaking, this would be a name given to a subject standing over against an object: a master is a master of something. Here, however, the Master does not refer to the subjectivity that stands over against objectivity. It is "Absolute Subjectivity," which transcends both subjectivity and objectivity and freely creates and uses them. It is "Fundamental Subjectivity," which can never be objectified or conceptualized and is complete in itself, with the full significance of existence in itself. To call it by these names is already a mistake, a step toward objectification and conceptualization. Master Eisai therefore remarked, "It is ever unnamable."

Perforce Master Zuigan gave the name "Master" to this ever unnamable Reality; Master Gutei stuck up one finger; Master Eno called it "Original Face"; Master Rinzai named it "True Man of no title." All these different names that Masters are compelled to use try to point to one and the same Reality. (I would take it that the "I" in "Before Abraham was I am" also refers to the ever unnamable Reality.)

Zen is nothing other than the experience each of us has of opening his spiritual eye to this Absolute Subjectivity, and of coming to be it ourselves. Satori is this experience. One has to give oneself body and soul to it. Mumon emphasized this point when he said in the first koan: "In studying Zen, one must pass the barriers set up by the ancient Zen Masters. For the attainment of incomparable satori, one has to cast away his discriminating mind."

Master Gudo of Myoshinji in Kyoto wrote a poem entitled "Original Face":

> This is the youth of natural beauty.
> If you have not had a heart-to-heart smile with him
> Your heart must bleed.
> Seishi's beauty loses its color,
> Yoki's gracefulness is cast into the shade.

The Absolute Subjectivity that can never be objectified or conceptualized is free from the limitations of space and time; it is not subject to life and death; it goes beyond subject and object, and although it lives in an individual it is not restricted to the individual. Master Gudo calls this Absolute Subjectivity "the youth of natural beauty," which is genuine beauty undefiled by any artificiality. Referring to Seishi and Yoki, who are noted as the most beautiful women in the history of China, Gudo illustrates the absoluteness of the youth's natural beauty by saying that even such rare Chinese beauties would look faded beside it. Because of this, Gudo says, one has to cast all his intellection away and have a heart-to-heart smile with him, that is, grasp him experientially even at the risk of life. If one fails to do so, it will be a matter of the greatest regret throughout life.

Zuigan is a Zen Master who had a heart-to-heart smile with the youth of natural beauty after long and hard training under the noted Master Ganto. Ever after this experience, Zuigan kept on calling out to "it," or the "Master," which was the name Zuigan gave to the youth of natural beauty. He lived, enjoyed, and used the Master in himself, and his Zen life was much admired by Zen students of later generations. The calling Master and the answering Master cannot be two, but must be the One Absolute Master of Absolute Subjectivity. Lucid indeed was his Zen mind; deep indeed was his Zen experience. He certainly deserves our sincere admiration.

Zuigan continues his questioning and answering in living-enjoying-using "it." "Are you awake?" "Yes, I am." "Never be deceived by others under any circumstances." "No, I will not." If we just superficially and literally read this soliloquy or self-dialogue, it may sound very simple: "Oh, Master, is your subjectivity clear and firm?" "Yes, it is." "Don't let anybody, at any time, obscure your subjectivity." "No, never." We must clearly see here, however, in his calling out to himself and answering himself, how firm and transparent his Zen was. We have to read the story again with the Zen eye acquired through our training and experience.

"Are you awake?" "Yes, I am." "Never be deceived by others." "No, I will not." What does this asking himself and definitely answering himself on the part of Zuigan mean? A Zen Master said, "It is the lord of lords who ably carries it through." Zuigan's Master was ever transparent in his eating, dressing, talking, and smiling, and could never be deceived by anything. If he stands, there he is awake; if he sits, there he is awake.

It was because of such transparency in Zuigen's Zen, the Zen he lived, that "all the people loved and respected him, and they invited him to the Zuigan Monastery as the abbot."

An ancient Zen Master commented figuratively on how genuinely and precisely Zuigan carried and lived his Zen, by saying, "A dragon enjoys a jewel." How wonderful it is that Zuigan lived, enjoyed, and used "it" in himself by calling out to himself and answering himself. It is wonderful, like a dragon loving and enjoying a jewel.

Such deep and lucid Zen spirituality of living, enjoying, and using "it" in himself can never even be glimpsed by superficial and literal interpretations, which take it as an ethical teaching of self-examination and introspection.

Why did Master Zuigan lead such a strict life of living-enjoying-using "it"? We should not fail to see his overflowing compassion toward succeeding generations as well as the transparency of his Zen. That is also the reason why Mumon presented this koan to his disciples. In short, Zuigan's Master is your Master, my Master, here and now.

There is another koan which is a sequel to this koan of "Master." One day a monk came to see Master Gensha. Gensha asked the newcomer, "Where have you been recently?" "With Master Zuigan, Sir," replied the monk. "I see. In what manner does Master Zuigan instruct his disciples?" asked Gensha. The monk reported in detail how Zuigan would every day call out "Oh, Master!" and would answer himself. Listening to the monk, Gensha asked again, "Why didn't you stay longer with Zuigan to continue your training?" The monk said, "Master Zuigan died." At this reply, Gensha asked the monk an unexpected question, "If you call out to him now, 'Oh, Master!' will he answer?" Unfortunately, the monk could not say a word in reply and remained silent.

Master Zuigan is already dead, and Gensha asks, "If you call out to him now, 'Oh, Master!' will he answer?" Why did he dare ask such a question? Master Gensha's Zen is at work behind it: he is trying to awaken the monk to the true Master that transcends space and time, I and you, life and death. Regrettable is the incapability of this monk who failed to respond to the kind questioning of Gensha.

In the age of civil wars in Japan there was a feudal lord named Ota Dokan who built his castle in Edo, the present Tokyo. He studied Zen under Master Unko, who lived in a nearby temple called Seishoji and assiduously disciplined himself in Zen. Master Unko gave Dokan the koan of "Zuigan the Master" and made him work very hard at it. He went through a sincere and earnest searching for a long time with this koan, and one day penetrated into the essence of the Master. Unko wanted to test further his attainment and asked, "Now, at this very moment, where is the 'Master'?"

> Mountains respond
> To the temple bell
> In the moonlight.

was the reply Dokan gave at once, and it received his teacher's approval.

Is this poem of Dokan's the same as Zuigan's answering himself? Or are they different? The true Master is ever alive, with Zuigan or with Dokan, now or in the past; he is never a lifeless concept. The Master is always here now, and is "awake" in your standing and sitting. You who have the eye to see, see him now, immediately; you who have the ability to use, use him directly— Mumon urges us.

TEISHO ON MUMON'S COMMENTARY

Mumon said, "Old Zuigan himself sells and himself buys. He has a lot of masks of goblins and demons to play with. Why? Nii! A calling one, an answering one, an awake one, and one who will not be deceived by others. If you take these different appearances as really existing, you are altogether mistaken. If, however, you would imitate Zuigan, your understanding is that of a fox."

This commentary consists of three parts. The first is the part where Mumon seemingly abuses Zuigan for his conduct of "every day calling out to himself and answering himself." "You are yourself selling and yourself buying. What do you mean by such one-man play, bringing out all sorts of monsters one after another on the stage?" Thus Mumon grills Zuigan. This is, however, the familiar traditional method in Zen of praising most highly with abusing or teasing expressions. He is in fact admiring Zuigan's Zen at work.

"Nii!" is an exclamatory word to stress the meaning. Here it has the meaning of "There!" or "Look!"—demanding an answer, because of his allusion to goblins and demons. There was an old folk belief in China that if a slip of paper with the character *nii* written on it was fastened to the gate, it would charm away all fiends.

We are to read between the lines in the first part of Master Mumon's eulogy on Zuigan's lucid and transparent Zen life that he was the Master himself through and through, and carried it on in his coming and going, sitting and lying down.

In the second part Mumon says, "A calling one, an answering one, an awake one, and one that will not be deceived by others. If you take these different appearances as really existing, you are altogether mistaken." He refers to each different kind of behavior of Zuigan: now he calls out to himself, now he answers himself; now he tells himself to be awake; now he says he will not be deceived by others. "Never become attached to all these different faces," Mumon strictly warns the monks. Fundamentally the Master is the Master no matter what appearances he may present. An ancient wise man commented, "A donkey in the east house; a horse in the west house." With a willow it is green, with a flower it is red; wherever he may be, he always lives the Truth and never fails to be the Master. By way of compassionate commentary, Mumon encourages his disciples to see the essence of Zuigan's Zen.

The last sentence: "If, however, you would imitate him, your understanding is that of a fox." Some may conclude that the Master means the Absolute which is beyond all description; what we should do is just call out, "Oh, Master! Oh, Master!" If they imitate Zuigan like this, without their own creative Zen at work, their understanding is certainly a dead one. It is a lifeless and false understanding of Zen, which is called fox-Zen. Thus railing at them, Mumon shows the true, living Master to his monks. Kind indeed is Mumon's admonition.

TEISHO ON MUMON'S POEM

> Those who search for the Way do not realize the Truth,
> They only know their old discriminating consciousness.
> This is the cause of the endless cycle of birth and death,
> Yet ignorant people take it for the Original Man.

This is a poem written by Master Chosa. Mumon borrowed it here exactly as Chosa wrote it, and used it with his own Zen capability as a commentary on this koan. The "Original Man" corresponds to Zuigan's "Master." Mumon must have used the poem in his compassionate attempt to smash the illusory dream of those people who cling to the discriminating consciousness as if it were the Original Man, which is exactly the cause of ignorance forever.

In my training days I started to recite this poem in front of my teacher. I had barely finished the first line, "Those who search for the Way do not realize the Truth," when he assailed me, saying, "Leave aside the poem. Now what is *your* Truth?" I remember that I was quite speechless at his severe, demanding question.

In this one word "Truth" lies the essence of Zen, and also the life of this poem. In other words from this one word the Master, or the Original Man, is born.

Many people in search of the Way do not realize the true Master. It is because they cling to arayashiki (the source of all human consciousness), which they have long believed to be the root of their existence. This is in fact the very cause of their continuing cycle of birth and death forever, and should be immediately smashed and cast away. What a pity to see them mistake it for the true Master, the Original Man! With this verse Mumon wants us to open our eyes to the true Master.

If one objectifies this Master and takes him as an existence outside oneself, it is already an attachment and becomes the cause of ignorance. An old Zen Master left the following poem of admonition for later generations:

> A water bird comes and goes,
> Leaving no traces at all.
> Yet it knows
> How to go its own way.

13

Tokusan Carried His Bowls

Tokusan one day came down to the dining room carrying his bowls. Seppo said, "Old Master, the bell has not rung and the drum has not yet been struck. Where are you going with your bowls?" Tokusan at once turned back to his room. Seppo told this incident to Ganto, who remarked, "Great Master though he is, Tokusan has not yet grasped the last word of Zen." Hearing of it, Tokusan sent his attendant to call Ganto in, and asked, "Do you not approve of me?" Ganto whispered his reply to him. Tokusan was satisfied and silent. The next day Tokusan appeared on the rostrum. Sure enough, his talk was different from the usual ones. Ganto came in front of the monastery, laughed heartily, clapping his hands, and said, "What a great joy it is! The old Master has now grasped the last word of Zen. From now on nobody in the world can ever make light of him."

MUMON'S COMMENTARY

As for the last word of Zen, neither Ganto nor Tokusan has ever heard of it, even in a dream. If I examine it carefully, they are like puppets set on a shelf.

MUMON'S POEM

If you understand the first word of Zen
You will know the last word.

99

The last word or the first word—
"It" is not a word.

TEISHO ON THE KOAN

It may be necessary, in the case of this koan in particular, to give some supplementary explanations before giving teisho on the koan itself.

Koan are originally sayings or doings in the form of mondo, instructions, talks, etc., left by great Zen Masters. In other words, drawing on their deep Zen experiences they freely expressed their Zen under different circumstances. The significance of koan varies greatly one from another, and they cannot be classified by any forms or rules. Some may encourage training; some may be mondo between two people to test closely and refine each other; some may express profound and lucid spirituality; some may stress the truth of equality, or the working aspect of the Truth in differentiation; some may emphasize the truth that "one is all; all is one"; some may wipe off all the stinks and even smacks of Zen; some may not fit under any category.

There are, of course, simple and direct koan and intricate ones, since they are actual sayings and doings that come directly out of the life of a Zen Master. In the case of "Tokusan Carried His Bowls" the import is especially complex and the spirituality is unusually lofty and profound; it is regarded as the most typical nanto koan. Unless one has gone through the training to a considerable degree and has a clear Zen eye opened, he will not be able to grasp what it is all about.

There is hardly any Zen book which has a proper teisho on this koan, though many books on the *Mumonkan* are available in Japan. When it comes to those written by scholars who do not have actual training in Zen, their explanations all miss the point and none of them can be recommended.

Once my own teacher explained the role of the koan in Zen training with an easy simile, and I shall quote it here as it ably explains what the koan is: "Needless to say, the task or role of the koan is to help a student open his Zen eye, to deepen his Zen attainment, and to refine his Zen personality. It is a means in Zen training, but in actual practice the koan does not lead a student along an easy and smooth shortcut, like other ordinary means. The koan, on the contrary, throws a student into a steep and rugged maze where he has no sense of direction at all. He is expected to overcome all the difficulties and find the way out himself. In other words, the koan is the most difficult and rough means for the student to go through. Good koan, called nanto, are those that are most intricate, illogical, and irrational, in which the most brilliant intellect will completely lose its way.

"Suppose here is a completely blind man who trudges along leaning on his stick and depending on his intuition. The role of the koan is to mercilessly take the stick away from him and to push him down after turning him around. Now the blind man has lost his sole support and intuition and will not know where to go or how to proceed. He will be thrown into the abyss of despair. In this same way, the nanto koan will mercilessly take away all our intellect and knowledge. In short, the role of the koan is not to lead us to satori easily, but on the contrary to make us lose our way and drive us to despair."

I should like to apply those remarks to the koan of "Tokusan Carried His Bowls." Completely blind and weak-sighted men will be deprived of all they have, driven into the dark abyss of despair, and will not know what to do. Those capable students whose Zen eye is opened will immediately find the direction, however complicated the labyrinth may be—will be able to see through the darkness and with their own ability come out of the intricate maze.

"Tokusan Carried His Bowls" is indeed an intricate maze and sheer darkness. Mumon presented this koan to his disciples so that they might have really deep and penetrating Zen ability. The same is required of Zen students today, too. If you have a Zen eye firmly opened, you can see a way clearly leading through the impregnable barrier.

In this koan three characters appear. The main figure is Master Tokusan Senkan, who is famous for swinging his stick. Whoever might come to him, he used to say, "Whether you can say a word or not, all the same: thirty blows of my stick!" Thus he encouraged the monks to plunge directly into the Truth. Tokusan was first a noted student of the *Diamond Sutra,* but when he came to the south to oppose the teachings of Zen he gave up his sutra studies and became a disciple of Ryutan Soshin. Later he became one of the greatest Masters in the history of Zen in China. Tokusan died in 866 in his eighty-third year. The incident in this koan took place three years before his death, when Ganto was in his thirty-fifth year and Seppo in his forty-first.

Master Ganto Zenkatsu was a successor to Tokusan and an equally great Master, not yielding even to his teacher. During the period of the great persecution of Buddhism in China, in 845, he became a ferryman on a lake. He left many famous sayings. He was born in 828, in Senshu, where Seppo also was born, and died in 887 in his sixtieth year.

Master Seppo Gison was also a disciple of Tokusan. At the monastery he worked for a long time in the kitchen, refining his attainment while taking care of cooking for all the monks. Even today, the room in the monastery where monks in charge of cooking live is called "Seppo's room." He was born in 822 in the T'ang dynasty and died in his eighty-seventh year, in 908, just at the end of the dynasty.

It is well known that Ganto, like a true friend, showed consideration for his junior, Seppo, and encouraged and helped him to break through the barrier of Zen. The Zen drama developed in this koan took place toward the end of Tokusan's life, when Ganto and Seppo were staying at his monastery.

"Tokusan one day came down to the dining room carrying his bowls. Seppo said, 'Old Master, the bell has not rung and the drum has not yet been struck. Where are you going with your bowls?' Tokusan at once turned back to his room."

One day, probably, lunch was a little delayed. Old Tokusan came down to the dining room with his bowls. (The monks staying at a monastery all have their own set of bowls and at mealtime come to the dining room carrying their bowls.) His disciple Seppo saw this and asked, "Master, the bell has not yet rung nor the drum been sounded to announce the mealtime. Where are you going, carrying your bowls?" Hearing it, as if to say, "Oh, is that so?" Tokusan quite meekly and quietly turned back to his room in silence. This is the beginning of a Zen drama to be developed by the three characters.

Tokusan was a great and most capable Zen Master. Why did he quite naïvely turn back to his room at the remark made by Seppo, without saying a word? Here we have to enter into Tokusan's heart. This is the first point in the koan. Granting that he committed a blunder by coming down to the dining room before the mealtime was announced, there has to be his Zen at work here, worthy of a great Zen Master.

A Zen Master admired Tokusan's innocent and discreet behavior and noble personality, saying, "He stealthily goes under heaven and quietly walks on earth." Another Master symbolically and poetically praised his innocent, ingenuous, and artless behavior of no-mind:

> As the wind sways the pussy willows
> Velvet beads move in the air.
> As the rain falls on the pear blossoms
> White butterflies fly in the sky.

There is no stink of Zen. He lives with no pretension, no affectation. His transcendental purity is like that of an infant. Nobody can easily reach such spirituality.

On the other hand, Seppo was still young and full of vigor. His Zen attainment was not yet sufficiently refined to appreciate Tokusan's life of no-mind, so serene and innocent. He was, on the contrary, pleased with his own remark, which made old Tokusan go back. Seppo was here too young to realize that Tokusan's spirituality was far beyond his ability to see it. Seppo therefore told the incident to his good friend Ganto in an elated manner. Here the story makes the second development.

Ganto was already an accomplished monk whose Zen ability was greater than that of Seppo. Listening to his report, Ganto felt sorry for Seppo, who did not realize his inability to appreciate Tokusan's Zen at work. He attempted to inspire his good friend, availing himself of this opportunity to break through another barrier and refine his spirituality.

He resorted to extreme measures. Having listened to Seppo's story, he said, "Great Master though he is, Tokusan has not yet grasped the last word of Zen."

Obviously enough, Ganto was well aware that old Tokusan was a truly accomplished Master who no longer had to be concerned about "the last word of Zen." The koan here gets very intricate. There was no way for Seppo and the rest of the monks at Tokusan's monastery to know what Ganto really intended. "The last word of Zen" now stands in front of them as a barrier they must break through.

The "last word of Zen" can be interpreted as "Ultimate Word" or "Absolute Word" or "Absolute Essence to be finally reached in training." Zen demands that we grasp it as a fact personally experienced and as the actual spirituality with which we live all the time. It should not be conceptually dealt with or philosophically speculated about.

Literally the koan seems to say, "Seppo sent old Tokusan back to his room with his remark and told his senior, his good friend Ganto, about this mondo rather elatedly. Listening to Seppo's report, Ganto declared that the reason Tokusan had to yield to Seppo was that Tokusan had not yet grasped the last word of Zen."

The great question here for everybody is whether the world-famous old Tokusan had not in fact grasped the last word of Zen. Consequently, another question is "What is this last word of Zen?" Also it has to be asked whether there is really a so-called last word in Zen or not.

Not only Seppo and the monks at the Tokusan Monastery, but we ourselves today have to solve these vital questions and get fundamental peace of mind. How then can we solve them? The significance of this koan lies here, and the whole complication was worked out by Ganto out of his compassion.

The koan here makes the third development. Tokusan, hearing of Ganto's unexpected statement, sent his attendant to call Ganto in and asked, "Do you not approve of me?" Ganto came closer to Tokusan and whispered "a word" in secret into his ear. The secret he whispered apparently satisfied old Tokusan, who quietly sent Ganto away. Here the koan reaches its climax. Being asked by Tokusan, "Do you not approve of me?" why did not a great and capable Zen monk like Ganto give him a proper answer clearly and directly? Unexpectedly, he whispered a word in secret into Tokusan's ear. Furthermore, the secret he whispered satisfied old Tokusan so that he remained silent! The whisper must have had an extraordinary significance. Let me ask you here, what kind of whisper could this be? Further, tell me if there is anything in Zen that has to be whispered in secret, or not. We have to inquire thoroughly into this secret whisper, for this is the heart and core of the koan.

In actual training, the Zen Master will closely press the student, asking, "What is the secret Ganto whispered?" With this question Zen deprives a student not only of all his knowledge and intellect but even of the last smack of Zen. It will open up for him a true Zen vista, pure, lucid, immaculate, and simple.

According to the literal meaning of the koan, it seems as if Ganto conveyed "the secret of the last word of Zen" to Tokusan. Let me warn you not to be misled by the superficial context. Actually, is there anything to be conveyed at all in Zen? If you say "No," however, I ask you, "What was the secret, then, that Ganto whispered?" Zen does not want you to give a logical or conceptual answer to it, but urges you to grasp the secret experientially as a concrete fact testified to by yourself personally.

The koan here makes the last development. The next day Tokusan appeared on the rostrum to give teisho. Sure enough, the merit of the whispered secret was apparent, for his teisho was really very good and different from before. Noticing it, Ganto stood in front of the assembly, laughed heartily, clapping his hands, and cried out so that every monk would hear, "To my great joy, old Tokusan seems to have grasped the last word of Zen. From now on nobody in the world can make light of him." Why this change in Tokusan? Here is another question for you to answer. Ganto ran a grand play, carrying around "the last word of Zen" until the end and demanding that Seppo and the rest of the monks at the Tokusan Monastery break through this barrier.

If you are a real Zen man, how will you respond to Ganto's call, and how will you express your appreciation for his efforts in producing such a grand play? If you are unable to greet him properly you have missed the point of the koan altogether. Here your concrete grasp of the koan based on your own training and experience is required.

Master Kodo Genju of Jojiji made the following poem on "Tokusan Carried His Bowls":

> If you help others, do it up to the hilt.
> If you kill others, be sure you see the blood.
> Tokusan and Ganto,
> Solid iron all through!

This act of Zen drama for training had very complicated developments and has finally come to its end. Why in the world did the great Tokusan in his old age have to be concerned about the last word of Zen with Ganto? They are both far too great and capable to be measured by such an immature yardstick.

Both Tokusan and Ganto "did it on purpose." They worked out an act of Zen drama, acted as its heroes, and upholding the last word of Zen out of their boundless compassion, did not even seem to mind their ugliness in doing so. Tokusan and Ganto are really solid iron all through. Pure gold. They are one in body and spirit in producing the drama. How can we today answer their overbrimming compassion?

I ask you again: "What is the last word of Zen? What secret did Ganto whisper to Tokusan?" When you clearly open your Zen eye and break through this invulnerable barrier, you can live a new and free and creative life. And this is how you can really thank them for their compassion.

TEISHO ON MUMON'S COMMENTARY

"As for the last word of Zen, neither Ganto nor Tokusan has ever heard of it, even in a dream. If I examine it carefully, they are like puppets set on a shelf." Mumon's commentary is very short and simple compared with the koan, which is long and very intricate. "As for what is called the last word of Zen, neither Tokusan nor Ganto has ever heard of it even in a dream." Thus Mumon casts away the very question of the last word of Zen. Whether it be the last word or the first word, the less said the better. Best not to have it at all! This is Master Mumon's view and his compassionate commentary. He adds a few more words and says, "If you closely examine the koan, the last word, the whisper in secret, the grasping or not-grasping, the crying and laughing, all these are in an act of a puppet play." With this compassionate remark, Mumon illustrates the most refined and lucid spirituality of the true Zen man, wiping away everything, leaving no traces whatsoever.

TEISHO ON MUMON'S POEM

> If you understand the first word of Zen
> You will know the last word.
> The last word or the first word—
> "It" is not a word.

Mumon says that if you understand the first word, then you have already got the last word. Essentially, there is no question of first or last—or is there? There is no discussion about understanding and not-understanding. No first, no last: only man in ignorance gives plausible names to the ever unnamable "it," and calls it now first, now last.

Master Mumon too had no other means but finally to say, " 'It' is not a word." Master Tozan said, "I am always most sincere right here." Let me ask you, "Where is 'right here'?"

14

Nansen Kills a Cat

KOAN

Once the monks of the Eastern Hall and the Western Hall were disputing about a cat. Nansen, holding up the cat, said, "Monks, if you can say a word of Zen, I will spare the cat. If you cannot, I will kill it!" No monk could answer. Nansen finally killed the cat. In the evening, when Joshu came back, Nansen told him of the incident. Joshu took off his sandal, put it on his head, and walked off. Nansen said, "If you had been there, I could have saved the cat!"

MUMON'S COMMENTARY

You tell me, what is the real meaning of Joshu's putting his sandal on his head? If you can give the turning words on this point, you will see that Nansen's action was not in vain. If you cannot, beware!

MUMON'S POEM

> Had Joshu only been there,
> He would have taken action.
> Had he snatched the sword away,
> Nansen would have begged for his life.

TEISHO ON THE KOAN

This is a very famous koan in Zen circles, one that has been included in many Zen books because of the unusual story, which denies all rational or intellectual approaches. It is therefore extremely difficult for scholars, except those who themselves have gone through Zen training, to understand the koan correctly. In most cases they interpret it from the standpoint of ethics alone, or from a common-sense point of view, since they do not have the authentic Zen eye and experience to grasp the essence.

Once more I should like to point out that koan are Zen Masters' sayings and doings in which they have freely and directly expressed their Zen experiences. We have to realize that they are fundamentally different from instructions in ethics and common sense. If we are not aware that koan belong to quite another dimension than the ethical or the prudential and practical activities of men, we shall forever be unable even to glimpse their real significance.

Some may criticize this statement by saying it implies that Zen ignores ethics and common sense. This is an extreme misunderstanding. Zen, on the contrary, frees us from our suffering and restraints caused by ethics and common sense. This does not mean to ignore or defy ethics and common sense, but to be the master of them and to make free and lively use of them. Unless this point is clearly understood, Zen sayings and doings can never be correctly appreciated.

The main figures in this koan are Nansen Fugan and his disciple Joshu Junen, two great Zen Masters who played active leading roles toward the end of the T'ang dynasty when Zen flourished most notably. In *Hekigan-roku* the same koan appears as two koan: "Nansen Kills a Cat," and "Joshu Puts a Sandal on His Head." In the *Mumonkan* it is introduced as a single koan.

"Once the monks of the Eastern Hall and the Western Hall were disputing about a cat. Nansen, holding up the cat, said, 'Monks, if you can say a word of Zen, I will spare the cat. If you cannot, I will kill it!' No monk could answer. Nansen finally killed the cat."

The first half of the koan quite simply states the incident. It is recorded that at the monastery where Master Nansen was the abbot, there were always hundreds of monks who had come to study under him. One day the monks staying at the Eastern Hall and the Western Hall were having a dispute about a cat. The koan does not tell us what the real issue of the dispute was, and there is no way for us to know it today. From the context it may be inferred that they were engaging in some speculative religious arguments referring to a cat.

Master Nansen happened to come across this dispute. His irresistible compassion as their teacher burst forth to smash up their vain theoretical arguments and open their spiritual eye to the Truth of Zen. He seized the cat in one hand, a big knife in the other, and cried out, "You monks, if you can speak a word of Zen, I will spare the cat. If you cannot, I will kill it right away!" He challenged the monks to the decisive fight.

Setting aside the monks at the Nansen Monastery, I ask you, "What is the word to save the cat in response to Nansen's demand?" The koan is asking for your answer which would stop Nansen from killing the cat. This is the key point in the first half of the koan. In actual training, the Master will press the monk: "How do you save the cat right now?" And if you hesitate even for a moment, the Master, in place of Nansen, will at once take decisive action.

Commenting on the koan, an old Buddhist said, "Even Nansen's knife can never kill the Fundamental Wisdom. It is ever alive even at this very moment." Even though this statement is undoubtedly true, it still smells of religious philosophy, for the term "Fundamental Wisdom" is an extremely philosophical expression which means "the Fundamental Truth that transcends all dualism." Master Nansen is actually holding up a cat in front of you. He is not inviting you to philosophical discussion or religious argument. If you refer to the Fundamental Wisdom, he will demand, "Show me that cat of the Fundamental Wisdom right here!" He insists on seeing your Zen presentation.

Be no-self; be thoroughly no-self. When you are really no-self, is there a distinction between you and the world? You and the cat? You and Nansen? Is there a distinction between the cat killed and Nansen the killer? At any cost, first you have to be actually no-self; this is the first and the absolute requisite in Zen. The word to save the cat will then naturally come out of you like lightning. Actual training and experience are definitely needed in Zen.

There are seldom truly capable men, either in the past or today. Many disciples were there with Nansen, but none of them could speak out to meet their teacher's request. "No monk could answer," the koan says. Keeping back his tears, probably, Nansen "finally killed the cat." We can read from the word "finally" with what a bleeding heart he killed it.

Be that as it may, "Nansen finally killed the cat" is a precipitous barrier in this koan which has to be broken through in actual training and discipline. The Zen Master will certainly grill the student, "What is the real meaning of Nansen's killing the cat?" If you are unable to give a concrete and satisfactory answer to him, your Zen eye is not opened. Only those who grasp the real meaning of killing the cat are the ones who can save the cat.

Master Toin said, "What Nansen killed was not only the cat concerned, but cats called Buddhas, cats called Patriarchs, are all cut away. Even the arayashiki, which is their abode, is completely cut away, and a refreshing wind is blowing throughout." Though rightly stated, it still sounds very much like an argumentative pretext not based on actual training and experience.

Master Seccho of *Hekigan-roku* commented on Nansen's killing the cat quite severely, "Fortunately Nansen took a correct action. A sword straightway cuts it in two! Criticize it as you like." However, referring to the comment, "A sword straightway cuts it in two!" Dogen said, "A sword straightway cuts it—no-cut!" and pointed out a quite different standpoint. In other words, he is asking us to see "it," which no sword can ever cut, in Nansen's work of Zen.

In my training days I took sanzen with my teacher who suddenly asked, "Setting aside Nansen's killing the cat, where is the dead cat cut by Nansen right now?" A moment's hesitation in replying to his severe demand would immediately result in thirty blows of his stick, for it would clearly show that neither Nansen's killing the cat nor Dogen's "A sword straightway cuts it— no-cut!" is really understood. Sanzen in Zen training is not so easy as outsiders may generally think.

A Zen man should be able freely to express and live his Zen in his killing, if he kills the cat. If the cat is killed, the whole universe is killed, and his Zen is at work in the dead cat. Otherwise he has not got even a glimpse of the real significance of this koan. Traditionally, he can never study Zen apart from his actual self—here, now. Intellectual and common-sense interpretations of koan may be possible, but they are all by-products.

The scene of the koan changes here. In the evening Joshu, well known as an outstanding monk under Nansen, came back to the monastery. Nansen told him what had happened while he was away. Hearing it, Joshu took off his sandal, put it on his head, and walked out of the room without a word. Nansen, seeing this, praised Joshu, saying, "If you had been with us there on that occasion, I could have saved the cat!" "The father well understands his child, and the child his father." They are in complete accord in silence.

Now, what is the real meaning of Joshu's putting a sandal on his head? Further, how can it save the cat? This is the vital point in the latter half of the koan. Here again, unfortunately, there are hardly any books that show an authentic Zen point of view on what Joshu did, because these authors themselves have not actually broken through the barrier of Nansen's killing the cat.

Master Dogen very aptly said, "Death: just death all through—complete manifestation!" When you die, just die. When you just die thoroughly and completely, you will have transcended life and death. Then, for the first time, free and creative Zen life and work will be developed. There, cats and dogs, mountains and rivers, sandals and hats, will all transcend their old names and forms and be given new birth in the new world. This is the wonder of revival.

In this new world the old provisional names all lose their significance. Listen to an old Master who says,

> A man passes over the bridge.
> Lo! The bridge is flowing and the waters are unmoving.

It is said that Jesus Christ rose from death after his crucifixion. As I am not a Christian, I do not know the orthodox interpretation of the resurrection in Christianity. I myself believe, however, that Jesus' resurrection means to die in human flesh, and to revive as the Son of God transcending life and death. His resurrection means the advent of the Kingdom of God. It is the mysterious work of God to create the new and true world. There everybody, everything, lives in God, and all the provisional names and defilements of this earth are never found in the least.

Joshu availed himself of Nansen's killing the cat (i.e., the Great Death) as the opportunity for resurrection. Do not be deluded by old fixed names such as sandal or hat, a mountain or a river. A name is a temporary label given to Reality at one time at one place. Only when your attachments to such provisional given names are cast away will the Reality, the Truth, shine out. Joshu directly presented the Reality that can never be cut by anything. In this new world everything is revived with new significance. Why on earth do you have to cling to old provisional names? Joshu's action is the direct presentation of his Zen, which Master Nansen highly praised, saying, "If you had been there, I could have saved the cat!"

Master Shido Bunan illustrated the mystery of Zen working in his poem:

> Die while alive, and be completely dead,
> Then do whatever you will, all is good.

The first line, "Die while alive, and be completely dead," well describes Nansen's Zen at work, and the second line, "Then do whatever you will, all is good," refers to the working Zen of Joshu. Nansen's and Joshu's Zen are two yet one, one yet two. Master Mumon used this koan so that his disciples would grasp this mystery of Zen. Master Daito made the following poems on the koan. First, on "Nansen Kills a Cat":

> Nansen seizes the cat: lo! one, two, three!
> He kills it: behold, just solid iron!

Here all has been thoroughly cast away. The whole universe is just one finger. All has returned to One. Then, on "Joshu Puts a Sandal on His Head" Master Daito wrote:

Joshu goes with a sandal on his head: lo! three, two, one!
Heaven is earth; earth is heaven!

Where Absolute Subjectivity works, the old fixed ideas are of no avail. This is the world of Reality, or Truth, which transcends provisional names and labels, where everything is born anew with creative freedom.

TEISHO ON MUMON'S COMMENTARY

"You tell me, what is the real meaning of Joshu's putting his sandal on his head? If you can give the turning words on this point, you will see that Nansen's action was not in vain. If you cannot, beware!"

Master Mumon asks his disciples, "What is the real meaning of Joshu's putting his sandal on his head?" Master Daito, as I have quoted, admired the free working of Joshu in his poem, saying, "Heaven is earth; earth is heaven!" Where in the world is the source of this creative freedom? Cut, cut, cut! Cut everything away! When not only the cat, but Buddhist views and Dharma concepts are all cut away, leaving no trace behind, this creative freedom is yours. However, without actual hard searching and discipline you cannot expect to attain it. Mumon's address to his disciples is always from the standpoint of actual training. It is from this standpoint that he asks you to see the real significance of Nansen's action of Truth in Joshu's free presentation of Zen. In other words, he tells us to appreciate the wonder of resurrection in the fact of the Great Death. Then the killed cat will bloom in red as a flower; flow in blue as a stream. It is ever alive, not only with Master Joshu, but with you in your hand and in your foot today.

There is an old haiku poem in Japan:

A frog leaps into the water;
With that strength
It now floats.

It is interesting to read the poem in connection with this koan.

In the end Mumon admonishes his monks, "If you cannot, beware!" If you fail to grasp Nansen's and Joshu's Zen alive, and keep on chopping logic, you are in danger. You had better be killed once and for all by Nansen's sword.

TEISHO ON MUMON'S POEM

> Had Joshu only been there,
> He would have taken action.
> Had he snatched the sword away,
> Nansen would have begged for his life.

Mumon says that if Joshu had been there when Master Nansen demanded, holding up the cat, "If you cannot say a word of Zen, I will kill the cat right away," it would have been Joshu who took the action of Truth of "One cut, all is cut!" Is it because they are both birds of the same feather? Only he who is capable of giving life is able to kill. Joshu was utterly free either to revive or to kill, to give or to take away. Such was the preeminent Zen ability of Joshu.

Placing wholehearted confidence in Joshu's Zen ability, Mumon says that if he had snatched the sword from Nansen even the great Master Nansen would have been unable to hold up his head before Joshu. Do not jump to the conclusion, however, that Joshu's work is good and Nansen's is not. When a Zen man wins, he just wins; that's all. When he loses, he just loses; that's all. No trace is left behind.

Master Mumon says, "If he had snatched the sword away." Let me ask you, "What kind of sword is this?" If it is the sword of the Fundamental Wisdom, not only Nansen but the cat, monks, mountains, and rivers all have to ask for their lives. Perhaps I have spoken too much.

15

Tozan Gets Sixty Blows

When Tozan came to have an interview with Unmon, Unmon asked, "Where have you been recently?" "At Sado, Master," Tozan replied. "Where did you stay during the last ge-period?" "At Hozu of Konan," replied Tozan. "When did you leave there?" "On the twenty-fifth of August," Tozan answered. Unmon exclaimed, "I give you sixty blows with my stick!" The next day Tozan came up again and asked the Master, "Yesterday you gave me sixty blows with your stick. I do not know where my fault was." Unmon cried out, "You rice-bag! Have you been prowling about like that from Kosei to Konan?" At this Tozan was enlightened.

MUMON'S COMMENTARY

If Unmon at that time, by giving Tozan the fodder of the Truth, had awakened him to the vivid, dynamic Zen life, Unmon's school would not have declined. In the sea of yes-and-no, Tozan struggled all through the night. When the day broke and he came to see the Master again, Unmon helped him break through. Though Tozan was immediately enlightened, he was not bright enough. Let me ask you, "Should Tozan be beaten, or not?" If you say he ought to be beaten, trees and grasses and everything ought to be beaten. If you say he should not be beaten, then Unmon is telling a falsehood. If you can be clear on this point, you and Tozan will breathe together.

MUMON'S POEM

> A lion trains its cubs this way:
> If they walk ahead, it kicks them and quickly dodges.
> Against his will, Tozan had to be struck again;
> The first arrow only nicked him, but the second went deep.

TEISHO ON THE KOAN

This koan tells us of the first interview Tozan Shusho had with Master Unmon Bunen and how he attained his satori.

Master Unmon Bunen, who lived at Koho-in on Mount Unmon, was a successor to Seppo and was active from the end of the T'ang dynasty to the Five Dynasties (he is said to have died in 949). His strict and lofty Zen greatly influenced Zen circles in his day, and later he came to be admired as the founder of the Unmon School, one of the five schools of Rinzai Zen. He turned out many great Zen Masters who succeeded him, and Master Tozan Shusho was one of them.

Master Shusho is usually called Master Tozan because he lived at Tozan in Joshu. He is often confused with Master Tozan Ryokai, the founder of Soto Zen, but the latter lived at Tozan in Kinshu. They are two separate Masters who lived at different places at different times.

Master Tozan of Joshu was born in 910 at Hosho, in the western part of Sensei-sho in present China, and died in 990. Hosho, together with Choan and Rakuyo, had been a center of academic studies of Buddhism ever since its introduction into China and on through the T'ang into the Sung dynasty. Born in such a district, Tozan must have had considerable contact with Buddhist studies. Not being satisfied with them he left Hosho, crossed the great Chinese continent, traveling thousands of miles from the northwestern corner of the country to the south near Kanto, to see Master Unmon and to study under him. It may be easily imagined how ardent his searching was.

The traveling conditions in those days were not easy. There is no record of the hardships he had to go through, how long it took, what kinds of experiences he had on his journey after the Truth from his distant home in northwest China until he finally reached Mount Unmon. Yet it must have been a very hard and trying trip, and if he had not had a most ardent and determined will to seek the Truth, he could not have endured it.

One day, after traveling literally thousands of miles, Tozan had an interview with Master Unmon. Unmon asked this newcomer from afar most commonplace questions, such as can be asked of any stranger.

UNMON: Where have you been recently?

TOZAN: I was at Sado, Master.

UNMON: Where did you stay during the last ge-period?

TOZAN: At Hozuji in Konan.

UNMON: When did you leave Hozuji?

TOZAN: On the twenty-fifth of August, Master.

In those days the question "Where have you been recently?" was often used, not only as an ordinary greeting to a newcomer but also as a typical question in mondo to test the Zen ability of the monk. "Where have you been recently?" may refer to a place, but it also asks about one's inner Zen spirituality. Tozan's reply was most naïve and ordinary, and did not seem to have anything of Zen in it. A naïve response, of course, can be a genuine and interesting Zen expression, but in this case Tozan had not yet attained such spirituality.

Master Unmon proceeded with his question, "Where did you stay during the last ge-period?" [the traditional annual ninety-day "rainy season" period of meditation for monks]. Still Tozan showed no change in his response. Unmon took another step forward in his questioning and asked, "When did you leave there?" Tozan still answered in the same naïve way, and nothing of Zen came flashing out of him. Master Unmon now could not contain himself any longer. His Zen suddenly burst out working. "You stupid fool!" So crying, he knocked Tozan down with the stick he had in his hand.

In this mondo the questions are quite ordinary and the answers are very innocent. No fault to be criticized or deserving a beating can be found anywhere. Why, then, did Master Unmon rebuke and beat Tozan? Unmon was a great Zen Master, well known throughout the country. He could not possibly use his stick unreasonably. Then where in Tozan's answers could be the reason to beat him? You have to have a Zen eye to answer this question, and this is where the key of the koan is.

About Master Unmon's severe blows with the stick, people almost uniformly give the following interpretation: "Tozan's attitude as seen in his journey was not earnest enough. The severe blows of Unmon's stick were given as moral condemnation of Tozan for his lazy attitude in training and to inspire him to bestir himself." They all fail to grasp the real Zen significance of this koan, and that is because they do not have actual training and experience of their own.

If it were meant to be a moral admonition, Master Mumon would not have taken it up as a koan and presented it for his disciples to study in their training.

Master Unmon has another famous mondo. Once a monk asked him, "What is Unmon's tune?" That is, "What is your Zen?" Unmon answered, "The twenty-fifth of December." We should carefully study this mondo together with the koan of "Tozan Gets Sixty Blows."

Now back to Tozan. An old Zen Master commented on Tozan's response to Unmon, saying, "Being on the finest horse, he does not know how to ride it." He is in fact on the finest horse right now, yet he is not aware of it. In other words, he says, "You are living in the midst of Zen every day, and yet you do not realize it. What a fool!" The Zen eye of Master Tozan was not yet opened at this time.

How sad it is that Tozan does not come to the realization while himself answering, "At Sado, Master." [Sado is the name of a village along the way.] He says, "At Hozu of Konan," and is still unawakened. Master Unmon asks for the third time, "When did you leave there?" "On the twenty-fifth of August," and he does not realize it! Everywhere the Truth is all revealed. Everything as it is, is Zen. Because it is too close nobody knows it! Unmon could not help bursting out with his stick.

An old Zen Master commented on this stick of Unmon's as follows:

> In front of the Goho Palace
> He was asked where Rakuyo was.
> With a golden stick
> He pointed to the long, grand palace avenue.

In front of the White House he was asked where the capital of the United States is. With his stick he pointed to the street stretching before him. Yet those whose eyes are not opened will not know. Master Hakuin clearly sings:

> Your going and returning takes place nowhere but where you are;
> Your singing and dancing is none other than the voice of Dharma.

It is the same old world, and what is required of us is to open our spiritual eye to the new vista of quite a different dimension.

Here the koan moves into the second important scene, the sixty blows. (The original Chinese says "three 'ton' of blows." One ton is twenty, therefore three ton would be sixty, but here it does not refer to an exact number; it just means many blows.) Tozan received sixty blows of the Master's stick and retired to his place. He must have felt as if he had been driven into the bottom of a ravine ten thousand feet deep. The koan simply states, "The next day Tozan came up again and asked the Master, 'Yesterday you gave me sixty blows with your stick. I do not know where my fault was.' " Nothing is mentioned of the intense inner struggle and pain Tozan must have had after he had been beaten by Unmon and until he came to question him again the next morning. Consequently most people seem to overlook the spiritual process Tozan went through during this vitally important night. It simply shows that they have never sought after the Truth or disciplined themselves with such intensity even at the risk of their lives.

Mumon was a great Master who had gone through a hard searching and training process himself and did not overlook this point. He entered into Tozan's heart and said, "In the sea of yes-and-no, Tozan struggled all through the night." All through the night he must have lain awake and wondered about the Master's blows. He wondered and wondered with such intensity that he was not aware when morning broke. I should like to press my hands together in deep appreciation for this one night. Only those who have had similar hard and painful training days can put themselves in Tozan's place on that night. A Zen Master, seeing monks disciplining themselves most assiduously, could not help feeling the exact pain himself, and sang:

> For years I suffered in snow and frost;
> Now I am startled at pussy willows falling.

If you read the lives of the ancient Masters, you come across sentences like these: "At that moment he attained satori," or "At that he was enlightened." Though nothing is mentioned of the difficulties and hardships they had to experience prior to their attainment of satori, you have to be able to appreciate them. I daresay that unless you have felt the same pain they must have felt from this one word "satori," you are not yet qualified to read their biographies perceptively. The koan here is no exception in this regard.

Tozan undertook the long and most difficult journey across the Chinese continent looking for the right Master, and had now finally arrived at Mount Unmon in the southern part of the country. It was literally a life-and-death journey of searching. With what intense suffering and agony he would have struggled in the sea of dichotomy all through that night! We feel awestruck to think of his spiritual struggle.

The next morning Tozan asked Unmon, "Yesterday you gave me sixty blows with your stick. I do not know where my fault was." It was not an easy, casual question. It was a bleeding question, on which his searching life was staked. If a student is not able to read such a spiritual struggle in Tozan's question, it means he does not have the experience of life-and-death searching and training himself. It is also the aim of this koan to encourage and lead the student to sincere and earnest searching and discipline.

Master Unmon was a capable old campaigner. He reviled Tozan, "You rice-bag! Have you been prowling about like that from Kosei to Konan?" [Rice-bag: a good-for-nothing, an idler.] The denunciation was certainly harder and more severe than the sixty blows with a stick. As mentioned before, this seeming moral admonition is not to be interpreted in a superficial ethical sense.

Fortunately Tozan's long discipline came to its fruition; the most painful struggle overnight in the abyss of despair resulted in his breaking through the barrier. At Master Unmon's compassionate denunciation, the darkness in Tozan's heart was all dispersed. He attained satori. Everything as it is, is "it." What has been long sought is right here under my very feet! I-myself, the world —everything is "it," and cannot be otherwise! Only I was not awakened. Yet what a difference! It is quite another world.

I dare repeat, "Stop talking about satori, but first seek and discipline yourself with your body and soul." What is most important in Zen study is the sincere spiritual quest and hard inner struggle before satori is given you. How great was Tozan's joy! His biography tells us that with irresistible gratitude he thanked Master Unmon, saying, "In the future I will live far from villages without keeping a grain of rice or a piece of vegetable. Yet there I will guide all the people in the world." He said, in other words, "This great joy of mine today is not for me to keep within myself alone. Extremely poor though I am, what is poverty? I will let everybody know the happiness of Zen life." Unmon, his teacher, verified Tozan's attainment of satori and said, "You are no bigger than a coconut, yet how big you talk!" How beautiful it is to see the teacher and his disciple one in happiness and joy. It belongs to quite another dimension from ethical reflection or moral admonition.

TEISHO ON MUMON'S COMMENTARY

"If Unmon at that time, by giving Tozan the fodder of the Truth, had awakened him to the vivid, dynamic Zen life, Unmon's school would not have declined. In the sea of yes-and-no, Tozan struggled all through the night. When the day broke and he came to see the Master again, Unmon helped him break through. Though Tozan was immediately enlightened, he was not bright enough. Let me ask you, 'Should Tozan be beaten, or not?' If you say he ought to be beaten, trees and grasses and everything ought to be beaten. If you say he should not be beaten, then Unmon is telling a falsehood. If you can be clear on this point, you and Tozan will breathe together."

Seccho, a Master belonging to the Unmon School, comments on this koan, "Unmon's spirit is like that of a king. Once he works, everything crumbles away. Had he taken the right action at that time, his descendants would not have become extinct." The first part of Mumon's commentary is almost in the same tone as Seccho's. Mumon says, commenting on Master Unmon first, "What a pity that you did not give Tozan the fodder of the Truth straightway when he came to see you, so that he would have opened his spiritual eye much wider and more clearly. Then Zen of the Unmon School would not have declined." The fodder of the Truth is Zen food, Dharma food; or it may be blows, KWATZ! cries, or pointed questions; it is the ultimate means of Zen. Superficially it sounds as if Mumon is disparaging Unmon by referring to the decline of the Unmon School later. But in fact he is praising Unmon.

Next Mumon comments on Tozan, saying, "Unmon gave Tozan sixty severe blows with his stick, which drove Tozan into the midst of darkness." In the abyss of despair Tozan spent a sleepless night struggling with his inner spiritual anguish. This sea of yes-and-no, this Great Doubt or anguish of "sheer darkness all over," as Rinzai described it, is the most important and agonizing process one has to go through before breaking through the barrier. Master Mumon in his training days was in this agony for six years with Joshu's "Mu." Although Mumon simply states, "When the day broke Tozan came to see the Master again," we can well appreciate what a spiritual state he was in. His hard searching and striving for half a lifetime depended on this action. Because his struggle was hard enough, and his agony deep enough, the Master's thundering rebuke, "Have you been prowling about like that from Kosei to Konan?" penetrated through the darkness in his mind like lightning. What a happy and blessed moment this is! How great his joy was! I can only press my hands together in gratitude for this moment of breaking through. Mumon says, "Though Tozan was immediately enlightened, he was not bright enough." With those superficially disapproving words he is in fact praising Tozan.

In the third part of his commentary, Master Mumon suddenly turns to his disciples and directly asks them, "Now let me ask you monks: Tozan was given sixty blows of the stick. Should he really be beaten, or not?" He presses them further, "If you say he ought to be beaten, then everything including even trees and grasses ought to be beaten. If you say he should not be beaten, it means Unmon is telling a falsehood and deceiving people. If you can be clear on this point, you can then live the same Zen life with Tozan."

Setting aside Mumon's disciples, you right here now, how do you answer

Master Mumon? Here again Mumon points out that it has to be answered out of one's own discipline and experience.

TEISHO ON MUMON'S POEM

> A lion trains its cubs this way:
> If they walk ahead, it kicks them and quickly dodges.
> Against his will, Tozan had to be struck again;
> The first arrow only nicked him, but the second went deep.

There is an old legend in China to tell us how the lion, the king of animals, brings up its cubs. "A lioness, three days after she gives birth to her cubs, will kick her beloved ones from the precipice into an unfathomable valley. She brings up only those promising ones that have scaled the cliff, and she deserts those that are not brave enough to do so. The king of animals has its own hard rearing method suitable to the king, and does not bring up its cubs with rosewater." Master Unmon had an attitude like that of the mother lion toward Tozan, and harshly kicked him down from the precipitous cliff with sixty blows of his stick. Regrettably, Tozan did not have enough courage and strength to turn upon him and attack him immediately. Master Unmon therefore had to shoot the second arrow: "You rice-bag! Have you been prowling about like that from Kosei to Konan?" Tozan was no ordinary monk, and at this second blow he plucked up his spirits to break through the barrier and attained the joy of satori.

In the first two lines of his poem, by speaking of the unusual strictness of the mother lion in bringing up her cubs, Master Mumon indirectly refers to the encounter of Unmon and Tozan. In the last two lines he admires Master Unmon's live working of Zen. "Though the first sixty blows did not sufficiently serve their purpose, the second blow—'Rice-bag!'—was exactly to the point" —with this remark Mumon praises Tozan's attainment of satori as well as Unmon's capable methods.

16

Bell-Sound and Priest's Robe

KOAN

Unmon said, "Look! This world is vast and wide. Why do you put on your priest's robe at the sound of the bell?"

MUMON'S COMMENTARY

Now, in studying Zen and disciplining oneself in Zen, one must strictly avoid following sounds and clinging to forms. Even though one may be enlightened by hearing a sound, or have one's mind clarified by seeing a form, this is just a matter of course. It is nothing to talk about, either, if a Zen man is able to master sounds and control forms, and thus can clearly see the reality of everything and is wonderfully free in everything he does. Though it may be so, you tell me, does the sound come to your ear, or does your ear go to the sound? Even if you are able to transcend both sound and silence, how do you speak of that fact? If you listen with your ear, you cannot truly get it. When you hear with your eye, then you can really get it.

MUMON'S POEM

> If you understand "it," all things are One;
> If you do not, they are different and separate.
> If you do not understand "it," all things are One;
> If you do, they are different and separate.

TEISHO ON THE KOAN

This koan is taken from Master Unmon Bunen's teisho to the assembled monks and is not addressed to any particular monk. As Unmon is the famous Master who appeared in the previous koan, I will not refer to him in detail here.

One day, just as he ascended the rostrum to give teisho for his disciples, he heard the ringing of the bell. He at once took up this bell-sound for his teisho and said, "Look! This world is vast and wide. Why do you put on your priest's robe at the sound of the bell?" Master Mumon introduced this teisho by Master Unmon as a koan to his monks to help in their training.

Needless to say, Unmon's saying is to be studied as a Zen koan. Some commentators discuss Kegon philosophy, on which, according to them, Unmon's thought is based. Some argue about the robes Buddhist monks use. These questions are, however, all incidental; they have no direct connection with the true significance of the koan and are of secondary importance.

Unmon first declares, "Look! This world is vast and wide." Behold how vast and limitless this universe is! Not a particle to obstruct it, he says. This of course refers to inner Zen spirituality, and Master Unmon urges us to live actually in this spirituality now. If we interpret it conceptually or dogmatically, it ceases to be Zen.

From the standpoint of the world, I-myself am the world. From the standpoint of I-myself, the world is I-myself. When the world is I-myself, there is no self. When there is no self, the whole world is nothing but I-myself, and this is the true no-mind in Zen. When one lives with this no-mind, can there be anything to obstruct I-myself? What can there be, then, to restrict the world? "The world is vast and wide" refers to this no-mind. Students seeking after the Truth must first attain this no-mind themselves.

Master Unmon's Zen is really cutting and sharp. He pointedly asks, "Why do you put on your priest's robe at the sound of the bell?" It has to be the Truth, not as an idea, but as the fact actually lived by us. The one word "Why?" is the core of this koan, and it is the outflow of Master Unmon's ardent compassion. He asks it out of his wholehearted wish that we may be reborn as the subjectivity of seeing and hearing. Here, now, who can speak out in reply to Unmon's urge with the words that will satisfy him?

He referred to the robe only because the audience was made up of his monk disciples; there is no particular significance implied in the robe as such. It is the same as to say, "You go to the classroom with your books at the sound of the bell," or "You take up the receiver at the sound of the telephone." "The sound of the bell" is here to be taken as representing all sounds and hence all objective existences. While living in this world which is vast and wide we are not aware of it; we are constrained by varied phenomena in the objective scene. What a pity that we thus suffer—that we ourselves make our free subjectivity into constricted slavery! Both Unmon and Mumon are urging us, in their compassion, to throw off this restriction and return to our original freedom.

At the sound of the bell you put on your robe; at the sound of the bell you go to the dining room; at the sound of the telephone you take up the receiver. On answering the call, you have to see the wonderful work of Zen. An old Zen Master has described this mysterious work of Zen in a beautiful poem:

> So thick the bamboos grow,
> Yet they do not obstruct the running stream;
> So lofty the mountain is,
> Yet it does not impede the white cloud floating.

He is kindly pointing out for us the mystery of the free and creative working of no-mind.

TEISHO ON MUMON'S COMMENTARY

"Now, in studying Zen and disciplining oneself in Zen, one must strictly avoid following sounds and clinging to forms. Even though one may be enlightened by hearing a sound, or have one's mind clarified by seeing a form, this is just a matter of course. It is nothing to talk about, either, if a Zen man is able to master sounds and control forms, and thus can clearly see the reality of everything and is wonderfully free in everything he does. Though it may be so, you tell me, does the sound come to your ear, or does your ear go to the sound? Even if you are able to transcend both sound and silence, how do you speak of that fact? If you listen with your ear, you cannot truly get it. When you hear with your eye, then you can really get it."

While the koan itself is simple, Mumon's commentary is very kind and painstaking. Master Hakuin criticized it, saying, "I do not like this commentary. He did not have to make an unnecessary fuss about it, but should leave it to each individual whether he may get enlightened or not."

In the first sentence Master Mumon shows the key in Zen studies: "In studying Zen and disciplining oneself in Zen, one must strictly avoid following sounds and clinging to forms." In actual Zen training, students are most strongly warned against following sounds and clinging to forms, that is, against being deluded by discriminating consciousness and enslaved by objective phenomena. Zen's aim is that one should transcend both subject and object in the ordinary dualistic sense and establish the True Self, which lives as Absolute Subjectivity. Sounds and forms here refer to the six obstacles Buddhism talks about, namely, form (eye), sound (ear), smell (nose), taste (tongue), touch (body), and idea (mind). Here the first two of the six objective phenomena are mentioned to represent all the objectivities.

Mumon goes on to say, "Even though one may be enlightened by hearing a sound, or have one's mind clarified by seeing a form, this is just a matter of course." One may have his satori by hearing a sound, like Master Kyogen, who was enlightened when he heard a stone striking a bamboo; one may be awakened to his True Self by seeing a form, as Master Reiun did when, after many years, he broke through the barrier of Great Doubt when he saw peachblossoms. For a Zen man, such experience is just a matter of course and not to be specially mentioned. Primarily, a true Zen man will live the Truth as the subjectivity of forms if forms appear before him; will make free use of sounds as their subjectivity if sounds come to him. He will never be enslaved by any objectivity. He will always live the Truth in his seeing, hearing, feeling, or knowing. He will work the Truth in each movement of his hand and foot. Mumon declares that this is how a Zen man lives with absolute freedom and creativity.

Master Mumon changes the tone of his commentary and addresses his disciples, "Be that as it may, can you give the clear answer to the following question: 'A Zen man is said to master sounds; if so, does the sound come to the ear, or does the ear go to the sound?' Even if you are able to transcend the opposition of sound (voice, objectivity) and silence (ear, subjectivity), how can you express this fact in words? You will probably be unable to do so." With this question Mumon presses his disciples for their concrete answer. Now, how do you answer him? The essence of this koan lies here.

We have the following folk song in Japan:

> Is it the bell or the stick that sounds?
> It is the unity of the bell and the stick!

"The unity sounds"—what is it really? There is another song as if to negate the first one:

> Neither the bell sounds, nor the stick;
> This unity of unsounding bell and stick!

This of course points to the mysterious state where "sound and silence are both transcended"; yet I have to ask, how do you speak of that fact? Let me ask you also, what is the unity of the unsounding bell and the stick? Get hold of the stark-naked Truth of the sound! Be the sound through and through!

Master Mumon in conclusion presents the secret of Zen training in actuality: "If you listen with your ear, you cannot truly get it. When you hear with your eye, then you can really get it." He is saying, "Do not hear with your ear, but with your eye, for there is the secret of transcending subject-and-object dichotomy and attaining absolute freedom."

In short, transcend your body and spirit; transcend the body and spirit of others; cast away ears and eyes that would work in the dualistic world of subject and object. When the ear is truly transcended, the whole self is but an ear. When the eye is truly cast away, the whole universe is but an eye. It is no wonder at all for you then to hear with the eye and listen with the foot. Master Daito has a waka poem:

> If you see with your ear and hear with your eye,
> Then you will not doubt.
> These raindrops dripping from the eaves!

Let us deeply study it along with Master Mumon's commentary.

I should like to remind you here that if you deviate even a little from actual training and experience and start discussing the above commentary on the level of ideas and concepts, then it ceases to be Zen any longer. Master Hakuin's remark introduced at the beginning of this teisho on Mumon's commentary strongly warns you against that. Mumon's sentence, "If you listen with your ear, you cannot truly get it," is extracted from Master Tozan Ryokai's poem of satori:

> How wonderful, how wonderful, how wonderful indeed!
> The Dharma talk by the nonsentient is really splendid.
> If you listen with your ear, you cannot truly get it.
> When you hear with your eye, then you can really get it.

Tozan Ryokai studied under his teacher Master Ungan, who gave him the koan of "The Talk of the Nonsentient." Working hard at it, Tozan was finally able to attain satori, and the above poem was made on that occasion. "To hear with the eye" is to live in the state of absolute freedom in differentiation, with all one's six organs in complete harmony. In other words, it is the work of no-mind in Zen, but in order to avoid the possibility of a conceptual interpretation, an expression such as "to hear with the eye" is used.

TEISHO ON MUMON'S POEM

> If you understand "it," all things are One;
> If you do not, they are different and separate.
> If you do not understand "it," all things are One;
> If you do, they are different and separate.

In the first two lines and in the last two, exactly the same words are repeated with contrary sense, which makes the poem difficult to understand. Master Mumon writes the first two lines from our ordinary standpoint where the dualism of satori and ignorance prevails. If one opens his eye to the spirituality of "mastering sounds and controlling forms" and lives the wonderfully free Zen life of "hearing with the eye," then "all things are One," and he can live in the world of Oneness where subject and object are identified. If, however, his Zen eye is not opened, and he lives under the discrimination of I-and-you and suffers from the contradiction of yes-and-no, then things are "different and separate." Each stands over against the other, and he can never have peace.

There is still another barrier here for a Zen student to break through. The fact that he distinguishes satori from ignorance as if they were two different things just shows that his training is still immature. The last two lines tell us to scrape off such dirt as satori and ignorance, and throw our whole being into the Truth itself, the Reality itself. Then live naturally and freely as you will, Mumon tells us.

Whether one understands "it" or not, the world of differentiation is primarily One and in unity. Regardless of whether one understands "it" or not, in the world of Oneness and unity differentiation and multiplicity are—just as they are—free and unlimited. Oneness, if we are attached to it, is ignorance; differentiation, if we are not attached to it, is satori.

After all, where is the point? Though Mumon's wording is intricate and repetitive, what he emphatically asks us to do is to wipe away our discriminating mind, which distinguishes satori from ignorance. When our discriminating mind is cast away, the new vista of the Truth opens up to us. Leave all the reasoning and plunge directly into the Truth of "Why do you put on your priest's robe at the sound of the bell?" Get hold of the concrete Truth of Zen there.

17

The National Teacher Calls
Three Times

The National Teacher called to his attendant three times, and the attendant answered three times. The National Teacher said, "I thought I had transgressed against you, but you too had transgressed against me."

MUMON'S COMMENTARY

The National Teacher called three times, and his tongue dropped to the ground. The attendant answered three times, and softening his light he gave it out. The National Teacher, as he got old and was feeling lonely, pushed the cow's head down to the grass to feed her. The attendant would not simply accept it. Even delicious food cannot attract a full stomach. Now, tell me, how did they transgress?

> When the nation is at peace, men of talent are respected;
> When the family is well off, the children maintain their status.

MUMON'S POEM

> An iron collar with no hole, he has to wear it.
> It's no easy matter, the trouble passes on to his descendants.
> If you want to support the gate and sustain the house,
> You must climb a mountain of swords with bare feet.

TEISHO ON THE KOAN

The National Teacher in this koan is Master Echu of Nanyo. He had studied under Master Gunin, the Fifth Patriarch, and under Eno, the Sixth Patriarch, whom he succeeded. For forty years Echu lived a secluded life on Mount Byakugai, in Nanyo, while his reputation as a great Master spread. In 759 he moved to the capital at the imperial order; for sixteen years he was a teacher of Emperor Shuku-so and Emperor Dai-so, and was given the title of "National Teacher." He must have been well over one hundred years old when he died in 775.

Although no personal name is given, the attendant here is Oshin, who later succeeded Master Echu and became the abbot of Tangen Monastery. This incident took place when Master Oshin was still with his teacher, Master Echu, as his attendant, and Master Mumon introduced it as a koan with which his disciples might refine their spirituality.

The koan says that one day Master Echu called to his attendant, "Oshin!" In response to the call, the attendant answered, "Yes, Master." The Master again called "Oshin!" and Oshin again answered, "Yes, Master." The Master called to him, "Oshin!" for the third time, and the attendant answered him, "Yes, Master," for the third time. Then the Master remarked, "I thought I had transgressed against you, but you too had transgressed against me."

What does "calling thrice and answering thrice" mean? This is the first key point of this koan. The second is Master Echu's own comment on this "calling thrice and answering thrice" by himself and his attendant—that is, "I thought I had transgressed against you, but you too had transgressed against me." What are the transgressions of the Master and his attendant? These two points have to be clearly answered.

From the fundamental standpoint, it may not necessarily have to be "calling thrice and answering thrice." "Calling once, answering once" may very well do. Yet we should be able to see special significance in the "calling thrice and answering thrice" of the Master and his disciple. A Zen Master commented on Master Echu's calling three times with an old poem:

> Repeatedly she calls out, "Oh, Shogyoku!"
> It is for no other purpose
> Than that her lover
> May recognize her voice.

The meaning of the poem is that a young lady repeatedly calls out to her maidservant, "Oh, Shogyoku, Shogyoku!" and keeps on talking aloud to the servant—not, however, because she has any particular business to discuss with the maid; her sole wish is that her lover, who happens to be near, may recognize her voice and know she is there.

Master Echu's calling thrice sounds very much like that. By calling to his attendant, he is trying to accomplish quite a different objective. The attendant Oshin, however, read his teacher's mind. Quite innocently he answered "Yes, Master," and did not seem to be the least bit disturbed.

This is calling with no-mind; answering with no-mind. No-mind is responding to no-mind in lucid Oneness. Even if a thought of discrimination moves, then subject and object are thousands of miles apart. This mystery of Oneness can be achieved only by actual training, where discipline is at once satori.

If you take up a flower, you yourself are a flower; if you see a mountain, you yourself are a mountain; if you look at a pillar, you yourself are a pillar through and through. Whatever you see, whatever you hear, and wherever you go, no-mind works in Oneness and Suchness. Where then is such a distinction as satori and discipline?

I remember that my teacher, when he gave teisho on this koan of "calling thrice and answering thrice," said, "You monks, I do hope your training will be as scrupulous and thoroughgoing as this!" An old Master made a beautiful poem commenting on this wonderful working of Oneness in calling and answering three times:

> A mirror reflects candle lights in the Golden Palace.
> A mountain responds to the temple bell in the moonlight.

Candle lights in the mirror, reflecting one another—which are the true lights and which are the reflections? In sheer brightness they can hardly be distinguished. The mountain echoes the temple bell in the moonlight. Responding to each other in the quiet sky, the bell and the echoes are indistinguishable. The calling Master and the answering disciple are working together in Oneness.

Echu was a Zen Master with a gentle, open, and forthright personality. He lived and worked in Oneness of satori and discipline. Master Echu has another famous mondo: "A government officer by the name of Kyogunyo once asked the National Teacher, 'When you stayed on Mount Byakugai for years, what kind of training did you have?' The Master called up a young boy attendant and, patting him on his head, said, 'If you are this, directly say you are this. If you are that, straightway say you are that. Don't be deceived by people at any time!'"

The open and forthright characteristic of his Zen living in satori-disciplined Oneness can be seen in this mondo, which has much resemblance to the koan of "calling thrice and answering thrice."

Once, in the age of civil wars in Japan, there was a loyal samurai named Kusunoki Masashige. When he was on a trip, he happened to travel with a Zen monk, of whom Masashige asked what the secret of Zen might be. The monk asked, "What is your name please?" "My name is Kusunoki Masashige," replied the other. "Oh, Masashige!" the monk called out. When Masashige replied, "Yes?" the monk asked, "Is there any secret there?" This question impressed him deeply and made him study Zen seriously from then on.

The National Teacher, after calling out three times and being answered three times, commented, "I thought I had transgressed against you, but you too had transgressed against me." How did they transgress?—you have to answer. The Master called to the attendant—how and why is it a transgression? The attendant answered, "Yes, Master"—how and why is it a transgression?

Listen to the following mondo: "A monk asked Master Joshu, 'What is the meaning of the National Teacher's calling to his attendant?' Joshu replied, 'It is like a man writing characters in darkness. Characters may not be formed, yet the traces have already been left.' " What does he mean by "Characters may not be formed, yet the traces have already been left"? If the Master calls, "the trace has already been left," that is, the ever unnamable "it" has already been stained.

To call the Truth "it" is already staining it. There is no such distinction as subject and object in the Truth. It has neither form nor name. If I call out "Oshin!" I have already committed the transgression of giving a false name to the unnamable. And if you answer "Yes, Master" to my calling a false name, you have certainly transgressed against me. This is what Echu says. The father well understands his son. This transgression of the father and the son in Oneness beautifully depicts the characteristic of Master Echu's Zen.

TEISHO ON MUMON'S COMMENTARY

"The National Teacher called three times, and his tongue dropped to the ground. The attendant answered three times, and softening his light he gave it out. The National Teacher, as he got old and was feeling lonely, pushed the cow's head down to the grass to feed her. The attendant would not simply accept it. Even delicious food cannot attract a full stomach. Now, tell me, how did they transgress?

> When the nation is at peace, men of talent are respected;
> When the family is well off, the children maintain their status."

"To call once is enough. To call thrice—how grandmotherly kind he is! His tongue may melt away." With this somewhat sarcastic remark Mumon shows the gentle, open, and forthright characteristics of Echu's Zen. Then Mumon goes on to praise Oshin's answering three times, saying, "Softening his light, Oshin gave it out." Oshin is wonderful in softening his light and with no-mind responding to the call of his teacher. His pure and sincere spirituality does not yield even to that of his teacher. Mumon is admiring the beautiful spiritual identity of father and son.

Mumon continues to comment, "The National Teacher is getting older and apparently feeling lonesome. With excessive kindness he pushes the cow's head down to the grass forcing her to eat. The attendant, however, does not seem to pay any heed to it at all. He is thoroughly aware of the secret of Echu's hand, for he is a completely matured and accomplished Zen monk. A man with a full stomach does not even turn his face to food however delicious it may be." This is Mumon's comment on Echu and on Oshin, respectively.

Finally Mumon, referring to the transgression, asks his monks, "The National Teacher talks about transgression: tell me, how did they transgress?" Thus indicating the key point of the koan, Mumon encourages the training of his disciples. It is not, of course, to Mumon's disciples alone but to Zen students today that this question is addressed. Mumon then quotes a poem:

> When the nation is at peace, men of talent are respected;
> When the family is well off, the children maintain their status.

The poem, originally ascribed to Taikobo, means that when the state is well ruled and thriving, men of talent are esteemed. When the family is well off and flourishing, even the children in the household become noble and refined. Wealth prevails everywhere, and there is no shadow of lowliness or destitution.

Essentially, is "it" subject to transgression or nontransgression? What do you lack here and now? Can there be any greater richness than not caring even for satori? There is an old haiku poem:

> Nothing inside,
> Light is my pocket.
> This evening's cool!

TEISHO ON MUMON'S POEM

> An iron collar with no hole, he has to wear it.
> It's no easy matter, the trouble passes on to his descendants.
> If you want to support the gate and sustain the house,
> You must climb a mountain of swords with bare feet.

Long ago a heavy iron collar was placed around the neck of a felon. It was a horrible burden. But the iron collar mentioned here is one with no hole. It is an extraordinary thing, absurd beyond description. Here it means the Truth of Zen transmitted from Buddhas and Patriarchs. It also refers to the koan of "The National Teacher Calls Three Times."

This iron collar with no hole, which rejects all attempts to comprehend it, has to be borne at any cost. To bear this collar however is no easy task, for its trouble will affect even the descendants of the man who attempts it. He can never do it with ordinary determination. Mumon thus emphasizes how serious, important, and difficult it is to experience Zen Truth, and also points out how one is to discipline oneself with this koan.

His ardent encouragement to his disciples continues: "If you wish to re-build the declining gate of Zen transmitted from your ancestors, it is not enough to bear the iron collar with no hole. You have to stir up your spirit and strength to go through the tortures of hell, of climbing with bare feet a hill of knives and a mountain of swords."

Mumon's admonition and encouragement were of course addressed to his disciples in the late southern Sung dynasty, when Zen was obviously on the decline, but he is asking us today for even stronger determination in studying Zen, which is definitely required through all the ages.

18

Tozan's Three Pounds of Flax

A monk asked Master Tozan, "What is Buddha?" Tozan said, "Three pounds of flax."

Old Tozan studied a bit of clam-Zen, and opening the shell a little, revealed his liver and intestines. Though it may be so, tell me, where do you see Tozan?

> Thrust forth is "Three pounds of flax!"
> Words are intimate, even more so is the mind.
> He who talks about right and wrong
> Is a man of right and wrong.

Although this koan is very short and simple it is famous, being introduced in many Zen texts. In *Hekigan-roku* it is included as the twelfth koan.

The main figure in the koan is Master Tozan Shusho, a successor to Master

Unmon, both of whom have appeared here in the fifteenth koan. One day a monk asked Master Tozan, "What is Buddha?" Tozan, who may have been working with flax just then, answered, "Three pounds of flax." Because this answer is so splendid it has ever since been very popular in Zen circles.

"What is Buddha?" is of course one of the most representative questions in Zen mondo. In the *Mumonkan* alone it is asked on four occasions: namely, in this eighteenth and in the twenty-first, thirtieth, and thirty-third koan. Innumerable mondo on this subject are recorded in various Zen books.

Some explanation of the term "Buddha" may be necessary here. "Buddha" is "Butsu" in Chinese, originally a transliteration of the Sanskrit *buddha*. Etymologically it is a common noun meaning "an enlightened man."

While Sakyamuni Buddha, the founder of Buddhism, was alive, because he was such a great enlightened man the term "Buddha" came to be used as the title for Sakyamuni alone. After his death, however, the transformation in significance of Buddha from the historical Buddha to the conceptual Buddha naturally took place. In the course of its long history, as the thought and teaching of Buddhism spread over wide areas, various views of Buddha—religious, dogmatic, or philosophical—developed. Today, views concerning Buddha are so intricate and extensive that even specialists in the field may find it difficult to sum them up. I shall leave such studies to the specialists and shall not go into details here.

Although the Buddha the monk asks about in the koan is naturally closely related to the general concepts of Buddha in the broad sense, here it refers more directly to the Zen view of Buddha, that is, the fact of Sakyamuni Buddha's satori which he attained under the bodhi tree. In other words, Buddha in Zen is unique and not necessarily connected with various views concerning Buddha in other Buddhist schools. Buddha in Zen is to be grasped by each individual through his own realization experience.

Many great Zen Masters have given various answers to the question "What is Buddha?" Although superficially they look different, they are all expressions directly coming out of their realization experience. In studying them we must not confine ourselves to the answers alone, but must directly grasp the Zen experience from which these expressions emanate. If we miss this, the real Zen significance of the koan is lost. Unfortunately, however, most people turn their eyes to the superficial meanings of the answers and fail to grasp the point.

The monk here who asked, "What is Buddha?" is of course seeking Buddha as the fact of Zen experience. Like the great Master with deep, genuine experience that he was, Tozan at once answered, "Three pounds of flax!" How lucid and direct his Zen working is! This answer is to be appreciated as a free expression of Master Tozan's Zen at work. It is not a lukewarm philosophical statement such as "The Buddha body pervades the universe and manifests itself before all sentient beings," or "Every single thing is nothing but Buddha." If it remained only a philosophical statement like that, it could never be praised as an especially outstanding mondo in Zen circles. In this answer we see the Truth vividly working, penetrating through space and time, life and death, subject and object, and transcending all intellect and reasoning. If you cannot see it, you have not grasped the life and spirit of Master Tozan.

Master Toin in his teisho on "Three Pounds of Flax" said, "Just this three pounds of flax. Just this live three pounds; just this dead three pounds; just this adverse three pounds; just this favorable three pounds. Wherever you may go, it is the same amount. How vast is this three pounds! How remote is this three pounds! Even Buddhas and Patriarchs beat a retreat, to say nothing of devils." Because of the strange phrases he used, some might complain that Master Toin is marshaling words that do not make sense. It is not so, I tell you. He is urging you to transcend life and death, favorable and adverse, space and time, Buddhas (satori) and devils (ignorance), all with this "three pounds."

In the *Bannan-sho* it is said, "Tozan said, 'Three pounds of flax!' This is certainly a solid iron wedge that refuses all our attempts and approaches. You may have to struggle in the abyss of darkness for ten years, for twenty years. Cast away all discriminating consciousness and be no-mind, be no-self; otherwise you will not be able to grasp the essence of this koan." Zen students must give serious attention to this commentary, as well as to the one above of Master Toin.

Master Tenkei made a waka poem commenting on "Three Pounds of Flax":

> "What is Buddha?"
> "Three pounds of flax," he answers.
> Not increasing, not decreasing;
> Just as it is!

The latter half of the poem, "Not increasing, not decreasing;/Just as it is!" refers to the "three pounds of flax," but as it is so lightly mentioned, the reader may misinterpret it and say, "Three pounds of flax is just three pounds of flax. When three pounds of flax is accepted just as it is without a thought of discrimination, it is Buddha." Let me repeat: if you try to find the meaning in the expression itself, you have made an irreparable mistake. Unless you directly see into Master Tozan's Zen, from which this answer sprang out, you can never get the true significance of the koan.

There is another comment on this koan by an old Zen Master. Master Dogen sings,

> The color of the mountain and the sound of the stream,
> Each as it is, is Sakyamuni Buddha's figure and voice.

"Therefore, some may say, three pounds of flax is Buddha. What absurd nonsense!" We should listen carefully to this remark in conjunction with Master Tenkei's poem.

This mondo has a sequel, though it is not recorded in the *Mumonkan:* The questioning monk to whom Master Tozan answered "Three pounds of flax" later called on Master Chimon and asked, "What is the true significance of Master Tozan's answer 'Three pounds of flax'?" In reply to this, Master Chimon said,

> Flowers in abundance;
> Brocade in brilliance.

Then he asked the monk, "Do you understand?" When the monk confessed that he did not, Chimon further remarked,

> Bamboos in the south,
> Trees in the north.

On his return to Tozan's monastery the monk reported to the Master what Chimon had said. Tozan took the rostrum, saying, "I will talk not to you alone but to all the monks on the subject," and gave the following kind instruction: "It is impossible to express exactly the reality of things in words, and to show correctly the truth of inner spirituality in language. If you keep on clinging to words, you will lose your True Self. If you cling to letters and are not able to transcend them, your spiritual eye will never be opened."

Tozan was trying to point out that Buddha in the true sense of the term in Zen is not to be found in words and letters, and that to study Zen correctly is to transcend words and letters.

An old Zen Master commented on Tozan's answer, praising him from the same standpoint:

> Pure gold!
> Solid iron!

TEISHO ON MUMON'S COMMENTARY

"Old Tozan studied a bit of clam-Zen, and opening the shell a little, revealed his liver and intestines. Though it may be so, tell me, where do you see Tozan?"

On Tozan's answer, "Three pounds of flax," Mumon comments that Tozan seems to have studied a little bit of clam-Zen. Shellfish immediately show all their inward parts if they open their mouth even slightly. Just like an open clam, Master Tozan revealed all of himself in his short answer. As usual, Mumon sounds as if he were bantering—how can "three pounds of flax" be so great as to reveal his liver and intestines? Mumon, to be sure, has penetrated the heart of the koan, though he may sound cynical. He therefore emphatically asks his disciples in the next sentence, "Where do you see Tozan?" He is urging his disciples to get hold of Tozan's Zen, which is so great and thoroughgoing in his answer, "Three pounds of flax!" Mumon is so direct and clear in pointing out the core of the koan because he is himself a capable Master with deep experience.

TEISHO ON MUMON'S POEM

Thrust forth is "Three pounds of flax!"
Words are intimate, even more so is the mind.
He who talks about right and wrong
Is a man of right and wrong.

In summing up the koan in the form of a poem, Mumon first says, "Thrust out is 'Three pounds of flax!' " Those who can see Tozan will immediately see through "it" in this "thrust out is three pounds of flax." They will grasp the True Buddha alive and appreciate Master Tozan's Zen at work in this first line.

The second line says, "Words are intimate, even more so is the mind." The answer itself is wonderful, but the spirit of the answer is even more wonderful, a spirit that revealed Tozan's liver and intestines. Buddha, three pounds of flax, and Tozan are all One, and this Oneness pervades the universe. Thus Master Mumon highly praises Tozan's "Three pounds of flax." How can such profound significance be found in this answer? As the *Bannan-sho* tells you, you may have to struggle in the abyss of darkness for ten years, for twenty years. Casting away all discriminating consciousness, you have to be no-mind, no-self. Then you can appreciate it personally yourself. If you try to deal with Zen intellectually or conceptually, you can never get hold of it.

Mumon's kind comment continues: "He who talks about right and wrong is a man of right and wrong." Master Seccho's comment in his poem is also in the same vein:

> If you try to see Tozan
> By clinging to the event and following the expressions,
> You are like a lame terrapin or a blind turtle
> Going into a deep valley.

Let me warn you once again. Those who would variously argue about this koan, clinging to Tozan's words, are after all men of right and wrong (dualism). They are no better than a lame terrapin or a blind turtle. I ask you, "What are Tozan's liver and intestines?" In the three pounds of flax get hold of his inner experience itself. Appreciate it not as Tozan's experience, but as your own.

19

Ordinary Mind Is Tao

Joshu once asked Nansen, "What is Tao?" Nansen answered, "Ordinary mind is Tao." "Then should we direct ourselves toward it or not?" asked Joshu. "If you try to direct yourself toward it, you go away from it," answered Nansen. Joshu continued, "If we do not try, how can we know that it is Tao?" Nansen replied, "Tao does not belong to knowing or to not-knowing. Knowing is illusion; not-knowing is blankness. If you really attain to Tao of no-doubt, it is like the great void, so vast and boundless. How, then, can there be right and wrong in the Tao?" At these words, Joshu was suddenly enlightened.

MUMON'S COMMENTARY

Questioned by Joshu, Nansen immediately shows that the tile is disintegrating, the ice is dissolving, and no communication whatsoever is possible. Even though Joshu may be enlightened, he can truly get it only after studying for thirty more years.

MUMON'S POEM

> Hundreds of flowers in spring, the moon in autumn,
> A cool breeze in summer, and snow in winter;
> If there is no vain cloud in your mind
> For you it is a good season.

TEISHO ON THE KOAN

This koan, like the fourteenth, is a mondo between Master Nansen and Master Joshu. In this koan however Joshu, still named Junen, is a very young monk in training, probably a little over twenty years old, while Nansen, his teacher, must be around fifty. The young truth-seeker Junen had given up his scholastic studies of Buddhism, traveled from his homeland in North China all the way to South China, and had been concentrating on Zen training under Master Nansen. The incident in the koan took place around this time. This is a very significant mondo by which young Joshu was able to open his Zen eye. Master Mumon presents it as a koan to help and encourage his disciples in their training.

"Tao," asked about in the mondo, is a term that plays an important role in Asian thinking. Its significance cannot be fully explained in language, nor can it be simply replaced by other words. It was in use in China before the introduction of Buddhism. Etymologically, *Tao* means a way, or a passage where people come and go. It can also be used in the sense of the right path for man to follow. It thus refers to the moral code, or more broadly, the fundamental principle and reality of the universe, and has been used as an essential word in Taoism. As its etymological meaning—"a passage where people come and go"—indicates, Tao is basically a very practical and realistic word, reflecting the pragmatic and ethical characteristics of traditional Chinese culture. Indian culture, by contrast, is much more philosophical. Indians use such words as *bodhi* (satori of true wisdom), *nirvana* (satori of no-life, no-death), *prajna*, or *sunyata*, which are all distinctly metaphysical and speculative. When Buddhism with its Indian tradition was introduced into China, the Chinese people had great difficulty in translating the Indian Buddhist terms, and finally they used *Tao* as a Chinese equivalent for *bodhi*, *prajna*, and similar words. Although the final meaning of the originally Chinese word is the same as its Indian equivalents, the nuances are naturally different, reflecting their respective cultural backgrounds. Tao gradually came to be used with its Chinese practical connotations.

Later as the Zen of Bodhidharma's line, which stresses the importance of experience and is the most practical in nature among all Buddhist teachings, spread and flourished as a new type of teaching in China, the old traditional term *Tao*, with its experiential connotations, began to be used as a Zen term referring to the Truth of Zen. Incidentally, it is often called Great Tao, Ultimate Tao, or True Tao.

One day, Joshu, a young monk in training, asked his teacher, Master Nansen, "What is Tao?" As I have explained above, Tao has characteristically

Chinese connotations. Here, however, it can be taken to mean "the fundamental Truth in Zen" or "the essence of Zen," in the same sense as the Ultimate Truth or the Great Tao.

It must have been this "What is Tao?" that made young Joshu give up his academic studies of Buddhism and prompted him to travel all the way from North China to Nansen's monastery in South China. To realize experientially "What is Tao?" was his most urgent and important task. To this question of Joshu, Master Nansen quite plainly answered, "Ordinary mind is Tao." Literally it means, "Everyday mind as it is without any discrimination is Tao." This Tao, which from ancient times has been treated by many saints and wise men as a fundamental principle and reality, is nothing other than our ordinary mind as it is, Nansen says. But who can simply and immediately accept this instruction and say, "Yes, so it is"? If Tao is literally our everyday mind as it is, farmers and fishermen's wives would all know it, and we would not have to wait for saints and wise men to teach us and save us. This means we have to transcend our ordinary mind to attain the true ordinary mind, and in order actually to transcend our dualistic ordinary mind, sincere searching and hard discipline are required. When we have broken through the barrier where our ordinary mind is not at all ordinary mind, we can for the first time return to our original ordinary mind, which Nansen upholds.

"Tao is near at hand, yet people look for it afar," said an old wise man. It is also said, "Tao is never away from us even for a moment. If it is, it is not Tao." Yet for those who are not awakened to this fact, the ordinary mind, Nansen teaches, naturally belongs to the unknown world beyond the barrier, and they cannot help looking for it afar. It was just natural that young Joshu, who had not yet broken through the barrier, could not simply accept the instruction of Nansen, for whom the whole universe was nothing but himself and for whom there was no Tao apart from his ordinary mind.

Joshu had to ask Nansen, "Should we direct ourselves toward it or not? In what direction should we strive in order to open our spiritual eye to the fact that ordinary mind is Tao?" This is a natural and proper question for one who has not yet attained this spirituality, and only if one pursues this sincere and earnest quest can he have true training.

Master Nansen answers sharply out of his absolute Zen life, "The more you try to direct yourself toward it, the further you go away from it." Your very striving and trying to get it is already discrimination and contrivance that alienates you from Tao. Nansen is kindly pointing out that if one tries to seek after Tao, in which he himself already is, his very searching alienates him from it.

There is an old anecdote of a Japanese steamship which went up to the lower reaches of the great Amazon River in South America. The width of the river was over a hundred miles, and the crew thought they were still in the ocean. They saw a British ship far out and asked them by signal to please spare some drinking water for them. To their surprise the British ship signaled back, "Put your buckets down into the water."

"You are in the midst of 'it' right now. If you try to direct yourself toward it, you go away from 'it'!" What a kind instruction this is! Yet such a compassionate teaching as Nansen's cannot be accepted by those whose spiritual eyes are not yet opened.

Joshu's stiff question continues, "If we do not try, how can we know it is Tao?" We might say it is quite reasonable of Joshu to ask, "Without striving to get it, without speculating about it, how can we be convinced that ordinary mind is Tao?"

There are many who simply conclude from these questions that Joshu was a philosophically minded, argumentative youth. However, do not take the young questioning Joshu in that sense. He has already given up his studies of religious philosophy and traveled all the way from North to South China to study under the famous Zen Master Nansen. He is here a sincere and earnest truth-seeker who is giving himself to training in Zen.

In his persistent questions to his teacher Nansen, "Should we direct ourselves toward it or not?" and "If we do not try, how can we know that it is Tao?" we hear the bleeding cry of a truth-seeker who has been driven to a desperate deadlock. The quest in his mind urges him to break through it even at the cost of his life; yet no approach is possible. If a reader is unable to enter into Joshu's inner anguish, but just literally reads his questions, he must be one who has never really sought after Truth or disciplined himself. Any Zen man without exception has to experience excruciating inner anguish before he finally attains satori, which fundamentally changes his whole personality. Satori in Zen is thus totally different from intellectual understanding, which belongs to the world of human knowledge and thought. Joshu's irresistible questions came out of his inner desperation. Later he became a great Zen Master who could declare, "You are being used by the twenty-four hours, but I am using the twenty-four hours." At this time, however, he was still a young truth-seeker who was being used by the twenty-four hours.

Master Nansen's instruction here is extremely kind. He says, "Tao does not belong to knowing or to not-knowing. Knowing is illusion; not-knowing is blankness. If you really attain to Tao of no-doubt, it is like the great void, so vast and boundless. How, then, can there be right and wrong in the Tao?"

In the Japanese language, the word for Tao is *michi,* which has the meaning of "abounding." When it is abundant everywhere, how can it be sought after? The seeking mind itself is already the sought-after Tao. If we try to know it, it turns out to be a relativistic objective and ceases to be the Reality. It is therefore said, "Tao does not belong to knowing or to not-knowing." What is known is only a conceptual shadow of the Reality. If, however, it is not known at all, it is dead blankness. Cast away all the discriminating consciousness and attain to the Tao of no-doubt. It will then be like the great void, so vast and boundless. There is no room for discrimination to enter here. With painstaking compassion Nansen tries to enlighten Joshu.

Master Hakuin criticizes Nansen saying, "I do not like such grandmotherly mildness. He ought to beat Joshu severely, without a word." Nansen's inculcation, however, has the live strength naturally coming out of his experience, while words of mere scholars and philosophers cannot be expected to have such convincing power.

The koan says, "At these words Joshu was suddenly enlightened." The fortunate moment came upon him. His self and the whole universe crumbled away, and he was reborn to the Tao of no-doubt. How happy he was! This happiness, however, did not just accidentally visit him. Let me remind you that behind the simple sentence there is the stern fact of his long and hard discipline and deep inner struggle.

"Blessed are those who hunger and thirst for righteousness, for they shall be satisfied" (Matthew 5:6) is a Christian saying. The expressions may be different, yet in actually seeking after Truth in any religion, one has to go through the darkness of spiritual struggle.

Young Joshu broke through the barrier and awoke in the great void, vast and boundless. In other words, his spiritual eye was opened for the first time to Nansen's Zen, where ordinary mind as it is is Tao. The ordinary mind Zen upholds is not our dualistic ordinary mind, but it has to be the ordinary mind attained by satori.

Master Keizan, of Soto Zen in Japan, was suddenly enlightened when he listened to his teacher Master Tettsu's teisho on "Ordinary Mind is Tao." Keizan declared, "I have got it!" to which his teacher retorted, "How have you got it?" "A jet-black iron ball speeds through the dark night!" This reply points to the Absolute Oneness where all discriminations are transcended. It is nothing else but the experience of the great void, vast and boundless. Master Tettsu, however, did not easily approve it, and demanded, "It is not enough. Speak further!" Keizan answered again, "When I am thirsty, I drink. When I am hungry, I eat." Master Tettsu was now satisfied and verified Keizan's satori, saying, "In the future you will certainly promote Soto Zen."

For the ordinary mind of drinking tea and eating rice to be Tao and Zen, it has to go once and for all through the absolute negation of "A jet-black iron ball speeds through the dark night." Unless one has personally experienced the Absolute Oneness, vast and boundless, and has returned to his ordinary mind, his Tao is not true Tao which he can freely and creatively use and enjoy every day.

TEISHO ON MUMON'S COMMENTARY

"Questioned by Joshu, Nansen immediately shows that the tile is disintegrating, the ice is dissolving, and no communication whatsoever is possible. Even though Joshu may be enlightened, he can truly get it only after studying for thirty more years."

Master Mumon first comments on Master Nansen's earnest instruction, "Being questioned by young Joshu, Nansen verbosely states this and that. How clumsy! It is not a tolerable answer at all." As usual, Mumon sounds as if he is disapproving Nansen's reply. In fact, however, he is trying, with this abusive language, to warn truth-seekers, who are liable to fall into intellectual interpretation that the true ordinary mind can never be fully expounded in words, however wonderful the explanations may be. He is at the same time admiring Nansen's masterly efforts.

Next Master Mumon goes on to comment that even though Joshu may be enlightened, he can really and truly get it only after disciplining himself for thirty more years. Mumon negates Joshu's awakening. Why? Because Zen has to be the fact of personality and be lived actually in one's everyday life. Otherwise it will be just the idle talk of a conceptual philosopher. Mumon kindly reminds us that "ordinary mind" should be the aim of our lifelong training. In our "upward" or "ascending-the-mountain" training there will be the time when we may reach the goal. In our "downward" or "descending-the-mountain" training, however, there will be no end, for it is the training of "ordinary mind," and the training in differentiation will infinitely develop. There is no termination for true training, or Zen life.

"Thirty years" does not refer to a fixed length of time to be counted as thirty, but means infinitely or forever.

TEISHO ON MUMON'S POEM

> Hundreds of flowers in spring, the moon in autumn,
> A cool breeze in summer, and snow in winter;
> If there is no vain cloud in your mind
> For you it is a good season.

Describing the beauties of the four seasons, Master Mumon illustrates what ordinary mind is. Beauty in spring, however, with hundreds of flowers in bloom, is accompanied by the sorrow of falling flowers. The clear and serene moon in autumn brings also the grief of interruption by clouds and rain. The cool breeze in summer is followed by the unpleasantness of intense heat. Snow in winter brings with it the regret of bitter cold. In fact, ordinary mind is in the vortexes of good and evil, beautiful and ugly, happy and sad, joy and pain.

In the third line Master Mumon brings out an important phrase: "If there is no vain cloud in your mind." "Vain cloud" means a foolish and useless thing; more concretely, it is our discriminating working, which is a worthless fuss, to no fundamental purpose. In order to attain the personality that has no vain cloud in the mind, one has to plunge once and for all into the vast and boundless great void and have the experience: "a jet-black iron ball speeds through the dark night." When one has actually experienced it, for the first time he has fundamental peace and freedom. For him, then, to live is one aspect of his ordinary mind, to die is also an aspect of his ordinary mind. He always lives in the blessing of his noble ordinary mind in his sickness if he is sick, in his poverty if he is poor. He will never waver in decision, or cling to right and wrong, but is the absolute subjectivity under every circumstance.

Master Unmon taught his disciples that "every day is a good day." He lived every day as a good day, whether it was right or wrong, good or bad. It was a good season for him. It is not at all easy, however, for anyone to live "ordinary mind is Tao." He certainly has to study for thirty more years. Master Bukkan said to his disciples, "If you want to get 'ordinary mind is Tao,' you must not leave it to chance. In order to row a boat you have to use oars. In order to race a horse you have to give it the whip." I want you to read these words carefully.

In connection with Master Mumon's poem on the four seasons, Master Daito made the following interesting poems. The first is entitled "A Poem of True Words":

> Neither flowers in spring
> Nor a cool breeze in summer;

No moon in autumn,
No snow in winter.

"A Poem of False Words" says:

Flowers in spring,
A cool breeze in summer;
The moon in autumn
And snow in winter.

Why did he make such contradictory poems? Isn't he telling us to live the Truth transcending affirmation and negation, this and that? An old Zen Master said, "Tao with no-mind is in accord with man. Man with no-mind is in accord with Tao." He is joining Master Daito in illustrating for us the wonder of "ordinary mind is Tao."

20

A Man of Great Strength

KOAN

Master Shogen said, "Why is it that a man of great strength cannot lift his leg?" Again he said, "It is not with his tongue that he speaks."

MUMON'S COMMENTARY

Of Shogen it must be said that he emptied his intestines and turned his belly out. Yet no one understands it. Even though there is a man who immediately understands it, I will give him severe blows with my stick if he comes to me. Why? Nii! If you want to know pure gold, see it in the midst of fire.

MUMON'S POEM

Lifting his leg he kicks up the Scented Ocean,
Lowering his head, he looks down on the Four Dhyana Heavens.
There is no place to put this gigantic body.
You please add another line.

TEISHO ON THE KOAN

This koan is taken from Master Shogen's teisho to his disciples, and is not in the form of a mondo.

Master Shogen Sugaku of Reiin, Koshofu, was a man of integrity—sincere, precise, and attentive. After some years of study as a lay disciple, he was ordained in his thirties. He died in 1202 at the age of seventy-one, and at that time Master Mumon was a young monk twenty years old. Although there is a difference of a half-century between them, for twenty years these two Masters lived in the same southern Sung dynasty, and developed true dynamic Zen life in Zen circles at a time when the signs of decline were gradually becoming apparent. Among the Zen Masters who appear in the forty-eight koan of the *Mumonkan*, Master Shogen historically belongs to the latest period.

The koan consists of two parts. First Shogen asks, "Why is it that a man of great strength cannot lift his leg?" "A man of great strength" is here a man spiritually outstanding as well as physically strong. It is a matter of course that a man of great strength can freely and easily lift his leg. Shogen flatly negates this fact and asks, "Why is he unable to do so?" The essence of the koan is to be grasped at this point. With this negative "Why?" is he asking his disciples to forget their legs and be awakened to the mysterious work of no-leg? Or is he saying with the negative "Why?" that the true man of great strength is one who has transcended the dualistic discrimination of "lifting" and "not lifting"? With this "Why?" he is urging you to completely cast away yourself and the universe. When there is no self, there can be nothing that would restrict the self. On the contrary, so-called free legs will cause the self to stumble.

There is a funny story: Once a centipede was asked how he could operate all his numerous feet in such an orderly manner without ever getting them confused. Strangely enough, from that time on the centipede became unable to move and finally died.

By depriving you of everything, Master Shogen expects you to revive as a truly free man of great strength and to develop your unconstricted life as an enlightened man.

An old Zen Master said, "A green mountain is always walking!" When one is thoroughly a green mountain of no-mind, and walks with no-mind, he is truly a man of great strength worthy of the name. Let me stress once again: plunge into this "Why?" and cast away not only your leg but your very self with this "Why?"

The second part of the koan says, "It is not with his tongue that he speaks," which means literally, "In speaking words he does not use his tongue." In order to stress the point of the koan, I should like to put this sentence in the form of the first question, "Why is it that a man of great strength does not use his tongue in speaking?"

Needless to say, the man of great strength is an enlightened one who has cast away both himself and the universe with this negative "Why?" When there is truly no self, what can there be that would interfere with speaking and silence? All day long he may speak, yet he never moves his tongue. Master Shogen is asking us to attain this mysterious work of no-tongue and to freely use and enjoy it.

I dare to suggest to you again: plunge into this "Why?" and with it cast away not only your tongue but your very self.

Master Dogen said, "Extinction of thinking and doing is nothing other than every form of doing and acting. Abandonment of words and letters is nothing other than every word and phrase." For Master Dogen, extinction of thinking and doing did not mean to be like wood or a stone by annihilating his thinking and doing, but for him it was to be Absolute Subjectivity and to be free in all doings and actings. For Dogen, abandonment of words and letters was not to be dead silent without moving his tongue; it was, for him, to be the free master of speech and silence. Yet he leaves no trace of any doing or speaking. This is certainly the wonderful life of the man of great strength.

Master Shogen in his teisho is asking each of his disciples to be the man of great strength and to live the truly free life transcending speaking and silence, activity and stillness, in the midst of speaking and silence, activity and stillness. He is encouraging his disciples in their actual training and is not talking about speaking and silence, action and stillness as such. (On this point, see the twenty-fourth koan, "Abandon Words and Speaking.")

Some Zen books refer to Shogen's "*Three* Turning Phrases," although their source is not indicated. Those works have another sentence in addition to the two recorded in this koan, namely: "Why is it that a man of satori cannot cut off the red thread under his feet?"

"A man of satori" is the one whose spiritual eye is clearly opened. It is the same in meaning as "a man of great strength," though they may make different impressions. "The red thread under his feet" refers to illusions and discriminations, which naturally must have already been cut off by the man of satori. Master Shogen dares to ask why he is unable to cut off the red thread under his feet. What does he mean by "the red thread" of the man of satori? In the third statement, as in the two earlier ones, Master Shogen tries to arouse his disciples to actual discipline and experience. In other words, with the negative "Why?" he deprives them of satori and ignorance, cutting off and not-cutting off, so that they may be reborn as men of real freedom. When one has this realization, the red thread under his feet turns into a working aspect of free subjectivity, and the question of cutting off and not-cutting off is all transcended.

So far I have shown the traditional Zen attitudes toward Shogen's Three Turning Phrases. But those who try to interpret them literally or superficially will be unable to appreciate them.

Most of the commentaries fail to get at the real significance of Master Shogen's teisho and simply interpret the Three Turning Phrases as ethical admonitions, giving the following explanations:

First, on "Why is it that a man of great strength cannot lift his leg?" they say that this is Shogen's warning to those Zen men who remain in their static zazen in quietude. He is rebuking them by saying that after they have attained the great strength of satori through having disciplined themselves assiduously for years, they must not remain satisfied in the cave of quietistic zazen, but ought to come out into the world of differentiation to work. It is a very plausible opinion, but from the beginning such quietistic monks could not be called men of great strength.

Second, on "It is not with his tongue that he speaks," they may say, "Master Shogen is giving a sharp rebuke to those monks who, neglecting their primary objective of clarifying their True Self, busy themselves in boastfully arguing about the Buddha's teachings or the koan of the old Masters. He points out the flippancy of these letter-bound monks." This also sounds plausible. Yet these monks, to begin with, are not true Zen men.

Third, on "Why is it that a man of satori cannot cut off the red thread under his feet?" their interpretation may be as follows: "Shogen admonishes immature monks, saying, 'With your Zen ability, which you have attained after years of hard training, why are you unable to cut off your illusions and attachments? Why can't you wipe off the stink of Zen, the smack of satori?' " This may be a good suggestion, but these monks are not at all men of satori.

Of course these interpretations give important ethical teachings which Zen men too ought to keep in mind. Yet if Shogen's Three Turning Phrases are no more than ethical admonitions, they need not be taken up as koan with their unique Zen role to play.

As I have emphasized at several previous points, the role of koan is to take away all established ideas and accumulated knowledge from the student and drive him into extremity and beyond. Then from the abyss of Great Death he revives as a new man in the new world. A completely new vista opens up to him. Zen has the depth and transparency to bring about the fundamental change of one's whole personality in the realm where ethics has not yet started to work. If this essential point is missed, a collection of koan turns out to be a book of mere speculation or ethics and ceases to be a genuine Zen writing. This does not mean that ethics and morals are unnecessary in Zen; on the contrary, ethics has to be the natural outcome of Zen life. When one lives and enjoys his Zen life of no-mind, ethical actions automatically develop.

TEISHO ON MUMON'S COMMENTARY

"Of Shogen it must be said that he emptied his intestines and turned his belly out. Yet no one understands it. Even though there is a man who immediately understands it, I will give him severe blows with my stick if he comes to me. Why? Nii! If you want to know pure gold, see it in the midst of fire."

Master Mumon's commentary is severe, and free as usual either to praise or to denounce. First he admires Shogen, saying, "Master Shogen, in giving teisho, emptied his intestines and turned his belly out. He thrust out all his Zen ability right in front of his disciples." Mumon fully appreciates Master Shogen's energetic Zen working. In order to illustrate the absolute freedom of the true man of great strength, Shogen used drastic means. "Yet no one understands it." How regrettable! They interpret it as an ethical admonition, and nobody seems to get Shogen's true meaning. There are not many, either today or in the past, who have their Zen eye clearly opened.

Mumon continues, "Even though there may be someone who immediately understands Shogen's teisho, if he comes to me, I will give him severe blows with my stick. I will not easily approve him. Why is it? Have you any objections?"

Why this negation? Because the true man of great strength is utterly free and works in a realm different from that of the intellect and reasoning. An old Zen Master cried, "Under the clear blue sky, get another blow!" He is telling you to smash up satori if you ever get satori.

Mumon ends his commentary with a kind instruction, "If you want to know genuine gold, see it in the midst of fire." Unless it is once thoroughly tested by raging flames, we cannot tell for sure whether it is genuine gold or sham. Unless you study under a really strict Master and taste once and for all his deadly blow in raging flames, you cannot be called a man of great strength. Master Mumon is urging us to be true Zen men of actual training and experience.

TEISHO ON MUMON'S POEM

> Lifting his leg he kicks up the Scented Ocean,
> Lowering his head, he looks down on the Four Dhyana Heavens.

There is no place to put this gigantic body.
You please add another line.

Master Mumon tries to depict, in the poem, the working of the man of great strength. We should note that he does not give any ethical preaching at all. He asks us to concentrate ourselves on our actual training.

Mythologically, in the tales of primitive Buddhism, the universe is supposed to consist of Mount Sumeru and the Scented Ocean that surrounds it, over which there are Four Dhyana Heavens. The Scented Ocean may be interpreted here as infinite extension and the Four Dhyana Heavens as infinite height.

Mumon describes the man of great strength, saying, "Just lifting his leg a little, he turns the Scented Ocean over. So great is he that he looks down upon the Four Dhyana Heavens far below, lowering his head." He is an extraordinary giant who could put the great universe into his bosom. Where could such a gigantic body be put? Nowhere can there be such a place.

Nothing can interfere with the freedom of the man who has transcended the restriction of time, who has gone behind the limitation of space and no longer lives in the dualistic world of big and small. But be careful and do not make the vital mistake! Listen to what the compassionate Master Mumon has to say at the end: "You please add your final words to complete the poem."

You now raise your finger. You now utter a word: if you turn your eye away from it and look for the man of great strength outwardly, you have missed "it" completely. The mysterious working of Zen is right here and now in your every doing. An old Zen Master was eager to make this point clear when he put the question, "All things return to One; where does One return to?" Zen thoroughly negates actual facts, yet at the same time Zen yields to none in affirming actual facts.

21

Unmon's Shit-Stick

A monk asked Unmon, "What is Buddha?" Unmon said, "A shit-stick!" (Kan-shiketsu!)

MUMON'S COMMENTARY

Of Unmon it must be said that he is so poor that he cannot prepare even plain food; he is so busy that he cannot write properly. Very likely they may bring out the shit-stick to support the gate. The outcome is just obvious.

MUMON'S POEM

> A flash of lightning!
> Sparks struck from a flint!
> If you blink your eye
> It is gone.

TEISHO ON THE KOAN

As Master Unmon Bunen has already appeared in the fifteenth and the sixteenth koan, no further introduction to him is needed. I should, however, like to mention here another of his characteristics: he was noted for his short and terse answers, directly to the point. Often he gave a one-word or one-phrase reply, sharp and pointed, bursting out of his spiritual strength, apart from the literal meaning of the answered word itself. Let me give you some examples of his pithy replies:

MONK: "What is the talk that transcends Buddhas and Patriarchs?"

UNMON: "Kobyo!" (Rice cake!)

MONK: "No thought has been stirred. Is there any fault there, or not?"

UNMON: "Shumi-sen!" (Mount Sumeru!)

MONK: "What is the eye of satori?"

UNMON: "Fu!" (Pervading!)

MONK: "If one kills his father and mother, he will make a confession before Buddha. If he kills Buddhas and Patriarchs, how can he confess?"

UNMON: "Ro!" (Revealed!)

The mondo in this koan ("A monk asked Unmon, 'What is Buddha?' Unmon said, 'Kan-shiketsu!' ") is also an example of his terse response. As for the question, "What is Buddha?" I have already given my teisho on it in discussing the eighteenth koan, "Tozan's Three Pounds of Flax," and detailed explanations are omitted here.

Needless to say, the questioning monk is not asking about dogmatic Buddhist views, nor is he inquiring about philosophical concepts of Buddha. What he asks about is Buddha in Zen, that is, Buddha as the fact of one's realization experience. He wants to know it and get it. Even so, what an unexpected reply Master Unmon gave: "A shit-stick!"

Just a shit-stick! For Master Unmon, here, the whole universe was a shit-stick; he himself was a shit-stick. No room is there for such an idle distinction as dirty and clean.

From olden days, there have been varied interpretations of "shit-stick," and it is difficult to know which may be correct. One says it is a bamboo tool used in ancient China to pick up and take away feces from the road. Apparently in those days in the country they excreted outside. Anyway, it is the dirtiest and most contemptible thing in the world.

Most commentaries would say about this reply of Unmon, "It is expounded in the *Kegon-kyo* that 'Buddha pervades the universe and is revealed before all sentient beings.' According to this view of Buddha in Buddhism, there is not a single item that is not a Buddha. A shit-stick is not an exception; it is a manifestation of Buddha."

We have to remember that to know the truth as an idea or a concept is one thing, and to have the actual experience of Truth in oneself which makes one declare that "each and every thing is Buddha," is quite another. Between the two there is all the difference in the world. If one lacks this inner experience of realization, his wonderful thought is without reality, just like a painted lion.

Zen insists that this realization experience is essential. Whether the Master's reply is "Three pounds of flax" or "A shit-stick!" is of secondary significance depending on external conditions. The Zen Master tries with a mondo to awaken the student to this realization experience and let him attain a new and creative Zen personality in order to live freely in this world. This is the sole aim of koan studies.

Master Daie taught one of his lay disciples as follows: "What is the shit-stick? It can neither be grasped nor tasted. When you have intense inner struggle, you are in the right course of training." Daie is also trying to point to the experiential fact that precedes all thoughts and philosophies.

Master Unmon's "shit-stick" has another role to play apart from its primary significance just mentioned. His reply would root out any possible preoccupation in the student's mind such as "virtuous Buddha, inviolable holiness" and the like, and would lead him directly to the absolute spirituality, utterly lucid and transparent. We must not overlook Unmon's compassionate intention here.

"All through his life he pulls out nails and wedges for others," is a phrase characterizing Master Unmon. This is a good description of his Zen, for his mondo always show the compassionate means he uses to encourage his monks in their training.

TEISHO ON MUMON'S COMMENTARY

"Of Unmon it must be said that he is so poor that he cannot prepare even plain food; he is so busy that he cannot write properly. Very likely they may bring out the shit-stick to support the gate. The outcome is just obvious."

As usual, Master Mumon admires this koan by severely denouncing it. Commenting on Unmon's reply he says, "The way you answer the monk makes us think you are in such dire poverty that you cannot offer even the plainest meal to a visitor, and that you are altogether too busy to write sentences with care. You must be speaking and writing just offhand." By way of severe criticism Mumon is in fact praising Unmon.

Mumon continues to comment on "a shit-stick": "By the way, students of Zen in later generations may hold up the shit-stick and claim that they would sustain Dharma with it. However, what they would be doing would surely predict the decline of the true spirit of Buddhism." This is Master Mumon's admonition to the students in later generations. He is telling them how vitally important and serious this shit-stick is, and also how essential it is that each in himself should have the realization experience on which this answer is based.

TEISHO ON MUMON'S POEM

> A flash of lightning!
> Sparks struck from a flint!
> If you blink your eye
> It is gone.

In this very short poem Mumon beautifully describes the wonderful quality of Master Unmon's answer. To "What is Buddha?" he had no hesitation in replying "Kan-shiketsu!" Not only did he not allow any room for discriminating argument, but also he wiped away any smacks of Buddha. His capability and tact are outstanding and quick as a flash of lightning or the sparks of a flint struck with iron. Blessed are you if you have enough ability to get into Unmon's heart. If you cherish a thought of discrimination, the real significance of his shit-stick will be lost forever. Praising Unmon most highly, Mumon is thus cautioning his disciples.

22

Kasho and a Flagpole

Ananda once said to Kasho, "The World-Honored One transmitted to you the brocade robe. What else did he transmit to you?" Kasho called out, "Ananda!" Ananda answered, "Yes, sir." Kasho said, "Pull down the flagpole at the gate."

MUMON'S COMMENTARY

If you can give the exact turning word to this koan, you will see that the meeting at Mount Grdhrakuta is definitely present here. If not, then know that Vipasyin Buddha is still unable to get the Truth even though he began his seeking in remote antiquity.

MUMON'S POEM

> The calling out is good, but even better the answering.
> How many are there who have opened their true eyes?
> The elder brother calling out, the younger brother replying,
>   the family shame is revealed.
> This is the spring that does not belong to Yin and Yang.

The sixth koan of the *Mumonkan* presents the truth of teacher-disciple transmission between Sakyamuni Buddha and the Venerable Kasho. This twenty-second koan shows the teacher-disciple transmission between the Venerable Kasho and the Venerable Ananda. This is therefore a companion to the sixth koan, "Sakyamuni Holds Up a Flower."

The real life and spirit of Zen is in the religious experience attained by each individual. In Zen it is transmitted directly from mind to mind and not by writing or rituals such as prayers or chanting of mantras and sutras. While its tradition and transmission are maintained solely by the religious experience of each individual, the genuineness of the experience of the disciple must be identified with that of his teacher. In other words, while Zen insists on the one hand that the religious experience of the individual is the fundamental requisite, at the same time Zen holds that the teacher's verification of his disciple's attainment is absolutely necessary. The mind-to-mind transmission in Zen thus has to be teacher-disciple identification. This is exactly the case with the Dharma transmission from Sakyamuni to Kasho, and also from Kasho to Ananda. I want you to read again the sixth koan, "Sakyamuni Holds Up a Flower," for a more detailed exposition.

Master Mumon introduces here the fact of Dharma transmission from the Venerable Kasho, the teacher, to the Venerable Ananda, the disciple, as a koan to encourage his monks in their training.

According to the general opinion of scholars, Sakyamuni Buddha died in 486 B.C. at the age of eighty. The Venerable Kasho, although he was Sakyamuni's disciple, was the same age as his teacher or even a little older, and the Venerable Ananda, Kasho's successor, was a middle-aged monk forty-six years old.

Ananda was Sakyamuni's attendant for over twenty years, from the time he was twenty-three years old until the latter's death. Through his youth and middle years he always waited on Sakyamuni; he is known as the disciple of "the best hearing and remembering" among the Buddha's Ten Great Disciples and is said to have been very sincere, honest, and brilliant.

The fact that he was a man of "the best hearing and remembering" and was very brilliant, however, turned out to be the intellectual obstruction that prevented him from awakening to the True Self that transcends all restrictions. At the time of Sakyamuni's death he had not yet experienced the Great Joy of breaking through the barrier. He naturally continued his search after the True Self under the Venerable Kasho, and finally attained the happy experience of self-realization. This koan consists of a mondo between the Venerable Kasho and the Venerable Ananda that shows the reality of teacher-disciple identification.

One day Ananda asked the Venerable Kasho, "What did the World-Honored One give you besides the brocade robe?" Needless to say, the transmission of something in material or ritual form in Zen is just a shadow of the transmission of the untransmittable, which is formless and invisible. The vital question here is how this invisible Dharma is to be conveyed and how its transmission and identification can be verified. Ananda, with his brilliance and long discipline, must have been well aware of that, yet he could not help asking the question. We should not fail to see Ananda's agonizingly hard searching. He was almost craving. How is communication possible at this critical moment? How can identification be accomplished? The mondo between the Master and the disciple takes place on this plane. In that extreme situation the Venerable Kasho uttered one word, "Ananda!" Here is the working of no-mind, the work of no-work. What an outstanding and concrete instruction this is! So direct and penetrating that there is no room for intellection at all.

Ananda simply answered, "Yes, sir!" So direct and penetrating is the reply that there is no room for any intellection. This is the moment when the teacher-disciple identification has been accomplished. An old Zen Master commented on this teacher-disciple identification of calling and answering, in a poem:

> Two mirrors reflect each other,
> There is no image in between!

I myself would like to comment further with much emphasis: "Kasho calls Kasho; Ananda answers Ananda. The whole universe is Kasho who is calling; the whole universe is Ananda who is answering. Kasho calls Ananda, and Ananda answers Kasho. The universe calls, and the universe answers." Can there be more intimate calling and answering than this? I am afraid I have said too much; for once expressed in words, "it" has already been marred and ceases to be the Reality itself any longer. "It" can only be experienced and testified to personally by oneself.

The Venerable Kasho at once declared, "Pull down the flagpole at the gate!" All has been completed, for this is Kasho's verification of Ananda's attainment.

When a talk is given, a flag is hoisted to announce its opening. To pull it down is to declare that the teisho and mondo are over. In other words, it is Kasho's word of approval to Ananda: "You have got it!" The Second Patriarch of Dharma transmission in India has thus been born here. But those who are unable to read into the experiential truth of the Dharma transmission in this calling and answering of the teacher and the disciple may think this is just a meaningless exchange between them.

Let us set aside the mondo of teacher-disciple identification between Kasho and Ananda for a while. In actual training at the monastery, the Master may suddenly cry out: "I do not ask you about Kasho's 'Pull down the flagpole'! You, at this moment, pull down the flagpole at the monastery gate!" A moment of hesitation will result in thirty blows of his stick. To pull down the flagpole is to pull down I-myself. To pull down I-myself is to pull down the universe. Here, now, without moving even one finger, can you perform this wonder? Studies in Zen can never be separated from I-myself here and now. To study koan must always be to get hold of Zen alive and dynamically working. Ananda's answer must be resounding throughout the universe through I-myself. Zen is fundamentally different from intellectual understanding or conceptual interpretation.

TEISHO ON MUMON'S COMMENTARY

"If you can give the exact turning word to this koan, you will see that the meeting at Mount Grdhrakuta is definitely present here. If not, then know that Vipasyin Buddha is still unable to get the Truth even though he began his seeking in remote antiquity."

Master Mumon says to his disciples: "If you can clearly give the words of Truth directly pointing to the fact of teacher-disciple identification between Kasho and Ananda, you are then free in Dharma and will know that the great teaching of the World-Honored One at Mount Grdhrakuta is still definitely going on today. In other words, you can see face to face the World-Honored One and the Venerable Kasho here and now." Mumon is telling us that the untransmittable True Dharma is ever brightly shining at this very moment, transcending time and space, and that it has to be experientially grasped here by each one of us. Experience in Zen transcends history, yet it always works as a concrete fact in history. Otherwise it is not a live Truth.

Mumon's commentary continues, "If you are not capable of living in such spirituality, then no matter how long you may train yourself, you can never get the Truth of Zen." With this denunciation Mumon tries to encourage his disciples in their training.

In the Dharma genealogy of Zen, generally the Venerable Maha Kasho is regarded as the First Patriarch of Dharma transmission in India. Prior to him, at the very beginning of the Dharma genealogy there are "Seven Past Buddhas." The seventh of these Past Buddhas is Sakyamuni, who is a historical personage, but the rest are mythological Buddhas placed before Sakyamuni in order to glorify the transmission and exalt its origin. Vipasyin comes as the first Buddha. In other words, Vipasyin Buddha is the mythological Buddha in the past, ancient beyond calculation. Here the reference to Vipasyin Buddha is to be interpreted as indicating an infinite length of time.

"Vipasyin Buddha is still unable to get the Truth even though he began his seeking in remote antiquity"—this saying is ascribed originally to Master Joshu. The sentence has a Zen significance, different in dimension from its apparent common-sense meaning. In training at a monastery this is studied as an independent koan in itself. The literal meaning of the sentence is: "Vipasyin Buddha, who is the Buddha of time immemorial, has kept on disciplining himself for an infinite length of time, yet he is unable to get the Truth." The Master will give this to his disciple as a koan and demand, "What is the Truth that cannot be attained after long training? Show it to me right here."

This is the wonder of Reality shining at this absolute moment here-now, transcending time and space. It is the mystery of Truth at the meeting on Mount Grdhrakuta, which is ever present here and now. If you should fail to see into this wonder, it means your Zen eye is not opened and you are not qualified to read Zen books. Neither will you be able to see the real significance of Kasho's calling and Ananda's answering.

TEISHO ON MUMON'S POEM

> The calling out is good, but even better the answering.
> How many are there who have opened their true eyes?
> The elder brother calling out, the younger brother replying,
>   the family shame is revealed.
> This is the spring that does not belong to Yin and Yang.

"The Venerable Kasho's calling is excellent, but the Venerable Ananda's answering is even more wonderful." From ancient times it has been a live Zen mondo, in which the question is in the answer and the answer is in the question. Mumon is indirectly admiring the exquisite teacher-disciple identification demonstrated by Kasho's calling and Ananda's answering. In the second line Mumon points out the outstanding quality of this koan by saying, "From ancient times, how many have there been whose Zen eyes are clearly opened to see the essence of this mondo? Only a few, I must say."

"To open the true eye" is to have the capability of penetrating through the Truth. In the form of a rhetorical question Mumon stresses the point.

"Brother disciples Kasho and Ananda, by calling and answering, exposed the secret of the family to the public." In the third line, with a rather sarcastic expression, Master Mumon tells us how beautifully the transmission of the untransmittable took place. "The family shame" originally meant a dishonorable secret or private matter in the family that one would withhold from the public. Later it was used as a Zen term meaning the important and invaluable secret of the family.

The fourth line says that this "family shame" is the eternally bright spring that is not subject to climate or season. Mumon is speaking of "it," which never changes through all ages and places. He is also kindly pointing out for us that we are right now in that beautiful spring, day and night. "Why don't you open your true eye to the beauty of the eternal spring?" he is asking us.

In China, it has been a traditional belief that the four seasons change and develop through the work of Yin and Yang. "Not being subject to Yin and Yang" therefore means not being affected by the changes of the four seasons, which is to live the Absolute, transcending time and space.

23

Think Neither Good Nor Evil

KOAN

The Sixth Patriarch was once pursued by the Monk Myo to Daiyurei. The Patriarch, seeing Myo coming, laid the robe and bowl on a stone, and said, "This robe symbolizes faith; how can it be fought for by force? I will leave it to you to take it." Myo tried to take up the robe, but it was as immovable as a mountain. Myo was terrified and hesitated. He said, "I have come for Dharma, not for the robe. I beg you, please teach me, O lay brother!" The Sixth Patriarch said, "Think neither good nor evil. At such a moment, what is the True Self of Monk Myo?" At this, Myo was at once enlightened. His whole body was dripping with sweat. With tears he made a bow and asked, "Beside these secret words and meanings, is there any further significance or not?" The Patriarch said, "What I have just told you is not secret. If you will realize your True Self, what is secret is in you-yourself." Myo said, "Although at Obai I followed other monks in training, I did not awaken to my True Self. Thanks to your instruction, which is to the point, I am like one who has drunk water and actually experienced himself whether it is cold or warm. You are really my teacher, lay brother!" The Patriarch said, "If you are so awakened, both you and I have Obai as our teacher. Live up to your attainment with care."

MUMON'S COMMENTARY

Of the Sixth Patriarch it has to be said that in an emergency he did something extraordinary. He has a grandmotherly kindness; it is as if he had peeled a fresh litchi, removed its seed, and then put it into your mouth so that you need only swallow it.

MUMON'S POEM

You may describe it, but in vain, picture it, but to no avail.
You can never praise it fully: stop all your groping
and maneuvering.
There is nowhere to hide the True Self.
When the world collapses, "it" is indestructible.

TEISHO ON THE KOAN

The incident in the koan is taken from the biography of the Sixth Patriarch Eno, one of the greatest Masters in the history of Zen. After its introduction into China, Buddhism developed by stressing the importance of bibliographical and philosophical studies. Although the Buddhism that emphasized religious experience flourished after the time of Bodhidharma, it still retained a strong Indian influence in its teachings. It was Eno, the Sixth Patriarch, who almost completely wiped away the remaining Indian characteristics and laid the foundation for the new Buddhism in China called Zen. Before taking up the koan presented here by Mumon for his disciples, it may be helpful to sketch briefly Eno's life and explain how the incident in the koan took place.

Master Eno was born in 638, during the T'ang dynasty, in a poor family of Kanto-sho in South China. He lost his father when he was still very young, and after that earned his livelihood and supported his mother by selling firewood in the town. He must have been born with rich religious endowments. His active Zen life started when he was about forty years old at Hosshoji, Koshu, and he died in 713 in his seventy-sixth year.

One day when Eno was walking along the street as usual, selling firewood, he happened to hear someone chanting *Kongo Hannya-kyo* (the *Diamond Prajna Sutra*), and somehow it appealed to him. While listening to the chanting he heard the passage, "No mind, no abode, and here works the mind!" It strongly impressed Eno. He could not leave without inquiring about it further, and asked the chanter where he had obtained such a superb sutra. The man told him that he had received it from Master Gunin of Mount Obai of Kinshu in North China, who was propagating the teaching of Bodhidharma and was much respected as the Fifth Patriarch.

From that moment Eno wished to see Master Gunin and tried to find a way to do so. It happened in the course of time that a benevolent man gave him a certain sum of money. Leaving it with his mother to take care of her living expenses, Eno set out on his long journey to the north to see Master Gunin.

Master Gunin Daiman, the Fifth Patriarch, lived at Mount Obai in Kinshu. His encounter with the Fourth Patriarch, Master Doshin, must have taken place when Gunin was about twenty-three years old. After studying under the Fourth Patriarch for years, he finally succeeded him and developed his activities at Mount Obai until he died in 675. The two great Masters Shinshu and Eno, founders of the Northern and the Southern Schools of Zen, were both his disciples. It happened that Zen began to flourish about this time, and there were always over seven hundred monks studying under Gunin at Obai.

Eno, when he arrived at Mount Obai, was twenty-four years old, an insignificant, poor, shabby-looking youth. Poor though he was, he must already have had within himself some kind of spiritual insight which inspired and encouraged him to carry out this great and most difficult undertaking. The following are the mondo that took place when he first met Master Gunin at Mount Obai after the long and trying journey:

GUNIN: Where did you come from?

ENO: From Reinan, Master.

GUNIN: What are you seeking for?

ENO: I want to become a Buddha.

GUNIN: You monkeys of Reinan do not have the Buddha Nature. How can you expect to become a Buddha?

ENO: There is a distinction of south and north for man. How can there be such a distinction for Buddha Nature?

From these mondo Master Gunin recognized Eno's religious genius and allowed him to stay in the monastery as a rice-cleaner and to train himself. For eight months Eno silently concentrated on his discipline while working in the grain mill.

One day Master Gunin announced to his more than seven hundred disciples, "In studying Dharma, you must not remain satisfied by just copying my words. Make a poem, each one of you, to show your own realization experience, demonstrate your Zen ability, and show whether you are worthy to be the Dharma successor."

In response the first monk, Shinshu, who was the most senior of over seven hundred monks and much respected by all, made the following poem and wrote it on the monastery wall:

> The body is the tree of bodhi,
> The mind is like the stand of a bright mirror.
> Moment by moment wipe the mirror carefully,
> Never let dust collect on it.

Seeing it, Eno thought that it was a good poem beautifully expressed, but that it was not quite penetrating yet. He made a poem to express his own spirituality and also wrote it on the wall. (Since he was born in a poor family, Eno was not well educated and was illiterate. It is said that he asked a young acolyte to write it for him.)

> Bodhi is not originally a tree,
> Nor has the bright mirror a stand.
> Originally there is nothing,
> So where can any dust collect?

Monk Shinshu's poem may be excellent, yet it remains ethical and does not go beyond a static religious view. On the other hand, Brother Eno's poem is transcendental and penetrating and reflects a dynamic religious view of a higher order. Where these two poems are concerned, there is definitely a great difference in the Zen ability of Shinshu and Eno.

Master Gunin recognized Eno's superior spirituality, but Eno was then a mere young lay brother working for the monastery, not acceptable to some of the monks as the Dharma successor. In secret on a dark night, Gunin advised Eno to leave Mount Obai, giving him his robe and bowl as a proof of the Dharma transmission. He advised Eno to hide himself until the right opportunity should come, in the meantime refining and deepening his spirituality. Such was the deep compassion of the teacher for this promising seedling that would flourish in the future.

In accordance with Gunin's advice, Eno left Mount Obai. But the monks learned that a young, rustic, and nameless lay worker had received Master Gunin's sacred robe and bowl, the symbols of Dharma transmission, and had left the monastery. Some of them simply could not accept the fact; they were startled and felt most indignant. So they decided to pursue Eno and take back the holy robe and bowl. Among the group of monks who pursued Eno was Myo. He was a guileless, impulsive man with a sharp temper and had once been a general before becoming a monk at Mount Obai in middle age. He caught up with Eno on the ridge of Mount Daiyurei and demanded that he return the robe and bowl given him by Master Gunin. Mumon has taken this incident as a koan to instruct his monks.

Brother Eno was coming near the ridge of Mount Daiyurei when the pursuing Monk Myo finally caught up with him. Myo intimidated Eno, saying, "We cannot afford to see an illiterate rustic like you carry away the holy bowl and robe. I have come here to take them back from you. Give them to me without making a fuss." Hearing this, Eno quietly put the transmitted robe and bowl on a stone nearby and said to Myo, "This bowl and this robe are symbols of trust in the Dharma transmission. They must not be fought for with self-interest or by force. If you dare to take them by violence, do as you like."

Being rebuked like this with good reason, Myo could not find a word to reply. As he was originally an honest and simple-hearted man, so straightforward in his action as to have pursued Eno to Mount Daiyurei, he must have experienced even greater compunction. Eno's words "This robe and bowl symbolize trust; how can they be fought for by force?" must have penetrated his mind and driven him to his final extremity. Even though he touched the robe and bowl as they lay there on the stone, in his emotional agitation he could not lift them up. Hesitating and trembling, he simply stood there, petrified. This unexpected spiritual impulse must have thrown the sincere and forthright Myo into the bottomless abyss of Great Doubt. His ego-centered and enraged self was at once completely smashed. This inner conversion, which fundamentally changed Myo's personality, was the most important moment in his whole life. Yet there are scarcely any commentators who make mention of it. This is because they have not gone through actual searching and training themselves. At this moment the enraged Myo was changed to one of those who "hunger and thirst after righteousness."

With a quite different attitude Myo now frankly implored Brother Eno, saying, "It is indeed the supreme Dharma that I am seeking, and a visible article with a form like a robe or a bowl is not what I want. I beseech you, O lay brother, please teach me." Throwing his whole being at Eno's feet, Myo thus entreated him.

Eno cuttingly asked, "When you think neither good nor evil, what is the True Self of Monk Myo at that very moment?" This opportune question asked in direct accord with the present situation is the core of this koan.

When all the dualistic oppositions such as good and evil, right and wrong, love and hatred, gain and loss, and the like are completely transcended, and when one lives in the realm of the Absolute, where even a thought of consciousness does not work, where is Eno? Where is Monk Myo? What there is, is "the

Reality of body and mind have dropped away." This is the moment when one's searching has been forever set at rest. At such a time the Reality of the True Self is vividly and thoroughly revealed. At this extreme moment, Monk Myo could fortunately be awakened to his True Self. He could at last have fundamental peace and freedom. Dripping with sweat, he shed tears of gratitude. Reverently Myo bowed to Eno and asked, "Beside the secret words and meanings you have just told me, is there any other instruction?"

The experience he has now personally attained is clear and evident. As it was so simple and direct, Myo felt a little uncertain and suspected that there might be some other special teaching to be secretly transmitted. An old Zen Master said, "If there is secret teaching, he cannot be saved after all." A long one is a long Buddha; a short one is a short Buddha. Those who know will immediately know "it." This is exactly the case with Zen experience.

Eno's reply is given with great authority and already has the dignity of the great capable Zen Master he later turned out to be: "What I have just told you is not secret. It is thoroughly lucid and transparent. If you are truly awakened to your True Self, everything you see, everything you hear is nothing but 'it.' What else can there be? If you think there is some secret, it is of your own making."

Monk Myo was made to realize even more clearly how spiritually blind he had been. He could not help expressing his heartfelt gratitude and joy, saying, "For years I disciplined myself at Mount Obai together with other monks, but have so far been unable to realize my True Self. Now, thanks to your direct instruction, I have intimately experienced 'it' myself, just like one who knows warmth or coldness of water himself by actually drinking it. You are indeed my Dharma teacher." We can well appreciate how Monk Myo felt. His humble and sincere attitude toward Eno, expressing greatest thanks and admiration, is a natural and beautiful consequence. As mentioned before, transmission in Zen from teacher to his disciple is from mind to mind and is always personally handed down.

Eno here was still a young lay brother and very modestly answered, "If you have really awakened to your True Self, both you and I are brother disciples of the Fifth Patriarch. Master Gunin is our teacher. Please carefully live up to 'it' which you have personally attained." Eno thus gave his hearty blessing and encouragement.

After parting from Eno, Myo lived alone on the mountain for a while and later moved to Mozan of Enshu, where he developed his active Zen life.

For over ten years after this incident Eno lived in hiding, and it was when he was about forty years old that he appeared at Hosshoji in Koshu. (The twenty-ninth koan deals with an event that took place when he came out of this long period in hiding.)

TEISHO ON MUMON'S COMMENTARY

"Of the Sixth Patriarch it has to be said that in an emergency he did something extraordinary. He has a grandmotherly kindness; it is as if he had peeled a fresh litchi, removed its seed, and then put it into your mouth so that you need only swallow it."

Master Mumon's commentary is only on Eno's attitude toward Monk Myo, and he does not directly comment on Myo.

Pressed by Monk Myo's fervent pursuit, Eno spoke out from the extreme standpoint in direct accord with the actual situation at the moment. "Think neither good nor evil. At such a moment, what is the True Self of Monk Myo?" On this reply of Eno, Master Mumon comments with a sarcastic tone, "You were driven into a corner, O Sixth Patriarch, and in desperation you came out with a preposterous answer." Mumon is in fact admiring Eno's capability, which brought about an unexpected result. It may be true that Eno gave this answer under pressure, yet it was really an excellent answer, right to the point and coming out of his experience.

Mumon continues, "Be that as it may, how grandmotherly kind is your answer given in an emergency! It is as if you had hulled and cored the litchi, and put it in his mouth so that he can just swallow it without any effort." Here again Mumon speaks with his usual sarcastic and teasing tone. Eno's answer at the critical instant—"Think neither good nor evil. At such a moment, what is the True Self of Monk Myo?"—was most apposite and produced the happy result of awakening Monk Myo to his True Self. Master Mumon is praising it in his unique way. We must not, however, lightly read Mumon's commentary, for Eno's instruction is neither light nor easy, and it is addressed to us today, too, as well as to Monk Myo.

In other words, his question is a stern barrier to Zen, one that rejects all the contrivances of the student. Master Mumon has given this commentary in the hope that his disciples will put all their strength into breaking through this barrier.

TEISHO ON MUMON'S POEM

> You may describe it, but in vain, picture it, but to no avail.
> You can never praise it fully: stop all your groping
> and maneuvering.
> There is nowhere to hide the True Self.
> When the world collapses, "it" is indestructible.

Mumon's poem does not directly refer to the koan; he only sings of the True Self, which is the core of the koan.

Eno pressed Monk Myo: "Think neither good nor evil. At such a moment, what is the True Self of Monk Myo?" Fortunately Myo could be enlightened by these words. Yet this True Self which he realized is completely beyond all description. It can be neither copied nor pictured in any form; it can never be expressed in words or sung about in poetry. If one dares to do so casually, he may end in depicting a lifeless shadow. Mumon therefore strongly asks you to stop all the discriminating functions and to cast away all attachments. A sword does not cut the sword itself; water does not drench water itself. "It" has to be appreciated just as it is; one has to be "it" oneself.

Thus Mumon says, "There is nowhere to hide the True Self." When you see, everything you see is nothing but "it." When you hear, everything you hear is no other than "it." If you cover "it" trying to hide it, the very cover is nothing but "it."

Therefore, "when the world collapses, 'it' is indestructible." The term "world" in China and Japan carries two meanings: the moving and changing that is temporal, and direction, which is spatial. The term thus already connotes limitation, change, and collapse. The True Self which, as Absolute Subjectivity, freely makes use of time and space, knows no such dichotomy as collapsing or not-collapsing. Therefore the meeting at Mount Grdhrakuta is definitely present here, and even when the world collapses the True Self is ever indestructible.

Let me stress the point once more: the True Self is one's original True Nature, in which not a thought of discrimination is working. It is the True Self awakened to the Buddha Nature. It is the True Self that is one with Reality. From ancient times various names have been given to it, such as "the True Self," "the True Man of no title," "the Absolute Being," or "it." Ultimately speaking, however, the True Self can never be experienced in the realm of intellect or knowledge. There is no method for you to attain it other than to thoroughly cast away your intellect and reasoning, and personally plunge into the experiential fact which "you may describe, but in vain; you may picture, but to no avail." That is why Master Mumon cries out, "Stop all your groping and maneuvering."

Master Gudo calls this True Self "the youth of natural beauty" in his poem. (Please refer to the twelfth koan: "Zuigan Calls 'Master,' " where I have introduced Master Gudo's poem with my detailed commentary.)

The True Self has to be the experiential fact, and it is not an abstract truth or philosophical principle. Because it is a living personality, Master Gudo avoided using any conceptual term to describe it, appropriately calling it "the youth of natural beauty"; he also referred to historical beauties such as Seishi and Yoki by way of comparison, to illustrate the absoluteness of the youth of natural beauty.

24

Abandon Words and Speaking

A monk once asked Master Fuketsu, "Both speaking and silence are concerned with ri-bi relativity. How can we be free and nontransgressing?" Fuketsu said,

> "How fondly I remember Konan in March!
> The partridges are calling, and the flowers are fragrant."

MUMON'S COMMENTARY

Fuketsu's Zen works like lightning. He has his way and marches along. But why does he rely on the tongue of the ancient poet and does not get rid of it? If you can clearly see into this point, you may attain absolute freedom. Abandon words and speaking, and say a word!

MUMON'S POEM

> He used no high-flown words;
> Before the mouth is opened, "it" is revealed.
> If you keep on chattering glibly,
> Know you will never get "it."

TEISHO ON THE KOAN

Master Fuketsu Ensho, the hero in this koan, was the Master four generations after Rinzai. He was born in 896 and spent his early years in Confucian studies, but when he took the examination for a government position was not successful, so he turned from his desire to be a government official and became a monk. First he studied Tendai Buddhism, but later changed to Zen and started his training under Master Kyosho when he was about twenty-five years old. The time was not yet ripe for Fuketsu's spiritual eye to be opened while he was with Master Kyosho, and he moved over to Master Nanin, who was reputed to be a great and capable Master. After studying for years under Nanin, Fuketsu finally became his successor. Later he reopened Fuketsuji Monastery, where he guided many monks and greatly enhanced Rinzai Zen. He died in 973.

One day a monk put a highly theoretical question to Master Fuketsu: "Both speaking and silence are concerned with ri-bi relativity. How can we be free and nontransgressing?" This monk must have been a philosophically oriented scholar monk.

The "ri" and "bi" referred to are quoted from *Hozo-ron,* by Sojo. This was an exceptionally talented religious genius who was punished by death in 414 at the age of thirty-one. He had been born in a poor family and his work as a scribe had made it possible for him to read many books and documents. By nature he was philosophically inclined and much interested in metaphysical and religious studies. First he was attracted by Lao-tzu's *Dotoku-kyo (Tao-te ching),* but when he later came across the *Vimalakirti Sutra* he was so overjoyed that he decided to be a Buddhist monk. Sojo studied under Kumarajiva and was respected as one of his most able disciples. When he was thirty-one years old, for reasons that are not known he was condemned to death. It is said that Sojo asked for seven days' reprieve before the execution and during that period wrote *Hozo-ron.* The poem he composed at his death is very famous:

> The four elements essentially have no master,
> The five functions are fundamentally nothing.
> Even if the naked sword cuts off my head,
> It will be like cutting a spring breeze.

Sojo's *Hozo-ron* has a chapter entitled "Ri-Bi Taijo-bon," in which he expounded a religious view using the terms *ri* and *bi*. The Truth of the universe, or the Reality of Dharma, is separate from all names, forms and distinctions. Because of the fundamental activity of equality or oneness in Reality, everything returns to the Self, or One. This is called *ri* (separateness).

This fundamental activity of equality in the Truth of the universe freely works and develops in infinitely different ways, in accordance with varied situations and circumstances of differentiation. This creatively free working is called *bi* (subtle, mysterious). Although it acts in infinitely varied situations of differentiation, yet it is fundamentally pure and undivided. Its working is therefore always creative, subtle, profound, mysterious, and knows no contradiction.

The Truth of the universe, or the Reality of Dharma, once it is expressed in words becomes bi, that is, phenomena. If it is expressed by silence it comes under ri, which is fundamental equality, unification. In other words, if you are in "silence" you are committed to equality, harmony; if you speak, you are committed to differentiation. Thus "both speaking and silence are concerned with ri-bi relativity."

The monk here dares to ask Master Fuketsu, "How can we be free and nontransgressing?" He is asking, "How can we live a truly free life that comes under neither differentiation nor oneness, that is committed neither to fundamental equality nor to phenomena, that is concerned neither with speaking nor with silence?" Needless to say, the questioning monk is not asking for logical or intellectual explanations, but is seeking the Zen solution based on Fuketsu's own experience as a Zen Master. The core of this koan lies here.

As long as one remains on the common-sense plane, the monk's question can never be satisfactorily answered. If one speaks, he is concerned with bi and commits himself to relativistic differentiation. If he remains silent, he is concerned with ri and commits himself to relativistic equality. This contradiction can never be solved in our ordinary domain of intellect.

$$
\text{Great Tao} \begin{cases} \text{ri} \rightarrow \text{silence} \rightarrow \text{entering} \rightarrow \text{negation} \rightarrow \text{oneness} \rightarrow \text{fundamental equality} \\ \text{(separateness)} \\ \\ \text{bi} \rightarrow \text{speaking} \rightarrow \text{emerging} \rightarrow \text{affirmation} \rightarrow \text{differentiation} \rightarrow \text{phenomena} \\ \text{(subtle)} \end{cases}
$$

Great Tao, or Truth, is thus an absolutely contradictory fact. Contemporary Japanese philosophers explain it in such terms as: "The philosophy of 'affirmation is at once negation,'" or, "The self-identity of absolute contradiction," or, "Oriental Nothingness." These terms, however, remain abstract and metaphysical and do not go any further than philosophical interpretations.

Master Fuketsu was certainly a true and capable Zen Master. Without hesitation he quoted a beautiful poem in reply to the monk's question:

"How fondly I remember Konan in March!
The partridges are calling, and the flowers are fragrant."

He is saying, "Look and behold! This is how I am free and nontransgressing!" Fuketsu presented right before the monk the fact of his nontransgressing Zen at work. Capable students must be able to grasp immediately the wonder of Fuketsu's free and nontransgressing Zen through this presentation.

This poem was originally written by Toho (712–770), a famous Chinese poet of the T'ang dynasty. Toho is singing of the picturesque spring scenery of the south bank of the Yangtze River, renowned as one of the most lovely parts of China. So much for Toho's poem; let us return to the main subject.

When one completely forgets himself in the beauty of spring, and the self, the world, and everything are transcended and not a thought is moving, is there any such distinction as speaking and silence, ri and bi? It is just the beauty of spring through and through: there is no room at all for any discrimination. That beauty, as it is, is the whole of Master Fuketsu's life. In his pure speaking, just as it is, we should see the wonderful demonstration of his Zen at work, where he transcends the dualistic distinction of transgression and nontransgression and freely makes use of speaking and silence, ri and bi.

My teisho has gone too far, and I am afraid I have turned Master Fuketsu's Zen into philosophical exposition without live and dynamic working.

It may be in accord with Fuketsu's mind not to add any further idle explanations, but just to recite:

How fondly I remember Konan in March!
The partridges are calling, and the flowers are fragrant.

Once a famous Japanese haiku poet went to Mount Yoshino to see cherry blossoms. What he sang was simply:

How wonderful, how wonderful
These cherries of Yoshino!

The seer himself is a flower. The objects seen are flowers. There is no argument about transgression or nontransgression here.

In actual training at a monastery, the Master may suddenly ask you, "Is this not Toho's poem?" If you inadvertently answer, "Yes, it is," the severe blows of his stick will immediately fall upon you. Unless you can directly show the fact of your having transcended ri-bi relativity, this mondo ceases to be a Zen koan and will be just a nonsensical story. (Please refer to the twentieth koan: "It is not with his tongue that he speaks.")

In this connection, I should like to tell the following story: Master Daito (1282–1337), the founder of Daitokuji in Kyoto, was called Myocho, and when he was young he lived among beggars, hiding himself from society in order to deepen and refine his Zen spirituality. The emperor of the time heard that Myocho was an outstanding Zen Master and wanted to find him so that he might invite him to be his own teacher. He told his officials to work out a way to discover him among the beggars.

Because it was known that Myocho was very fond of muskmelons, one day it was announced that a melon would be given to every beggar. A lot of muskmelons were piled up on the riverbank at a favorite gathering place of beggars and whenever a beggar about Myocho's age came along, the officer would test him, saying, "Take the melon without using your hand." The beggars were surprised at these words and did not know what to do, though finally each was given one. At last another rather suspicious beggar came, and the officer said, "Take the melon without using your hand." The beggar immediately retorted, "Give me the melon without using your hand!" Because of this unguarded spontaneous reply Myocho was found out. He was thus brought into the world again and finally invited to be the emperor's teacher.

This may very well be a made-up story without historical basis. Yet the exchange, "Take the melon without using your hand," "Give me the melon without using your hand!" is not just a play on words. Myocho's answer was the free working of Zen, which transcends both transgression and nontransgression.

TEISHO ON MUMON'S COMMENTARY

"Fuketsu's Zen works like lightning. He has his way and marches along. But why does he rely on the tongue of the ancient poet and does not get rid of it? If you can clearly see into this point, you may attain absolute freedom. Abandon words and speaking, and say a word!"

Master Mumon first criticizes Fuketsu, "Master Fuketsu's Zen is very severe, straightforward, and as quick and direct as lightning. He always makes beautiful use of his Zen capability and never shows any relaxation. Here, however, what is the matter with him? He is so clumsy as to rely on an old poem made by Toho." This is Mumon's usual disparaging comment, but his real intention is not necessarily found in the literal meaning of his words. Fuketsu seems to have been a Master with deep poetic feeling. There are a number of other cases where he freely made use of beautiful poems by other people to express his own Zen spirituality.

Not only Fuketsu but many Zen Masters have used poems written by others as a means of expressing their own Zen attainment. In such an instance, even though the poem was originally made by another poet, and the Master is expressing his own Zen through it, he is not regarded as borrowing it. The general evaluation or criticism accepted in literary circles does not apply here, for poems here are not treated as literary works but used as means of expressing Zen experience which belongs to quite a different order. Master Mumon is well aware of this, and his teasing tone implies, on the contrary, his admiration of Master Fuketsu.

Mumon now turns directly to his disciples and says, "If you can really grasp the wonderful working of Fuketsu's Zen in this mondo, you may open your own Zen eye and attain the same free and creative Zen working as that of Master Fuketsu."

Mumon now demands of his disciples with renewed emphasis: "Set aside the old story. Here now, any one of you, say a word, abandoning speaking samadhi! Say a word without using your mouth! Can any of you be free and nontransgressing?"

To be in "speaking samadhi" means to be speaking itself through and through, transcending the distinction of speaking and silence. Further, to abandon "speaking samadhi" is to transcend even this "speaking itself through and through."

The Master will throw the nyoi he has held in front of you and demand, "Do not call it a nyoi, or not a nyoi; what do you call it?" (Leave affirmation and negation, and what do you call it?) The Master is asking you to show him the live fact of your transcending speaking and silence, ri-bi relativity.

TEISHO ON MUMON'S POEM

> He used no high-flown words;
> Before the mouth is opened, "it" is revealed.
> If you keep on chattering glibly,
> Know you may never get "it."

This poem is not original with Master Mumon but is a teisho given by Master Unmon. Mumon quotes Master Unmon's teisho exactly as it is and uses it as a commentary poem on the koan of speaking and silence, ri-bi relativity.

The first two lines refer to Master Fuketsu's answer. "High-flown words" are words of dignity and majesty, and more plainly here, high-sounding words, showing off satori. The monk put a grandiose and argumentative question: "Both speaking and silence are concerned with ri-bi relativity. How can we be free and nontransgressing?" In reply Fuketsu naïvely recited a beautiful poem, without showing any satori-smacking pretensions:

> "How fondly I remember Konan in March!
> The partridges are calling, and the flowers are fragrant."

Thus he presents the fact of how free and nontransgressing he is.

Following the first line, the second line says, "Before the mouth is opened, 'it' is revealed." The Truth of Zen, which is not concerned with ri-bi relativity, is vividly revealed in front of you, now, as well as when light and darkness were not yet separated. Even before you open your mouth, therefore, it is clear and perfect, and all is there. In other words, satori is not something to be attained in the future; it is one's realization that he is already and always in "it." An old Zen Master therefore declared, "Training and enlightenment are one."

The last two lines are Mumon's warning to his disciples, "If you fail to open your eyes to 'it' which is revealed even before opening your mouth, and if you keep on chattering glibly, know that you may never get 'it.' " If you play with intellect where intellect is of no avail, and rattle on talking nonsense and arguing, such a wastrel as you are will finally lose the right direction and have to realize that you can never know the wonder of free and nontransgressing Zen. This is of course a severe warning to each student who is studying Zen today.

25

Talk by the Monk of the Third Seat

KOAN

Master Gyozan had a dream: He went to Maitreya's place and was given the third seat. A venerable monk there struck the table with a gavel and announced, "Today the talk will be given by the monk of the third seat." Gyozan struck the table with the gavel and said, "The Dharma of Mahayana goes beyond the Four Propositions and transcends the One Hundred Negations. Listen carefully!"

MUMON'S COMMENTARY

Tell me, did he give a talk or did he not? If you open your mouth, you will lose "it." If you shut your mouth, you will also miss "it." Even if you neither open nor shut your mouth, you are a hundred and eight thousand miles away.

MUMON'S POEM

Broad daylight under the blue sky!
In a dream he talks of a dream.
Humbug! Humbug!
He deceived the whole audience.

TEISHO ON THE KOAN

Gyozan was a great Master who played an important role in Zen circles toward the end of the T'ang dynasty. He studied most assiduously under Master Isan, and they finally reached a perfect teacher-disciple identification. They are respected as the founders of a unique Zen school called Igyo-shu. Gyozan died in 890 at the age of seventy-seven.

This koan consists of a story about Master Gyozan's dream that he went to Maitreya's place and gave a talk there. There are some critics who say it is quite senseless to bring a dream story into a serious Zen book. There are also some who make lengthy remarks about what significance the idea of Maitreya's future advent might have. These are questions to be discussed in the field of religious philosophy and I will leave them to specialists in that field. In actual training in Zen they do not have any basic significance, and the point of this koan is not there at all.

As Master Mumon says in his commentary, the key point of this story as a Zen koan is: "Did Master Gyozan really give a talk or not? If he did, what kind of a talk was it?" Students must concentrate their efforts to open their Zen eye on this point. The rest, whether a dream or a reality, is an outer setting for the story and not important.

Now, according to the koan Master Gyozan once had the following dream: he went to Tosotsu Heaven where Maitreya lived and entered into the inner auditorium. Many venerable monks were seated there and only the third upper seat was unoccupied, and Gyozan was given that seat. One of the venerable monks in the hall stood up, struck the wooden table with a gavel, which is the practice at a monastery when an announcement is made, and said that today's talk would be given by the monk in the third seat. Master Gyozan then stood up, struck the wooden table with the gavel, and said, "The Dharma of Mahayana goes beyond the Four Propositions and transcends the One Hundred Negations. Listen carefully!"

This koan is not recorded in *Keitoku Dento-roku*, but *Goto Egen* has it. In *Goto Egen* a few more sentences are added: "All the monks were dispersed. When Gyozan awoke from the dream, he told of the event in the dream to Master Isan, who said, 'You have now reached the holy rank.' At this Gyozan made a bow."

It may be because of these last sentences that the koan is criticized as being a made-up mythological story and not a historical event. Be that as it may, Master Mumon in his *Mumonkan* ended the koan with "Listen carefully!" and omitted the rest. He must have thought that the last few sentences do not have any vital significance as a koan in the actual training of monks.

The "Four Propositions" and the "One Hundred Negations" are terms used in ancient Indian philosophy and logic. The Four Propositions are the basic terms: one, many, being, nonbeing. The One Hundred Negations are reached by saying that each of the basic four terms has four particular negations, making a total of sixteen; then by introducing the past, present, and future, we have forty-eight. These are doubled, as having already arisen, or being about to arise, which makes ninety-six. By adding a simple negation of the original four, we have One Hundred Negations.

"To go beyond the Four Propositions and transcend the One Hundred Negations" are terms used in scholasticism, but here they mean, plainly speaking, "Words and letters are unable to express 'it'; ideas and thoughts are unable to reach 'it.'" Master Gyozan declared, "The Dharma of Mahayana goes beyond the Four Propositions and transcends the One Hundred Negations. Now hear it clearly, listen to it carefully!" What kind of talk did he give here? You have to show it concretely and clearly. If you say he did not give a talk, why then did he demand of the audience, "Listen carefully"? The essence of this koan lies here, and students must concentrate their efforts in training to see through this point. Conventional interpretations that discuss Master Gyozan's artifices, or faith in rebirth in Tosotsu Heaven, are all meaningless from the Zen point of view.

TEISHO ON MUMON'S COMMENTARY

"Tell me, did he give a talk or did he not? If you open your mouth, you will lose 'it.' If you shut your mouth, you will also miss 'it.' Even if you neither open nor shut your mouth, you are a hundred and eight thousand miles away."

Master Mumon in commenting on this koan directly points to its core and pressingly questions his monks, "Tell me, did he give a talk, or did he not?" To "go beyond the Four Propositions" and to "transcend the One Hundred Negations" are phrases that just explain the characteristics of the Dharma of Mahayana. How is the Reality of the Dharma of Mahayana itself demonstrated? Did Master Gyozan thoroughly illustrate it in his striking the table with the gavel? Master Mumon presses the monks for their direct and concrete answer.

Those who have eyes must have seen it; those who have ears must have heard it. Master Mumon echoes Gyozan's "to go beyond the Four Propositions and transcend the One Hundred Negations" with a different wording and says, "As for the Dharma of Mahayana, if you open your mouth and talk, its truth is lost. Yet if you shut your mouth and are silent, its truth is also missed. Whether you talk or are silent, you are one hundred and eight thousand miles away from it. You are completely mistaken."

As Master Fuketsu said in the twenty-fourth koan, certainly "both speaking and silence are concerned with ri-bi relativity. How can we be free and nontransgressing?"

Now tell me, how was Master Gyozan free and nontransgressing in giving his talk? We, too, have to be free and nontransgressing in giving a clear and concrete answer. Thus we may be able to respond to the compassion of the old Masters.

TEISHO ON MUMON'S POEM

> Broad daylight under the blue sky!
> In a dream he talks of a dream.
> Humbug! Humbug!
> He deceived the whole audience.

Master Mumon sums up the essence of the koan in a short and concise poem. "Broad daylight under the blue sky!" He thrusts this direct line at the very beginning. Bright sunny day! It is so clear and fresh. There is nothing hidden or vague. The Dharma of Mahayana is vividly revealed right in front of you. Those who have eyes see it, those who have a mind appreciate it, Mumon tells us. There is no idle argument about giving a talk or not giving a talk. In this one line the essence of this koan is thoroughly disclosed.

When it is so absolutely clear, who would listen to a dream story in a dream? Mumon goes on to ask in the second line. It is said, however, "A shrimp may jump, yet he doesn't get out of the bucket." A dream, too, is "it" and cannot be otherwise.

Long ago in China there was a philosopher named Soshu. In a dream he became a butterfly and was flying and dancing in the air. When he awoke from the dream he was not sure whether he was Soshu who became a butterfly or a butterfly that became Soshu. An interesting story, isn't it? Is it a dream or is it a reality? It is the wonder of Zen to have a clear insight here.

In the third and fourth lines Mumon seems to be flatly negating all that has been said: "Humbug! Humbug! He has wonderfully deceived all the five hundred venerable monks in Maitreya's abode."

Now tell me, with what kind of talk did Master Gyozan deceive all the venerable monks? Master Mumon made use of such paradoxical expressions only to show his hearty appreciation of Gyozan. Let me ask you once again: How was Master Gyozan free and nontransgressing in talking of the Dharma of Mahayana, which goes beyond the Four Propositions and transcends the One Hundred Negations? What kind of talk did he give? When you can truly appreciate this talk, you will also understand why Master Mumon said that Gyozan deceived all the audience.

As I mentioned before, in other Zen texts "Listen carefully!" in the koan is followed by "All the monks were dispersed." This sentence is generally interpreted as implying that all the audience left rejoicing at Gyozan's talk. An old Zen Master, out of his compassion, took this sentence up so that the students would study harder and deeper with it and firmly get hold of Master Gyozan's real intention. In the Sung dynasty, when Zen was still flourishing, Master Ekaku of Roya gave the following teisho to his disciples: "It is said that the five hundred venerable monks were all dispersed. Tell me, did they approve of Gyozan, or did they not? If you say they did approve of him, you have not understood Gyozan. If you say they did not approve of him, you may raise a disturbance in a peaceful land. I, a humble old monk, will most kindly expound it for you: 'The Dharma of Mahayana goes beyond the Four Propositions and transcends the One Hundred Negations.' If you tell it in this way to the people and if they accept it like that, they are sure to fall into the hell of death as fast as an arrow shot from a bow."

More plainly speaking, Master Ekaku says, "If you say that the whole audience in Maitreya's abode did appreciate Master Gyozan's talk, you will miss his real intention. If, however, you say that they did not agree with his talk, it will be like raising a disturbance in a quiet and peaceful land. With grandmotherly kindness I will now elucidate the point for you. Because it is said that 'The Dharma of Mahayana goes beyond the Four Propositions and transcends the One Hundred Negations,' it is a terrible mistake if you just swallow it blindly. You will then fall into the hell of death as fast as an arrow shot from a bow."

As far as this teisho is concerned, Master Ekaku, too, is deceiving his monks, isn't he? After all, there is no other way but for each one of you personally and intimately to appreciate Master Gyozan's "talk of no-talk."

In connection with a dream, there is an interesting story which I should like to tell you, though it has no direct connection with this koan. At the beginning of the Tokugawa period in Japan there was a Master named Takuan at Daitokuji, in Kyoto, who was very active in Zen circles in those days. When his death was near his disciples asked him to leave a swan poem. Takuan refused at first, saying, "I have no last words." At his disciples' repeated and earnest request, Takuan finally took up a brush and wrote one character, "Dream," and passed away. Master Takuan, while he was active, used to talk of "Dream Zen," and he wrote "One Hundred Dream Poems." The following is his famous poem on "Dream":

> Thirty-six thousand days in one hundred years.
> They talk of Maitreya and Avalokiteśvara, of right and wrong.
> Right is a dream; wrong too is a dream.
> Buddha said to take it this way.

With this one character for *dream* Master Takuan symbolized the Reality of the Dharma that goes beyond the Four Propositions and transcends the One Hundred Negations. This one character *dream* shows how free and nontransgressing Takuan was. When you realize this dream, you yourself and everything else are just a dream, and there is nothing in the universe that is not a dream. When you are alive, you are just alive through and through, and everything is alive. When you die, you are just dead through and through. An old Zen Master said, "When I live, I thoroughly and completely live; when I die, I thoroughly and completely die." He can therefore say there is neither life nor death.

Master Takuan says, "Right is a dream; wrong too is a dream." Certainly for him life is a dream and death is also a dream. Heaven and earth and all things under the sun are just a dream. Therefore it is the same to say there is no dream at all. "Dream Zen" is thus penetratingly transparent and thoroughgoing.

26

Two Monks Rolled Up the Bamboo Blinds

KOAN

The monks gathered in the hall to hear the Great Hogen of Seiryo give teisho before the midday meal. Hogen pointed to the bamboo blinds. At this two monks went to the blinds and rolled them up alike. Hogen said, "One has it; the other has not."

MUMON'S COMMENTARY

Tell me, which one has it and which one has not? If you have your Zen eye opened at this point, you will then know how Master Seiryo failed. Be that as it may, you are strictly warned against arguing about "has" and "has not."

MUMON'S POEM

When they are rolled up, bright and clear is the great emptiness.
The great emptiness does not yet come up to our teaching.
Why don't you cast away emptiness and everything?
Then it is so lucid and perfect that even the wind does not pass
through.

TEISHO ON THE KOAN

The Great Hogen of Seiryo mentioned in the koan is generally known as Master Hogen Buneki, the abbot of Seiryo-in at Kinryo. He was by nature very bright and began to study Buddhism at an early age. In particular he had a profound knowledge of Vijnaptimatrata philosophy and Kegon philosophy. The former teaches that all the three worlds exist because of the mind and every phenomenon exists because of recognition, while the latter develops the philosophy that principle and phenomena are interfused and limitless. These are certainly excellent Buddhist ideas, and Hogen was able later to attain the Zen experience that gives real life to these philosophies from within. Finally he developed his own unique Zen, which is called the Hogen School, and was respected as one of the leading figures in Zen circles toward the end of the T'ang dynasty. He died in 958 at the age of seventy-four.

The following interesting story is from Master Hogen's biography. While he was still a young training monk called Buneki, he went on a training journey with a few of his monk friends. On the way their pilgrimage was impeded by heavy rain and they were forced to stay at a temple called Jizo-in. After a few days, when the flood was over, they were ready to leave and bade farewell to the abbot of Jizo-in, Master Keishin. The Master pointed to the big stone outside the front gate and asked Buneki, "Venerable monk, 'All the three worlds exist because of the mind, and every phenomenon exists because of recognition'—this is your usual elucidation. Now tell me, is this stone out of the mind or in the mind?" "It is in the mind," Buneki replied immediately. Master Keishin then asked, "You, traveling monk, why do you carry around such a heavy stone in your mind?" Buneki could not say a word in reply. Finally he decided to give up his pilgrimage and stay at this temple to study under Master Keishin.

From that time on Buneki brought to Master Keishin, one after another, all the conclusions he had come to as a result of his profound philosophical studies. Each time the Master would laugh the proposition away, saying, "It is not real live Buddhism at all!" Buneki studied even harder, almost forgetting to eat and sleep, to solve his problems. But the more devotedly he searched, the more desperate he became.

One day, his energy exhausted, he confessed to his teacher, "I have no word to say and no thought to present." He was driven to the last extremity. Master Keishin calmly told him, "If Buddhism is to be shown, it is perfect and manifest." At this Buneki was at once awakened to the Truth of Zen and was free in Dharma thereafter. Finally he became Master Keishin's successor.

As mentioned before, Master Hogen was well versed in Buddhist philosophy. It was natural that he should teach, based on the Kegon philosophy, the oneness of Zen and scholarship. He said, "Buddhism so-called consists of ultimate Truth and phenomena. Ultimate Truth is based on phenomena, and phenomena are based on ultimate Truth. They are interfused in each other; they are like eyes and feet. If there were phenomena alone and no universal Truth, things would stagnate and not work through. If there were the Realm of Principle alone and no phenomena, things would go astray and not return to the origin." Also he said, "As for the view of the Dharma world, universal Truth and phenomena are thoroughly clarified, and form and emptiness of the self are transcended. The limitless ocean is embraced in a single hair, and Mount Sumeru, the greatest of mountains, is in a single poppy seed. Such are not particularly holy and mysterious works, but are natural occurrences as they ought to be. There is no principle that is not manifested as phenomena, and there are no phenomena that do not return to the Realm of all Elements. The universal Truth and phenomena are not two, and 'it' is neither a phenomenon nor a universal Truth."

These are excellent talks that we may read in his philosophy of "Zen and Scholarship are One." However, they will not show us the true picture of capable Zen Master Hogen with his deep and lucid Zen experience. Hogen's Zen is described in the saying that "a night watchman commits a crime at night." With his sharp, shrewd, and acute working he deprives the student of everything. The following mondo provide good examples of his skill.

Once a monk asked Hogen, "What is the one drop of water from Sogen?" In reply Hogen said, "It is the one drop of water from Sogen." (Sogen is the name of the place where the Sixth Patriarch lived. "Gen" in Sogen means "the foundation." The monk's question, "What is the one drop of water from Sogen?" is the same as asking, "What is the essence of Zen?")

Once a monk asked Hogen, "What is the ultimate Truth?" The Master replied, "First, I pray you will live it. Second, I pray you will live it!"

Keitoku Dento-roku has the following sentences to praise Hogen's Zen ability: "He frees stagnation and clears up confusion. If one earnestly asks for his instruction, he administers medicine suited to each disease."

These descriptions will tell us what kind of Zen Master Hogen was and will be helpful in studying the koan of "Two Monks Rolled Up the Bamboo Blinds."

Now let us return to the koan. One day some monks gathered in the hall to listen to Master Hogen's teisho before the midday meal. Hogen without a word raised his hand and pointed to the bamboo blinds, which were hanging down. At this, two monks stood up at the same time, walked to the blinds, and rolled them up alike. Looking at this, the Master said, "One has it; the other has not."

Obviously the point of this koan is: why did Hogen declare that one monk had grasped his mind and the other had missed it, while both of them did exactly the same thing at the same time? If there is no distinction of right ("has") and wrong ("has not") in the same action, why did Master Hogen say "One has it (right); the other has not (wrong)"? If there is a distinction of right and wrong in the same action, what kind of "right and wrong" did Hogen see there? The aim of this koan is to let the student clearly open his Zen eye to see through this dilemma. (Readers are advised to go through the eleventh koan once more, where Master Joshu saw the superiority and inferiority of the two hermits who equally held up their fists. What was his real intention?)

An old Zen Master commented on this koan as follows: "This koan aims to arouse the Great Doubt in the mind of the students. If they were to try to understand the significance of 'One has it; the other has not' with their intellect and reasoning, it would be like looking for horns on rabbits and horses." The real intention of Master Hogen's Zen working here is to arouse the religious Great Doubt in each student, so that he will immediately cut off the dualistic dilemma of gain and loss, right and wrong. If the students were to try to solve this question of gain ("has") and loss ("has not") logically or intellectually, they would be attempting the impossible—would be looking for horns on rabbits and horses.

Another Zen Master said, "Why did Hogen see the difference of right and wrong in the same act of rolling up the bamboo blinds? In equality there is differentiation; in differentiation there is equality. When snow is put in a silver bowl, or a snowy heron stands among white reed-flowers, all is just white and there seems to be no discrimination. Yet a silver bowl is a silver bowl, snow is snow, a snowy heron is a snowy heron, and reed-flowers are reed-flowers. They are definitely different. If, however, you should come to the illusory understanding that Master Hogen saw the two monks with a differentiating view, you would be unable even to stand beside the two monks."

The Zen Masters are urging us to transcend the opposition of right and wrong, but what is their real motive? Some may say, "The two monks went together and rolled up the blinds alike—this symbolizes equality and oneness, which is the universal Truth. Master Hogen said, 'One has it; the other has not'—this shows differentiation and two, which are phenomena. He is telling us to see the wonder of the oneness of universal Truth and phenomena, that in the universal Truth phenomena are included, and in phenomena is the

Truth." This is certainly a beautiful explanation. But wonderfully expressed though it may be, it is after all an intellectual interpretation and not direct, live Zen. Zen does not explain the truth of "the oneness of Truth and phenomena," but it lives actually day and night "the oneness of universal Truth and phenomena." Every movement of hand and foot at every moment must be the live proof of it. Let me ask you here, once again, "What is the Truth of the oneness of the universal Principle and phenomena?" Unless you can show me the live fact as your answer, it cannot be Zen. It will just be an idea and philosophical speculation.

TEISHO ON MUMON'S COMMENTARY

"Tell me, which one has it and which one has not? If you have your Zen eye opened at this point, you will then know how Master Seiryo failed. Be that as it may, you are strictly warned against arguing about 'has' and 'has not.'"

Master Mumon, commenting on this koan, talks to his disciples: "Master Hogen said, regarding the two monks who went and rolled up the blinds alike, 'One has it; the other has not.' Now tell me, which one had it, and which one did not? If you have your Zen eye clearly opened to see through the Ultimate Truth at this point, then you can certainly appreciate Master Hogen's real intention." ("Zen eye" means the Zen ability to make free use of gain and loss, right and wrong.)

Mumon says that Master Seiryo "failed." Usually the term "failed" means a mistake or a blunder. Here, however, its meaning is just the contrary and it is used in the sense of strong admiration. Zen men sometimes use it to mean "true intention," "essence," or "a vital point." Master Mumon is here taking up the key point of this koan and is repeating the question, "What is Master Hogen's real meaning in saying 'One has it; the other has not' when two monks did exactly the same thing in rolling up the blind?"

He is kind enough to give a warning to his disciples at the end: "Be that as it may, never make such an absurd mistake as to discriminate between right and wrong." Let me ask you here, how will you transcend "has" and "has not" when Master Hogen declares that "one has it; the other has not"? Grasp the truth of rolling up the blinds there!

There is a popular book in which the writer rather proudly introduces his opinion: "Since gain and loss are considered to be the same, if a gain is added and a loss is deleted from the same action, the result is apparent. It is just the same as adding one and deleting one; after all, therefore, there is neither gain nor loss." He is one of those who "argue about 'has' and 'has not' " with their sophistry, and needless to say this is not Zen at all.

There is a koan used in monasteries in Japan today, though I do not know its author:

> Two are going;
> One does not get wet.
> This autumn rain!

Some take it as a funny story with a play on words saying, "When two people are going together, both will get wet, and not only one." There is no contradiction or difficulty in solving it. Thus they just laugh it away. They also "argue about 'has' and 'has not' " and do not know what a Zen koan is. Their interpretation has nothing to do with Zen. They cannot even imagine that there is a live new Zen vista that transcends all dualism, such as two and one, getting wet and not getting wet. A Zen man lives this fact.

Master Tendo has a famous poem on this koan of "One has it; the other has not":

> A pine is straight and a bramble is crooked;
> A crane is long and a duck is short.
> People in the reign of Emperor Gi forget both peace and war.
> Their tranquility is with a dragon lying in the depths;
> Their comfort is with a phoenix released from its fetters.
> There is nothing in the teaching of the First Patriarch.
> Right and wrong are just equal, however they may be.
> Mugworts dance in the air with the wind;
> A boat goes across the river and reaches the bank.
> In this, you monk of realization,
> See through the working of Seiryo!

"A pine is straight and a bramble is crooked; a crane is long and a duck is short"—is there the distinction of right and wrong here, or not? "Mugworts dance in the air with the wind; a boat goes across the river and reaches the bank"—is there the distinction of gain and loss here, or not? Master Tendo says, "Right and wrong are just equal, however they may be." A Zen man must have his Zen eye clearly opened, based on the experiential fact, so that he may develop his own working.

When they are rolled up, bright and clear is the great emptiness.
The great emptiness does not yet come up to our teaching.
Why don't you cast away emptiness and everything?
Then it is so lucid and perfect that even the wind does not pass
through.

Master Mumon illustrates the essence of the koan in the four lines of his poem. First, commenting on the two monks who rolled up the blinds alike, he says, "When they are rolled up, bright and clear is the great emptiness." Blinds make a distinction between inside and outside. If this distinction is taken away, the great emptiness is all equal with no discrimination. It is clear and bright, and there is nothing to obstruct the view. It is the penetrating lucidity of universal Truth. In the second line, however, Master Mumon negates the first line and says, " 'The great emptiness does not yet come up to our teaching.' Even this purest spirituality of absolute equality does not come up to my fundamental true standpoint, with which I live the oneness of universal Truth and phenomena." ("Our teaching" refers to Buddhism in a broad sense, but more specifically to Zen.)

He emphatically maintains in the third line, "Why don't you cast away emptiness and everything?" Zen men often say, "No-mind is still far away beyond thousands of barriers." Great emptiness, no-mind, equality, and the like show the religious experience of absolute negation, and they are no doubt a pure and sacred spirituality. If, however, one stops with this spirituality, then it turns out to be one-sided relativistic emptiness, which means that he has gone astray and has missed the Truth. Master Mumon gives his careful warning to his disciples to cast away their attachment to such spirituality, and tells them to live the wonderfully open and guileless Zen life, where the universal Truth and phenomena are one. When one lives this free Zen life, it will then be "so lucid and perfect that even the wind does not pass through."

Here the new and wonderful vista that transcends both affirmation and negation opens up to him. This is the true spirituality, true Zen life, where there is neither right nor wrong, nor even oneness. Master Tendo sings of this spirituality and says, "People in the reign of Emperor Gi forget both peace and war." This is the truly free and boundless Zen life, where both universal Truth and phenomena are transcended.

Let me ask you again, why did Hogen say, "One has it; the other has not"? You have to show directly the actual live fact of transcending right and wrong as your answer. Otherwise you will be one of those who wander about in the world of right and wrong.

I will call your attention to another poem on this koan of "One has it; the other has not."

> Don't be overjoyed at the right.
> Don't be distressed over the wrong.
> For the ancient Masters, things are like flowers and blossoms;
> Peach blossoms are red, plum blossoms are white, and roses are pink.
> Though I ask the spring breeze why they are so, it knows nothing.

In accordance with this instruction, students today must open their Zen eye to realize where Master Hogen failed.

27

Neither Mind Nor Buddha

A monk once asked Master Nansen, "Is there any Dharma that has not yet been taught to the people?" Nansen said, "Yes, there is." The monk asked, "What is the Dharma that has not been taught to the people?" Nansen said, "It is neither mind, nor Buddha, nor beings."

MUMON'S COMMENTARY

Nansen, being asked the question, had to use up all his resources at once. How feeble and awkward!

MUMON'S POEM

> Too much courtesy impairs your virtue;
> Silence is certainly effective.
> Let it be so. Even if the blue ocean should change,
> "It" will never be communicated to you.

TEISHO ON THE KOAN

Master Nansen was introduced in the fourteenth koan, so biographical details about him are omitted here.

Hekigan-roku, another famous Zen text, has a similar mondo in its twenty-eighth koan: Nansen had an interview with Master Nehan of Hyakujo. Hyakujo asked, "Is there any Dharma that all the Patriarchs in the past have not yet taught to the people?" Nansen said, "Yes, there is." Hyakujo asked, "What is the Dharma that has not been taught to the people?" Nansen said, "It is neither mind, nor Buddha, nor beings." Hyakujo asked, "Have you finished talking?" Nansen said, "As for me, I am like this. How about you, Master?" Hyakujo replied, "I am not a great learned Master. What do I know about talking and not-talking, teaching and not-teaching?" Nansen said, "I do not understand." Hyakujo said, "I have thoroughly explained it to you."

In that mondo in *Hekigan-roku,* Master Hyakujo Nehan plays the chief role and Nansen the subordinate role. In the case of the *Mumonkan,* Master Nansen is the main figure and a nameless monk is the questioner. Also, only the first half of the mondo is introduced as a concise koan in the *Mumonkan,* and it naturally has a significance different from the koan of *Hekigan-roku,* even though they may look alike. Probably Master Mumon extracted this koan from the mondo in *Hekigan-roku* and rearranged it in a terse form for his disciples. It is to be studied independently of *Hekigan-roku.*

One day a monk asked Master Nansen, "Is there any Dharma that has not yet been taught to the people?" In order to understand clearly the meaning of this question, we must not overlook the word "yet." This "yet" plays a conjunctive role and implies something like the following: "Many Patriarchs so far must have taught the essentials of Buddhism for us, ordinary beings that we are, in various ways out of their compassion. Nevertheless, is there any special Dharma that has not yet been taught to the people?"

We can guess from the tone of the questioning monk that he probably expected to hear Master Nansen say, "No, there is not," which is a common-sense reply, and a correct answer too, in a way.

Master Nansen was, however, an outstandingly capable Master with a superb Zen standpoint that went beyond common-sense interpretation. With this Zen outlook, he must have read the monk's mind. Contrary to his expectation, Nansen replied with assurance, "Yes, there is." We can sense his intent to lure him on and then give him a Zen blow.

The monk was taken in, of course, and asked the next question, "What is the Dharma that has not been taught to the people?" This was the question Nansen anticipated. The Dharma that has not been taught is the Dharma that cannot be taught. A true Zen man always maintains the standpoint that transcends talking and not-talking, teaching and not-teaching, and lives the Truth, which is in fact the Dharma that has not been taught. Old Zen Masters insisted on "transmission outside scriptures" and "not relying on letters," and also said, "Not a word has been taught." They all uphold "the Dharma that has not been taught to the people." The vital question lies here. How do you actually live the essence of Zen, which upholds the Dharma that has not been taught to the people? Your answer has to be an experiential fact. Master Nansen said confidently, "It is neither mind, nor Buddha, nor beings."

In the *Lotus Sutra (Hoke-kyo)* there is a famous passage: "Mind, Buddha, and ordinary beings—these three are not different." Nansen's teacher, Master Baso Doitsu, also has a mondo similar to the one in this koan. So far as this answer is concerned, Master Nansen's saying here is not necessarily original. The deep significance of his answer nevertheless does not change because of that, for it casts away all dualism and presents directly before the student the essence of Zen, which transcends talking and not-talking, teaching and not-teaching. The key point of this koan is here, and Master Mumon asks us to get hold of it firmly.

Since this is the core of the koan, my teacher, Master Bukai, when he gave it to his disciples, used to press them, "What is the Dharma that has not yet been taught to the people?" Then he would ask them further, "Here, now, what is it that is in front of you? What is it that is under your feet?" Was he not telling his disciples that every movement of their hands and feet, whether they were silent or speaking, active or quiet, everything was nothing but the Dharma that has not yet been taught to the people? He was trying to awaken the students to this lucid and transparent fact.

Master Nansen was an outstandingly great Master with great compassion. He used his capable methods in guiding the monk, by first answering, "Yes, there is" and drawing him in. Then he thrust at him the live fact of the Dharma that has not been taught to the people, that is "neither mind, nor Buddha, nor beings." If you stick to Master Nansen's terminology and follow the literal meaning of his words, then you will never be able to get hold of the vividly working spirit of his Zen.

If you fail to get hold of Reality right in front of you here, now, you will forever miss Master Nansen's spirit and will be unable to see the significance of this koan after all. Master Hakuin said, commenting on this koan, "If I were asked, I would answer, 'Avatamsaka, Agama, Vaipulya, Prajna, Saddharma-pundarika, and Nirvana!' " He deliberately mentioned the names of the sutras Sakyamuni taught the people during his lifetime. Here again, you must not be deluded by Master Hakuin's terminology. For one who has his Zen eye clearly opened, whatever he sees, whatever he hears, is all the Dharma that has not been taught to the people. Everything is "it," which transcends talking and not-talking, teaching and not-teaching, and cannot be otherwise. Master Hakuin's comment is really superb.

Zen Masters may express their Zen experience by talking, by writing, by painting, by a sudden blow, or in many other ways. It is an iron-clad rule in Zen always to read the teaching, however it may be expressed, from within, based on the experiential fact, and never to try to reach the experiential fact by following any particular form of expression.

TEISHO ON MUMON'S COMMENTARY

"Nansen, being asked the question, had to use up all his resources at once. How feeble and awkward!"

Master Mumon's comment on this koan is pithy: "Dear Master Nansen: Being asked by a monk, 'What is the Dharma that has not been taught to the people?' you immediately replied, 'It is neither mind, nor Buddha, nor beings.' From my viewpoint, it looks as if you have delivered up all your possessions. How disgraceful! How awkward! I cannot bear to see it." It sounds as if Mumon is reviling Master Nansen. Such denunciation, as we have seen, is a favorite means in Zen circles of commenting on another Master's capability. With extreme abusive language they express the greatest admiration, which ordinary praise cannot fully convey. Mumon's real meaning is, "Dear Master Nansen: at the monk's question you threw out, right in front of him, the Dharma that has not been taught to the people and beautifully answered him. How wonderful! How splendid!"

Let me ask you here: Master Mumon says that Master Nansen used up all his resources. What kind of resources are they that he used up?

TEISHO ON MUMON'S POEM

Too much courtesy impairs your virtue;
Silence is certainly effective.
Let it be so. Even if the blue ocean should change,
"It" will never be communicated to you.

In the first two lines of the poem Master Mumon is commenting on Master Nansen's answer: "Master Nansen, your attitude is so kind and courteous as to stain the honor of a great Master. Too much is as bad as too little. As for the Dharma that has not been taught to the people, it is better to leave it unsaid. If you do not talk about it, its greatness will be brighter." Here again

Mumon uses his old paradoxical means of admiring Nansen by speaking ill of him.

"Too much courtesy impairs your virtue" refers to a mythological fable in China: Once upon a time there was a king called Kondon, who had none of the six organs, such as eyes, nose, and so on. Yet the nation was well governed by this king. Stupid ministers thought that if the king could have all his six organs opened there would be even greater peace throughout the land, so they forcibly tried to give King Kondon the six organs. The result was that the king died because of their efforts and the nation was thrown into confusion. Mumon, by referring to this old tale, satirized Master Nansen's answer.

In the last two lines Master Mumon emphatically states how absolute the essence of Zen is. Even though the world may collapse and the great blue ocean turn into a green field, yet the Dharma that has not been taught to the people will never be communicated by any techniques or logic. This is because it has to be personally experienced and testified to by each individual as his own live fact.

It is well known that Master Tozan said, "I am always most sincere right here." This Dharma is, for a Zen man, the fact of his everyday life. If he wants to go, he goes, and if he wants to sit, he sits. In this there is no argument about communicating or not communicating. What on earth do you want to communicate, after all?

There are some who interpret the last two lines differently: "Even though the great change may come on earth and the great blue ocean may turn into a green field, the real significance of Master Nansen's answer will never be understood by the questioning monk." They say that these two lines criticize the incapability of the questioning monk. I myself, however, am not inclined to agree with this interpretation.

28

Well-Known Ryutan

Tokusan once called on Ryutan to ask for instruction and stayed until night fell. Ryutan said, "It is getting late; you had better leave." At last Tokusan said good-by, lifted up the door curtain, and went out. Noticing that it was dark, he turned back and said, "It is dark outside." Ryutan thereupon lit a candle and handed it to him. Tokusan was about to take it when Ryutan blew it out. At this Tokusan was all of a sudden enlightened. He made a bow. Ryutan asked, "What realization do you have?" Tokusan replied, "From now on I will not doubt the sayings of any of the great Zen Masters in the world."

The next day Ryutan mounted the rostrum and declared, "Among the monks here there is a fellow whose fangs are like swords, and whose mouth is like a bowl of blood. You may strike him with a stick but he will not turn his head. Some day in the future, he will establish his way on a steep and lofty peak."

Tokusan then took out his notes and commentaries on the *Diamond Sutra,* and in front of the monastery hall he held up a burning torch and said, "Even though one masters various profound philosophies, it is like placing a single strand of hair in the great sky; even if one gains all the essential knowledge in the world, it is like throwing a drop of water into a deep ravine." Taking up his notes and commentaries, he burned them all. Then he left with gratitude.

MUMON'S COMMENTARY

When Tokusan had not yet left his home, his mind was indignant and his tongue sharp. He confidently came to the south in order to exterminate the "special transmission outside scriptures." When he reached the road to Reishu, he talked to an old woman who sold tenjin. The old woman said, "Venerable Monk, what books do you carry in your box?" Tokusan said, "They are notes and commentaries on the *Diamond Sutra.*" The old woman said, "It is said in the sutra that 'the past mind is unattainable; the present mind is unattainable; the future mind is unattainable.' Which mind, Venerable Monk, are you going to light up?" Tokusan was unable to answer this question and had to shut his mouth tight. Even so, he could not die the Great Death at the old woman's words, and finally asked her, "Is there a Zen Master in the neighborhood?" The old woman replied, "Master Ryutan lives five miles away." Arriving at Ryutan's monastery, he was completely defeated. It has to be said that his former words and his latter words do not agree. Ryutan is like the mother who, because she loves her child too much, does not realize how meddlesome she herself is. Finding a little piece of live coal in Tokusan, he quickly poured muddy water over him. Looking at it calmly, I would say that the whole story is just a farce.

MUMON'S POEM

> Far better seeing the face than hearing the name;
> Far better hearing the name than seeing the face.
> Though he saved his nose,
> Alas, he has lost his eyes!

TEISHO ON THE KOAN

The main figure in this koan is Tokusan Senkan, the Tokusan of the thirteenth koan. While that koan, "Tokusan Carried His Bowls," deals with an event which took place toward the end of his life, in this twenty-eighth koan he is still in his youth. It tells us how as a sutra scholar he met Master Ryutan and had his satori, which led later to his becoming a great Zen Master. "Ryutan Blows Out the Candle" would be a more suitable title, I think, than "Well-Known Ryutan."

The koan only tells us how Tokusan attained satori after seeing Master Ryutan. The story of how he came to see the Master is also interesting. Master Mumon refers to it in his commentary, but it may also be opportune to introduce it here.

Master Tokusan Senkan was born in the Shu family at Kennan in Shisensho, in a remote district of China. He was ordained as a Buddhist monk when he was still very young, went to the capital of the province, and studied the precepts *(vinaya)* and various sutras and scriptures. He had especially profound knowledge of the *Diamond Prajna Sutra* and was good at lecturing on it. People nicknamed him the "Diamond Shu" and respected him as a learned scholar-monk.

In those days Zen was flourishing in the Kosei and Konan area in South China. Tokusan heard that they were spreading the teaching that insisted on "special transmission outside scriptures," or "not relying on letters," or "this mind as it is is Buddha." He was indignant at such teaching, which sounded as if it ignored the sutras and scriptures. He made up his mind to exterminate such heretical Buddhists. Carrying his notes and commentaries on the sutras and scriptures, he left his home in high spirits. From his remote district in China he made a long trip down the Yangtze River to Reishu near Lake Dotei where Zen was flourishing. One day, feeling hungry, he stopped in a small teahouse by the roadside and asked for tenjin, a snack. The old woman of the teahouse saw an elated-looking young monk coming in with a big box on his shoulders, and asked him, "Venerable Monk, what books are you carrying in your big box?" Diamond Shu proudly replied, "I have notes and commentaries on the *Diamond Sutra* in it." At this the attitude of the old woman changed a little, and she said with rather a stern look, "Venerable Monk, if you can answer my question, I will treat you to tenjin. If you are unable to answer, you cannot have it here." Naturally Diamond Shu said, "You may ask me any questions!" The old woman said, "In the *Diamond Sutra* it is written that 'the past mind is unattainable; the present mind is unattainable; the future mind is unattainable.' You have just said that you would light up your mind. Which mind are you going to light up?" (The Chinese characters *tenjin* have another meaning: "to light up the mind.")

Diamond Shu, who had been absorbed in the study of religious philosophy, could not say a word in reply to this live question based on the experiential fact. An old Zen Master commented on this encounter, "What a pity! Diamond Shu could have had an opportunity of awakening here." Probably the time was not yet ripe.

Diamond Shu, however, must have felt something deep down in his mind.

Quietly he asked the old woman, "Is there any great Zen Master around here?"
"There is Master Ryutan, about five miles away," she told him. Diamond Shu
lost no time in calling on Master Ryutan.

As soon as he arrived at Ryutan's monastery he cried out, "I have long
heard of the well-known Ryutan. Having now arrived here I see neither a
dragon nor a lake!" (The Chinese character for *ryu* means a dragon, and *tan*
means a lake.) This was no doubt the best possible remark that Diamond Shu
could make, since he relied on the prajna philosophy of sunyata (emptiness).
Master Ryutan replied, "You have arrived at Ryutan in person." Master
Ryutan's incomparable spirituality is fully conveyed by the words "in person."
No dragon, no lake, this is the true Ryutan. Regrettably indeed, Diamond Shu,
who relied on philosophy, could not break through the barrier even at this
sharp blow of Ryutan's reply. The event of Ryutan's blowing out the candle
in this koan took place some time after this initial encounter.

Tokusan, or Diamond Shu, saw Master Ryutan again and asked for his
personal instruction, exchanging mondo until late at night. We can feel how
eager and even desperate he was. Zen, however, cannot be reached by logic
or argument. One has to make a leap into another dimension after going
through the crisis of desperation. A new vista will then be opened to him.

Master Ryutan at last told him, "The night is far advanced. You had better
take your leave." Tokusan finally bade his teacher good night, lifted up the
bamboo curtain, and went out. As it was dark outside, he turned around and
said, "It is pitch dark outside." Not only outside but within, his mind too must
have been like a dark abyss. Psychologically, he was in a touch-and-go situation. Master Ryutan quietly lit the candle and handed it to him. Just at the
moment when Tokusan was about to take it, he blew it out with one breath.
What superb working! What excellent instruction! In an instant the whole
universe was in sheer darkness again, and at this moment, all of a sudden
Tokusan's relativistic self was dispersed, like a barrel unhooped. This is the
great inner conversion which has been described in Zen: "The world has
collapsed and the iron mountain has crumbled!"

Tokusan prostrated himself before Master Ryutan and worshiped at his
feet. The Master, seeing through what had happened in Tokusan, asked him
as a test, "What realization do you have?" Tokusan, who was now thoroughly
enlightened, had no cloud in his mind. He simply replied, "From now on I will
not doubt the sayings of any of the great Zen Masters in the world." He finally
grasped "it," which does not rely on letters.

How great was the joy of Master Ryutan, the teacher! The next day he
gathered all the monks of the monastery, mounted the rostrum, and declared,

"Among the monks here, there is an extraordinary fellow. He has fangs as sharp as swords and his big mouth is crimson. Even though you may beat him or strike him, he doesn't even turn a hair, he is such a firm and reliable man. Some day in the future he will certainly be a great leader and will develop his severe and lofty teaching." This was Master Ryutan's great expectation and blessing for Tokusan's future.

In Zen, needless to say, even harder and more attentive training is needed after one has attained satori, in order to refine the personality in every aspect of daily life. That is why Master Ryutan said "some day in the future" and expected the development of Tokusan's great activities as a Zen Master in the time to come.

Tokusan, too, with irresistible joy and gratitude, took out all the notes and records he had made on the *Diamond Sutra*, which he had valued more than anything else, and in front of the monastery set fire to them, saying, "However thoroughly you may study and master profound philosophy, compared to the depth of experiential truth it will be like placing a single strand of hair in the great sky. However exhaustively you may learn essential theories in the world, compared to the absoluteness of the untransmittable Reality it will be like throwing a drop of water into a deep ravine. There is all the difference in the world between them." Burning his notes and records, Tokusan left Master Ryutan with deep gratitude. He was now a completely new man, with lucid and refreshing spirituality.

Sure enough, Diamond Shu fully lived up to Master Ryutan's expectation. After some decades of further refinement, he developed his activities at Tokusan Monastery in Konan-sho and played an important role as one of the greatest Masters in Zen circles in the T'ang dynasty.

Now we can understand the feelings of Tokusan, or Diamond Shu, who had long been enslaved by philosophy and sutra studies, when he burned his notes and sutras. I should like to comment here, however, that he did not in fact have to burn any sutras or commentaries. Zen is based on the fundamental Buddha mind. The sutras are the Buddha's sayings and the precepts are the Buddha's doings. A Zen man ought to be able to make free use of them as his own. Master Rinzai said, "There is nothing that I dislike."

TEISHO ON MUMON'S COMMENTARY

"When Tokusan had not yet left his home, his mind was indignant and his tongue sharp. He confidently came to the south in order to exterminate the 'special transmission outside scriptures.' When he reached the road to Reishu, he talked to an old woman who sold tenjin. The old woman said, 'Venerable Monk, what books do you carry in your box?' Tokusan said, 'They are notes and commentaries on the *Diamond Sutra.*' The old woman said, 'It is said in the sutra that "the past mind is unattainable; the present mind is unattainable; the future mind is unattainable." Which mind, Venerable Monk, are you going to light up?' Tokusan was unable to answer this question and had to shut his mouth tight. Even so, he could not die the Great Death at the old woman's words, and finally asked her, 'Is there a Zen Master in the neighborhood?' The old woman replied, 'Master Ryutan lives five miles away.' Arriving at Ryutan's monastery, he was completely defeated. It has to be said that his former words and his latter words do not agree. Ryutan is like the mother who, because she loves her child too much, does not realize how meddlesome she herself is. Finding a little piece of live coal in Tokusan, he quickly poured muddy water over him. Looking at it calmly, I would say that the whole story is just a farce."

Young Tokusan with his indignant mind left his home for the south in high spirits. But he was asked by the old woman of the roadside teahouse, "Venerable Monk, which mind are you going to light up?" Master Mumon first comments on this encounter, "Tokusan was unable to answer this question. Anyway it is much to be regretted that he could not die the Great Death at this acute question of the old woman, which could have cut away conceptual tangles and opened his Zen eye." This is a very good comment.

At the monastery the Master will demand of the monk in training, "You answer the old woman in place of Tokusan!" This is the barrier in studying this koan.

Tokusan was quite a character, and with his insight he must have perceived something deep in the old woman's question. He had to give in to her, and he asked, "Is there any great Zen Master in the neighborhood?" "Master Ryutan lives five miles away from here," the old woman told him. Tokusan lost no time in calling on Master Ryutan.

It has already been explained in the koan how Tokusan was able to attain satori. About this happy result Mumon says, "Arriving at Master Ryutan's monastery, Tokusan committed a blunder. It was a miserable failure quite contrary to the bombast he had made when he left his home." Tokusan, who had boasted that he would beat the Zen devils in the south, was suddenly enlightened by Master Ryutan's live instruction, and he then declared, "From now on I will not doubt the sayings of any of the great Zen Masters in the world." With his usual paradoxical way of expressing himself, Master Mumon is blessing the sudden great awakening of Tokusan to Zen Truth.

Master Mumon's cutting paradoxical language continues in his comment on Master Ryutan's attitude: "Dear Master Ryutan, doting on your child, you do not seem to notice how you meddle with him. Having found a little bit of hope (a live coal) in Tokusan, you recklessly poured muddy water right over his head." He is speaking of Ryutan's praising words of Tokusan, "Someday in the future, he will establish his way on a steep and lofty peak."

Finally Mumon refers to the whole circumstance, still in his favorite paradoxical way: "If I reflect on the whole matter calmly, it is after all just a farce." Mumon obviously is speaking from the absolute standpoint of Zen, which transcends both satori and ignorance. At the same time he is reminding Masters in Zen circles that they ought always to maintain strict and severe attitudes toward their disciples, and is encouraging Zen students to devote themselves to discipline with a zeal that would not yield even to that of their teachers.

TEISHO ON MUMON'S POEM

> Far better seeing the face than hearing the name;
> Far better hearing the name than seeing the face.
> Though he saved his nose,
> Alas, he has lost his eyes!

"Hearing the name" is repeated in the first two lines of the poem. Whose name is it? Depending on how you take it, the meaning of the two lines will be differently interpreted.

If we interpret this poem as a commentary poem on the title of the koan "Well-Known Ryutan," the name will naturally be Ryutan's. "For a long time I have heard the name of the great Master Ryutan. But it is far better to see him face to face personally. Once having personally met, and exchanged mondo with him, there is no particular secret there. It is just that I have grasped the True Self, or am awakened to the original Buddha Nature. There is nothing special there."

On the other hand, if we take the name as the essence of Zen, the significance of the first half of the poem will naturally be different. You must not like Diamond Shu, remain satisfied with just hearing of Zen, and understand it as "the special transmission outside scriptures" or the teaching of "this mind as it is, is Buddha." You have to see its face actually with your own eyes. In other words, unless you personally attain the experience, your talk will make no sense. Once however you have had satori and seen its face intimately, the "special transmission outside scriptures," or "this mind as it is, is Buddha," is nothing but what you see in front of you here, now. "Our ordinary mind is Tao," and there is nothing special.

The third line says, "Be that as it may, Tokusan fortunately saved his nose." Mumon congratulates Tokusan's attainment of satori through Ryutan's superb instruction by saying that "he saved his nose."

"What a pity, though, that he seems to have lost his precious eyes!" This comment in the fourth line refers to his act of burning up the notes and commentaries on the sutra in front of the monastery. It means that he seems to have fallen into one-sided equality if he thought he had to burn up the sutras. In other words, although he could realize the Truth (saved the nose), he lost the free working in differentiation (lost his eyes).

In *Shodoka* it is said, "Be free in the universal Truth, and be free in explaining it. Thus the Truth and its working are perfectly interfused and never fall into dead emptiness." Master Mumon is insisting that a true Zen man with his spiritual eye clearly opened ought to be free in both the Realm of Truth and working.

29

Neither the Wind Nor the Flag

KOAN

The wind was flapping a temple flag. Two monks were arguing about it. One said the flag was moving; the other said the wind was moving. Arguing back and forth they could come to no agreement. The Sixth Patriarch said, "It is neither the wind nor the flag that is moving. It is your mind that is moving." The two monks were struck with awe.

MUMON'S COMMENTARY

It is neither the wind nor the flag nor the mind that is moving. Where do you see the heart of the Patriarch? If you can see clearly, you will know that the two monks obtained gold intending to buy iron. Also you will know that the Patriarch could not repress his compassion and made an awkward scene.

MUMON'S POEM

The wind moves, the flag moves, the mind moves:
All of them missed it.
Though he knows how to open his mouth,
He does not see he was caught by words.

TEISHO ON THE KOAN

The main figure in this koan is Master Eno, the Sixth Patriarch, who is also in the twenty-third koan, "Think Neither Good Nor Evil." The twenty-third koan deals with the event that took place when Master Eno, as a lay brother, became the Dharma successor, was given the Fifth Patriarch's robe and bowl, and left Obai to hide himself in the south.

Nearly fifteen years after the events in the twenty-third koan Eno appeared, still as a layman, at Hosshoji, in Koshu. This koan introduces the story about Eno when, after these many years in hiding, he came to hear the Venerable Inju lecture on the *Nirvana Sutra* at Hosshoji. One day Eno happened to hear two monks arguing and pointing at the flag fluttering in the wind. The one said that the flag was moving; the other said that the wind was moving. When a flag is moving, our eyes perceive it as actually moving. If there is no wind, however, the flag does not move. There is some reason in the statement that the wind moves the flag, and it is therefore the wind that is moving and not the flag. On the other hand the wind is invisible, and it is beyond our capacity to perceive the wind itself moving. Thus there is some meaning in the statement that it is the flag that moves. Once a painter was asked to draw a picture of the wind. What he painted was a willow with its branches swinging in the wind.

Listening to this naïve discussion, which seemed to get them nowhere, Eno stepped up to them and said, "It is neither the wind nor the flag that is moving. It is your mind that is moving." This direct solution from the subjective standpoint put an end to the endless dualistic discussion, and the two monks hearing it were struck with awe and greatly impressed.

Since they were Buddhist monks in training, they must have known the basic Buddhist teachings, such as "Every phenomenon is only due to mind," or "Nothing exists outside mind." Brother Eno's statement, "Your mind is moving," came directly out of the experiential fact which has nothing to do with intellectual interpretation. In other words, it was the natural working of Eno's Zen. The two monks intuitively recognized it, and that is why they were so impressed and even overawed.

Master Mumon's real intention in introducing this koan is also to be grasped here: by this statement, "Your mind is moving," he wished his disciples to open their Zen eye to the experiential Truth which transcends intellectual understanding.

Setting aside the old story, how should we, here and now, grasp "It is your mind that is moving" as the living fact in our lives?

In the *Keitoku Dento-roku* ("The Transmission of the Lamp") there is another paragraph after the story in this koan, to the following effect: "The Venerable Inju heard from the two monks of the mondo of a lay Buddhist and was struck with awe and admiration. The next day he invited him into his room and asked him again about the discussion on the wind and the flag. The lay Buddhist gave a clear answer. The Venerable Inju spontaneously stood up and said, 'Lay brother, you must certainly be no ordinary person. Who in the world are you?' Brother Eno frankly told him, without concealment, how he had been given the Dharma sanction at Obai years before. Hearing it, the Venerable Inju looked up to Brother Eno as his teacher and begged him to be their Zen Master. Inju announced to the public, 'Though I am only an ordinary being dressed in a robe, I have now met a living Bodhisattva.' "

Brother Eno was then formally ordained by the Venerable Chiko and became a Buddhist monk. His life as the Sixth Patriarch Eno started here, and his great activities as a Zen Master developed from this time.

TEISHO ON MUMON'S COMMENTARY

"It is neither the wind nor the flag nor the mind that is moving. Where do you see the heart of the Patriarch? If you can see clearly, you will know that the two monks obtained gold intending to buy iron. Also you will know that the Patriarch could not repress his compassion and made an awkward scene."

Master Mumon's commentary on this koan "Neither the Wind Nor the Flag" consists of two parts. In the first part he says, "It is neither the wind nor the flag nor the mind that is moving. Where do you see the heart of the Patriarch?" The commentary points directly to the core of the koan. Whereas Master Eno says in the koan that "your mind is moving," Master Mumon flatly denies it, saying, "It is not the mind that is moving." Having squarely negated it, Master Mumon cuttingly asks us, "Where do you see the heart of the Patriarch?" What a superb comment this is! He is demanding of us that we grasp Master Eno's real intention.

It is moving, yet there is no movement. It is standing still, yet there is no standstill. For all that, moving will do and standing still will do. This is the freedom of Zen, which transcends subject and object, movement and nonmovement, and real peace is enjoyed only when one lives with this freedom. There is an old haiku poem by an unknown author:

This lace curtain
Just swinging
In the cool breeze!

Let us read into the heart of this poem.

Long ago in China there was a nun called Myoshin, who was a disciple of Master Gyozan Ejaku. She was in charge of a guest house outside the temple. One day seventeen monks came from the faraway country of Shoku to see Master Gyozan, and they stayed at her lodging house. In the evening they got together by the fireside and began discussing the koan of "Neither the Wind Nor the Flag." Nun Myoshin, listening to their talk, disapproved of all of them, saying, "You seventeen donkeys have never come across Buddhism even in a dream. What a pity!" In reply to their request for instruction, she declared, "It is neither the wind nor the flag nor the mind that is moving." Her clear voice went straight to their hearts, and the seventeen monks were all enlightened. They expressed their heartfelt gratitude and returned to Shoku without seeing Master Gyozan.

In his commentary, Master Mumon quotes Nun Myoshin's reply exactly from the story and then asks pressingly, "Where do you see the heart of the Patriarch?" If it is truly spoken, if it is truly heard, the awakening is right there.

In the second part of his commentary Master Mumon says, "If you can directly and clearly see through the koan of 'Neither the wind nor the flag nor the mind is moving,' you will know that the two monks who were engaged in the foolish argument made an unexpected big profit. It is as if they obtained gold while paying for iron. As for Master Eno, he could not help putting in a word, out of his compassion, and remarked, 'Your mind is moving.' You will realize that his meddling is just nonsensical." This is again Mumon's usual paradoxical way of expressing his admiration.

Master Seppo said, commenting on these words of Master Eno, "Great Master though he is, what an awkward statement Master Eno made when he said, 'Your mind is moving!' If I had been there, I would have given the monks thirty blows of my stick without saying a word." Why did Master Seppo make such a severe criticism? Let us take it sincerely as a warning to each one of us.

TEISHO ON MUMON'S POEM

The wind moves, the flag moves, the mind moves:
All of them missed it.

Though he knows how to open his mouth,
He does not see he was caught by words.

Master Mumon's poem on this koan is concise. The first line says, "The wind is moving, the flag is moving, and the mind is moving." He just repeats the argument of the two monks together with Master Eno's comment. In the second line he denies them all, saying, "From my viewpoint, the two monks and the Sixth Patriarch are equally at fault." They are all in the wrong, the poem says.

He goes on to say, in the third and fourth lines, "Though he knows how to open his mouth, he does not see that he was caught by words." As soon as you open your mouth and say, "Your mind is moving," you have already been caught by words and have completely lost the Truth. "Once you open your mouth," Mumon warns us, "the Truth is no longer there. Beware!"

The real Zen man, however, must be able to use freely both speaking and silence, and the truth of "The wind is moving, the flag is moving, and the mind is moving" is in this freedom.

Goto Egen has the following story. Once when Master Zensei of Sodo was studying under Master Soshin of Oryo, he was given this koan of "Neither the Wind Nor the Flag." For a long while he worked hard with the koan but could get nowhere. One day in his teisho Master Soshin told his disciples, "When a cat tries to catch a rat, it concentrates all of its energy and attention directly on the single aim." Hearing it, Zensei shut himself up in a room to sit single-heartedly with the koan and finally was able to break through it. He made the following poem on that occasion:

Zui, zui, zui, zui; shaku, shaku, shaku!
Zui, zui, zui, and nobody knows what is what.
At night the bright moon rises over the mountain.
Truly, it is only "it."

What a clear and splendid spirituality this is!

After all, you are to be "it" through and through, and directly and single-heartedly live "it" and enjoy "it," just like the cat trying to catch a rat. The ultimate significance of this koan is to be grasped there, in your actually doing it.

30

Mind Is Buddha

KOAN

Taibai once asked Baso, "What is Buddha?" Baso answered, "Mind is Buddha."

MUMON'S COMMENTARY

If you can at once grasp "it," you are wearing Buddha clothes, eating Buddha food, speaking Buddha words, and living Buddha life; you are a Buddha yourself. Though this may be so, Taibai has misled a number of people and let them trust a scale with a stuck pointer. Don't you know that one has to rinse out his mouth for three days if he has uttered the word "Buddha"? If he is a real Zen man, he will stop his ears and rush away when he hears "Mind is Buddha."

MUMON'S POEM

A fine day under the blue sky!
Don't foolishly look here and there.
If you still ask "What is Buddha?"
It is like pleading your innocence while clutching stolen goods.

TEISHO ON THE KOAN

This koan consists of a mondo between Master Baso Doitsu and his disciple Taibai Hojo.

Master Baso Doitsu was a great Zen Master in the T'ang dynasty, and the unique characteristics of his Zen were well known even while he was alive. He produced many famous Masters from among his disciples and was respected as one of the brightest figures in the history of Zen in China.

Doitsu was born in the Ba family, hence his name Baso, which literally means Patriarch Ba. Doitsu is his personal name. He succeeded Master Nangaku Ejo, who studied under the Sixth Patriarch. A famous story tells us how Baso first met Master Nangaku and became his disciple. When Master Nangaku was at Hannyaji in Kozan, Baso stayed at Denpo-in on the same mountain, doing nothing but zazen day and night. One day Master Nangaku asked Baso, "Reverend Sir, what are you doing here?" "I am doing zazen," answered Baso. "What are you going to accomplish by doing zazen?" asked Nangaku. Baso replied, "I am only trying to be a Buddha." Hearing that, Nangaku walked away without a word, picked up a piece of brick in the garden, and started to polish it with a grinding stone in front of his hut. Baso asked, wondering, "What are you trying to accomplish by polishing that brick?" "I am trying to make a mirror by polishing this brick," replied Nangaku. Baso asked again, "Can a piece of brick be made into a mirror by polishing?" Nangaku retorted, "Can one become a Buddha by doing zazen?" Baso went on to ask, "What should I do then?" Nangaku said, "It is like putting a cart to an ox. When the cart does not move, which is better, to beat the cart or the ox?" Baso was unable to answer. Nangaku then kindly explained to him, "You practice zazen and try to become a Buddha by sitting. If you want to learn how to do zazen, know that Zen is not in sitting or lying. If you want to become a Buddha by sitting, know that Buddha has no fixed form. Never discriminate in living in the Dharma of nonattachment. If you try to become a Buddha by sitting, you are killing Buddha. If you attach to the form of sitting, you can never attain Buddhahood."

Baso decided to study under Master Nangaku henceforth, and went through most assiduous training. Finally he became an exceptionally capable Zen monk and was chosen to be Nangaku's successor. Later he moved to Kosei, where he guided and trained many good disciples and was much respected as "Ba, the Great Master." He died in 788, probably about eighty, but his exact age is not known.

Master Taibai Hojo of Joyo was one of Baso's senior disciples. After receiving the Dharma sanction from Baso he lived in a humble hut on a secluded mountain away from worldly turmoil and devoted himself to deepening his spirituality. Once a visitor came to his hut to invite him to become the abbot of a big temple, and Taibai responded with the following poem:

> A dead old tree is left uncut in a remote forest.
> Often has spring returned, yet my mind is not changed.
> Woodsmen have come, but have not wanted me,
> Visitors never took the trouble to look for me.
> Leaves are always sufficient for my clothes,
> Seeds of pine are more than enough to nourish me.
> Since people have now found out my abode,
> I move my hermitage further into the mountain's heart.

Then he moved further up the mountain. But even so, many monks followed him to study under him, and finally the Taibai Monastery was built in an isolated spot on the mountain. Master Taibai died in 839 at the age of eighty-eight.

"Mind is Buddha" was not necessarily original with Master Baso. In *Shinno-mei,* written by Fu-daishi probably before Bodhidharma came to China, there is the following passage: "If you realize the origin, you will attain mind. If you attain mind, you will see Buddha. Mind is Buddha; Buddha is mind." He also says, "You truth-seeker, look into your own mind. If you realize that Buddha is in yourself, you will not seek after him outwardly. Mind is Buddha; Buddha is mind. If your mind is clear, you will realize Buddha." Clearly, the phrase "Mind is Buddha" was already in use before Baso's time.

"Mind is Buddha" is a very important philosophical saying which concisely depicts the essence of Zen. In other words, Zen is a teaching which contends that "Mind is Buddha," and training in Zen aims to make it possible to be personally awakened to this fact. "Mind is Buddha" had always been an important theory in Zen, but it was Master Baso who especially emphasized it. *Keitoku Dento-roku* records the following teisho by Baso. The Master one day talked to the monks, "I tell you, my disciples, your mind is Buddha. This very mind, as it is, is Buddha mind. The great Master Bodhidharma came to China to transmit the great teaching of One Mind, and he guided you to enlightenment. He also quoted the *Lankavatara Sutra* to clarify people's minds, for you are probably confused and are not convinced. This Dharma mind is in each one of you. It is therefore said in the *Lankavatara Sutra,* 'The Buddha mind is the basis, and gateless is the Dharma gate.' Again it says, 'He who seeks after Dharma will certainly attain nothing. Outside mind there is no Buddha; outside Buddha there is no mind.' "

Master Sekito, too, one day gave the following teisho: "This Dharma, which has been handed down from the Buddhas, does not teach dhyana and discipline. If one opens the Buddha eye, his mind is at once Buddha."

Master Obaku, also, writes in his *Denshin Hoyo:* "A monk asked, 'From earliest times they all say, "Mind is Buddha"; I wonder which mind could be Buddha?' Obaku said, 'How many minds do you have? If a thought of consciousness arises, you are at once in the wrong. From time immemorial until today, "Mind is Buddha" has never been changed. There is no other Dharma. It is therefore called the attainment of true satori.' "

In the sayings of Master Daito it is recorded as follows: "To see into one's nature [to attain satori] is to be awakened to the Buddha mind. Cast all thoughts and consciousness away and see that 'Mind is Buddha.' . . . The one who realizes that his true mind is Buddha is the man who has attained Buddhahood. He neither practices good nor commits evil; he has no attachment to his mind. His eyes see things but he does not become attached to them; his tongue tastes things, but he does not become attached to them. This mind that does not become attached to each and every thing is the Buddha mind. This is why Master Baso said, 'Mind is Buddha.' "

The above are all philosophical or theoretical explanations of "Mind is Buddha." But here Master Baso's answer, "Mind is Buddha," to Taibai's question "What is Buddha?" is to be taken up as a Zen koan. As for the question "What is Buddha?" I have already explained it in my teisho on the eighteenth koan, "Tozan's Three Pounds of Flax," and I shall not repeat it here. Needless to say, the Buddha asked about here is not unrelated to the concept of Buddha in the broad sense in Buddhism. But what Taibai asks about is Buddha as the fact of realization experience in Zen, which is not necessarily related to philosophical interpretations of Buddha. Many Zen Masters have given different answers to the question, but they are all direct presentations of their realization experiences. If you fail to grasp the Zen experience itself from these varied answers, they cease to be live Zen koan. Master Baso's answer here, "Mind is Buddha," is no exception in this regard, and in studying it as a koan you have to read into it his Zen experience.

What is "Mind is Buddha"? Plunge into "Mind is Buddha" direct. When you work with it in actual training, philosophical interpretations have to be definitely abandoned. You have to be especially careful on that point in this case, for this "Mind is Buddha" is an answer with strong philosophical implications as compared with "Tozan's Three Pounds of Flax," or "Shit-Stick," which are also answers to the same question.

Let me ask you once again: "What is 'Mind is Buddha'?" Don't get into reasoning or discrimination, but grasp it directly. Otherwise you are thousands of miles away from it.

An old Zen Master made the following poem as his answer to "Mind is Buddha":

> In winter I long for warmth,
> In rain I look for a fine day.
> Spring enraptures people with her beautiful moonlight.
> Repeatedly she calls out, "Oh, Shogyoku!"
> It is for no other purpose
> Than that her lover may recognize her voice.

Those whose spiritual eyes are clearly opened will immediately appreciate the essence of Master Baso's kind answer, "Mind is Buddha," in the first two lines of the poem: "In winter I long for warmth,/In rain I look for a fine day." In the last two lines he comments on "Mind is Buddha" with a metaphor. A lady is repeatedly calling out to her maidservant, "Shogyoku! Shogyoku!" and giving her orders one after another. Her real concern is not the orders; she only wants her lover, who happens to be nearby, to realize that she is near him. In other words, when Masters say, "Mind is Buddha," "Mind is not Buddha," or "No mind, no Buddha," their real intention is not in these words. They only want us to realize, by means of various words, "True Buddha," which is not really in the words.

Master Taibai was fortunately able to attain satori when he received the instruction of Baso, "Mind is Buddha." After this he went far back on Mount Taibai to deepen and refine his spirituality, shunning fame and wealth.

Later, Master Baso sent a monk to Mount Taibai to find out secretly how Taibai was doing. The following is the mondo exchanged between Master Taibai and the messenger. The monk asked Taibai, "Reverend Sir, I see you are living here on the mountain in this manner. What did you get from Baso when you saw him?" Taibai replied, "Baso told me 'Mind is Buddha.' I was enlightened by it, and I live here like this." "Recently Master Baso teaches differently," said the monk. "How differently does he teach?" asked Taibai. The monk said, "Recently he says, 'No mind, no Buddha!'" At this Taibai said, "This old monk keeps on confusing people. I will leave it to him to say 'No Buddha, no mind.' As for me, I definitely say, 'Mind is Buddha!'" The monk on his return reported the conversation to Master Baso who highly praised the unshakable Zen attainment of Master Taibai, saying, "O Monks, the plum is really ripe." (The character *bai* in Taibai means "plum," while *tai* means "great.")

In connection with this subject of "Mind is Buddha," there is the following interesting story found in *Nanbanji Kohai-ki* ("The History of Nanbanji"): About four hundred years ago a great religious debate was held at Nanbanji between Buddhists and a Portuguese Catholic Father who was much favored by Oda Nobunaga, an influential feudal lord of that time. The Portuguese Father was certainly a man of wide reading and learning and was quite familiar with the Buddhist sutras. Representatives of various Buddhist schools were all argued down by his eloquence. Finally Master In of Nanzenji, in Kyoto, was selected as the last debater. The Portuguese Father asked, "What is Buddha?" "Mind is Buddha," answered Master In. The Portuguese Father now unsheathed a dagger, thrust it at Master In's chest, and demanded, "What is 'Mind is Buddha'?" Master In, not disturbed in the least, uttered a great KWATZ! cry. The Portuguese Father fell into a swoon in spite of himself and the audience, including Oda Nobunaga, all paled.

TEISHO ON MUMON'S COMMENTARY

"If you can at once grasp 'it,' you are wearing Buddha clothes, eating Buddha food, speaking Buddha words, and living Buddha life; you are a Buddha yourself. Though this may be so, Taibai has misled a number of people and let them trust a scale with a stuck pointer. Don't you know that one has to rinse out his mouth for three days if he has uttered the word 'Buddha'? If he is a real Zen man, he will stop his ears and rush away when he hears 'Mind is Buddha.' "

At the beginning of his commentary Master Mumon says, "If you can at once grasp 'it,' you are wearing Buddha clothes, eating Buddha food, speaking Buddha words, and living Buddha life; you are a Buddha yourself." To "at once grasp 'it' " is to be "it" at that very moment, at that very place, without any intellection or consciousness intervening. It is the basic attitude of Zen, and not necessarily in the case of "Mind is Buddha" alone. An old Master said, "Zen is a name for mind; mind is the foundation of Zen." In Zen you are awakened to the Absolute Mind, which is prior to human intellection or discriminating consciousness.

If you actually attain this Absolute Mind as a fact of your own experience, then you are living the Buddha life, wearing Buddha clothes, eating Buddha food, and speaking Buddha words. Your whole life, as it is, is Buddha life. In accord with Master Nansen you can say, "Ordinary mind, as it is, is Tao."

"As it is," however, is a very misleading phrase. In *Zazen Wasan,* Master

Hakuin says, "Your going-and-returning takes place nowhere but where you are," and "Your singing and dancing is none other than the voice of Dharma." But this great assertion has a precondition: "if you testify to the truth of Self-nature—the Self-nature that is no-nature." "No-nature" is the same as no-mind, but this does not mean nihilistic nothingness.

In order to avoid possible misunderstanding of "as-it-is-ness," a Zen man often uses paradoxical expressions and says, "I wear clothes, but I do not have any body. I eat, but I do not have a mouth. I walk, but I do not have feet." You must realize that this is a fact actually experienced by the True Self. In any case, if you cling to words, you miss the Truth in either expression and you can never appreciate "Mind is Buddha." For a Zen man the fact of his daily life, each movement of his hands and feet, is the live proof of his True Self of no-mind. Every movement for him is the movement of creation. "Ordinary mind" and "as it is" really mean such spirituality.

Master Mumon's commentary continues: "Though this may be so, Taibai has misled a number of people and let them trust a scale with a stuck pointer." The pointer on a scale has to be free to move in accordance with the weight of the item to be weighed. If it is locked in place, it does not serve the purpose of a scale. That is to say, however precious the satori of "Mind is Buddha" may be, if it is a lifeless corpse it is of no use. Master Mumon is telling Master Taibai, "Dear Taibai, you say you had satori that 'Mind is Buddha.' Because of this statement of yours, many people became attached to it and lost real freedom." It is not, however, Master Taibai's fault that they became attached to the scale with a stuck pointer. It is the fault of those people who failed to grasp the essence of "Mind is Buddha" as their experiential fact. Master Mumon's criticism is also an admonition to us today.

"Don't you know that one has to rinse out his mouth for three days if he has uttered the word 'Buddha'?" Mumon goes on to ask, fervently, "Master Taibai, haven't you ever heard of the old Master who having uttered the word 'Buddha' rinsed out his mouth for three days, saying his mouth was polluted?"

If you speak of Buddha, Buddha already has a dualistic stench. For one who has really attained the true Buddha of no-form, no-shape, its name is already an obstacle and a pollution. If you were a true Zen man, you would be overwhelmed with shame if you even uttered the word "Buddha." A Zen man of spirit who has clearly opened his Zen eye and has thoroughgoing satori will stop his ears and rush away if he hears "Mind is Buddha." "Master Taibai, you are an unexpected snob who values names, aren't you!" With all his might Master Mumon sharply denounces Taibai. Here we can see how outstandingly penetrating Mumon's Zen ability is. Also we read his compassionate admonition to those who cling to words and the superficial meanings of "Mind is Buddha."

TEISHO ON MUMON'S POEM

A fine day under the blue sky!
Don't foolishly look here and there.
If you still ask "What is Buddha?"
It is like pleading your innocence while clutching stolen goods.

While Master Mumon's commentary on the koan is kind and detailed, his poem on it is short and direct. First he says, "A fine day under the blue sky! Don't foolishly look here and there." If you have really grasped "Mind is Buddha," there is nothing hidden or vague, all is just like the clear, cloudless sky. If you stand, at the very place where you stand "Mind is Buddha" is fully revealed. If you sit, at the very place where you sit it is fully revealed. Each movement of your hand and foot is nothing but "it." You need not look for "it" here and there. Thus Mumon directly presents the essence of "Mind is Buddha." Those whose spiritual eyes are opened will immediately appreciate it in these first two lines.

Master Mumon is kind enough to explain it further: "Yet if there be anyone who would still ask what is meant by "Mind is Buddha," he is like one who insists on his innocence while clutching stolen goods." If you truly live the life of no-mind, Reality is right in your hand. Once you have missed your original True Self of "Mind is Buddha" and start looking for Buddha outwardly, you are immediately turned into a man of ignorance and are hundreds and thousands of miles away from Buddha. You are then as silly and stupid as if you were to declare your innocence with the stolen goods in your hands.

Master Daichi has a poem on "Mind is Buddha":

Truth is fully revealed, beyond argumentation.
Green gentian is bitter; ice is cold—how clear!
Living up to "Mind is Buddha,"
Day and night his forehead gives off light.

Master Daichi declares in the first line, "Mind is Buddha, and the Truth is fully revealed, so lucidly and clearly presented in front of you here, now, that it is foolish to argue about this and that." He goes on to speak of "Mind is Buddha" with concrete facts: "Green gentian is bitter; ice is cold." Look and behold. There is nothing hidden. This second line is indeed an excellent comment which thoroughly discloses the essence of "Mind is Buddha." In the third and fourth lines Master Daichi describes the life of a Zen man who lives up to "Mind is Buddha" in his daily life: day and night he lives and develops the life of Buddha freely in accordance with the actual situation.

Master Yoka says in his *Shodoka:* " 'It' is ever present here, now. If you look for it outwardly, know that you will never be able to get 'it.' " He warns us that as soon as we start seeking for the Truth outside ourselves, we will miss it forever.

31

Joshu Saw Through the Old Woman

A monk asked an old woman, "Which way should I take to Mount Gotai?" The old woman said, "Go straight on!" When the monk had taken a few steps, she remarked, "He may look like a fine monk, but he too goes off like that!" Later, a monk told Joshu about it. Joshu said, "Wait a while. I will go and see through that old woman for you." The next day off he went, and asked her the same question. The old woman, too, gave him the same reply. When he returned, Joshu announced to the monks, "I have seen through the old woman of Mount Gotai for you."

MUMON'S COMMENTARY

The old woman knew how to work out a strategy and win the victory while sitting in her tent. Yet she is not aware of the bandit stealing into the tent. Old Joshu is skillful enough to creep into the enemy's camp and menace their fortress. Yet he does not look like a grown-up. Upon close examination, they are both at fault. Now tell me, how did Joshu see through the old woman?

MUMON'S POEM

The question is the same each time,
The answer, too, is the same.

In the rice there is sand,
In the mud there are thorns.

TEISHO ON THE KOAN

The central figure of this koan is again the famous Master Joshu, who has already appeared several times in previous koan, so no introduction is needed here. Another leading figure is an old woman who cannot be historically identified. It is very likely, however, that in those days when Zen flourished most in China there were some old women who had fully studied Zen (such as the old woman of the teahouse who had mondo with Master Tokusan as told in the twenty-eighth koan).

Mount Gotai mentioned here is a holy mountain in the northeastern part of present Sansei-sho in China, a holy mountain because it has been regarded as the abode of Manjusri. From ancient times famous monks have lived on this mountain, and Buddhists of all kinds as well as monks in training have made pilgrimages to it.

An old woman lived near Mount Gotai, probably running a small teahouse by the roadside. Whenever a traveling monk asked her, "Which way should I take to go to Mount Gotai?" she would always answer, "Go straight on!" She would not tell him to go either east or west. Seeing the traveling monk take a few steps forward, she would scoff at him, saying, "This monk again! He may look like a fine monk, but what an awkward figure he cuts!"

For a sincere truth-seeker, where could the way to Mount Gotai be? The way to Mount Gotai is the way to Zen; it is the way to the fundamental Truth, and it has to be the way to himself, his True Self. What is the use of looking for it outwardly away from his very self here and now? It is an old saying that all roads lead to Rome, also that "the Great Way leads to Ch'ang-an." There is no argument about east or west, right or left, time or space, for it is the One True Way. "Go straight on!" What else could we say about this Absolute Way? Sakyamuni taught Ananda, "The Truth is in all ten directions; straight is the Way to Nirvana."

Going astray from this inner way which is deep in himself, the traveling monk starts wandering along blindly, following the superficial meaning of the old woman's words. She could not help scoffing at him sadly, "He may look like a fine monk, but he too goes off like that!"

As this mondo between the old woman and a monk took place repeatedly, the report spread around and one day Master Joshu heard it from a monk.

Joshu said, "Wait a while, I will go and see through that old woman for you." The next day he equipped himself for a trip, and off he went determined to see through her.

Before long he came to her place and asked her, just as all the rest had, "Which way should I take to Mount Gotai?" The old woman, too, replied in exactly the same manner, "Go straight on!" As Master Joshu went a few steps on, the old woman remarked as usual, "He may look like a fine monk, but he too goes off like that!" In other words, exactly the same mondo was exchanged between the two as on all the previous occasions.

On his return to the monastery, Master Joshu gathered all the disciples and confidently announced, "I have clearly seen through that old woman on the road to Mount Gotai for you." He declared to his disciples that he did see through the old woman, but did not say how he had done it, made no detailed report—which naturally gives rise to various arguments and speculations.

Although Master Joshu himself did go over to the old woman's place on the way to Mount Gotai and did personally exchange mondo with her, he spoke and acted exactly as the rest of the monks had. The old woman also spoke and acted exactly as she had before. There was nothing whatsoever that was different or special. Nevertheless Master Joshu declares, on his return to the monastery, "I have seen through the old woman of Mount Gotai for you!"

Did he in fact see through her or not? If he did, how did he see through her? What kind of fact are you talking about when you say that Joshu saw through her? Unless you open your Zen eye on this ultimate point you are not able to stand beside Joshu, nor can you get the real significance of the koan.

Master Bokitsu of Isan said, commenting on this koan, "All the monks in the world only knew how to ask the old woman the way to Mount Gotai and did not realize what vital significance is involved in the question. If it were not for old Joshu, how could we expect such great success?"

All the monks ask the old woman the Way, and are busy looking for it outside themselves. They are not aware that the real problem is in themselves. It takes a true and capable Zen man like old Joshu to achieve such an incomparable success. Master Bokitsu is thus highly praising Master Joshu, yet he does not state at all how, in fact, Joshu "saw through the old woman."

Let me ask you, my students, "What is 'the old woman'? What does he mean by 'seeing through her'?" An old Zen Master asked, "How can water drench water? How can gold be changed into gold?" Be water through and through! Be gold through and through! In the all-pervading "seeing through" how can there be Joshu or the old woman? The whole universe has just been seen through.

TEISHO ON MUMON'S COMMENTARY

"The old woman knew how to work out a strategy and win the victory while sitting in her tent. Yet she is not aware of the bandit stealing into the tent. Old Joshu is skillful enough to creep into the enemy's camp and menace their fortress. Yet he does not look like a grown-up. Upon close examination, they are both at fault. Now tell me, how did Joshu see through the old woman?"

In commenting on the old woman, Master Mumon quotes a Chinese saying, "Making a plan of operations within the tent, he wins a victory on the battlefield a thousand miles away." This is how a great general fights. This old woman, too, Master Mumon comments, has a wonderful ability like that of a great general who leads to victory at a far distant front while he himself is sitting in the tent and working out his strategy at his table. Capable as she is, she does not seem to know that a thief has stolen right into her own room. In other words, Mumon criticizes the old woman, "Dear old woman, you make quite shrewd remarks like 'Go straight on!' or, 'He may look like a fine monk, but he too goes off like that,' yet your secret hand is all known to me!"

Why does Master Mumon so criticize the old woman, when she treated Joshu in exactly the same way she treated the other monks?

Master Hakuin's comment on this koan is famous, "You all understand that Joshu has seen through the old woman, but do not know that the old woman has seen through Joshu. Now, tell me, how did she see through Joshu?" I ask you, "How did the old woman see through Joshu?" If you cannot give me a clear and concrete answer to this question, you will be unable to understand Master Mumon's commentary, nor can you grasp the essence of this koan.

Master Mumon then comments on Master Joshu: "Old Joshu is skillful enough to capture the enemy's headquarters and menace their fortress. Yet in my eyes he is not yet grown up." Let me ask you: Even though Master Joshu talked and acted just like the other monks, why does Master Mumon criticize him like this? If you cannot give me a clear and concrete answer to this question, you will be unable to understand Master Mumon's commentary, nor can you grasp the essence of this koan.

Mumon goes on to say, "Upon close examination, Joshu and the old woman are both at fault." What does he mean by the "fault" for which both of them are to blame?

At the end Mumon asks his disciples, "Now tell me, how did Joshu see through the old woman?" Needless to say, when you realize how Master Joshu saw through the old woman, you will also realize how the old woman saw through Master Joshu. The key of the koan lies right here.

As Master Hakuin says, this is a very complicated, typical nanto koan, and its real significance cannot be easily grasped. A popular writer comments on it, "Both Master Joshu and the old woman are good friends with equal ability, and their encounter ended in a tie." He also says, "This is an admonition to the monks to see under their feet and to open their spiritual eyes clearly just as Master Joshu did." These interpretations miss the essence of the koan; they do not even understand what a koan is.

TEISHO ON MUMON'S POEM

> The question is the same each time.
> The answer, too, is the same.
> In the rice there is sand,
> In the mud there are thorns.

The first line simply says, "The question is the same." This is a comment on Joshu, who personally went out in high spirits declaring, "Wait a while. I will go and see through that old woman for you." But he did not try any special means, he just asked the same question as the rest of the ordinary monks, "Which way should I take to Mount Gotai?" The second line, "The answer, too, is the same," is a comment on the old woman, who gave Joshu her stereotyped answer, "Go straight on!" and "He may look like a fine monk, but he too goes off like that!"

The third and fourth lines refer to the attitudes of both Master Joshu and the old woman: "In the rice there is sand,/In the mud there are thorns." Sand in the rice and thorns in the mud are both dangerous items hidden in something soft. One can easily get hurt by them. So take good care, Mumon warns us.

Setting aside these literal meanings, what does he really mean by "sand in rice and thorns in mud" about which we have to be careful? In them is hidden the real significance of the old woman's "Go straight on!" and Master Joshu's "I have seen through her!" Can't you hear Master Mumon telling you, "Joshu has seen through the whole universe, not to speak of the old woman"? If you fail to grasp it here, the koan turns out to be nothing but a nonsensical farce.

Master Enan of Oryo has a poem on this koan:

Joshu stands preeminent in the world of Zen.
There is a good reason for his seeing through the old woman.
Since that time the four seas are calm as a mirror,
Travelers no longer have to worry about the journey.

Master Enan is saying, "Master Joshu certainly is a preeminently great Master in Zen circles. There is a good and profound reason for his seeing through the old woman by the roadside leading to Mount Gotai. Thanks to old Joshu, the world is now calm and peaceful like a mirror. You, student, go straight on the way to Mount Gotai in peace and confidence."

In spite of Master Enan's assurance, for those who have not personally and directly awakened to the real significance of Joshu's "I have seen through her!" the way to Mount Gotai is ever steep and difficult.

32

A Non-Buddhist Questions the Buddha

A non-Buddhist once asked the World-Honored One, "I do not ask for words, nor do I ask for no-words." The World-Honored One remained seated. The non-Buddhist praised him, saying, "The great compassion of the World-Honored One has dispelled the clouds of my ignorance and enabled me to be enlightened." Making a bow of gratitude, he departed. Ananda then asked Buddha, "What realization did the non-Buddhist have that made him praise you like that?" The World-Honored One replied, "He is like a high-mettled horse which starts at even the shadow of the whip."

MUMON'S COMMENTARY

Ananda is Buddha's disciple, yet his understanding falls far short of the non-Buddhist's. Now tell me, how different are they, the Buddha's disciple and the non-Buddhist?

MUMON'S POEM

He walks along the edge of a sword
And runs over the sharp ridges of an ice floe.
You need take no steps,
Let go your hold on the cliff!

TEISHO ON THE KOAN

The three characters who appear in this koan are Sakyamuni Buddha (the World-Honored One), who is the founder of Buddhism, his disciple, the Venerable Ananda, who faithfully served Sakyamuni for over twenty-five years and is known as the disciple of the best hearing and remembering, and an unnamed non-Buddhist. A "non-Buddhist" is what Buddhists call anyone who belongs to a religion other than Buddhism. Here he is probably a Brahman philosopher, for the Vedic tradition flourished widely in India in those days. Although there were many philosophical schools in India at that time, they tended to lean either toward materialism, emphasizing phenomena and the perceptions of the senses, or toward an extreme idealism that denied phenomenal differentiation. Mahayana Buddhism, on the other hand, upholds the teaching of the Middle Way. It transcends both negative and affirmative views, subjectivism and objectivism, and is based on Reality itself, which is neither dualistic nor monistic. The essential teaching of Mahayana lies here.

One day a Brahman philosopher came to see Sakyamuni Buddha and asked, "Please show me directly the Truth that is committed neither to an affirmative view with words nor to a negative view without words." (Compare this with the twenty-fourth koan, "Abandon Words and Speaking.")

If you speak, you have departed from the principle. If you do not speak, you are not in accord with phenomenal facts. The questioner acutely asks for the Truth which transcends this fundamental dilemma. In reply to the non-Buddhist's question, Sakyamuni showed "it" by remaining seated. He appealed neither to words nor to no-words, but just remained seated. An old Zen Master said, commenting on that response, "An iron wall, an impregnable fortress!" Another said, "Cutting off all the oppositions, illuminating is the one sword throughout the universe!" Thus Sakyamuni remained seated. Absolute was his remaining seated; incomparably superb was his working. Let us admire it; let us grasp his essence.

Once a word of explanation is uttered, it is already under the limitation of words. Needless to say, Sakyamuni's remaining seated was not mere silence. Master Tenne Gie therefore comments:

> Neither was Vimalakirti silent nor was he merely seated.
> To argue about his remaining seated is already to be at fault.
> Sharp and cold is the blade of the finest sword.
> Non-Buddhists and devils shall all fold their arms.

Master Tenne likens Sakyamuni's remaining seated to Vimalakirti's "sitting in silence" and warns us that if we were to take it as mere sitting we would be making a vital mistake. He is urging us to grasp the live Truth, which transcends affirmation and negation, speaking and silence, from this sitting of Sakyamuni. He compares it to the sharp blade of the finest sword, and says that even devils and non-Buddhists would have to withdraw, folding their arms.

The non-Buddhist who received Sakyamuni's incomparable instruction must have been a man of rare insight; he must have gone through the spiritual struggle, the relativistic dilemma of words and no-words. He must have been in the abyss of desperation and the time must have been ripe for an explosion. When he appeared before Sakyamuni he was at his final extremity in spiritual searching. At the direct instruction of Sakyamuni his inner struggle was at once dissolved, and he could be awakened to the Truth that transcends both negation and affirmation. The non-Buddhist could not help making a bow of sincere gratitude, and he praised Sakyamuni saying, "The great compassion of the World-Honored One has dispelled the clouds of my ignorance and enabled me to be enlightened."

Master Engo is truly a great Master who asks in relation to this praise of the non-Buddhist, "Now, you tell me what is the great compassion of the World-Honored One?" This is a question which students under actual training cannot lightly overlook. I ask you, my student, to give me your answer here, now, an answer not concerned with either words or no-words.

The non-Buddhist said, "You have enabled me to be enlightened." Fundamentally, however, the Truth that transcends affirmation and negation can be neither attained nor lost. The fact is that he was awakened to the Truth, which he had from the beginning. Here is nothing unusual—he only realized that he had originally been born with "it." This is the new vista where the World-Honored One and the non-Buddhist are not two. "He remained seated"—the stark-naked Truth is fully revealed, and how can it be different for different people?

Master Sesso has a poem:

> The eyes of Sakyamuni penetrate the three worlds.
> The sight of the non-Buddhist extends to the five heavens.
> Tender is the heart of the flower; the peach blossoms smile.
> The light of spring rests not on the willow leaves only.

The eyes of Sakyamuni, remaining seated, are bright and light up the three worlds of the past, present, and future. The eyes of the enlightened non-Buddhist illuminate the five heavens (the whole universe). The expressions may be different, but the Truth that transcends affirmation and negation can never be different. It is the beauty of a spring scene, where the heart of the flower is tender and peach blossoms are smiling. The peace and beauty of spring (which represents the truth of Sakyamuni's remaining seated) is not only on the willow leaves, but is equally on the peach blossoms. It is not only with Sakyamuni, but with the non-Buddhist as well.

Here the koan changes to the second part where Sakyamuni and Ananda have mondo. The Venerable Ananda, who always waited on Sakyamuni faithfully and was known as the disciple of "the best hearing and remembering," was at this time still a monk of mere "best hearing and remembering," and his spiritual eye was not yet opened. Witnessing this unusual exchange between Sakyamuni and the non-Buddhist in front of him, Ananda asked Sakyamuni, "What kind of attainment did the non-Buddhist have that made him praise you like that?" Calmly, Sakyamuni said, "He is very bright indeed, just like a spirited horse that starts running at the shadow of the whip."

In *Samyuktagama* there is a simile that explains the different qualities of Buddhist monks: "Bhikkhus can be compared to four different kinds of horses. The first senses the shadow of the whip and obeys the rider's will. The second reacts when its hair is touched. The third starts when its flesh is touched, and the fourth when its bones are shaken." Among Buddhist disciples there is the difference of bright ones and dull-witted ones. The non-Buddhist appearing here must have been one of the most brilliant and capable of men. Just like the horse of high mettle that starts galloping even at the shadow of the whip, he immediately attained the Truth upon seeing Sakyamuni remain in his seat. Thus Sakyamuni praised his brilliance.

An old Zen Master commented on Sakyamuni's answer to Ananda: "You are too mild and easy, World-Honored One. If I had been there, I would have slapped Ananda without a word. Then Ananada might have been revived with even greater vigor than the non-Buddhist." For a Zen Master, this is but a natural comment.

Be that as it may, in actual training the brilliance alone will never do. Attainment of satori is always preceded by hard and sincere seeking and discipline.

TEISHO ON MUMON'S COMMENTARY

"Ananda is Buddha's disciple, yet his understanding falls far short of the non-Buddhist's. Now tell me, how different are they, the Buddha's disciple and the non-Buddhist?"

Master Mumon's commentary on this koan is very interesting, since in pithy words he points directly at the core of it. First he comments on the Venerable Ananda, who was one of Sakyamuni's Ten Great Disciples and is noted for his "best hearing." "Buddha's disciple though he is, Ananda could not appreciate the true intention of Sakyamuni's remaining in his seat. He is in no way equal to the non-Buddhist in his understanding." This is certainly a good criticism. As Master Sesso says, "The light of spring rests not on the willow leaves only." The truth of "remaining seated" cannot be different for people or for places.

Master Hakuin said, referring to this "remaining seated": *"Daigaku* ["The Great Learning"] is a Confucian classic in which it is said, 'Stop in extreme good. Having once stopped, there is dhyana.' Realize, you students, that this dhyana and Sakyamuni's remaining in his seat are not a bit different." Master Bukai, my teacher, used to say, "It is written in the Bible, 'Blessed are the poor in spirit, for theirs is the kingdom of heaven.' This is exactly the same as the essential teaching of Buddhism."

The fundamental Truth that transcends subject and object, affirmation and negation—that is, the fact of religious experience—can never change by difference of religion. The sectarian differences on the part of the person who believes and lives the Fundamental Truth are of secondary importance.

Finally Master Mumon, looking over his disciples in the hall, asks, as if to put an end to this koan, "Now tell me, how different are they, the Buddha's disciple and the non-Buddhist?" This question shows Master Mumon's great compassion toward his disciples.

Needless to say, a silly argument such as, "If he understands, he is a Buddha's disciple, and if he cannot, he is a non-Buddhist," completely misses the mark. It is not a matter of such a connotation or definition. This is a question based on the One Truth; it is asked from the absolute Zen standpoint, based on the experiential fact. It is a question asked out of great compassion, trying to wipe away all our dualistic intellection. The Master will ask, "How different are they, a pole and a lamp? How different are they, the desk and the chair?"

TEISHO ON MUMON'S POEM

> He walks along the edge of a sword
> And runs over the sharp ridges of an ice floe.
> You need take no steps,
> Let go your hold on the cliff!

The first two lines describe a man who goes through the greatest danger and gets over the crisis at the risk of his life. It certainly is no easy task, and to accomplish it takes a man of unusual capability. Master Mumon likens the non-Buddhist to such a man. In other words, Master Mumon is highly praising the non-Buddhist who was at once awakened to the Truth at the sight of Sakyamuni remaining seated.

"One leap, and you are right in satori" is a Zen saying. In making this "leap" there is no distinction such as Buddha's disciple and non-Buddhist, man and woman, wise man and ordinary man. Go straight on! "You need take no steps."

Mumon does not forget to encourage his disciples to have an intrepid spirit, to be ready to "let go your hold on the cliff a thousand feet high!"

Master Hakuin has a poem:

> You, young fellow,
> If you don't want to die,
> Die now,
> Once dead, you don't have to die twice.

There is a well-known haiku poem:

> Having died one death,
> Here is a man,
> Free and serene.

Is there a distinction between Buddha's disciple and the non-Buddhist here?

33

No Mind, No Buddha

A monk once asked Baso, "What is Buddha?" Baso answered, "No mind, no Buddha."

If you can see into it here, your Zen study has been completed.

> If you meet a swordsman in the street, give him a sword;
> Unless you meet a poet, do not offer a poem.
> In talking to people, tell them three quarters only,
> Never let them have the other part.

In the thirtieth koan, when Taibai asked, "What is Buddha?" Master Baso answered, "Mind is Buddha." Here in this koan, when an unnamed monk asks, "What is Buddha?" Baso replies, "No mind, no Buddha." Thus Baso has given two different answers to exactly the same question, and furthermore, "Mind

235

is Buddha" and "No mind, no Buddha" sound quite opposite.

What reason could there be for Baso to give such contradictory answers? It must be his compassionate and creative means of wiping away all the attachment of his disciples and definitely awakening them to Reality. Earlier, Taibai had come to Master Baso seeking Buddha outside himself, and in order to break through his illusion Baso told him, "Mind is Buddha." Now that Baso sees that many disciples have become attached to "Mind is Buddha" he says "No mind, no Buddha" in order to smash and wipe away their attachment to "Mind is Buddha."

Master Jizai, who was Master Baso's successor, commented, " 'Mind is Buddha' is the phrase for one who wants medicine while he has no disease. 'No mind, no Buddha' is the phrase for one who cannot do away with medicine when his disease has been cured." For such people, who presume that they are diseased and look for medicine while actually they have no disease at all, "Mind is Buddha" is given to save them. For those who have been cured of disease but still cling to medicine, "No mind, no Buddha" is to be given. Thus they ought to realize that a truly healthy man knows neither disease nor medicine.

The following mondo between Master Baso and a monk is recorded: A monk asked Baso, "Why do you teach that 'Mind is Buddha'?" "It is in order to stop a baby crying," replied Baso. "What is it like when the baby stops crying?" asked the monk. "No mind, no Buddha," answered Baso.

That mondo may help you to penetrate Baso's "No mind, no Buddha."

Sugyo-roku gives the following theoretical explanations. First the question is raised: "Patriarchs and Masters of India and China have said that 'Mind is Buddha'; the principle is so clear and the teaching so direct that they speak as if with one mouth. Why, then, does Baso say, 'No mind, no Buddha'?" Then the philosophical answer is made as follows: "Mind is Buddha" is an affirmative statement; by straightforwardly stating that fact they make the student personally realize his own mind and lead him to attain satori. "No mind, no Buddha" is a negative statement. It protects against mistakes, shuts out faults, crushes attachments, and thus takes away all discriminating consciousness. To those who rely on intellectual interpretations and cling to them, Baso says "No mind, no Buddha" in order to take away their attachments.

That is a good philosophical explanation, but here Master Baso's answering "No mind, no Buddha"—which was his reply to a monk's asking "What is Buddha?"—has to be taken up as a Zen koan. (Concerning the question "What is Buddha?" refer to my teisho on the eighteenth koan, "Tozan's Three Pounds of Flax.") The Buddha asked about here is Buddha as the fact of one's religious experience in Zen, and there is no concern with its philosophical meaning or theoretical interpretation. "No mind, no Buddha" is of course a direct expression of Baso's religious experience, and if one fails to grasp his answer in this sense, it loses its life and real significance as a Zen koan. One has to work personally with it in his training and himself be "No mind, no Buddha." In this regard, what is required of students in training is the same as in the case of "Mind is Buddha."

I ask you, my students, "What is 'No mind, no Buddha!'?" Cast away all intellectual understanding and plunge into it with your whole being. Unless you grasp its truth as a fact of your own experience you can never really appreciate what Zen is.

Master Hakuin said, " 'Mind is Buddha' is like a dragon without horns; while 'No mind, no Buddha' is like a snake with horns." From what standpoint does he comment in this way?

A Zen Master asked, "Who holds the promissory note?" Unless you firmly hold it in your hand, you may be cheated, you may be deceived. That is to say, unless you have your Zen eye clearly opened, based on actual training, you may be deceived by "No mind, no Buddha!" Now tell me, what is the promissory note that can never be defaulted? What is the clear Zen eye acquired in training that will never be obscured?

TEISHO ON MUMON'S COMMENTARY

Master Mumon comments most briefly on this koan, "If you can see into it here, your Zen study has been completed." "It" here refers to Baso's true intention in saying "No mind, no Buddha!"—which sounds quite contradictory to his previous answer, "Mind is Buddha." When we clearly see into Baso's true intention and actually live the Zen life of "No mind, no Buddha!" the aim of our Zen training has been completely fulfilled.

As long as one is attached to mind and bound by Buddha, one can never attain the true Buddha. The aim of training in Zen can be fulfilled only when one is detached from the name and form of mind and Buddha, that is, when one is free from his attachment to mind and Buddha.

This shows what high respect Master Mumon paid to Baso's spirituality as shown in this koan, "No mind, no Buddha!" Master Daichi made the following poem on it:

> "No mind, no Buddha!"—the talk changes.
> Zen students all over the country can hardly see it.

If you can leap out of the thresher's mouth,
You are free to run barefoot over the sword-mountain.

Master Baso first said, "Mind is Buddha" and now answers "No mind, no Buddha!" His talk is inconsistent and his answers sound contradictory. Zen monks throughout the country can hardly see the truth. A thresher is an agricultural tool to clean rice by threshing it. Because Master Baso was born in a family whose occupation was to make threshers, it is used here as a symbol for Baso himself. The thresher's mouth means Master Baso's words. Thus— even though he first said "Mind is Buddha" and then "No mind, no Buddha!" —don't be dragged around by his words; leap out of the expressions! Then for the first time you will be a truly free man. You do not have to be equipped with iron sandals, but with your bare feet you will enjoy freely sauntering over and playing on the sword-mountain. Our daily life is full of pain and suffering, a mixture of anger, love, pleasure, and despair. Even though it is like walking over mountains of swords, you can go over them with joy and freedom. Your every step will create a refreshing breeze, and there will be no cloud in the mind. It will certainly be a life of supreme spirituality, where all striving has come to an end.

TEISHO ON MUMON'S POEM

If you meet a swordsman in the street, give him a sword;
Unless you meet a poet, do not offer a poem.
In talking to people, tell them three quarters only,
Never let them have the other part.

With a poem Master Mumon comments on the unrestricted compassion of Master Baso, who first said, "Mind is Buddha" and then could not stop but went on to say, "No mind, no Buddha!" The first two lines are quoted from an old poem. They mean that it is a waste to give a sword to one who is not an expert swordsman, and that if you offer a poem to one who is not a poet he may not appreciate it.

However excellent the answer—whether it be "Mind is Buddha" or "No mind, no Buddha!"—it will be quite useless and a waste if given to an incapable man. It has to be addressed to those who have the ability to grasp its essence. Referring to a swordsman and a poet, Master Mumon is illustrating how outstandingly superb Master Baso's answers are.

The last two lines are taken from an old adage in military tactics. Probably the word "sword" as used in the first line was a rhetorical reference to such tactics. It is an old tactical proverb that since secrecy must be strictly maintained in strategy, three quarters of a plan may be explained, but the last quarter must be left unexplained even among good friends. (There are some who take "the other part" in the last line of Mumon's poem to mean the whole, and not one quarter out of four. In this case the meaning of the last two lines of the poem will be: "You may explain three quarters to others, but never tell them all." It is more correct, however, to take "the other part" as meaning the last quarter, since this is the original saying used in tactics.)

Master Mumon is saying, "Dear Master Baso, you give a most excellent answer—such as 'Mind is Buddha' or 'No mind, no Buddha!'—to just anybody, regardless of whether he can appreciate it or not. You are really too kind and are explaining too much. A good teacher ought to leave the last quarter unspoken, so that each student may work hard with it himself and be personally awakened to it." Criticizing Master Baso in this manner, Mumon is in fact admiring how uniquely splendid Master Baso's answers are.

Now let me ask you, how and why is "No mind, no Buddha!" explaining too much?

34

Wisdom Is Not Tao

Nansen said, "Mind is not Buddha; wisdom is not Tao."

MUMON'S COMMENTARY

Of Nansen it has to be said that on getting old he was lost to shame. Just opening his stinking mouth a little, he reveals his family shame. Even so, only a very few feel grateful for it.

MUMON'S POEM

> The sky is clear and the sun appears;
> Rain falls and the earth is moistened.
> Without restraint he has explained everything,
> Yet how few are able to grasp it!

TEISHO ON THE KOAN

In this koan Master Nansen, since he has appeared several times on previous occasions, needs no introduction. Master Mumon must have had special affection for him, since in the *Mumonkan* he has given four koan about him.

The koan is, "Nansen said, 'Mind is not Buddha; wisdom is not Tao,' " and it sounds as if this were a saying by Master Nansen. This sentence, however, cannot be found either in *Keitoku Dento-roku* or in *Goto Egen* in the chapter about Master Nansen. On the other hand, in *Goto Egen*, volume 3, we read in the chapter about Master Nyoe of Toji: "The Master said, 'Mind is not Buddha; wisdom is not Tao. The boat goes on; having dropped a sword in the water, you then mark its location on the gunwale. How foolish!" The saying in this koan is therefore probably not original with Nansen. Since Master Nyoe of Toji and Master Nansen were fellow disciples under Baso, and it is likely that this saying was popular in those days in Zen circles and often used by Masters, it is not surprising that it is sometimes attributed to Nansen.

Whether it was originally Master Nansen's saying or first said by Master Nyoe is of bibliographical concern but not a vital question in actual training in Zen. The primary role of koan in Zen training is to actualize the spirituality of the Zen saying in the student himself, here and now.

This koan is very short and simple: "Mind is not Buddha; wisdom is not Tao." From what aspect does Master Nansen take up Zen Truth here? The key terms used in this short saying—"mind," "Buddha," "wisdom," and "Tao"—have their own different connotations. From the standpoint of Zen experience, however, they are all vital words expressing in their respective nuances the fundamental Zen Truth.

The old Zen Masters emphatically stated, "You do not realize that your very mind is Buddha, and you seek for it outside yourself!" or, "Realize your own mind. There is no Buddha outside your mind." In the *Mumonkan* too there are several koan which, at least conceptually, sound more or less alike, such as the nineteenth, "Ordinary Mind Is Tao"; the twenty-seventh, "Neither Mind nor Buddha"; the thirtieth, "Mind Is Buddha"; and the thirty-third, "No Mind, No Buddha."

Though these are very important terms for expressing the fundamental Truth of Zen, yet such words as "mind," "Buddha," "wisdom," and "Tao" are only names temporarily given to the "ever unnamable 'it.' " An old Zen Master therefore warns us, "Be sure to detach yourself from all your clingings. Be sure not to attach yourself to nonclinging either."

It is, however, an unfortunate tendency of man that he clings to traditional labels. Master Nansen cut off this deep-rooted attachment of man to given names with his single *No.* It is his earnest wish out of compassion to free human beings from all their delusions and attachments and revive them as true men of peace and freedom. Names and words are nothing but the result of man's discriminating intellection. To cast away our attachment to all such labels is to live the One Truth right in front of us just as it is.

The Truth has been revealed in full in its as-it-is-ness in the past, and so it is revealed in its as-it-is-ness today. In your going and in your sitting, in the redness of flowers and the green of the willows, live the Truth as it is. When you do so, your True Self works freely; it is the peace and freedom of the man who has transcended the distinction of subject and object, yes and no.

For one who lives the nonattached life of the True Self, certainly mind is not Buddha; the sun rises every morning in the east, and the moon sets at night in the west. For him, "Wisdom is not Tao. A melon is round and smooth; a gourd is curved and crooked." How clear and how lucid! How transparent and penetrating! An old Zen Master rightly said, "What a shame it is even to speak the word 'Buddha'!" When Master Dogen returned to Japan after making a difficult voyage across the ocean and studying in China for a long while, he was asked, "What kind of Dharma have you obtained abroad?" His reply was, "Empty-handed I have returned home. I have only realized that the eyes are horizontal and the nose is vertical." Admirable indeed is his lucid spirituality.

"Mind is not Buddha; wisdom is not Tao," is the statement flowing out of Master Nansen's great compassion. We should grasp the essence of his compassionate instruction with deep appreciation.

An old commentary says, "What is called mind or wisdom is the Absolute Mind and Absolute Wisdom with which every being is originally born. Mind is the foundation, and wisdom is its working. The working of wisdom to reveal this mind in every phenomenon is called Tao. Nansen's mind and wisdom which are beyond expression are nothing else than the Great Tao of the original Buddha. But if it is explained in this way, people will cling to the explanation and abide in it. Nansen therefore broke them loose from this clinging by saying, 'Mind is not Buddha; wisdom is not Tao.' " Though this explanation is certainly correct, Master Nansen's heart is not there. I do not want you to miss the live spirit of this koan in your training by busying yourself with such philosophical explanations, which are as useless as putting another hat on top of one that is already on your head. Zen has its own unique vista, ever new, fresh, and vivid.

TEISHO ON MUMON'S COMMENTARY

"Of Nansen it has to be said that on getting old he was lost to shame. Just opening his stinking mouth a little, he reveals his family shame. Even so, only a very few feel grateful for it."

Master Mumon, as usual, by severely criticizing him with abusive language expresses his utmost admiration for Master Nansen's lucid and penetrating spirituality and his compassion toward his disciples.

"By uttering stinking words, you have disclosed the family shame to the public. What a shameless old fool you are!" Mumon sharply reproaches him. "The family shame," as explained in the twenty-second koan, originally meant the shame within the household that must be kept private and secret, but the meaning shifted to "the most precious and important secret of the family."

What Master Mumon really means in his commentary is: "Dear Master Nansen, how utterly kind and good-natured you are to disclose the important secret of the family that 'Mind is not Buddha; wisdom is not Tao'!"

"Even so," Mumon continues, "how few there are who can truly appreciate Master Nansen's heart and respond to his great compassion. What a pity!" Thus Master Mumon admires and respects the great Zen working of Master Nansen and at the same time admonishes and encourages his own disciples to be sincere in their training.

TEISHO ON MUMON'S POEM

> The sky is clear and the sun appears;
> Rain falls and the earth is moistened.
> Without restraint he has explained everything,
> Yet how few are able to grasp it!

"The sky is clear and the sun appears; rain falls and the earth is moistened," sings Master Mumon and presents before us, as concrete facts without any discrimination, the essence of Master Nansen's teisho: "Mind is not Buddha; wisdom is not Tao." Mumon is a great Master who had undergone hard and sincere training himself. These two lines show his high and lucid spirituality. Certainly they are the words of one who does "feel grateful." Together with Master Dogen's "the eyes are horizontal; the nose is vertical," it is a live and wise saying. Its truth never changes through all ages.

"Without restraint he has explained everything, yet how few are able to grasp it!" In these last two lines Master Mumon repeats his regret already expressed in the commentary. "Only a very few feel grateful!"

The Truth thus presented by Master Nansen, who out of his irresistible compassion disclosed the ultimate secret with all his power, will rarely be appreciated by people. Will there be any who can really thank him for his instruction?

Indirectly, Mumon is telling us how incomparably outstanding Master Nansen's spirituality is, as revealed in this koan.

35

Sen-Jo and Her Soul Are Separated

KOAN

Goso asked a monk, "Sen-jo and her soul are separated: which is the true one?"

MUMON'S COMMENTARY

If you are enlightened in the truth of this koan, you will then know that coming out of one husk and getting into another is like a traveler's putting up in hotels. In case you are not yet enlightened, do not rush about blindly. When suddenly earth, water, fire, and air are decomposed, you will be like a crab fallen into boiling water, struggling with its seven arms and eight legs. Do not say then that I have not warned you.

MUMON'S POEM

Ever the same, the moon among the clouds;
Different from each other, the mountain and the valley.
How wonderful! How blessed!
Is this one, or two?

TEISHO ON THE KOAN

This koan consists of a question Master Goso asked his disciple, "Sen-jo and her soul are separated: which is the true one?" (The *jo* of Sen-jo means a girl, while *Sen* is a proper name.) At a glance it sounds very simple, yet from olden times this has been studied by Zen students as one of the nanto koans.

Master Hoen, commonly known as Master Goso because he lived on Mount Goso, was born in Shisen-sho and was ordained as a Buddhist monk when he was thirty-five years old. He started his academic studies in Buddhism at Seito, the capital of the province, and was known as a good scholar monk. One day, however, Hoen read the following sentences: "It is said in Buddhism that when a Bodhisattva sees with his satori eye, the working and the principle are fused, circumstances and the essence are unified, and subjectivity and objectivity are not separated. A non-Buddhist scholar argued against this, saying, 'If subjectivity and objectivity are not separated, how can that fact itself be proved?' No one could answer, but the Venerable Genjo spoke out, 'It is the same as if one realizes personally how cold or warm the water is by drinking it himself.' "

Hoen said to himself, "I know 'cold and warm,' but what is 'to realize it personally'?" Hoen put the question to his teacher, but his teacher could not clarify it for him and told him, "If you want to solve this question, go to the south and ask a Zen Master." With firm determination Hoen left his home to visit Zen Masters at various places. While he was studying under Master Hakuun Shutan, one day a monk asked the Master a question and was severely rebuked by him. This incident spiritually inspired Hoen, who happened to witness it. Later, Hoen heard the following teisho by Master Shutan: "There are several Zen monks from Mount Ro, all of whom have had satori. If you should let them speak, they could give beautiful talks. If you asked them regarding various koan, they could answer clearly. If you wanted them to write a pithy commentary, they could do so nicely. Yet they have not attained 'it.' " This teisho aroused the Great Doubt in Hoen, and after having worked hard with this koan for several days he was finally fully enlightened. Moreover, this realization experience wiped away the smack of Zen from his previous experiences. Thereafter Hoen's reputation as a great Zen Master gradually spread in Zen circles.

For forty long years Hoen earnestly instructed his disciples. One day he mounted the rostrum, declared his retirement, returned to his room and took a bath and shaved his head, and the next day he calmly died. It was in 1104, and Hoen was probably over eighty years old. Master Engo, who is famous as a compiler of *Hekigan-roku* ("The Blue Rock Records"), was a disciple of Master Goso Hoen.

The story of "Sen-jo and Her Soul are Separated" is taken from a T'ang dynasty legend. In Koshu in China in that dynasty there lived a man named Chokan. He had two daughters, but as the elder one died young he loved the younger daughter Sen-jo all the more and made much of her. Since she was an unusually beautiful girl, many young men wished to marry her. Sen's father selected a good youth named Hinryo from her many suitors and decided to give Sen-jo to him. Sen-jo, however, had a secret lover named Ochu, who was Chokan's nephew. When Ochu was a child, Sen's father had told him in jest, "Ochu and Sen-jo will make a well-matched couple. You two had better get married when you grow up." This remark made them believe that they were engaged, and in the course of time they found that they were in love with each other.

Sen-jo, who had suddenly been told by her father to marry Hinryo, was greatly cast down and depressed. As for Ochu, when he heard of it he was so distressed that he decided to leave the village, for he could not bear to live anywhere near her. One evening he secretly left his homeland by boat without even telling Sen-jo. At midnight he noticed a vague figure running along the bank as if to follow his boat. He stopped to see who it was, and to his great surprise and joy he found it was his beloved. He was overcome with joy at the truth of her heart, and they embraced each other in tears. As they could not now dare to return to Sen-jo's father, they traveled to the remote country of Shoku, where they were married.

Five years passed after they had left home. Sen-jo, who was now the mother of two children, could not forget her native country, and her longing for her parents and home increased day by day. One day, in tears, she confessed her painful longing to her husband. "Loving you and following you, I left my home without permission, and I have stayed with you in this remote country. I wonder how my parents are getting on. Having left home as I did, against my parents' wishes, an ungrateful daughter like myself may never be able to return home!" Ochu, who was in fact also longing for his homeland, calmed her saying, "Let us then go back to Koshu and beg your parents' pardon." Immediately they hired a boat and returned to Koshu, their dear old home.

Leaving Sen-jo at the port, Ochu first went to Chokan's house by himself, apologized for their ungrateful act, and told him the whole story. Chokan was astonished and asked Ochu, "Which girl are you talking about?" "Your daughter Sen-jo, Father," replied Ochu. Chokan said, "My daughter Sen? From the time you left Koshu she has been sick in bed and has been unable to speak." Ochu was equally taken aback and tried to explain, "Sen-jo certainly followed me and we have lived together in the country of Shoku. She has borne two children and is physically very well. If you do not believe what I say, please come with me to the port, for she is there in the boat waiting for me."

Chokan, mystified, sent an old servant to the boat to check, and he returned to report that it was unmistakably Sen-jo. Chokan then went to her room in his house, and sure enough, his daughter Sen was still there sick in bed. In bewilderment Chokan told the sick Sen-jo the whole story, whereupon, looking extremely delighted, she got out of bed still without saying a word. In the meantime the Sen-jo who had come ashore arrived at Chokan's house in a cart. The sick Sen-jo went out from her home to meet her, and just as the Sen-jo from the boat alighted from the cart, the two Sen-jos became one.

Chokan, the father, spoke to Sen-jo, "Ever since Ochu left this village, you have not uttered a word, and you have always been absent in mind as if you were drunk. Now I see that your soul left your body and has been with Ochu." To this Sen-jo replied, "I did not know at all that I was sick in bed at home. When I learned that Ochu had left this village in distress, I followed his boat that night, feeling as if it were a dream. I myself am not sure which was the real me—the one with you, sick in bed, or the one with Ochu as his wife."

This is a brief outline of a novel called *Rikon-ki* ("The Story of the Separated Soul").

Master Goso Hoen has presented this well-known story, and inquires, "Which is the true one?" Needless to say, he is not asking you a vulgar question as to which is the true Sen-jo in this tale, which is something like a ghost story. He refers to the story of Sen-jo, who with her one body turned out to be two, as a means of training his monks so that they will open their Zen eye.

Master Mumon, too, agrees with Master Hoen's intention and asks his disciples, "Which is the true one?" He is demanding that they have penetrating, clear Zen spirituality to see through it. Let me remind you, his question is addressed to you today as well.

If we reflect on ourselves, don't we realize that we are all in a situation similar to Sen-jo's, with her soul separated? There is the "I" that always wants to do just as "I" please, trying to satisfy "my" desires and enjoy life as much as possible. There is also another "I," who feels lonely in such a pleasure-seeking life and even finds it detestable. Which is the true "I"?

Saint Shinran, who is respected as the founder of Jodo Shinshu (the True Pure Land School of Buddhism) in Japan, is famous for his lamentation, "Deep and heavy are my sins; rampant are my passions. I am definitely destined for hell!" Shinran, who thus severely criticizes himself and struggles to be saved, cannot be different from the hopelessly sinful Shinran. "Which is the true one?" This is the question to be asked by each one of us in our life.

Now returning to the subject, is the Sen-jo sick in bed with her body alone the true Sen-jo, or is the Sen-jo with the separated soul alone the true Sen-jo? If we take up the body as the true Sen-jo, then the soul would turn out to be false. If we recognize soul as the true Sen-jo, then the body has to be false. In actuality, however, there is no human being with a soul alone without a body, or with a body alone without a soul. A living human being cannot be defined as soul or body. He is the Reality which is neither one nor two. There is no idle argument that can distinguish one from the other as true or false. In other words, what exists is the Reality of man, which is neither one nor two, and this Reality naturally develops its working in two aspects, as body and soul.

Buddhist philosophy explains the above problem as follows: we should transcend the dualistic oppositions of true and false and be based on the Absolute Oneness. From this standpoint, a new vista will be opened where we can live and enjoy true freedom to make use of the dualistic phenomena in the world. For this Absolute Subjectivity, or Oneness, which transcends true and false, the distinction of true and false has no significance. Master Yoka therefore says in his *Shodoka:*

> Delusions need not be removed;
> Truth need not be sought after.
> The Reality of ignorance is at once Buddha Nature;
> The illusory form is at once Dharma body.

Such Buddhist philosophical speculations may very well provide a reasonable intellectual interpretation, but they cannot be a Zen answer. Zen insists that each one of us must actually live the Absolute Subjectivity as a fact of his own experience. This is exactly the real motive of Master Mumon in presenting the story of Sen-jo as a Zen koan here.

The *Shoto-roku* contains the following poem written by a monk by the name of Fuyu Chizo, who after studying hard with this koan of "Sen-jo and Her Soul are Separated" under Master Hoen finally had his satori. The poem may help to give you a glimpse into the koan's real significance:

> The two girls were unified to become a young wife.
> The working has ended, no interfusing any more.
> Coming and going leave no traces at all.
> You travelers, please do not ask me which path I once took.

The meaning of the poem is: "The two Sen-jos came together and became one young woman. The Reality of this One Absolute Subjectivity can never be explained by words and letters. Just this Reality—and there is no room for intellect or reason here. Now that I am One Absolute Subjectivity through and through, there has actually been no coming or going, no subject or object. Please do not ask me, my fellow beings, which path I took in the past How can I ever recall such an old story?"

There is another poem written by an old Zen Master in reply to this koan:

> The moon on the waves,
> Now scattered, now unified!

TEISHO ON MUMON'S COMMENTARY

"If you are enlightened in the truth of this koan, you will then know that coming out of one husk and getting into another is like a traveler's putting up in hotels. In case you are not yet enlightened, do not rush about blindly. When suddenly earth, water, fire, and air are decomposed, you will be like a crab fallen into boiling water, struggling with its seven arms and eight legs. Do not say then that I have not warned you."

Master Mumon, in commenting on this koan, first points to the essence, "If you are enlightened in the truth of this koan, you will then know that coming out of one husk and getting into another is like a traveler's putting up in hotels." If you can be enlightened in the Truth of Zen (needless to say, the Truth of Zen is the Truth of I-myself) by this koan of "Sen-jo and Her Soul are Separated," you are then a truly free man under any circumstances. Transcending all the contradictions and limitations, you develop the dynamic working of your free life as the Absolute Subjectivity wherever you may be. Whatever appearance you may happen to take, the Absolute Subjectivity, or the True Self, remains the same. It will just take one form or another at one time or another, in accordance with the situation. It may be compared to a hermit crab which comes out of one husk or shell and gets into the next one. It may again be like a traveler who moves from one hotel to another. In other words, for one who lives his Absolute Subjectivity, the outer and inner Sen-jo are neither one nor two, but there is just the true Sen-jo.

Two of the phrases in the first sentence—"coming out of one husk and getting into another" and "a traveler's putting up in hotels"—seem to refer to the journey of our life, especially our journey from life to death, which is the ultimate question for man. The solution of this question of life and death will be the fundamental solution in a man's life.

If you can personally attain to the truth of this koan, then you will be able to declare that to live is to be a form of your True Self at one time and at one place; to die is also to be a form of your True Self at one time and at one place; life and death are not two different things.

It may be just like big and small waves in the ocean. The "true one," or the Truth, can be likened to the water itself, and husks and hotels to the numerous waves. The water can take various forms as waves—now a billow, now a ripple. From the standpoint of the water, each wave is its form at a certain time and place. After all, the fact that they are all water does not change. Master Dogen therefore taught us, "If there is Buddha in life-and-death, there is no life-and-death." "Buddha" here is another name for the "true one," which is forever unchanging.

Master Mumon's commentary continues, "In case you are not yet enlightened, do not rush about blindly." He says, "If you cannot yet grasp the 'true one,' in spite of my teisho above, stop making a fuss, looking after this philosophy and that, this teaching and that. Put a definite end to all these maneuvers and singleheartedly inquire into 'What is the "true one"?' Plunge directly into it!" Then he goes on to say, "When suddenly earth, water, fire, and air are decomposed, you will be like a crab fallen into the boiling water, struggling with its seven arms and eight legs."

People in ancient times thought that a human body was composed of the four basic elements: earth, water, fire, and air. "When suddenly earth, water, fire, and air are decomposed" therefore refers to death. Master Mumon vehemently warns the monks, "Those of you who have not awakened to the 'true one,' those of you who have not yet attained fundamental peace of mind, will not be able to pass away in peace when the time suddenly comes for you to die, but will be in miserable agony just like a crab fallen into the boiling water and struggling with its many arms and legs." Master Mumon ends his commentary with "Do not say then that I have not warned you." He did not forget to add his compassionate warning, "You may regret on your deathbed that you have not attained the 'true one,' but it will be too late." This is kind and vital advice for us today, too.

TEISHO ON MUMON'S POEM

Ever the same, the moon among the clouds;
Different from each other, the mountain and the valley.
How wonderful! How blessed!
Is this one, or two?

Comparing the "true one" to the moon among the clouds, and the illusory one to the mountain and valley, Mumon sings, "Ever the same, the moon among the clouds; different from each other, the mountain and the valley." The moon among the clouds is forever unchanging wherever you may see it. Views on earth vary from this valley to that mountain. If you once realize that the truth of the beautiful view of the valley is solely due to the moon, then you will know how foolish it is to argue about equality and differentiation, the true one and the illusory one, the outer Sen-jo and the inner Sen-jo. Just as it is, in its as-it-is-ness, whatever you see or whatever you hear is forever blessed. It is neither one nor two. This actual daily life of ours, as it is, is the blessed life in which we work and rejoice, hand in hand with all the Patriarchs. Can there be anything more wonderful, more remarkable?

Master Kido wrote the following famous poem on this koan:

> Peach branches and reeds in front,
> Paper money after the funeral cart.
> O disciples of the old foreigner,
> You will not enter into the realm of the dead.

The first two lines describe funeral customs in China. Those who lead the funeral procession carry in their hands peach branches or brooms made of reeds in order to keep away devils. After the coffin follow those who carry paper money to be burned to appease devils. These lines refer to funeral services. Speaking of the oneness of life and death, what an awkward picture you present! How could the devils attack you?

In the third line Master Kido speaks to the "students under Bodhidharma," or the "Zen man worthy of the name"; the "old foreigner" refers to Bodhidharma. In the fourth line Kido declares, "Those Zen men will never enter into the realm of the dead." What does the realm of the dead signify?

Master Hoen first presses you, "Sen-jo and her soul are separated. Which is the 'true one'?" Out of his compassion he could not help warning us not to take the "true one" as one-sided equality or empty nothingness. Master Mumon therefore sings with Master Hoen in one voice, "How wonderful! How blessed! Is this one, or two?"

For the one who has clearly opened his Zen eye, everything, as it is, is "it." If he stands, the very place where he stands is "it." If he sits, the very place where he sits is at once the "true one." It is, as it is, the whole universe.

36

Meeting a Man of Tao on the Way

Goso said, "If you meet a man of Tao on the way, greet him neither with words nor with silence. Now tell me, how will you greet him?"

MUMON'S COMMENTARY

If you can give an apt answer to the question, it certainly is a matter for congratulation. If you are not yet able to give one, be alert in every aspect of your life.

MUMON'S POEM

> If you meet a man of Tao on the way,
> Greet him neither with words nor with silence.
> I'll give him with my fist the hardest blow I can—
> Get it at once, get it immediately!

TEISHO ON THE KOAN

As Master Goso Hoen also appeared in the thirty-fifth koan, "Sen-jo and Her Soul Are Separated," details of his life are omitted here.

One day Master Hoen put a question to his disciples, "When you meet a man who has attained Tao, it is far from being adequate to greet him with words; it is completely irrelevant to greet him with silence. Under such circumstances, how will you greet him?"

Although the question "If you meet a man of Tao on the way, greet him neither with words nor with silence. How then will you greet him?" is introduced here as Master Hoen's saying, it is originally ascribed to Master Kyogen Chikan, who appeared in the fifth koan, "Kyogen's Man Up a Tree." In *Keitoku Dento-roku*, volume 29, the following poem is recorded together with a series of other poems, called "Talks on Tao," all by Master Kyogen:

> Clear, lucid, and no hindrance whatsoever;
> Standing all by yourself, you do not rely on anything.
> If you meet a man of Tao on the way,
> Greet him neither with words nor with silence.

Whether the saying in the koan originated with Master Kyogen Chikan or with Master Goso Hoen is a literary question and has, needless to say, nothing to do with its value as a Zen koan. Master Hoen probably was interested in the Zen significance of the saying and quoted it here as a koan to help in refining the Zen ability of his monks.

A "man of Tao" is one who has attained the essence of Zen, or the Truth, and he has naturally transcended the dualistic opposition of words and silence. "If you come across such a man, one who does not live in the dualistic domain of words and silence, how will you greet him?" By pressing his disciples with this question, Master Hoen drives them to the extremity of absolute contradiction, from which he hopes that they will revive as men of real freedom.

As already explained in the twenty-fourth koan, "Abandon Words and Speaking," the Truth of the universe, or the essence of Zen, is really separate from all names, forms, and relativistic distinctions. With silence, or no-words, only equality, which is half of Reality, can be expressed; while with speaking, or words, only differentiation, the other half of the Reality, can be expressed. A Zen man should be firmly based on Absolute Reality, which transcends equality and differentiation. Unless he is capable of making free use of speaking and silence without committing himself to equality or differentiation, he is not worthy to be called a Zen man.

With this challenging connotation, Master Hoen demands of his disciples, "Now tell me, how will you greet him?" There may be some who might declare with rash boldness, "It is easy enough. I can readily greet him without any difficulty." His greeting, however, has to have the lucidity and transparency that penetrates the foundation of his personality and transcends dualistic distinctions of space and time. No one can easily respond to this demand.

As words have no fixed forms and no binding meanings, a Zen man speaks without a tongue. As silence has no fixed form or meaning, when a Zen man is silent there is live working in his silence. This is how a true man of Tao works.

A Zen Master gave the following interestingly significant teisho: "If you do not speak out what is in your mind, you will feel heavy in the stomach. Yet if you speak, your tongue may cut your throat. Just speak as you should, and do not speak as you should not." This is indeed an excellent teisho, but because his instruction, "Speak as you should, and do not speak as you should not," sounds very much like an ethical admonition, I should like to warn students not to interpret it superficially in the ethical sense alone and thus fail to read into it its Zen significance.

In the *Vimalakirti Sutra* this question of "speaking and silence" is taken up in a mondo between Vimalakirti and Manjusri, the Bodhisattva of prajna wisdom. It is a very famous story in Buddhism: Bodhisattva Manjusri, together with many other Bodhisattvas, visited Vimalakirti to inquire about his sickness. Vimalakirti asked Manjusri, "How does a Bodhisattva attain the Dharma of nonduality?" Manjusri replied, "According to my view, the Dharma of nonduality is of no-word, no-speaking, no-presentation, no-realization, and is separate from all sorts of mondo. A Bodhisattva attains this Dharma of nonduality." Having thus answered, Manjusri then pressed Vimalakirti for his response to the same question, "We have all stated our views. What is your answer?" Vimalakirti then remained "silent"—he said not a word. Seeing this, Manjusri praised him ardently, "How wonderful, how wonderful! How can there ever be words and letters? He truly has attained the Dharma of nonduality!"

If the Dharma of nonduality is verbally explained as "no-word, no-speaking, no-presentation, no-realization," it is already committed to words and speaking. Once it is said to be "separate from all sorts of mondo," it is already committed to words and speaking. If, again, one should say that Vimalakirti's "silence" is the great response, his silence is already marred.

A Zen Master tries to eradicate the cause of human ignorance by an unexpected demand: "Greet him neither with words nor with silence!"

Master Soen, who was Dr. D. T. Suzuki's teacher in Zen, has a poem on "Vimalakirti's silence":

> For long, the old tune sounded throughout Viya in vain,
> But three thousand years later, here is his appreciator.

> Fluent is his speaking, both with pen and with tongue:
> This is the Truth of Vimalakirti's silence.

"The old tune" refers to the Dharma of nonduality, that is, the Truth that transcends speaking and silence. Vimalakirti has been playing the tune of the Dharma of nonduality in the city of Viya, but there has been nobody who could really appreciate it. Three thousand years later, here is one who has directly grasped the heart of the old tune. This man is fluent in speaking and in silence. With his pen and with his tongue he freely develops his working. In doing so he is living the Truth of Vimalakirti's silence.

Master Soen writes freely and speaks eloquently, and for him this pure act itself, just as it is, is nothing but the Truth of Vimalakirti's silence. Only when a person has transcended the dualism of speaking and silence can he attain real freedom and develop real creative working.

There are similar mondo by other Masters. For instance, in *Keitoku Dentoroku*, volume 13, in the chapter on Master Shuzan Shonen: "A monk inquired as follows: 'It is said that if one meets a man of Tao on the way, one must not greet him either with words or with silence. I wonder how one should greet him.' The Master said, 'I have seen through the three thousand worlds [the whole universe]!' "

And in *Goto Egen*, volume 7, in the chapter on Master Seppo Gison: "A monk put the question, 'An old Zen Master said that if one should meet a man of Tao on the way, one must not greet him either with words or with silence. I wonder how one should greet him!' The Master said, 'Have a cup of tea, please!' "

Master Shuzan says, "I have seen through the three thousand worlds," and Master Seppo says, "Have a cup of tea, please!" How and why can they be answers that are not committed to words and silence? Unless you can give a clear and concrete reply to this question, you are still one of those who are at the mercy of words and silence.

TEISHO ON MUMON'S COMMENTARY

"If you can give an apt answer to the question, it certainly is a matter for congratulation. If you are not yet able to give one, be alert in every aspect of your life."

Quoting an old Zen Master's saying, "If you meet a man of Tao on the way, greet him neither with words nor with silence," Master Hoen insistently asks his disciples, "Now tell me, how will you greet him?" Master Mumon, commenting on this koan, says that if you can give an answer exactly to the point of the question, that is, if you can correctly and pertinently greet such a man, you are really to be congratulated. Admiring most highly the working of such a capable Zen man, Master Mumon implies that there are not too many of them, and he tries to stimulate his disciples.

Mumon goes on to say, "If you are not able to greet him pertinently, and fail to give the apt reply to Master Hoen's request, your training is very incomplete. You should discipline yourself assiduously and be alert in every aspect of your life." "Every aspect" means "whatever you do at every moment in your life." What a painstakingly kind instruction this is! Master Mumon urges us to get firm hold of the live Truth that transcends words and silence in our walking and our lying down, that is, in every movement in our everyday life.

What is it that sees? What is it that hears? What is it that thinks? Keep on inquiring what it is, through and through, until there is no longer anyone who sees, hears, or thinks. When you have thus actually gone beyond the extremity of seeing and hearing, the new vista will open up to you.

Master Hakuin often wrote as his commentary poem on the picture of Bodhisattva Kwannon:

> With her eyes she hears the song of the spring;
> With her ears she sees the colorings of the mountain.

Is he telling us that a true Zen man must transcend hearing and seeing in his very hearing and seeing? We certainly must be alert in every aspect of our life. If you keep on working assiduously, with sincerity and devotion, the day will surely come when your eye is opened to the Zen Truth, which transcends words and silence.

TEISHO ON MUMON'S POEM

> If you meet a man of Tao on the way,
> Greet him neither with words nor with silence.
> I'll give him with my fist the hardest blow I can—
> Get it at once, get it immediately!

In his commentary poem on this koan, Master Mumon repeats the koan as it is, and sings, "If you meet a man of Tao on the way, greet him neither with words nor with silence." There is an old saying, "Each time it is presented, each time it is new." If one fails to appreciate, in these first two lines, Hoen's Zen freely at work transcending words and silence, he does not deserve to be called a Zen man. The last two lines are obviously unnecessary additions.

Here Master Mumon is excessively kind and puts in an extraordinary additional remark, "If I were to meet such a man, I would give him with my fist the hardest blow I could." This is quite a rough greeting, isn't it? He seems to assume a firm, straightforward, square attitude and says, "What nonsense are you still talking about!" Then he goes on to say, "Get it at once, get it immediately!"

Essentially, there is no such thing as getting it or not getting it in Zen. With your fist, transcend the fist; in your pain transcend the pain. Then look and behold! Truth is right there.

Master Hakuin criticizes Mumon, saying, "I do not like these last two lines. Master Mumon committed a blunder." Rather than calling it a blunder, I should say that Master Mumon is here unnecessarily rough, showing off his Zen-monkishness. A Zen man has to be able to act more decently and peacefully in developing his Zen working.

Now, if *you* meet a man of Tao on the way, greet him neither with words nor with silence. How do you greet him? I want your direct answer.

37

The Oak Tree in the Front Garden

A monk once asked Joshu, "What is the meaning of the Patriarch's coming from the West?" Joshu answered, "The oak tree in the front garden."

MUMON'S COMMENTARY

If you can firmly grasp the essence of Joshu's answer, for you there is no Sakyamuni in the past and no Maitreya in the future.

MUMON'S POEM

> Words do not convey actualities;
> Letters do not embody the spirit of the mind.
> He who attaches himself to words is lost;
> He who abides with letters will remain in ignorance.

TEISHO ON THE KOAN

Master Joshu left many koan, and this is one of his most famous; another is "Joshu's 'Mu.'" As I introduced him in that first koan, I shall not repeat it here.

One day a monk asked Master Joshu, "What is the meaning of the Patriarch's coming from the West?" and Master Joshu answered, "The oak tree in the front garden." This is a very short and terse koan.

Some explanations may be necessary for the phrase "the meaning of the Patriarch's coming from the West." The Patriarch here is Bodhidharma, who is regarded as the First Patriarch of Zen in China. Bodhidharma came all the way by ship from India, in the West, to Kanto-sho in South China, and then moved to Suzan in North China, where he stayed for nine years. He rejected all the scholastic approaches to Buddhism, insisted on the primary importance of realization experience in Buddhism, and laid the foundation of Zen in China. "The meaning of the Patriarch's coming from the West" refers to Bodhidharma's true intention in coming to China.

As Zen flourished as a new school of Buddhism in China, in the course of time the phrase "the meaning of the Patriarch's coming from the West" became a traditional expression in Zen circles, and the sense of it came to be "the Truth of Zen" or "the essence of Zen."

You will often come across the question "What is the meaning of the Patriarch's coming from the West?" in Zen writings after the T'ang dynasty. In all but a few exceptional cases it can be taken in the same sense as "What is the Truth of Zen?" It is a unique Zen question, directly asking what is the essence of Zen.

The answers given to this question by various Masters recorded in Zen writings may amount to several hundred, yet they are so varied that there seems to be no consistency whatsoever. It is utterly impossible for general readers to come to any logical conclusion. Furthermore, these answers are surprisingly free and unexpected, and to all appearances seem to have no relation at all either to the First Patriarch or to Zen teachings. Those whose Zen eye is not open will be completely at a loss as to how to understand them. I should like to remind you however that in these illogical and extraordinary answers, the old Masters' free Zen working is vividly presented.

Now let us return to the koan. In reply to a monk's question, "What is the meaning of the Patriarch's coming from the West?" Master Joshu answered, "The oak tree in the front garden." How and why is the essence of Zen in "the oak tree in the front garden?" How and why can the oak tree be Joshu's Zen? Here is the core of this koan.

According to the *Sayings of Joshu*, this mondo develops as follows:

A monk asked, "What is the meaning of the Patriarch's coming from the West?"

MASTER: "The oak tree in the front garden."

MONK: "Please, O Master, do not teach us referring to objectivity."
MASTER: "I do not teach you referring to objectivity."
MONK: "What is the meaning of the Patriarch's coming from the West?"
MASTER: "The oak tree in the front garden."

Oak trees are tall, and there are a lot of them in the northern part of China. There must have been many oak trees growing around the monastery where Master Joshu lived.

As we can see in this mondo, the questioning monk apparently presupposed that a holy, fundamental Truth like "the meaning of the Patriarch's coming from the West" must have very sacred, lofty, and profound significance. Master Joshu saw through the monk's mind and tried to smash his bias. People usually think of the Buddha mind in contrast to the ignorant mind, interpret objectivity as standing over against subjectivity, and understand the oak tree as a visible thing in front of them. This is the actual situation with ordinary people who live within the dualistic limitations of human life. Zen demands that we break through these fixed limitations and be reborn in the new world of quite another dimension.

Master Mumon extracted only the first half of the mondo from the *Sayings of Joshu,* namely, "A monk once asked Joshu, 'What is the meaning of the Patriarch's coming from the West?' Joshu answered, 'The oak tree in the front garden,' " and presented it to his monks as a koan. "The oak tree" is certainly an unapproachable fortress. This answer, "the oak tree," must have been his compassionate means to deprive his disciples of all their knowledge and intellect so that they would cast away all dualistic distinctions such as subject and object, I and you. He wished somehow to awaken them to the absolutely free and ever new Zen spirituality. An old Zen Master commented, "The answer of 'the oak tree' is like a solid iron wedge that refuses all interpretations and baffles understanding. You can never even touch it with your tongue or words. Arouse the Great Doubt within yourself, and singleheartedly work at it."

Master Rinzai, being asked by his disciple, "What is the meaning of the Patriarch's coming from the West?" said, "If there is any meaning at all, you can never save yourself." Is there no meaning? Alas! you have missed it altogether. If you say there is no meaning in the Patriarch's coming from the West, you have definitely lost sight of the Truth and you have to be severely beaten by the Master.

Master Joshu declares that it is just "the oak tree in the front garden." When the whole universe is the oak tree, there is nothing that is not the oak tree—or there is not even I-myself. How can there be room for the subject-object distinction? How can there be any names and forms to be attached? At this very moment when you are thus reborn as your True Self which is no-self, you can get hold of the Reality of the oak tree, and of Master Joshu, who is so vividly alive.

Let me remind you that Zen cannot be a lifeless conceptual conclusion. In actual training, if you should say to the Master, "It is just the oak tree in the front garden," he might immediately retort, "Show me the color of that oak tree! How deep is its root?" If you hesitate even for a moment, the Master will immediately make a raid on you: "Nay, this is a dead monk!" and drive you out of the room of sanzen.

There is a famous waka poem by an ancient Zen Master.

> Colorings of mountains and songs of the stream—
> All are the voice and features of our dear Sakyamuni!

Wonderful poem though it is, never lightly come to the easy conclusion and say, "Since the Buddha Nature pervades the whole universe, each phenomenon in differentiation is nothing but a manifestation of the original Buddha Nature. The oak tree in the front garden is therefore also the Buddha Nature itself." If you busy yourself with such idle reasoning, you can never expect to have even a glimpse of Master Joshu's superb spirituality.

Another famous mondo has developed from this koan. After Master Joshu passed away, Master Hogen asked Kakutesshi, who for a long time had devotedly studied under Master Joshu, "I have heard that your teacher, Master Joshu, had the koan of the oak tree. Is it true or not?" Kakutesshi replied, "My late teacher had no such koan. I hope, Venerable Sir, you will not slander my teacher." Kakutesshi was Master Joshu's good disciple who closely attended on him. He could not possibly have been ignorant of his teacher's famous koan of "the oak tree." From what standpoint did he assert, "My late teacher had no such koan?" Further, why is it slandering Master Joshu if he is said to have had the koan of the oak tree? Kakutesshi's answer is an excellent koan, not even yielding to Joshu's "oak tree."

An old Zen Master commented about Kakutesshi, "A good son does not live on his father's money." From olden times Masters have spoken in the highest possible terms of Kakutesshi's Zen ability, shown in his reply to be even greater than that of his teacher. Why? Just this "oak tree in the front garden"! Those who know, know it. Those who ask, do not know it.

A Zen Master made this waka poem as a commentary:

> Nothing whatsoever to say:
> This singing of the pine trees,
> Answering without being asked.

Be no-mind through and through. Then whatever work you do is good.

There is still another famous koan associated with the koan of "The Oak Tree." Master Egen, the founder of Myoshinji in Kyoto, was a great Zen Master who became a teacher of the emperor. Though he is very famous, no talks of his have been handed down except one single sentence: "The koan of 'The Oak Tree' has the working of a bandit—so shrewd, terrifying, and robbing us of everything." When Master Ingen, who came to Japan from China in the Tokugawa period, visited Myoshinji he was disappointed to learn that no talks of Master Egen, the founder, had been preserved. He was filled with awe, however, when he came across the only saying left by Master Egen: "The koan of 'The Oak Tree' has the working of a bandit—so shrewd, terrifying, and robbing us of everything." Ingen said, "This single saying excels a hundred volumes of talks," and prostrated himself before the Hall of the Founder in ardent admiration.

What is the "working of the bandit" in the koan of "The Oak Tree"? Grasp it directly and use it as your own. Otherwise this koan will remain a lifeless talk about concepts. I am afraid I have again spoken too much.

TEISHO ON MUMON'S COMMENTARY

"If you can firmly grasp the essence of Joshu's answer, for you there is no Sakyamuni in the past and no Maitreya in the future."

Commenting on Master Joshu's reply, Master Mumon asks us to "firmly grasp the essence." To "firmly grasp the essence" is to plunge directly into the oak tree and be the oak tree through and through. When one is thoroughly "it," and all of himself is cast away, everything is he-himself. Time is he-himself; space is he-himself; and each and every thing is he-himself—not to speak of the oak tree.

Master Joshu has another mondo on the oak tree. A monk asked, "Has the oak tree the Buddha Nature or not?" Master Joshu replied, "Yes, it has." The monk asked, "When does the oak tree attain Buddhahood?" The Master said, "Wait until the great universe collapses." Then the monk asked, "When does the great universe collapse?" And the Master answered, "Wait until the oak tree attains Buddhahood."

In line with Master Mumon's "firmly grasp the essence," the above mondo is very interesting. Be that as it may, Master Mumon says, "If you can firmly grasp the essence, for you there is no Sakyamuni in the past and no Maitreya in the future." The advent of Sakyamuni is nothing else than the oak tree; the coming of Maitreya is nothing else than the oak tree—what else can there be?

Standing alone all by yourself, your singing and dancing are nothing but the oak tree! Master Mumon's commentary is full of power and authority.

TEISHO ON MUMON'S POEM

> Words do not convey actualities;
> Letters do not embody the spirit of the mind.
> He who attaches himself to words is lost;
> He who abides with letters will remain in ignorance.

You may speak the word "fire," but your mouth is not burned; you may say "water," yet your throat is not moistened. Truly words do not represent facts. Truth has the creative power to produce verbal expressions, whereas verbal expressions once created are only descriptions of the Truth. Words work within their own limitations and cannot reproduce the Truth.

"Letters do not embody the spirit of the mind." However beautiful expressions may be, they remain concepts and thoughts unless the transcendental leap has been made into quite another dimension and the Truth has been grasped. Mere concepts without experience cannot be in accord with the live working of man's mind.

"He who attaches himself to words is lost." If one clings to verbal expressions and lacks the ability to grasp the essence that transcends them, he will forever miss the Truth.

"He who abides with letters will remain in ignorance." If one clings to the superficial meaning of sayings and is unable to go beyond verbal limitations, he will lose sight of the Truth and will have to live in ignorance forever.

The talk of "the oak tree in the front garden" must never be mere talk. It is the live Joshu working here, now, face to face with you. It is the Truth that penetrates through me-myself and the world. Be awakened to the One Truth, Master Mumon is urging us.

Incidentally, this poem was originally written by Master Tozan Shusho, and Master Mumon quoted it unchanged for his commentary poem on this koan. Needless to say, the scholarly concern as to who the original author was and how that other Master made use of it in upholding his Zen, are two different questions which must not be confused.

38

A Buffalo Passes Through a Window

Goso said, "To give an example, it is like a buffalo passing through a window. Its head, horns, and four legs have all passed through. Why is it that its tail cannot?"

MUMON'S COMMENTARY

If you can penetrate to the point of this koan, open your Zen eye to it, and give a turning word to it, you will then be able to repay the four obligations above and help the three existences below. If you still cannot do so, work with the tail singleheartedly until you can really grasp it as your own.

MUMON'S POEM

If it passes through, it falls into a ditch;
If it turns back, it is destroyed.
This tiny tail,
How extremely marvelous!

TEISHO ON THE KOAN

This is famous as a typical nanto koan in Zen circles. A Zen Master, at the beginning of his teisho on this koan, said, "The key to a koan lies in completely casting oneself away, and being awakened to the spirituality of absolute freedom in every differentiation. This koan is one of 'Hakuin's Eight Nanto Koans.' Be it 'Mu' or 'the sound of one hand clapping,' once one has truly broken through the barrier [the koan], he must be able to break through any koan. There is no distinction of easy and difficult in Dharma. People say, 'One cut, and all is cut.' I will say, 'One cut, and no cut!' Dharma is something that can never be cut, however you may try. If your first breaking through is not thoroughgoing, your study will forever be halfway and lukewarm." This is a penetrating remark that the student in training ought not to pass over.

The Goso in the koan is Master Hoen of Mount Goso, who has appeared on several previous occasions. Master Mumon extracted this paragraph from Master Hoen's teisho, "To give an example, it is like a buffalo passing through a window. Its head, horns, and four legs have all passed through. Why is it that its tail cannot?" And he presented it as a koan to his monks as a means of refining their spirituality.

This koan takes the form of a simile, which is apparent from the way it starts, "To give an example. . . ." From ancient times literary scholars have suggested several possible sources for this story, which has been subjected to a variety of ethical and philosophical interpretations. I will leave the issue to specialists in the field, for it has no important significance when the story is taken up as a Zen koan. The sole concern of a koan is how directly it points to the essence of Zen and how aptly it can be used to encourage the students' training.

Now let us return to the koan. Master Hoen says, "To give an example, it is like a buffalo passing through a window. Its head, horns, and four legs have all passed through." "It" essentially has no name, no form. What in the world does the buffalo symbolize? What is it that is given the temporary name of a buffalo? Whether your Zen eye is opened to see through it or not is the first barrier of this koan.

An old Master commented on "Its head, horns, and four legs have all passed through" with a noble and graceful poem.

> First I went out after the fresh green grass;
> Then I returned, pursuing the falling blossoms.

The acme of Zen is beautifully expressed here, but no immature students can get even a glimpse of it. It certainly is no easy task to attain such supreme spirituality.

"The huge tame buffalo leisurely passed through the window, yet why is it that its tiny tail cannot pass through?" With this extraordinary question Master Hoen cuts asunder all possible reasoning on the part of all the Zen students in the world. From olden times this demand, "Why is it?" has been greatly revered as the ultimate secret of Hoen's Zen. In other words, it is the bleeding cry of compassion trying to eradicate the cause of human ignorance all at once. Now you tell me, why is it that its tail cannot pass through the window?

This tail is nothing else than the formless form of Reality.

> You may describe it, but in vain,
> Picture it, but to no avail.
> When the world collapses,
> "It" is indestructible.

It symbolizes the ever unnamable "it." Alas! My explanation above is nothing more than a vain effort to play the ape.

Master Dogen has a poem commenting on this koan:

> This world is but the tail of a buffalo passing through a window.
> The tail is the mind,
> Which knows neither passing nor not-passing.

Does he mean that there is no coming and going for "the tail," or mind, and that its going-and-returning takes place nowhere but where you are?

Listen to Master Eisei, who first introduced Zen to Japan from China, when he speaks of "the True Mind that has no form": "It is impossible to measure how high the sky is; yet the mind soars above it. It is impossible to fathom how deep the earth is; yet the mind plunges further than that. It is impossible to surpass the light of the sun and the moon, yet the mind goes beyond it. How boundless is this mind!"

Is Eisei also speaking of the tail that cannot pass through? Master Daito's commentary on this koan, "Why is it that the tail cannot pass through?" is very terse: "How can there be any public office that has no secrecy? How can there be any water that has no fish?" There is no place where this tail is not. What nonsense to argue about its passing and nonpassing!

Master Hakuin left a famous commentary poem on this tail:

> Always the same is the moon before the window.
> Yet if there is only a plum branch,
> It is no longer the same.

If to this tail anything at all, however infinitesimal it may be, is added, its true form of no-form is forever lost.

Master Hakuin also makes this comment on the koan: "Goso likes the tail that cannot pass through. As for me, I like the tail that can pass through." Are Hakuin's and Hoen's standpoints the same or different? The old Zen Masters were never negligent in disciplining themselves to deepen and refine their spirituality with any one koan. Let me remind you,

> He who attaches himself to words is lost.
> He who abides with letters will remain in ignorance.

Now set aside philosophical interpretations and tell me, "What is the tail that cannot pass through the window?" You have to attain the answer experientially with your own soul and body.

In actual training the Master may suddenly ask you, "Is that buffalo male or female? Is it red or white? What does it live on? Where does it live now?" —and so on and on. Though these questions may sound extremely absurd and eccentric, you have to be able to show your Zen freely at work at each question. Otherwise all your study will be a vain and idle fuss. Zen should never be an empty argument apart from this I-myself, here, now.

TEISHO ON MUMON'S COMMENTARY

"If you can penetrate to the point of this koan, open your Zen eye to it, and give a turning word to it, you will then be able to repay the four obligations above and help the three existences below. If you still cannot do so, work with the tail singleheartedly until you can really grasp it as your own."

Master Mumon asks you to make sure your spiritual eye is even clearer than your teacher's, to see through the essence of this koan and give a turning word that will bring about the fundamental change of personality. In other words, it is an absolute requisite for a Zen student to have his Zen eye clearly opened and have the Zen ability, not even yielding to his teacher. When this requirement is met, then, Mumon says, for the first time he will be able to repay the four obligations above and help the three existences below, that is, he is capable of carrying on genuine religious activities.

"To repay the four obligations above, and help the three existences below" refers to this Zen life of gratitude and compassion. The four obligations are to one's parents, to the sovereign, to people in general, and to the three Buddhist treasures (the Buddha, the Dharma, and the Sangha). The three existences refer to the three realms in the old Indian traditional belief—desire, form, and no-form—through which beings transmigrate in accordance with their karma. More concretely, they represent three aspects of human life for those who have not yet been emancipated from ignorance.

In training in Zen, stress is always placed on negating our actual life. This is because Zen tries to free us from the contradictions and limitations of our relativistic life, so that we may develop ideal religious activities of gratitude and compassion.

Master Mumon ends his commentary with renewed emphasis: "In case you still cannot do so, work with the tail singleheartedly until you can really grasp it as your own." The tail is not simply an old story of Master Hoen but is your own question, to which you have to give the fundamental solution. Master Mumon fervently warns every Zen student, as well as his own monks.

TEISHO ON MUMON'S POEM

> If it passes through, it falls into a ditch;
> If it turns back, it is destroyed.
> This tiny tail,
> How extremely marvelous!

Describing the tail, Master Mumon sings, "If it goes through, it will fall into a ditch; if it turns back, it will be destroyed." This tail is with each one of us. It goes through heaven above and penetrates earth below. There can never be any passing through or turning back for it.

He concludes his poem with "This tiny tail,/How extremely marvelous!" This tail is neither small nor large, is neither purified nor defiled. It neither increases nor decreases. It has no name and no form. How extremely marvelous! How utterly extraordinary! He thus thrusts it out right in front of you.

Master Hakuin, however, negates what Master Mumon says in his poem with his kind admonition: "In such a way you can never really grasp the essence of this koan. O my disciples, your attainment must be the true attainment, with great joy at the very first step. Otherwise your Zen will be forever half-baked."

An old Zen Master left a poem on this koan of "A Buffalo Passes Through a Window":

> The summit of Tozan people can hardly reach.
> Those who reach it have to grope their way through clouds, in a fog.
> Night falls, and the half-moon is seen among the pine trees.
> The village to the south is dark, the village to the north is shrouded
> in mist.

Here Tozan is another name for Mount Goso, and it refers to Master Hoen. To reach the summit of Tozan, that is, the essence of this koan, one has to go through the hard, assiduous training of groping his way through clouds and being lost in the fog. One must not expect to attain this spirituality easily.

"Night falls, and the half-moon is seen among pine trees. The village to the south is dark, the village to the north is shrouded in mist." Both light and dark, the south village and the north village are all thoroughly embraced in the moonlight of the tail, aren't they?

39

Unmon Says "You Have Missed It!"

A monk once wanted to ask Unmon a question and started to say, "The light serenely shines over the whole universe." Before he had even finished the first line, Unmon suddenly interrupted, "Isn't that the poem of Chosetsu Shusai?" The monk answered, "Yes, it is." Unmon said, "You have missed it!"

Later Master Shishin took up this koan and said, "Now tell me, why has this monk missed it?"

MUMON COMMENTARY

In this koan, if you can grasp how lofty and unapproachable Unmon's Zen working is, and why the monk missed it, then you can be a teacher in heaven and on earth. In case you are not yet clear about it, you will be unable to save yourself.

MUMON'S POEM

> A line is dropped in a swift stream;
> Greedy for the bait, he is caught.
> If you open your mouth only a little,
> Your life is lost!

TEISHO ON THE KOAN

This mondo is different from the majority of other koan in the sense that it shows the keen, sharp, and masterly working of a capable Master in eradicating the root of the human ailment (ignorance), which really is no ailment at all.

For the biography of Master Unmon, who plays the main role in this koan, please refer to the fifteenth koan, "Tozan Gets Sixty Blows."

Chosetsu Shusai was a high government official who studied under Master Sekiso Keisho, and opened his Zen eye. *Cho* is his family name; *Setsu,* which means literally "unskillfulness," is his given name. "Shusai" was an honorific title bestowed on those officers who passed the government civil service examination in the T'ang dynasty. One day when Chosetsu came to see Master Keisho, the Master asked, "Shusai, what is your name?" "My family name is Cho, and the first name is Setsu," replied Chosetsu. The Master lost no time in asking further, "Skill is unattainable by seeking. Where does *Setsu* (unskillfulness) come from?" At this Chosetsu was awakened to his True Self, or no-self, and made the following poem:

> The light serenely shines over the whole universe,
> Ignorant, wise, and living creatures—all are in my abode.
> When no thought arises, the whole is fully revealed;
> If the six organs move even a little, it is obstructed by clouds.
> If you cut off your ignorance, your ailment will increase;
> If you look for the Truth, you are also in the wrong.
> Living in accordance with worldly affairs, you will have
>   no obstructions.
> Nirvana and life-and-death are like colors in a dream.

One day a monk came to Master Unmon, and trying to ask a question he started to say, "The light serenely shines over the whole universe." Before he had finished even the first line, Master Unmon cuttingly asked him, "Isn't that the poem of Chosetsu Shusai?" What a surprisingly great Master Unmon is! The phrase "before he had even finished the first line" graphically shows his incomparable capability. It is this phrase that makes the koan superb, and if one fails to appreciate it he has not only missed the koan's intrinsic value but has failed to appreciate Master Unmon's wonderfully drastic means, which overflow with compassion. Master Hakuin admiringly comments, "Such sharpness! Such shrewdness! If one is not astounded at Unmon's marvelous working, he is not yet a true Zen man." The questioning monk naïvely answers,

"Yes, it is." How regrettable! Why couldn't he at least say, "I do not know"? Being a Zen monk, he ought to be able to give a live Zen answer of his own.

Sure enough, Unmon's denunciation immediately fell upon him, "You have missed it!" An ancient Master commented on Unmon's remark, "You are too mild. With such a good opportunity you ought to have severely beaten the monk without saying a word. Then it might have given him the chance of awakening!" Why does the monk have to be rebuked like this?

"The light serenely shines over the whole universe": isn't this precisely the true picture of all beings, of how they essentially are? Master Hakuin declares at the beginning of his "Zazen Wasan":

> All beings are essentially Buddhas.
> As with water and ice
> There is no ice apart from water,
> So, apart from beings, there are no Buddhas.
> Not knowing how close to them the Truth is,
> Beings seek it afar—what a pity!

This monk, while his whole body is in the midst of the light, is foolish enough to seek it outside himself. How stupid it is if, while living in one's own house, one is obsessed with the idea that he is in somebody else's house, and pays the rent! This is the ignorance that is described as "binding oneself without a rope."

"The light serenely shines over the whole universe"—before Chosetsu Shusai, before the advent of Sakyamuni. More exactly, there is no before, no after, for it is the original Truth of the universe. Hence as soon as he moves his tongue he has already missed it. Asking a question is of course missing it forever; answering it is of course missing it altogether. A Zen man has no time for such absurd spirituality.

As for anyone who clings to an old saying and carries it about, he is utterly out of the question. The foolishness of the inquiring monk is even pitiable. On the other hand, how extremely compassionate Master Unmon is to give the sharp blow precisely to the point.

In actual training, you may start reciting "The light serenely shines over the whole universe," and if the Master asks you, "Isn't that the poem of Chosetsu Shusai?" how can you avoid missing it? We have to discipline ourselves harder in training to make our spirituality deeper, our ability greater, and our Zen working more genuine. Each student has to do it himself carefully and sincerely.

Master Houn has the following teisho: "If anyone asks me, 'What is the meaning of the Patriarch's coming from the West?' I will tell him, 'You have missed it!' " Master Houn says that even before any answer is given, he will say, "You have missed it!" Why and how is it missed? Carefully study it together with Master Unmon's reply.

The koan here makes its second development. Later, Master Shishin of Oryo presented this koan of "Unmon Says 'You Have Missed It!' " to his monks and asked them, "Now tell me, why has this monk missed it?" Master Shishin thus pointed out the direction for his disciples to follow, showing them how they should carry on with their training.

Master Shishin of Oryo was a successor of Master Maido Soshin and was born approximately one hundred and seventy years after the death of Master Unmon. When Shishin first came to see Master Maido, the latter held up his fist and asked, "If you call it a fist, you are committed to the name. If you call it not-a-fist, you negate the fact. What do you call it?" Shishin was completely at a loss for an answer. For two years after this, Shishin most assiduously worked with this koan of the fist, and finally became fully enlightened. The date of his death is unknown, but his last poem is famous:

> When you talk, it is crumbled to seven and eight,
> When you are silent, it falls into two and three.
> So I advise you, Zen men in the country,
> The mind of satori is ever free; stop all contriving.

Master Shishin, presenting the koan of "Unmon Says 'You Have Missed It!' " asks us, "Now tell me why has this monk missed it?" If you say a word, you have missed it; if you do not say a word, you have missed it all the same. Certainly "when you talk, it is crumbled to seven and eight; when you are silent, it falls into two and three." How can you be free and nontransgressing, so that your mind of satori is absolutely free in its working? Unless you can give your answer based on your training and experience, you have to remain a stranger to Zen.

"The light serenely shines over the whole universe!" It is just so, ever clear and true. How can there be the vain argument of now and then, of missing it and not-missing it? Let me warn you, however, "Don't be so careless as to swallow it blindly!"

TEISHO ON MUMON'S COMMENTARY

"In this koan, if you can grasp how lofty and unapproachable Unmon's Zen working is, and why the monk missed it, then you can be a teacher in heaven and on earth. In case you are not yet clear about it, you will be unable to save yourself."

In studying this koan, first of all you have to be able to appreciate the terrific strength of Master Unmon's sharp and cutting response, "Isn't that the poem of Chosetsu Shusai?" which gushed out even before the monk had finished reciting the first line. You have to be able to see clearly where this outstandingly superb, even scathing Zen working comes from and what its real significance is. You have to be able also to point out definitely where and why the questioning monk missed it. Master Mumon says that such a capable Zen man is worthy of being a teacher in heaven and on earth.

The reference here to "in heaven and on earth" originates in the old traditional Indian concept of the world. According to the Indian belief, the world of living creatures consists of six realms: those of hell, hungry spirits, beasts, fighting beings, men, and celestial beings. "Heaven and earth" here refer to the last two, which are above the other four. In order to be a teacher of men and celestial beings, to show them the way to transcend these six realms and save them from transmigrating through them, one has to be an enlightened Buddhist who has established supreme satori in himself and is capable of working for others and helping them. In other words, only he who has seen through the essence of this koan can guide beings as a truly enlightened teacher. This is in fact Master Mumon's high tribute to Master Unmon's great Zen ability. At the same time he is indirectly warning those who attach themselves to the superficial meaning of the sayings of the ancient Masters and who busy themselves with their philosophical and conceptual interpretations without having attained any true realization experience of their own.

Master Mumon adds another sentence of warning to his monks: "In case you are not yet clear about it, you will be unable to save yourself." If you fail to grasp through your own experience the lofty and unapproachable Zen working of Master Unmon, and also to see why the monk missed it, you are a stupid ass, unable to save yourself, not to speak of saving others. He is dashing a flood of icy water of admonition right over the monks' heads.

A Zen Master emphatically comments, "Whatever you may say, you miss it if you ever say it. Sakyamuni missed it; Bodhidharma missed it. We cannot afford to leave it to Master Unmon alone. Every one of us has to be as high-spirited as a king."

Let me point out here: If you have really grasped it, "it" can never be missed no matter what you say, no matter how you say it. Unless you are awakened to this absolute freedom, your Zen will be a lifeless concept. I tell you, it is not easy!

TEISHO ON MUMON'S POEM

> A line is dropped in a swift stream;
> Greedy for the bait, he is caught.
> If you open your mouth only a little,
> Your life is lost!

"A line is dropped in a swift stream." Figuratively Master Mumon comments on the unapproachable strength of Master Unmon's sharp retort—"Isn't that the poem of Chosetsu Shusai?"—which gushed out of his mouth even before the monk could finish the first line. The questioning monk, being ignorant of the bare fact that he himself and the whole universe are all in that line, betrayed his stupidity by answering, "Yes, it is." Master Mumon figuratively comments on his ignorance, "Greedy for the bait, he is caught."

Master Sosho, Master Mumon's teacher, has the following mondo, and most likely the first half of Master Mumon's poem is based on it: One day a monk quoted the koan of "Unmon Says 'You Have Missed It!' " and asked Master Sosho, "I wonder why this monk missed it?" In reply, Master Sosho said, "A sweet fish is caught!"

If you do not want to be caught, you have to discipline yourself and have the Zen ability in yourself not to miss it.

Master Mumon ends his poem with, "If you open your mouth only a little, your life is lost!" You would miss it if you say anything at all. And if you just silently remain seated, you have all the same already missed it. A true Zen man ought to have his own creative way out and make Master Unmon surrender completely. Now you tell me, what is your creative way out, so that you will never miss it?

40

Kicking Over the Pitcher

When Master Isan was studying under Hyakujo, he worked as a tenzo at the monastery. Hyakujo wanted to choose an abbot for Daii Monastery. He told the head monk and all the rest of his disciples to make their Zen presentations, and the ablest one would be sent to found the monastery. Then Hyakujo took a pitcher, placed it on the floor, and asked the question: "This must not be called a pitcher. What do you call it?" The head monk said, "It cannot be called a wooden sandal." Hyakujo then asked Isan. Isan walked up, kicked over the pitcher, and left. Hyakujo said, "The head monk has been defeated by Isan." So Isan was ordered to start the monastery.

MUMON'S COMMENTARY

Extremely valiant though he is, Isan could not after all jump out of Hyakujo's trap. Upon careful examination, he followed what is heavy, refusing what is light. Why? Nii! Taking the towel band from his head, he put on an iron yoke.

MUMON'S POEM

> Throwing away bamboo baskets and wooden ladles,
> With a direct blow he cuts off complications.
> Hyakujo tries to stop him with his strict barrier, but in vain.
> The tip of his foot creates innumerable Buddhas.

TEISHO ON THE KOAN

This koan gives us an example of a Zen test by which a Master is selected. In the case of scholars, those with deep and excellent learning and scholastic attainments are respected. In the case of Zen men, creative and absolutely free Zen working is most admired, and this koan is interesting because it clearly illustrates this point. But a word of caution may be necessary here: natural and free working flowing out of true Zen spirituality and unusual or eccentric behavior with a stink of Zen should never be confused. Unfortunately there are some who expect Zen men to look different, showing off Zen-monkishness, and even to be abnormal. What is essentially required of a Zen man is that he once and for all cast himself away thoroughly and completely. True Zen working will naturally and automatically flow out of this fact of his being no-self, or True Self, in his everyday life.

The koan starts with, "When Master Isan was studying under Hyakujo, he worked as a tenzo at the monastery." Regarding Master Hyakujo, I have given a brief biography in the second koan, "Hyakujo and a Fox," and it will not be repeated here. Master Isan Reiyu (770–853) was one of the greatest Zen Masters in the T'ang dynasty, and later he was regarded as the founder of the Igyo School of Zen. He was born in Fukushu and became a Buddhist monk when he was fifteen years old. First he undertook philosophical studies of Mahayana and Theravada Buddhism, but later he made up his mind to study Zen and came to Master Hyakujo's monastery. Reiyu (he was known as Isan after he became a Master) was then twenty-three years old, and Master Hyakujo was already seventy-four.

It is not known how many years after Reiyu came to Hyakujo that the following incident took place. One evening Reiyu was sitting in zazen like a piece of dead wood without realizing how far the night had advanced. Old Hyakujo broke the silence and asked, "Who are you sitting there?" "It's Reiyu, Master," he replied. "Oh, Reiyu, rake up the fire in the hearth there," Master Hyakujo ordered. Reiyu went to the hearth with the tongs as ordered. When he could find no embers, he said, "There is no fire left, Master." Hyakujo then came himself to the hearth, took up the tongs, raked deep down and found a small burning ember. Picking it up and holding it in front of Reiyu, Hyakujo cried, "What is this? Nii!" At this moment, Reiyu was all of a sudden enlightened. He was awakened to his original live fire in himself. It is recorded that Reiyu spontaneously prostrated himself in front of Hyakujo and presented his attainment to him.

Reiyu studied under Master Hyakujo for a long while even after this experience. The incident in the koan took place when, as one of Hyakujo's senior disciples, he was working as a tenzo at the monastery.

Incidentally, the tenzo in a Zen monastery holds an important post with responsibility for the supply of food and the cooking. Even today the shika, or general administrator; the fusu, or accountant; and the tenzo, or steward-cook, are regarded as the three most important posts in the monastery, and senior monks are appointed to them in turn.

At the suggestion of one of his followers, Master Hyakujo had decided to send a capable monk to Mount Daii to start a monastery there, and he had tenzo Reiyu in mind for the task. Zenkaku, who was the head monk, heard of it and wondered why priority was given to a tenzo, sidestepping the head monk. Master Hyakujo consequently decided to have an open test in front of all the monks to select the first abbot of Daii Monastery. This is the background of the story in the koan.

"Hyakujo wanted to choose an abbot for Daii Monastery. He told the head monk and all the rest of his disciples to make their Zen presentations, and the ablest one would be sent to start the monastery." Master Hyakujo took up a pitcher that happened to be at hand, showed it to the monks, placed it on the floor, and asked them, "This must not be called a pitcher. What do you call it?"

First the head monk stepped out and said, "It cannot be called a wooden sandal." The head monk Zenkaku's answer is quite a clever one, neither attaching to the name "pitcher" nor negating the pitcher. An ancient Zen Master said, "Both attaching and negating will never do." The Truth of Zen transcends both attaching and negating. No verbal expressions can ever reach it. A pitcher is here right now. If you call it a pitcher, you are attached to its name; if you call it not-a-pitcher, you negate the fact. Both attaching and negating will never do. The head monk Zenkaku barely managed to find his way out. A Zen Master comments on him, "A shrewd hawk, but what a pity that it is tied!" Zenkaku's answer shows that he is not yet completely free in his working.

Master Hyakujo called tenzo Reiyu and asked him the same question. Without saying a word, Reiyu quietly walked up, kicked over the pitcher, and withdrew. Reiyu knew no such idle argument as to whether or not it should be called a pitcher. His stark-naked True Self had no shadow of discrimination at all, and this True Self, or no-self, naturally developed the wonderful working of no-mind. A Zen Master comments with admiration, "How wonderful! Everything is broken to pieces. As there is no self, there is naturally no attachment to fame; so what he does is pure and transparent. The head monk must have been greatly impressed."

The following poem is a tribute by an ancient Master to Reiyu's working:

With one blow, he knocked down Kokakuro [the great tower].
With one kick, he turned over Omuju [the big island].

You should be able to appreciate this commentary couplet. If, however, you understand that what Reiyu kicked over was a "pitcher," you are thousands of miles away from the Reality of what has been kicked over. The key to it lies right there.

Master Hyakujo, laughing, gave his decision, "The head monk has been completely defeated by Reiyu," and ordered Reiyu to be the founder of Daii Monastery.

Reiyu thus left Haykujo's monastery and went to Mount Daii in Konan. For several years after this event nothing is known of him. Most likely he lived like a hermit, far from human habitations, eating wild nuts and berries, with animals as his friends. While he was thus deepening and refining his spirituality, his reputation as a great Zen Master spread around, and finally at the request of the governor he founded a Zen monastery called Dokeiji on Mount Daii.

Zenkaku, who was beaten by Reiyu, though he appears in this koan to be inferior to Reiyu, also became one of the great Zen Masters of the time. Later he moved to Mount Karin and enjoyed the free and sequestered life on the trackless, secluded mountain, and people respected him as Master Karin. The following interesting story is told of him. One day a high government officer who greatly admired him came all the way to his solitary hermitage on the mountain and said, "Dear Master, living all by yourself like this without an attendant, your life must be very inconvenient." "No, it is not, for I have a couple of attendants," replied Master Karin, and turning around he loudly cried out, "Oh, Daiku and Shoku!" (The names mean "small-emptiness" and "large-emptiness.") In reply to the call, with terrific roars two fierce-looking tigers appeared from the back of the hermitage. Imposing high officer though he was, the visitor was frightened out of his wits. Zenkaku told them, "Listen, this is my important guest. Be quiet and courteous." At this command, the two tigers crouched at his feet and were gentle as two kittens.

No detailed biography of Zenkaku is known.

TEISHO ON MUMON'S COMMENTARY

"Extremely valiant though he is, Isan could not after all jump out of Hyakujo's trap. Upon careful examination, he followed what is heavy, refusing what is light. Why? Nii! Taking the towel band from his head, he put on an iron yoke."

Here again Master Mumon is railing at Master Isan from the beginning to the end of his commentary, and in doing so is, on the contrary, praising Isan's Zen ability and personality.

First Mumon says, "Extremely valiant though he is, Isan could not after all jump out of Hyakujo's trap." Plucking up all his courage and giving full play to his ability, Isan won the victory over head monk Zenkaku. Though his capability deserves admiration, he could not after all jump out of the trap set by Master Hyakujo. Mumon is thus praising Isan's capability with which he beautifully passed Hyakujo's test without difficulty. He goes on to comment, "Upon careful examination, he followed what is heavy, refusing what is light. Why? Nii!" Although Isan did win the victory, upon careful examination it is seen that his victory resulted in his taking up the heavy duty of founding Daii Monastery and turning down the light position of tenzo at Hyakujo's monastery. After criticizing Isan like this, Mumon calls the attention of his disciples by asking, "Why? Nii!" Finally he concludes by saying, "Taking the towel band from his head, he put on an iron yoke." From ancient times, several different interpretations have been given to this concluding sentence, and it is difficult to decide which is the most appropriate. I will take it as Master Mumon's usual ironical method of praising Isan's Zen ability and personality most highly by mocking him, "What a fool you are to be the founder of Daii Monastery, leaving the post of tenzo at Hyakujo!"

TEISHO ON MUMON'S POEM

> Throwing away bamboo baskets and wooden ladles,
> With a direct blow he cuts off complications.
> Hyakujo tries to stop him with his strict barrier, but in vain.
> The tip of his foot creates innumerable Buddhas.

The tone of Master Mumon's poem is completely different from that of his commentary, for here, without using any teasing or ironical expressions, he directly and plainly comments from his Zen standpoint on Master Isan's working of "kicking over the pitcher."

The first line figuratively refers to the circumstances when Isan left the post of tenzo: he lightly threw away bamboo baskets and wooden ladles, which are necessary utensils for cooking. The second line praises the wonderful Zen working of Master Isan, who straightforwardly and gallantly kicked over the pitcher and thus cut off all idle dualistic conflicts. These two lines show Master Mumon's admiration for Isan's outstanding ability.

The third line refers to Master Hyakujo's question, "What do you call it?" Even such a strict barrier as Hyakujo posed was of no avail before Isan's Zen at work, Mumon points out with admiration.

Mumon ends his poem singing, "The tip of his foot creates innumerable Buddhas." Isan kicked over the pitcher. So wonderful indeed is his Zen that every movement of his foot and hand is shining with the Truth.

A monk once asked Master Seihei Goson, "What is uro?" (ignorance; literally, "leaking"). "A bamboo basket leaks. This is Buddhism," replied the Master. The monk went on to ask, "What is muro?" (satori; literally, "non-leaking"). "A wooden ladle scoops. This is Buddhism," was his reply. For Master Seihei, leaking (ignorance) and nonleaking (satori) were both Buddhism. Once one's spiritual eye is opened, every movement of his hand and foot creates a fresh breeze, and countless Buddhas will spring from it.

Let me remind you here. Those who study Zen today must not just be attracted by Master Isan's unique Zen working; they should first of all appreciate his lucid and penetrating spirituality from which his working flew out.

Master Tanzan, who was one of the greatest Zen Masters of the Meiji period in Japan, gave the following teisho on this koan: "Master Isan kicked over the pitcher. You monks might be able to kick it over, too, if it were a pitcher. My question is, 'Do not call Mount Fuji Mount Fuji. What do you call it?' Now what will you do?" This is a good koan which serves as a strong warning to those mimics who blindly imitate the sayings and doings of ancient Masters, spreading the stink of Zen around.

41

Bodhidharma and Peace of Mind

Bodhidharma sat in zazen facing the wall. The Second Patriarch, who had been standing in the snow, cut off his arm and said, "Your disciple's mind is not yet at peace. I beg you, my teacher, please give it peace." Bodhidharma said, "Bring the mind to me, and I will set it at rest." The Second Patriarch said, "I have searched for the mind, and it is finally unattainable." Bodhidharma said, "I have thoroughly set it at rest for you."

MUMON'S COMMENTARY

The broken-toothed old foreigner proudly came over—a hundred thousand miles across the sea. This was as if he were raising waves where there was no wind. Toward his end, Bodhidharma could enlighten only one disciple, but even he was crippled. Ii! Shasanro does not know even four characters.

MUMON'S POEM

Coming from the West, and directly pointing—
This great affair was caused by the transmission.
The trouble-maker who created a stir in Zen circles
Is, after all, you.

TEISHO ON THE KOAN

This koan, though it looks simple, deals with the most serious and important point in truth-seeking. It tells us how the Second Patriarch (Shinko), who was already middle-aged, after many years of rigorous seeking after the Truth came to see Bodhidharma. Unless one has actually gone through hard and painful truth-seeking himself, he will not be able to appreciate the real significance of this koan. An old Zen Master sang:

> For years I suffered in snow and frost;
> Now I am startled at pussy willows falling.

Bodhidharma was the third son of a king in southern India. He studied under Hannyatara in India and became his successor. After his teacher's death, Bodhidharma, in order to transmit correct Buddhism to China, came over to Koshu in South China, a hard three years' voyage by ship. First he had an interview with Emperor Wu of Liang, who was called "the Emperor with the Buddha mind," but the opportunity was not yet ripe and he moved on to Suzan in North China. There, at Shorinji, for nine long years he just kept on doing zazen and thus laid the foundation of Zen in China. The exact date of his death is not known, but generally it is said that he died in 527 when he was approximately one hundred and fifty years old.

The Second Patriarch Eka was at first called Shinko. In his early childhood he was a boy with unusual inspiration; he was particularly fond of reading. One day while reading a Buddhist text he had a great insight, which made him decide to become a Buddhist monk. He then studied Mahayana and Theravada Buddhism extensively, and was already a middle-aged monk when the incident in the koan took place. In spite of his great learning, his mind was not quite at peace. In order to have the fundamental emancipation he went to see Bodhidharma, and was finally given the Dharma sanction. Later he lived among the poor, hiding his brilliance. Though it is said that he was over a hundred years old when he died, no definite record of him is left.

In the koan, Master Mumon simply states in the first two short sentences, "Bodhidharma sat in zazen facing the wall. The Second Patriarch, who had been standing in the snow, cut off his arm and said. . . ." Let me quote here the original sentences in *Keitoku Dento-roku* ("The Transmission of the Lamp"), which give us the impressive description of how Shinko showed his eagerness in seeking the Truth and how he was first permitted to have sanzen with Bodhidharma: "He [Shinko] went over there [Shorinji] and day and night beseeched Bodhidharma for instruction. The Master always sat in zazen facing the wall and paid no attention to his entreaties. On the evening of December 9, heaven sent down a heavy snow. Shinko stood erect and unmoving. Toward daybreak the snow reached above his knees. The Master had pity on him and said, 'You have long been standing in the snow. What are you seeking?' Shinko in bitter tears said, 'I beseech you, O Master, with your compassion pray open your gate of Dharma and save all of us beings.' The Master said, 'The incomparable Truth of the Buddhas can only be attained by eternally striving, practicing what cannot be practiced and bearing the unbearable. How can you, with your little virtue, little wisdom, and with your easy and self-conceited mind, dare to aspire to attain the true teaching? It is only so much labor lost.' Listening to the Master's admonition, Shinko secretly took out his sharp knife, himself cut off his own left arm, and placed it in front of the Master. The Master, recognizing his Dharma caliber, told him, 'Buddhas, when they first seek after the Truth, give no heed to their bodies for the sake of Dharma. You have now cut off your arm before me. I have seen sincerity in your seeking.' The Master finally gave him the name Eka. Shinko asked, 'Is it possible to listen to Buddha Dharma?' The Master replied, 'The Buddha Dharma cannot be attained by following others.' [That is, one has to see directly into his own nature.] Shinko said, 'My mind is not yet at peace. I beg you, my teacher, please give it peace for me. . . .' "

The above account is not in accordance with historically traceable facts. It may be a mythological description by the author of *Keitoku Dento-roku*. But the painful and desperate struggle in seeking after the Truth, even at the risk of one's own life, is not a mythological fabrication by an old Zen Master. He who has experienced the same pain and hardship in really seeking the Truth cannot read it just lightly as an old story.

> The snow of Shorin is stained crimson,
> Let us dye our heart with it
> Humble though it may be.

This is a waka poem by an old Zen Master. We cannot read the above story without tears.

The koan here develops into the mondo between Bodhidharma and Shinko. Shinko pleads, "Your disciple's mind is not yet at peace. I beg you, my teacher, please give it peace." The forms and the expressions of asking may differ, yet is this not the search that every man must make? Through all ages, human beings have made this search even at the cost of their lives. It is not a personal desire entertained only by Shinko over a thousand years ago. Not only Zen, but any religion in the world must have the reason for its existence in the guidance it gives to those who pursue this quest. By making this search one may finally be led to the realization that every effort is in vain. True peace of mind, however, can be obtained only when one is personally awakened to the stark-naked fact that every effort *is* ultimately in vain. Seek, struggle, and despair! He who has never wept all night in struggle and despair will not know the happiness of satori.

I do not remember who it was, but these words of a Western theologian, which I once read, have been clearly imprinted on my mind: "You who have not spent sleepless nights in suffering and tears, who do not know the experience of being unable to swallow even a piece of bread—the grace of God will never reach you."

There is an excellent metaphor made by a Zen Master: "To try to find a man on an uninhabited island may prove fruitless. Once, however, it is definitely established that there is no man there, the island comes into the discoverer's possession. This is international law. It is the universal law effective through the ages. The whole universe now comes into his possession!"

"My mind is not yet at peace. I beg you, my teacher, please give it peace." This is the Great Doubt penetrating his whole being. The whole universe, and he-himself, was just this one Great Doubt. Only those who break through the extremity of this sheer darkness can have the great joy of being the true master of the whole universe. Bodhidharma said, "Bring your mind here, and I will set it at rest." What an exceedingly great Master Bodhidharma is! His sharp reply directly penetrates the questioner's heart.

Where is the mind that is not at peace? Who is it that is seeking it? Is the mind square or round? White or red? Does it exist or not? The mind does exist, but it is so absolutely affirmative that it is at the same time negative, is it not? If it does exist, bring it right here! How cuttingly sharp this demand is! So shrewd he is to "kill the enemy with the spear he has snatched from the enemy himself." Shinko must have been pushed down into the abyss of despair by this demand of Bodhidharma. He was driven to the wall. Intellect was of no avail, reasoning was no help. He was not aware whether he was alive or dead. He could not even utter a moaning cry. This must have been Shinko's actual situation.

The koan simply states, "Bodhidharma said, 'Bring the mind to me, and I will set it at rest.' The Second Patriarch said, 'I have searched for the mind, and it is finally unattainable.' " Those who have not themselves had the experience of searching and training will naturally interpret these sentences literally and will be unable to read between the lines the spiritual agony of actual search. They will consequently fail to realize that there is an interval of painful dark nights for weeks, for months, or even years, between Bodhidharma's demand, "Bring your mind to me, and I will set it at rest," and Shinko's answer, "I have searched for the mind, and it is finally unattainable."

Master Rinzai was described as "the monk of pure, singlehearted discipline" for three years. Later he spoke of those training days of his own: "Years ago, when I was not enlightened, I was in sheer darkness altogether." Master Hakuin said, "I felt as if I was sitting in an ice cave ten thousand miles thick." I myself shall never forget the spiritual struggle I had in sheer darkness for nearly three years. I would declare that what is most important and invaluable in Zen training is this experience of dark nights that one goes through with his whole being.

Once I read a criticism by a Japanese philosopher on this koan: " 'Bring your mind to me, and I will set it at rest.' 'I have searched for the mind, and it is finally unattainable.' How nonsensical and naïve Zen people are, that they can have satori through such a play of words." He who can only read Zen books in this superficial way is not a first-rate, respectable scholar, for he himself has had no experience of really seeking the Truth even at the risk of his own life. "I have searched for the mind, and it is finally unattainable"— this reply comes from the experience of plunging into another dimension. It is the cry of the person who has experienced that "the whole universe has collapsed and the iron mountain has crumbled." How many are there who can see a flood of tears shed by the Second Patriarch in this one word "finally"? The key to the koan is in the experience of grasping the live significance of this word "finally" as one's own.

It is no exaggeration to say that Zen is, after all, the search for the mind and for the attainment of real peace of mind. "Joshu's 'Mu,' " "Zuigan Calls 'Master,' " "A Buffalo Passes Through a Window," and of course, "Mind Is Buddha" are koan seeking the mind.

The Second Patriarch says, "I have searched for the mind, and it is finally unattainable." Master Rinzai declared, "The mind has no form, and, pervading the whole universe, it is vividly working right in front of you!" One has to actually experience it and testify to that fact to really appreciate these sayings, for it is not a matter of mere understanding or knowing.

Bodhidharma was certainly a great Master based on his deep, penetrating experience. He positively verified Shinko's attainment, "I have thoroughly set it at rest for you." This was the moment when the Second Patriarch of Zen in China was born.

Later the Second Patriarch received the following instructions in a poem from Bodhidharma:

Outside, cut off all relations.
Inside, have no panting in your mind.
Make your mind like a wall,
And thus you may attain Tao.

"A wall" cuts off all objective dust and illusions. To "make the mind like a wall," and to "find it unattainable," experientially refer to one and the same spiritual state. A Zen Master says in his teisho, "If you realize that there is no such thing as the mind, you no longer have to look for it. If your seeking mind is set at rest, then you are relieved of a great load. . . . You cannot even talk of pacifying the mind for it implies that body and mind are separate. Whenever it may be, wherever you may be, your mind is at peace, because there is no mind outside your body; because there is no body outside your mind. Since your body and mind have already dropped away, what is there to be pacified or not pacified? How wonderful is this mind that is always just at peace!"

Let me add my words here. It is said, "However wonderful a thing it may be, it is better not to have it at all!" A Zen man ought not to be easily self-satisfied.

TEISHO ON MUMON'S COMMENTARY

"The broken-toothed old foreigner proudly came over—a hundred thousand miles across the sea. This was as if he were raising waves where there was no wind. Toward his end, Bodhidharma could enlighten only one disciple, but even he was crippled. Ii! Shasanro does not know even four characters."

Commenting on the koan, Master Mumon first says, "The broken-toothed old foreigner proudly came over—a hundred thousand miles across the sea." When Bodhidharma came to China, people in Buddhist circles in China were interested only in philosophical studies of Buddhism, and Bodhidharma flatly disapproved of that trend of the time. Because of his firm stand against scholastic Buddhism he was hated by traditional Buddhists in China. According to the legend, they finally tried to kill him and he narrowly escaped poisoning. It is said that his front teeth became broken because of the poison, and that is why he is called "the broken-toothed old foreigner."

Although it is not certain, it is said that when Bodhidharma came to China he was already well advanced in years, probably nearly a hundred and fifty years old. I should like to take "the broken-toothed old foreigner" as a friendly nickname given to this old toothless Bodhidharma. It was very daring of him that in old age he did not hesitate to make the hard voyage of over a hundred thousand miles, spending three years on the sea, to come over to China.

Commenting on this praiseworthy undertaking, Master Mumon says, "This was as if he were raising waves where there was no wind. I certainly appreciate your tremendous efforts and the hardships you went through in coming over to China. But actually, is there any place where there is no Dharma? It is only so much labor lost. What a meddler you are!" Mumon is, of course, speaking from the absolute standpoint of the Truth itself.

Mumon goes on to say, "Toward his end, Bodhidharma could enlighten only one disciple, but even he was crippled." After much vain effort, what have you accomplished? You could save only one disciple, but even he was a cripple with only one arm! Thus by severely denouncing what the First Patriarch did, Master Mumon is in fact highly praising his incomparable achievements.

Finally, after the emphatic exclamation of warning—"Ii!"—Mumon concludes his commentary with "Shasanro does not know even four characters." What Master Mumon really wants to say in his commentary was perhaps this last sentence. He asks us to see, in this last sentence, the fact of "the mind if finally unattainable," the fact of "just sitting with one's mind like a wall."

There are various interpretations given to "Shasanro does not know even four characters." I would take Shasanro as an illiterate fisherman who does not know even the alphabet. The sentence therefore points to the unknowable, unattainable Reality.

Master Hoen has a mondo: "Once a monk asked Master Hoen, 'What is a Zen monk?' Hoen replied, 'Shasanro on a fishing boat.' "

TEISHO ON MUMON'S POEM

Coming from the West, and directly pointing—
This great affair was caused by the transmission.
The trouble-maker who created a stir in Zen circles
Is, after all, you.

An ancient Zen Master explained the first line, "People gave themselves up to words and letters, and were greatly absorbed in nonsensical business, such as counting the sands of the sea. They did not look for the Truth. At such a point the First Patriarch came over and taught, 'Directly pointing to one's mind, attain Buddhahood by seeing into one's Nature,' and 'transmission

outside the scriptures.' The ancient Master tried to depict the unique characteristics of Bodhidharma as the First Patriarch of Zen. Master Mumon refers
to these characteristics of Bodhidharma in his pithy first line, 'Coming from
the West, and directly pointing—' "

"This great affair" of raising waves where there is no wind was all caused
by the Dharma transmission, which is the transmission of the untransmittable,
from mind to mind. The second line, of course, refers to the fact of the Dharma
transmission by Bodhidharma from India to China, and to the Second Patriarch Eka.

In the third and fourth lines, Mumon reviles Bodhidharma, "The trouble-
maker who created a stir in Zen circles is, after all, you." Insisting on "sitting
facing the wall, and setting the mind at rest," or "pointing directly to one's
mind," you have made such a fuss in Zen circles. What an agitator you are!
Again, with his strong, abusive language, Master Mumon is on the contrary
illustrating the incomparably great accomplishments of Bodhidharma as the
First Patriarch of Zen.

42

A Woman Comes Out of Meditation

Once long ago, the World-Honored One came to the place where many Buddhas were assembled. When Manjusri arrived there, the Buddhas all returned to their original places. Only a woman remained, close to the Buddha seat in deep meditation. Manjusri spoke to the Buddha, "Why can a woman be close to the Buddha seat, and I cannot?" The Buddha told Manjusri, "You awaken this woman from her meditation and ask her yourself." Manjusri walked around the woman three times, snapped his fingers once, then took her up to the Brahma Heaven and tried all his supernatural powers, but he was unable to bring her out of meditation. The World-Honored One said, "Even hundreds of thousands of Manjusris would be unable to bring her out of meditation. Down below, past one billion, two hundred million countries, as innumerable as the sands of the Ganges, there is a Bodhisattva called Momyo. He will be able to awaken her from meditation." In an instant Momyo emerged from the earth and worshiped the World-Honored One. The World-Honored One gave him the order. Momyo then walked to the woman and snapped his fingers only once. At this the woman came out of her meditation.

MUMON'S COMMENTARY

Old Sakya put on a clumsy play and was no better than a child. Now tell me: Manjusri is the teacher of the Seven Buddhas; why could he not bring the woman out of her meditation? Momyo is a Bodhisattva of the initial stage; why could he do so? If you can firmly grasp this point, then for you this busy life of ignorance and discrimination will be the life of supreme satori.

MUMON'S POEM

The one could awaken her, the other could not;
Both are completely free.
A god mask and a devil mask,
The failure is wonderful indeed.

TEISHO ON THE KOAN

In an Indian sutra, *Shobutsu Yoshu-kyo* ("Sutra of the Buddha Assembly"), there is an allegory from which this koan was adapted. The story here, however, is quite different from that in the original, since it has been rewritten as a koan for monks so that they may use it to refine their spirituality. We need not be concerned about the original, but should take up the story as a koan that has a unique role in Zen training. The particular aim of this koan is to make the monks' Zen eye thoroughly clear regarding fundamental wisdom versus attained wisdom, philosophical teaching versus Zen experience, or equality versus differentiation, and in this respect it is a very interesting koan.

Once Sakyamuni Buddha with his supernatural power went over to the World of Pervading Light, where many Buddhas were assembling. Manjusri alone was not permitted to join the assembly and was sent far over to Mount Chakravada. Finally he was allowed to come. When, however, he appeared where the many Buddhas had assembled, they all returned to their respective original places.

Now, when Manjusri arrived why did all the other Buddhas disappear and return to their original dwelling places? Also, what are the Buddhas' original dwelling places? Students in training first have to direct their inquiry to these points. They must have their experiential understanding apart from philosophical interpretations.

After the various Buddhas had all returned to their original dwelling places, the only person who remained was a woman who was in deep meditation near the Buddha seat. In olden times in Asian countries, women were generally considered to be deeply defiled creatures who live in ignorance. It is therefore simply common sense to understand that they were not to come close to the Buddha seat. Manjusri asked the World-Honored One, "Why can't I come close to the Buddha seat, whereas a woman can?"

Two questions have to be asked here. First, why can a defiled woman be close to the Buddha seat? Second, why is Manjusri, who is highly respected as the teacher of the Seven Buddhas, unable to come close to the Buddha seat? The student in training has to be able to answer these questions from the Zen standpoint.

Manjusri is an idealized Buddha in Buddhist mythology. Although he attained the highest Buddhahood, he did not remain in Buddhahood but came down to the status of a Bodhisattva because of his infinitely great compassion, which moved him to save all beings. Here he is called, with much respect and adoration, the teacher of the Seven Buddhas. (As to the Seven Buddhas, please refer to the second koan, "Hyakujo and a Fox.")

The World-Honored One told Manjusri, "You awaken this woman from her meditation and ask her yourself." Manjusri thereupon "walked around the woman three times, snapped his fingers once, then took her up to the Brahma Heaven and tried all his supernatural powers," yet he could not wake her from her deep meditation. The World-Honored One said, "Even if hundreds of thousands of Manjusris were to get together, they could not awaken her from meditation."

Now, why is it that Manjusri with his high rank as teacher of the Seven Buddhas is unable to awaken the woman from her meditation? Students in training must also inquire into this question from the Zen standpoint.

The World-Honored One continued, "Down below, past one billion, two hundred million countries, as innumerable as the sands of the Ganges, there is a Bodhisattva called Momyo. He will be able to awaken her from meditation." As soon as he said this, Bodhisattva Momyo emerged from the earth and made a bow in front of the World-Honored One, who ordered him to awaken the woman. Momyo walked to her, and when he simply snapped his fingers once in front of her, she readily came out of meditation.

Though Momyo is a Bodhisattva of just the initial stage, how could he so easily accomplish what was impossible for Manjusri to do? This is another question students have to study carefully from the Zen standpoint.

In the preceding paragraphs I have pointed out the essentials of this koan. Students must strive to refine their Zen eye so as to see clearly through these essential points. Master Mumon makes an enlightening commentary on this koan in which he sums up its key points and gives instructions as to how students should discipline themselves. I will therefore go on to my teisho on Mumon's commentary without getting into details about the koan itself.

TEISHO ON MUMON'S COMMENTARY

"Old Sakya put on a clumsy play and was no better than a child. Now tell me: Manjusri is the teacher of the Seven Buddhas; why could he not bring the woman out of her meditation? Momyo is a Bodhisattva of the initial stage; why could he do so? If you can firmly grasp this point, then for you this busy life of ignorance and discrimination will be the life of supreme satori."

Master Mumon first gives a general comment on the koan, "Old Sakya put on a clumsy play and was no better than a child." Sakyamuni put on a silly, rustic play, but it is not a tolerable piece at all. Here again Mumon uses his usual paradoxical language. He then changes his tone, "Now tell me," and indicates where the points of this rustic play are. The first point is: "Manjusri is the teacher of the Seven Buddhas; why could he not bring the woman out of her meditation?" Manjusri is a highly respected Buddha as the teacher of the Seven Buddhas. Buddhist philosophy teaches that Manjusri symbolizes Fundamental Wisdom, that is, Absolute Wisdom. This wisdom is the One Truth to which everything returns and from which everything is born. If there is no dust in the eye, there should be nothing in the universe to interfere with the sight. Is there a distinction between satori and ignorance? Male and female? Entering into meditation and coming out of meditation? There, just as it is, Manjusri's real worth is vividly revealed. Don't be deluded by words. The live Manjusri pervades the universe. How wonderful it is that he could not bring the woman out of her meditation!

Another point this: "Momyo is a Bodhisattva of the initial stage; why could he bring the woman out of her meditation?" Momyo is only a very new hand at Bodhisattva training. Buddhist scriptures explain that there are fifty-two stages in the training of a Bodhisattva before he finally attains to Buddhahood. Momyo is a Bodhisattva at the beginners' stage, the very lowest of the fifty-two. He is a Bodhisattva of differentiation wisdom, one who goes about clarifying truths and phenomenon in accordance with the teachings of differentiation. "Differentiation" one may call it, but where the differentiation wisdom shines, each and every thing, as it is, is the entrance to emancipation.

There is an interesting allegory regarding the relationship of Manjusri and Momyo. One day a university professor noticed that his son, who was a kindergarten pupil, was reading a picture book incorrectly, and he said, "Son, you're misreading that part." The little boy replied, "Daddy, I don't think you know anything about this book. I'll ask my teacher at kindergarten tomorrow." The professor father nodded with a smile, "That's a good idea." For the child, a university professor is no match for a kindergarten teacher.

Finally, Master Mumon concludes with much emphasis, "If you can firmly grasp this point, then for you this busy life of ignorance and discrimination will be the life of supreme satori." This is Mumon's final blow. The true Zen man must never be deluded by labels such as "Manjusri," "Momyo," "the teacher of the Seven Buddhas," or "a Bodhisattva of the initial stage."

"This busy life of ignorance and discrimination" refers to our actual everyday life, which is a mixture of gain and loss, right and wrong, life and death. Master Mumon boldly declares that such a life as ours, just as it is, is the life of supreme satori. He says that the true Zen life is nothing other than this busy life of ours. This does not mean that right and wrong or life and death will cease to exist. When right and wrong or life and death no longer disturb one at all, he has truly transcended right and wrong, he is free from life and death. If equality is stuck at equality, it ceases to be true equality. If differentiation is stuck at differentiation, it is no longer true differentiation. Equality is the basis of differentiation; differentiation is the working which is dynamically developed from, but firmly based on, equality, Oneness. When this is realized, both equality and differentiation shine out with real life; then you may truly declare that "this busy life of ignorance and discrimination is the life of supreme satori."

Master Sogyo sings this comment on the koan:

> Taking along Sakyamuni the Tathagata, Manjusri, and Momyo,
> I enjoy the mountain spring
> Visiting one truth after another.

This beautifully describes the spirituality and working of a true Zen man. For him, this is exactly "the life of supreme satori."

TEISHO ON MUMON'S POEM

> The one could awaken her, the other could not;
> Both are completely free.
> A god mask and a devil mask,
> The failure is wonderful indeed.

Master Mumon sings, "The one could awaken her, the other could not; both are completely free." If it is your interpretation that Manjusri could not do it while Momyo could, your understanding is completely off the point. In the life of supreme satori, can there be such idle distinctions as "could" and "could not"? Can't you see that "both are completely free" as they are? When one is awake, he is just awake, through and through. When he is not awake, he is just not awake, through and through. Each fully reveals the true picture of Reality. Only if you have lucid spirituality and superb capability that will never be shaken by discrimination can you say that "everything shines with Dharma, and each phenomenon reveals ever-unchanging Truth." Is there anything that you lack here? Master Mumon is really high-spirited.

He goes on to sing, "A god mask and a devil mask, the failure is wonderful indeed." A Zen man is at peace in both favorable and adverse conditions, and his mind is not disturbed under any circumstances. This is the secret of Zen. Everything as it is, is glorifying the Dharma Truth in its own way. A god mask is wonderful; a devil mask is also wonderful. The one could awaken her—that is interesting; the other could not—that too is interesting. Each, as it is, is wonderful and interesting in its own way. Is there anything you dislike? Is there anything you have to hold fast to? Master Mumon's Zen ability is fully demonstrated here.

An actor plays different parts on the stage in accordance with the roles assigned to him. The characters he plays vary widely, but the actor is always the same person. There is a poem written by an old Zen master:

> He carries a bottle
> And goes out himself to buy village wine.
> On his return, putting on a robe,
> Now he is the host.

What a free life this is!

43

Shuzan and a Staff

KOAN

Master Shuzan held up his staff, and showing it to the assembled disciples said, "You monks, if you call this a staff, you are committed to the name. If you call it not-a-staff, you negate the fact. Tell me, you monks, what do you call it?"

MUMON'S COMMENTARY

If you call it a staff, you are committed to the name. If you call it not-a-staff, you negate the fact. You cannot talk; you cannot be silent. Quick! Speak! Speak! Quick!

MUMON'S POEM

> Holding up a staff,
> He is carrying out the orders to kill and to revive.
> Where committing and negating are interfusing,
> Buddhas and Patriarchs have to beg for their lives.

TEISHO ON THE KOAN

Man, once and for all, has to be driven to the abyss of dualistic contradictions and completely die to his small self in the depths of spiritual struggle.

Unless he is reborn, breaking through this barrier, he cannot be really free in living his actual everyday life. To be a free master, or Absolute Subjectivity, he is required in this koan to transcend the contradiction of committing himself to the name and negating the fact.

Master Mumon presents here as a koan the teisho Master Shuzan made on an earlier occasion. Master Mumon intends to use this koan as a means to drive his disciples to the abyss of dualistic contradictions, and expects them to find their way out, to be reborn with a completely new point of view.

Master Shuzan was born in the Santo area of China and was ordained while he was a boy. His personality was sincere, honest, and dignified, and he was quite different from ordinary people. He was active as a Zen Master when the Sung dynasty was established in 960 A.D. Zen of the Rinzai School in those days showed signs of gradual decline, and it was Master Shuzan who revived the true spirit of Rinzai Zen. He was born five generations after Master Rinzai and was sixty-eight years old when he died in 993. One day he mounted the rostrum and recited the following poem, and that afternoon died in peace:

A golden body in the pure silver world!
The sentient and the nonsentient are both of One Truth.
At the extremity of light and darkness all working is transcended.
The sun reveals its true body in the afternoon.

One day Master Shuzan appeared on the rostrum to give his teisho. Holding up a bamboo staff about three feet long, he addressed his disciples, "You monks, if you call this a staff, you are committed to the name. If you call it not-a-staff, you negate the fact. Tell me, you monks, what do you call it?"

An old Zen Master said when commenting on this koan, "Those who can grasp it do so when Master Shuzan holds up his staff, before he utters a word! If a tongue moves at all, you have missed it already!" Why? The whole universe is just One. Everything is just One. If, however, a thought of discrimination moves here, the absolute lucidity of this spirituality is already lost.

Be that as it may, so long as you live in the world of ordinary dualistic logic, the question "If you call it a staff, you are committed to the name. If you call it not-a-staff, you negate the fact. What do you call it?" can never be answered. Zen demands that you transcend this contradiction, find a clear and definite way out, and be a person of real freedom.

Readers may recall Master Hyakujo's question in the fortieth koan, "Kicking Over the Pitcher," and the dynamically free Zen working shown by Master Isan. Let me remind you, however, that what is vitally important here is the absolute lucidity of Master Isan's spirituality from which his unique working developed as the natural outcome. If you are attracted by the novelty of his expressed action alone, you are a hopeless fool.

Master Kisei of Sekken, who later became Master Shuzan's successor, has the following mondo: "Master Shuzan held up his staff and said, 'If you call this a staff you are committed to the name. If you call it not-a-staff, you negate the fact. Now tell me, what do you call it?' Kisei lost no time in snatching the staff, and throwing it on the ground he demanded in return, 'What is this?' Master Shuzan uttered a big, scolding cry, 'Blind!' at which Kisei was suddenly enlightened." In actual training we can always see such a live and dynamic display of Zen spirit.

Now tell me, my students, what do you call it? You have to give me the answer that will fully satisfy Master Shuzan and Master Mumon as well.

Master Shian symbolically comments on this koan in a poem:

> Hundreds of mountains with no birds flying at all,
> Thousands of lanes with no human traces whatever.
> An old man in a solitary boat, in his straw hat and coat,
> Is angling alone on a snowy river.

In essence you are transcendentally alone and do not rely on anything. Leap out of both committing and negating. Then look and behold, what obstruction is there?

In actual training at a monastery, the Master may suddenly ask you, "Clear away the two characters 'committing' and 'negating' for me!" Those without sufficient ability will make an unexpected blunder and will have to be tripped up. This is quite a shrewd koan.

TEISHO ON MUMON'S COMMENTARY

"If you call it a staff, you are committed to the name. If you call it not-a-staff, you negate the fact. You cannot talk; you cannot be silent. Quick! Speak! Speak! Quick!"

Master Mumon quotes Master Shuzan's statement as it is given in the koan and then adds, "You cannot talk; you cannot be silent. Quick! Speak! Speak! Quick!" With this extremely simple commentary Mumon is asking for an answer that will perfectly satisfy him.

Master Koboku Gen comments, "Not being committed to the name, and not negating the fact—much useless fuss, only creating doubts. If you open your mouths and start arguing you are hundreds of thousands of miles away from 'it.' " I fully agree with what he says.

TEISHO ON MUMON'S POEM

> Holding up a staff,
> He is carrying out the orders to kill and to revive.
> Where committing and negating are interfusing,
> Buddhas and Patriarchs have to beg for their lives.

Master Mumon comments that by holding up his three-foot-long bamboo staff, called a shippei, Master Shuzan is carrying out the terrific orders to kill and to revive. This bamboo staff, when it kills, kills whether it be Buddhas or Patriarchs. When it revives, it revives even the broken shoe thrown away by the roadside and makes it shine with new life. This staff has such wonderful power because it is nothing else than "it," which transcends committing and negating. If you try to describe "it" by saying that committing and negating are interfusing each other, you already have missed its Reality. Even Buddhas and Patriarchs cannot have a glimpse of "it."

Master Mujaku Bunki once worked as tenzo when he was still in training at a monastery. One morning Bunki was stirring gruel in a big iron pot when the noble image of Manjusri clearly appeared in a cloud of steam. Seeing it, Bunki immediately raised overhead a big spoon he had in his hand and struck directly at the image. Then a voice in the steam said, "I am Manjusri, I am Manjusri!" Bunki, with renewed vigor, cried out, "Manjusri is naturally Manjusri. Bunki is naturally Bunki! Even if Sakyamuni or Maitreya come, I will strike him down at a blow!" So saying he raised the big spoon overhead again. The image of Manjusri at once disappeared, whereupon a solemn voice declared:

> Green gentian is bitter even to its root,
> Sweet melon is thoroughly sweet all through.
> Disciplining myself for three long kalpas,
> Here, I am disliked by the old monk!

This story, of course, is not based on historical fact. Yet when a spoon in the hand freely carries out the orders to kill and to revive, Buddhas and Patriarchs have to beg for their lives! The tale is interesting in clearly depicting this lucid and transparent spirituality.

44

Basho and a Stick

Master Basho said to the monks, "If you have a stick, I shall give one to you. If you do not have a stick, I shall take it away from you."

It helps you cross the river where the bridge is broken. It accompanies you as you return to the village on a moonless night. If you call it a stick, you will go to hell as fast as an arrow.

The deep and the shallow wherever they may be
Are all in my hand.
It sustains heaven and supports the earth,
And promotes Zen Truth wherever it may be.

Zen refuses all forms of attachment and clinging. This is because it wants us to live in real peace and with absolute freedom, and because of this wish

Zen Masters resort to their whips of infinite compassion. This koan gives us an example of how such drastic measures are actually taken. As the wording used in the koan is unusual, various interpretations have been made of it. I warn you, however: don't be caught by words!

Master Basho Esei was a Korean who later lived on Mount Basho in Kohoku-sho, China. He came over to China looking for a true teacher of Zen, and after visiting several Masters he became a disciple of Master Nanto Koyu, who was a successor of Master Gyozan of the Igyo School. No other biographical details are known about Master Basho, and this koan of "A Stick" is the only teisho recorded as his saying.

The stick here is a kind of cane about seven feet long. It was at first a practical walking stick carried by a Zen monk on his training journey. Now it is often used in ceremonies, and Zen Masters frequently make use of it in mondo and teisho. In some cases it symbolically represents "the One Truth pervading the universe," "original Buddha Nature," "True Self," or "the fundamental 'it.'"

One day Master Basho mounted the rostrum, and holding up a stick he had in his hand, said to the monks, "If you have a stick, I shall give one to you. If you do not have a stick, I shall take it away from you." Having thus spoken, he leaned the stick against the rostrum and immediately withdrew. Master Basho made quite an extraordinary declaration when he said he would give him a stick if the monk had one and would take it away if he did not have one; obviously this has given rise to serious discussion.

Master Daii Bokitsu further complicated the matter by giving the following teisho on Master Basho's statement: "I, Daii, am different from Master Basho. If you have a stick, I shall take it away from you. If you do not have a stick, I shall give one to you. I am like this. You monks, can you make use of the stick or not? If you can, you may be Tokusan's vanguard and Rinzai's rearguard. If you cannot, return it to me, its original master." Master Bokitsu's comment naturally aroused much controversy. For instance, some say, "Once a person is awakened to the Buddha Nature, for which ignorance and satori are one, the giving or taking away of a stick, or whether one has it or not, do not come into question." Others may say that the real significance of a stick can be grasped depending on whether you can use it or not, and has nothing to do with "giving" or "taking away." These are conceptual interpretations attached to the superficial meanings of the words. The fact that such opinions are not based on actual training and experience has resulted in these unexpected misconceptions.

In actual training in Zen, by giving you may take away, and by taking away you may give. What is essential here is the live Zen Truth working, which is not at all concerned with conceptual interpretations or common-sense understanding. From the standpoint of actual training, Master Bokitsu's stick and Master Basho's stick are one and the same in developing the working of compassion, and we must not be bound by the superficial meanings of the words. If one is attached to satori, the Master will beat him and take his satori away. If one is in ignorance, the Master will beat him and take the ignorance away. In this manner the Master freely deals his severe blows of compassion, trying to awaken his disciples to absolute spirituality, which is utterly lucid and transparent. One has to be able to read clearly between the lines the live significance of words, drawing upon his own training and experience; otherwise, the Truth of ancient Masters' sayings will be lost forever. Master Mumon's real intention in presenting this koan to his disciples is also to be found here.

An ancient Master's commentary poem on this koan says:

> He robs a farmer of his plowing ox
> And snatches food from a hungry man.

This poem may help you to get a glimpse of what the koan is telling you. Let me repeat: with a stick the Master gives you severe blows of compassion. He leads you to real emancipation by taking away from you what is most important to you and inseparable from you.

TEISHO ON MUMON'S COMMENTARY

"It helps you cross the river where the bridge is broken. It accompanies you as you return to the village on a moonless night. If you call it a stick, you will go to hell as fast as an arrow."

How freely and wonderfully this stick works! With it you can cross the unbridged river; with it you are safe on a dark, moonless night. There can be nothing more helpful than this stick in passing through the difficulties of our everyday life. Why? Because with its wonderful working it smashes all obstructions and brings about transparently lucid spirituality with no hindrances whatsoever. If, however, a name is given to this stick, it restricts the stick, which immediately turns out to be an obstruction, and true freedom is lost. Listen to Master Mumon, who emphatically warns you, "If you call it a stick, you will go to hell as fast as an arrow."

TEISHO ON MUMON'S POEM

> The deep and the shallow wherever they may be
> Are all in my hand.
> It sustains heaven and supports the earth,
> And promotes Zen Truth wherever it may be.

According to an old saying, "In order to sound the depth of water, a measure is needed; in order to test a man, words are needed." Checking the depth and shallowness of the spirituality of Zen men throughout the land, Master Mumon says he will give a stick and a beating to one who does not have a stick; he will take the stick away from one who has a stick and give him a beating; he will take the stick away from one who does not have a stick and give him a beating; he will give a stick and a beating to one who has a stick. It is the wonderful working of the stick that it leads everyone to the absolute spirituality which is utterly lucid and free. This working of compassion is capable of sustaining heaven and supporting the earth, and of promoting true Dharma wherever it may be. When you are a stick through and through, transcending yourself, nothing in the world can disturb you.

Master Yu of Honei has the following poem commenting on this koan:

> If he has a stick, take it away in front of him.
> If he does not have a stick, snatch it away behind him.
> Jet-black darkness emits light—what a spectacle!
> It strikes and opens hundreds and thousands of gates.

In the last line Master Yu thoroughly and most pertinently describes the wonderful working of a stick.

45

Who Is He?

Our Patriarch Master Hoen of Tozan said, "Sakyamuni and Maitreya are but his servants. Now tell me, who is he?"

MUMON'S COMMENTARY

If you can see him and are absolutely clear about him, it will be like coming upon your own father at the crossroads. You do not have to ask someone else whether you are correct or incorrect in recognizing him as your father.

MUMON'S POEM

> Do not draw another man's bow;
> Do not ride another man's horse;
> Do not defend another man's fault;
> Do not inquire into another man's affairs.

TEISHO ON THE KOAN

This koan, though it is very simple, is full of the sharp and lofty spirit characteristic of Hoen's Zen. Have faith as firm as that seen in this koan!

Cultivate Zen ability as stable as that seen in this koan! With his overflowing compassion, Master Hoen warns you not to debase yourself, not to lose sight of the incomparably great light you were originally born with. As for Master Hoen, please refer to the thirty-fifth koan, "Sen-jo and Her Soul are Separated."

The present koan starts with "Our Patriarch Master Hoen." As Master Mumon is Master Hoen's Dharma grandson, it is with respect and affection that he calls him "Our Patriarch Master Hoen."

One day Master Hoen gave a striking teisho, which even sounds shocking: "Sakyamuni and Maitreya are but his servants. Now tell me, who is he?" All Buddhists pay their utmost homage to Sakyamuni, giving him such titles as the Buddha, or the World-Honored One. They equally respect Maitreya as the future Buddha, who will be born in this world to save all beings of the generations yet to come. Yet before "him," they are only lowly servants. Now tell me who this "he" is, Hoen demands.

Do you know "him," who makes the noblest, the holiest, and the most revered saints in the world his servants? Anyone would naturally be astounded at this extraordinary question.

A Japanese Zen writing, *Seihaku-sho,* says, "Sakyamuni and Maitreya are Patriarchs of the present and the future, and they also are past Buddhas. Buddhas of these three worlds (past, present, and future) are the most revered in Buddhism, and dogmatic and doctrinal Buddhists adore and venerate them devotedly. Now, this is not the case with Zen. They are the lowly underservants and undermaids employed by 'him.' They are 'his' most humble footmen. Who is this 'he'? Arouse the Great Doubt in yourself and see!"

The Great Doubt and the Great Satori are two sides of the same coin. An ancient Master says, "Under the Great Doubt is the Great Satori. If the mountain is high, the valley is deep. If the object is large, its shadow is also large." Inquire, inquire, and inquire exhaustively until the whole universe is just one lump of Great Doubt. At this extremity, if you do not stop but go on doubting and inquiring further, then, when the opportunity is ripe, the time will come when the Great Doubt will naturally be broken through by itself, and you will directly come upon "him." You will then really know that the old Masters did not deceive you. (Please read once more the forty-first koan, "Bodhidharma and Peace of Mind.")

The ancient Masters were never tired of pointing out that "he" is not somebody standing over against "I," that "he" is the one who is alone in the universe unaccompanied by anything, that "he" is the "True Man of no title," that "he" is the Master, or Absolute Subjectivity, that "he" is one's original True Self. However precisely you may describe "him," you will miss him if

you ever try to describe him at all; you have to grasp him and be him yourself
if you want to really know "him."

It is recorded that as soon as Master Hoen asked, "Who is he?" Master
Kaisei Kaku replied, "Kochosan and Kokurishi," which is the same as "Jack
and Betty." These are the commonest names of ordinary people. From what
standpoint did Master Kaku make them "the Only One," or "he" who em-
ploys Sakyamuni and Maitreya as his servants? Let me warn you once more:
Don't be deluded by names. Only he whose spiritual eye has been clearly
opened, who transcends the holy and the lowly, can really know "him." You
have personally and intimately to know "him," or be "him."

TEISHO ON MUMON'S COMMENTARY

"If you can see him and are absolutely clear about him, it will be like
coming upon your own father at the crossroads. You do not have to ask
someone else whether you are correct or incorrect in recognizing him as your
father."

To really see "him" is for one to be "him" through and through, and have
the clear realization of it. When you are actually "him," how can there be room
for correct or incorrect judgments about him? Even Master Mumon with his
sharp tongue could not give any other comment, but could only say, "You do
not have to ask someone else what your father looks like."

Another Zen Master says, "You know your own thing best yourself. Nothing can be more certain. If you see, what you see is yourself; if you hear, what
you hear is yourself; if you think, what you think about is yourself. 'Your
father' is just an example of what is most intimate with you. The fact is,
everything is you. Then how can there be room for any doubt?"

TEISHO ON MUMON'S POEM

> Do not draw another man's bow;
> Do not ride another man's horse;
> Do not defend another man's fault;
> Do not inquire into another man's affairs.

"Another man," repeated in the poem, is the relativistic other standing
over against "I." The four lines here can be summarized in any one line. When
all of the "other" or objectivity is thoroughly cast away, all of the "I," the

subjectivity, is also gone. And when this takes place, "he," the Only True One, will be fully manifested.

> A cuckoo sings;
> At its rare song
> I have forgotten the dream I had just now.

"The dream" here means I-myself, and the universe, and everything. What does this poem try to tell us? The following are some famous words of Master Dogen:

> To attain Buddha Dharma is to attain myself.
> To attain myself is to forget myself.
> To forget myself is to be testified to by everything in the world.
> To be testified to by everything is to have the body and mind of my self and of another's self dropped away.

You may intellectually understand what Master Dogen says, but to grasp and live in this spirituality yourself, experientially, is not at all easy.

46

Step Forward From the Top of a Pole

KOAN

Master Sekiso said, "From the top of a pole one hundred feet high, how do you step forward?" An ancient Master also said that one sitting at the top of a pole one hundred feet high, even if he has attained "it," has not yet been truly enlightened. He must step forward from the top of the pole one hundred feet high and manifest his whole body in the ten directions.

MUMON'S COMMENTARY

If you can step forward and turn back, is there anything you dislike as unworthy? But even so, tell me, from the top of a pole one hundred feet high, how do you step forward? Sah!

MUMON'S POEM

The eye in the forehead has gone blind,
And he has been misled by the stuck pointer on the scale.
He has thrown away his body and laid down his life—
A blind man is leading other blind men.

TEISHO ON THE KOAN

The top of a pole one hundred feet high is the summit of the highest mountain; which signifies the purest spirituality in which no thought has started to move. To be at the top means that he has opened his spiritual eye. If he settles down there, however, it turns out to be a cave. He has to go into the defiled world, hiding his brilliance. With his face covered with sweat and his head with dust, he has to live and work on the busy and crowded street. A Zen man of real attainment and capability is one who has cast off the holy smack of satori. If you have any satori at all, cast away every bit of it! This is why humble attitudes and compassionate working are to be developed. To talk about such a Zen life may be easy, but to live up to it in actuality is not easy at all, and that is why Master Mumon stresses this point in the koan.

The koan starts with "Master Sekiso said," and there have been various opinions as to who this Master Sekiso could be. On Mount Sekiso in Konan-sho, there was a Zen monastery that had been famous since the T'ang dynasty, and the many Zen Masters who lived in this monastery as its successive abbots were all called "Master Sekiso." After careful studies it is now agreed that the Master Sekiso in this koan is Master Sekiso Soen (968–1039). Master Mumon belongs to his Dharma line.

Master Sekiso Soen was born in South China and ordained when he was twenty-two years old. He traveled extensively looking for the right teacher and became a disciple of Master Funyo Zensho, to whom he finally succeeded. He was influential in promoting the true spirit of Rinzai Zen and played an important part in the history of Zen in China.

Although the koan takes the form of Master Soen's teisho, his own words are very few, "From the top of a pole one hundred feet high, how do you step forward?" The latter half of the koan is an ancient Master's saying added by Master Mumon.

"From the top of a pole one hundred feet high, how do you step forward?" had been a popular saying in Zen circles prior to the time of Master Soen, and its meaning was well known among Zen monks. Its significance, however, is ever new in actual training, for it indicates an essential point that every Zen student has to keep always in mind while carrying on his Zen studies.

"To be at the top of a hundred-foot pole" or "to sit on the summit of the highest mountain" means that one has fulfilled his upward or "ascending-the-mountain" training. As the result of his ardent training even at the risk of his own life, he has now opened his spiritual eye. If, however, one settles down in this attainment and becomes intoxicated with this pure spirituality, where there is neither satori nor ignorance, life or death, I or you, then he has fallen into a static oneness. It is but a lifeless, empty nothingness which, like a dead, scorched seed, produces nothing. It can never be the true satori of Zen.

The Zen student has to step out of this oneness. He has to live in the midst of people and work under thousands of varied conditions in differentiation. He has to get rid of all the stink of Zen, or the smack of satori, and as an ordinary man live the Truth of Oneness. How can he do this? How can he take this step forward? In order to answer this question experientially, never-ending actual training is needed in Zen.

Master Soen's few words are sufficiently to the point, but Master Mumon added a saying of an ancient Master to emphasize what had been said. "An ancient Master" here is Master Chosa Keishin. Little is known about Master Chosa, but he left excellent sayings and poems and is respected in the history of Zen as a great Master with poetic endowments and lofty spirituality.

There is an old mondo that will show you one aspect of Master Chosa. Master Chosa and Master Gyozan were good friends. One evening in autumn they were admiring the moon together. Suddenly Master Gyozan pointed to the sky and said, as if to himself, "This clear, bright moon! Though everyone has it, there is scarcely anyone who can freely use it." "Yes, there are some who can use it," said Master Chosa, "I can show it to you, if you wish." "That is interesting. I should like to see it," Gyozan answered. Even as Gyozan spoke, Chosa sprang upon him like lightning and knocked him down. Rising to his feet, Gyozan commented with admiration, "You are really a tiger!" Hence Master Chosa was given the nickname, "Shin the Tiger." Master Chosa's saying quoted here by Master Mumon as that of "an ancient Master" serves to emphasize what Master Sekiso said.

There is a unique Zen text called "The Ten Oxherding Pictures." This work explains the processes of training in Zen by comparing them to those of oxherding, and in doing so Master Kakuan, the author, introduces ten pictures showing different stages of training and spirituality, so that ordinary people can easily follow them. The eighth picture of "The Ten Oxherding Pictures" consists of an empty circle, by which Master Kakuan symbolizes the exquisite spirituality in which there is neither satori nor ignorance, and saint and fool are transcended. An early Master, however, comments on this absolute oneness, "The great emptiness does not yet come up to our teaching." This is the same as to say, "One sitting at the top of a pole one hundred feet high, even if he has attained it, has not yet been truly enlightened."

The ninth picture of the "Ten Oxherding Pictures" is "Returning to the Origin, Back to the Source," which refers to the spirituality of the one who accepts and lives with the ups and downs of changing circumstances in the world, just as they are. Master Kakuan then adds the tenth picture "Entering the City with Bliss-Bestowing Hands," and in this last picture he depicts a man who lives with the poor and lowly, enjoying with them and sorrowing with them. His head is covered with dust and his face is soiled with sweat. This life of compassion of a sacred fool is the ideal life in Zen. To "step forward from the top of the hundred-foot pole and manifest his whole body in the ten directions," refers to nothing other than this downward or "descending-the-mountain" training. Let us remember that if we live the life of an obviously wise and holy man, or behave with apparent Zen likeness, we are still immature and should be ashamed of that immaturity. I tell you, it is not easy to live a real Zen life.

TEISHO ON MUMON'S COMMENTARY

"If you can step forward and turn back, is there anything you dislike as unworthy? But even so, tell me, from the top of a pole one hundred feet high, how do you step forward? Sah!"

Master Mumon says, "If you can really step forward from a hundred-foot pole and turn back, that is, if you can return to your everyday life and live as an ordinary man, then every movement of your hand and foot will create a new breeze. No matter what you may do, you cannot but develop your working of the Truth." Let me remind you that this statement can only be made by one who has achieved the top of the pole. Those who have not yet attained it must not carelessly imitate the words. The attainment here has to be the actual experience of each student, and it is never the subject of conceptual discussion.

Master Mumon then changes his tone and asks exactly as in the koan, "Tell me, from the top of a pole one hundred feet high, how do you step forward?" At the end he cries, "Sah!" "Don't hesitate! Jump straight down! Go!" shouts Master Mumon. This is his shout of encouragement for you to cast off all of the smack of holiness and the stink of Zen.

TEISHO ON MUMON'S POEM

> The eye in the forehead has gone blind,
> And he has been misled by the stuck pointer on the scale.
> He has thrown away his body and laid down his life—
> A blind man is leading other blind men.

"The eye in the forehead" is not an ordinary eye, but is the third eye to see through the world of another dimension. In other words, it is the eye of satori. This is certainly a precious and sacred eye, but if one becomes intoxicated with its blessedness and gives himself to its wonder and grows addicted to it, then it immediately turns into the eye of ignorance. "The eye in the forehead has gone blind, and he has been misled by the stuck pointer on the scale," symbolizes this stupidity. The pointer on the scale can serve its purpose only if it is free to move. The scale with a stuck pointer can no longer work as a scale. In other words, satori loses its working and is no longer satori.

Master Mumon does not forget to add his words of warning. "You may have trained yourself well, throwing away your body and laying down your life, and you may now have reached the top of the pole one hundred feet high; but I tell you, if you have any attainment at all, cast away every bit of it." Unless you step forward from the hundred-foot pole—that is, unless you are so well trained as to live peacefully as an ordinary man in the world of differentiation—your attainment is of no real use. It will be like a blind man leading other blind people. Not only will you be unable to save yourself, but you will lead others to the sea of wrong teaching where you will all be drowned. Zen students have to take this strict admonition to heart.

47

Tosotsu's Three Barriers

Master Juetsu of Tosotsu made three barriers to test monks.

To inquire after the Truth, groping your way through the underbrush, is for the purpose of seeing into your nature. Here, now, where is your nature, Venerable Monk?

If you realize your own nature, you certainly are free from life and death. When your eyes are closed, how can you be free from life and death?

If you are free from life and death, you know where you will go. When the four elements are decomposed, where do you go?

MUMON'S COMMENTARY

If you can rightly give the three turning words here, you will be the master wherever you may be, and live up to the Dharma no matter how varied the circumstances. If, however, you are unable to give them, I warn you, you will get tired of the food you have bolted, and well-chewed food keeps hunger away.

MUMON'S POEM

This one instant, as it is, is an infinite number of kalpas.
An infinite number of kalpas are at the same time this one instant.
If you see into this fact,
The True Self which is seeing has been seen into.

TEISHO ON THE KOAN

This koan has been famous from ancient times as the one to help in establishing transparent spirituality, absolutely free and sublime. Although three barriers are presented, needless to say they are ultimately but one barrier to seeing into one's nature. "Seeing into one's nature," or *kensho* in Japanese, is an inner experience of awakening to one's True Self of no-form. This experience is possible only when one personally realizes his original nature, or the Buddha Nature. In Zen training this experience of seeing into one's nature is the first and the last requisite, since the wonderful Zen life of having transcended life and death, or of free working in differentiation, is but a natural outcome of this fundamental experience.

Master Tosotsu Juetsu was born in the southern part of Kosei-sho and was ordained while he was still a young boy. First he studied the sutras of Mahayana and Theravada Buddhism, but later he decided to study Zen. He visited Masters at various places and finally became Master Hobo Kokumon's Dharma successor. Later he moved to Tosotsu Monastery in northern Kosei-sho, where he began his teaching activities. In order to test visitors and newcomers he used these three barriers, but there was hardly anyone who could rightly pass through them. It was toward the end of Master Tosotsu's life that the famous Zen layman, Mujin, who was a high governmental official in the Sung dynasty, became his disciple and studied Zen under him. Mujin's poems are introduced later.

Although I have just said, "Toward the end of Master Tosotsu's life," he was only forty-eight years old, with great promise for the future, when he died in 1091. One day he gathered his disciples around his bed, showed them this, his last poem, and died serenely.

> Forty-eight years!
> I am all done with the ignorant and the wise.
> I am not a hero.
> My way to Nirvana is serene and peaceful.

"The Gateless Barrier!" Master Mumon declared at the beginning. How ridiculous it is, then, to say there are three barriers! This is certainly the barrier of barriers. Those who are able to pass through it will not ask, and those who ask are unable to pass through it. Master Hakuin, too, set his own barrier, "Listen to the sound of one hand clapping!" Hakuin says this is a means of "waiting for a brave warrior by setting a high prize." Master Tosotsu's three barriers must also be a means of waiting for a brave warrior by setting a high prize.

Master Tosotsu's first impregnable barrier: "To inquire after the Truth, groping your way through the underbrush, is for the purpose of seeing into your nature. Here, now, where is your nature, Venerable Monk?"

A Zen student spares no pains in seeking after the Truth. Trying to find a good Master, he may sleep in the open air and eat berries in the field. His eager search and training are only for the purpose of "seeing into his nature," says Master Tosotsu. This experience of "seeing into one's nature" is called satori. It is the most important and basic experience in Zen—an experience each student must attain for himself.

What is this experience of "seeing into one's nature"? It is to see into one's original true nature and be awakened to one's True Self. When this is accomplished, the student has transcended life and death, and his mind is thoroughly at peace. Established in this absolute freedom he will freely live in this busy world of ours. Everyone in this world has to face this fundamental question at least once in life.

Most people give themselves up to the pressure of temporal affairs and blindly pass through their days and nights. On some occasions, however, one may reflect on the ever-changing pictures of human life. He will realize the inevitable limitations and restrictions of man's everyday living. Once he has realized this actual human situation, he can no longer be indifferent, but feels an urge to solve this fundamental problem; he has to see into his nature at any cost.

This is indeed the fundamental problem, not only for Zen students but for everybody in the world. In other words, it is my fundamental problem to see into my nature; it is your fundamental problem to see into your nature. Master Tosotsu's question, "Here, now, where is your nature, Venerable Monk?" is thus addressed to each one of us.

Some may explain that this nature is one's original true nature with which he was born; that it is one's True Self that is revealed here, now, penetrating the three worlds (past, present, and future) and pervading the whole universe; that it is only this formless True Self restricted by nothing; or that it is the Reality which is neither alive nor dead. Needless to say, Master Tosotsu is not asking for these speculative explanations. He wants you to show it directly and concretely, here and now. What you can do here is to present the fact of your seeing into your nature in front of the Master, and what the Master can do here is to say either Yes or No. Unless you are established in your own definite experience, you can never answer his question. Yet if you give an affirmative answer, such relativistic affirmation has to be smashed away; if your answer is negative, such dead negation has to be cast away. Certainly the barrier set by Master Tosotsu is impregnable.

Let go your hold on the edge of the precipice and die to this small self. Then what is naturally revealed is the Buddha Nature, or the true nature, in which there is neither life nor death, long nor short, I nor you, time nor space. What definitely is there is the fact of your body and mind having dropped away. At any cost you have to have this experience of absolute self-realization once and for all. Without it you can never expect to see Master Tosotsu face to face.

Sakyamuni Buddha's enlightenment at seeing the glittering morning star, Master Reiun's awakening at the sight of plum blossoms, or Master Mumon's breaking through the barrier at the drumbeat are all nothing other than the experience of having their body and mind drop away. The forty-eight barriers of the *Mumonkan* are also barriers for you, to help you have your body and mind drop away.

An ancient Master comments on this first barrier:

> It is on this mountain.
> Because of the heavy mist, the exact location is unknown.

Let me warn you, never busy yourself seeking after it outwardly. Every one of the students has to be awakened to it personally, after hard and sincere discipline. There is no easy shortcut to it.

Master Tosotsu now sets his second barrier demanding a Zen response from his monks. "If you realize your own nature, you certainly are free from life and death. When your eyes are closed [and you are dead], how can you be free from life and death?" "To be free from life and death" is to be free from the dualistic restrictions of life and death. In other words, one now lives with absolute freedom because for him life and death are at once no-life and no-death. The *Nirvana Sutra* says, "All beings equally have the Buddha Nature and are in essence emancipated. Because of their attachment to their egoistic minds, they go astray in ignorance and suffer various restrictions. If they return to the Truth, shaking off their ignorance and transcending the restrictions, they become free, they are enlightened just as all Buddhas are. They are not different from Buddhas."

In fact, if one has truly broken through Master Tosotsu's first barrier, the second barrier has already been passed through also. That is because satori, or seeing into one's own nature, is the realization that life and death, coming and going, are all formless. With life, just as he lives, he has transcended life. With death, just as he dies, he has transcended death. There is nothing to dislike in life and death; there is nothing to welcome in Nirvana. He knows no useless distinctions such as transcendence or nontranscendence, emancipation or nonemancipation.

Once a monk came to see Master Egen, the founder of Myoshinji in Kyoto, and said, "I have come to train myself in order to solve the question of life and death." Master Egen drove him away saying, "At Egen's place there is no such thing as life and death!" This is a famous story in Zen circles. The same Master Egen passed away while talking with his successor, Master Juo, as they were standing by the pond in the Myoshinji garden.

Master Tosotsu asks, "When your eyes are closed, how can you be free from life and death?" He is not expecting to hear any logical explanations. He is urging you to show him concretely how you will die here and now, setting aside all conceptual arguments.

An ancient Zen Master said simply, "A poisoned arrow has gone straight to your heart!" This illustrates how directly he has broken through the barrier. Yet unless you yourself are established in the experiential fact, your appreciation is not real.

Master Daimin was the founder of Nanzenji and as a teacher of the emperor was much respected. At the moment of death, with the emperor close by his bed, Master Daimin wrote the following farewell poem and serenely died.

> In coming I have no abode,
> In leaving I have no fixed direction.
> How is it ultimately?
> Here I am all the time!

Master Ryutan in his last moments cried out and struggled in agony. When the disciples tried to stop him from crying out, Master Ryutan said, "I tell you, my agonized crying is not different at all from my joyful singing."

Master Bankei was visited by an old man who begged, "My last hour is approaching; please teach me how to prepare myself for death." "No preparation is needed," answered Master Bankei. "Why is it unnecessary?" asked the old man. "When the time comes for you to die, just die," was Bankei's reply.

The sayings of the Masters vary widely, but the fact that all of them are free from life and death is clear and decisive. If your eye of satori is not thoroughgoing, you cannot expect to pass through the second barrier.

Master Tosotsu's third barrier insistently asks, "If you are free from life and death, you know where you will go. When the four elements are decomposed, where do you go?" This barrier again illustrates points that are likely to be misinterpreted by many people. It is addressed not only to Zen students but to everybody, and it stands in front of us as the most difficult barrier of all.

Though it may be extremely difficult, if you have truly broken through the first barrier and live in the spirituality that enables you to say that "life and death, coming and going—these are all workings of the True Self," then your breaking through one barrier must be the same as breaking through hundreds and thousands of barriers. You will realize that you are coming and going where in reality there is no coming and going. Seeing into one's nature is to have this absolute freedom that can never be disturbed. Though you may understand this Truth intellectually, yet various obstructions and illusions will interfere with your actually living up to it. This is why Master Tosotsu's compassionate third barrier is needed.

According to ancient understanding the four elements composing a human body are earth, water, fire, and air. The phrase here, "the four elements," is therefore equivalent to a physical human body. The third barrier asks, "When your flesh is decomposed and your physical form perishes, where do you go?" We all have feelings and emotions that are deeply rooted in our minds. Master Tosotsu, out of his compassion, tries to eradicate such emotional attachments as ours.

In actual training the Master will not listen to any conceptual or philosophical arguments. The only answer that will satisfy him is the concrete fact of your having broken through the barrier. An early Master commented on the koan in this poem:

> The corpse is here.
> Where is the man?
> Truly, I know
> The spirit is not in this bag of skin.

Master Daie disapproved of the poem as a heretical view that recognized spirit apart from flesh, body apart from spirit. Daie's own famous commentary poem reads:

> This corpse, as it is, is the man.
> The spirit is the bag of skin,
> The bag of skin is the spirit.

"Life-and-death, as it is, is Buddha life," is Master Dogen's famous saying. Realize therefore that this is the Truth at one instant, that is the Truth at another instant. Each and every thing is I-myself in the Dharma world. How can there be anything that is not the newly born True Self? Listen to Master Ryokan's death poem:

> Showing now its front side,
> Now its back,
> Falls the maple leaf.

In training at the monastery, the Master may suddenly ask you, "Where do you go when you are dead?" He will not tolerate even a moment of hesitation in your reply.

Master Ekkei commented on Master Tosotsu's third barrier, "All say the bag of skin is the spirit; the spirit is the bag of skin. Totsu! Where are you leaving for? I will return, if not to Kanan (south), then to Kahoku (north). How can you say such a thing? Mountain after mountain, I just go on my long journey. Do I come to its end some day? All the green bamboos in the yard are greeting me."

Master Ekkei then added his own poem.

> The night advances, the whole body is piercingly cold;
> The corpse lies still under the light.
> At dawn, clouds are scattered over Mount Hokubo;
> With a bamboo stick and straw sandals he now goes in his travel
>   clothes.

Mount Hokubo is the mountain of the grave; the cold corpse lying motionless last night is now dressed in traveling clothes with a bamboo stick and straw sandals, and goes on pilgrimage in the morning light.

For the True Self pervading the universe, everything is the live manifestation of the Truth. At each moment he is born anew.

The high government official Mujin, as I said earlier, was a lay disciple of Master Tosotsu. He made a poem on each of his teacher's three barriers.

On the first barrier:

> The summer woods are full of cuckoos singing.
> The sun breaks through floating clouds, clear is the universe.
> Do not ask Sosan about his father Sotetsu,
> For a good son refrains from mentioning his father's name.

On the second barrier:

> The messenger of death has come to take away a life;
> The beautiful countenance has faded away.
> Now it is time to turn round.
> Do not easily let the king of death know of your turning round.

On the third barrier:

> The wives of the village have all gathered.
> In the wilderness the west wind blows, their sleeves are wet with
>   tears.

On the bank of Konan, the reeds are blue and the smartweeds red.

He is here now as Chosan, and drops a fishing line.

"If you can rightly give the three turning words here, you will be the master wherever you may be, and live up to the Dharma no matter how varied the circumstances. If, however, you are unable to give them, I warn you, you will get tired of food you have bolted, and well-chewed food keeps hunger away."

In the first sentence of his commentary Master Mumon says, "If you can give the right turning words to each of Master Tosotsu's three barriers, that is, if you can beautifully pass through the three barriers, you are then really free in life and death. You will be capable of being Absolute Subjectivity under any circumstances. As the master at each moment at each place, whether it be favorable or adverse, you are firmly established in your basic point of view and make free use of the various conditions in which you find yourself." Thus Master Mumon pays the highest tribute to the one who beautifully passes through the three barriers.

I wholeheartedly agree with an ancient Master who said,

Immediately I passed through the serenity of the bright moon and the fresh breeze;

I enjoy myself and am happy in the extreme agony of boiling water and scorching fire.

The universe is a great cathedral of satori. Each and everything in the universe is nothing else but I-myself.

Master Mumon concludes his commentary with the following finishing stroke: "If, however, you are unable to give them, I warn you, you will get tired of the food you have bolted, and well-chewed food keeps hunger away."

An old Zen Master said, "This iron cake, you chew, chew, and chew it away!" It is an awful saying, isn't it? When you have chewed it away, your training will be matured. Master Mumon, out of his grandmotherly compassion, advises us, "If you swallow it blindly without chewing it well, it can never be really useful in your everyday life. Chew it and digest it attentively and diligently, and with sincerity, and grasp it as your own!"

TEISHO ON MUMON'S POEM

> This one instant, as it is, is an infinite number of kalpas.
> An infinite number of kalpas are at the same time this one instant.
> If you see into this fact,
> The True Self which is seeing has been seen into.

Master Mumon seems to have had the following passage from *Kegon-kyo* in mind when he made this commentary poem:

> In one instant infinite numbers of kalpas are realized.
> There is no leaving, no coming, and no abiding.

The meaning here is, "Bodhisattva Manjusri's prajna wisdom directly penetrates the phenomena of the three worlds. In one instant here, now, infinite numbers of kalpas of time are included and boundless space is taken in. It is never disturbed by leaving, coming, or abiding."

If a person opens his satori eye, the whole Dharma world is he-himself. For him, infinite kalpas of time are nothing but this one instant here and now. This instant, here, now, is at once an infinite number of kalpas. This instant is the absolute Now. For the person who lives this absolute instant, every place, wherever it may be, is the one instant—every time, whenever it may be, is the one instant.

In the third and fourth lines Master Mumon says, "If this one instant is seen into here, now, the one who sees into it has been seen into." If this one instant is truly seen into, there is actually neither the seer nor the seen. All names and labels are transcended, and the Reality is fully manifested. There is just "it" through and through, and no room for idle speculation to work. As no instant can be named as such, there can be no nature to be seen into. How, then, can there be life and death to transcend? Actually the seer to see into is the seen to be seen into. Ultimately, how foolish it is to argue about seeing into and being seen into!

> Empty-handed I have returned home.
> I know only that the eyes are horizontal, the nose is vertical.

I have noted earlier this famous saying of Master Dogen when he returned from his long study in China. You have to read into his heart; otherwise you will be unable to appreciate Master Mumon's painstakingly kind instruction.

48

Kempo's One Way

A monk once asked Master Kempo, "The Bhagavats of the ten directions have one way to Nirvana. I wonder where this one way is." Kempo held up his stick, drew a line, and said, "Here it is!"

Later the monk asked Unmon for his instruction on this mondo. Unmon held up his fan and said, "This fan has jumped up to the Thirty-third Heaven and hit the nose of the deity there. The carp of the Eastern Sea leaps, and it rains cats and dogs."

MUMON'S COMMENTARY

The one goes to the bottom of the deep sea and raises a cloud of sand and dust. The other stands on the top of a towering mountain and raises foaming waves to touch the sky. The one holds, the other lets go, and each, using only one hand, sustains the teachings of Zen. What they do is exactly like two children who come running from opposite directions and crash into each other. In the world there is hardly anyone who has truly awakened. From the absolute point of view, the two great Masters do not really know where the way is.

MUMON'S POEM

Before taking a step you have already arrived.
Before moving your tongue you have finished teaching.
Even if at each step you may be ahead of him,
Know there is still another way up.

TEISHO ON THE KOAN

The mondo in this koan quotes a sentence in the *Suramgama Sutra*, "The Bhagavats of the ten directions have one way to Nirvana." In the case of this koan, what is most important is whether the student has correctly grasped the real significance of the question. The student has to study the question thoroughly before worrying about its answer. This koan is unique in illustrating that the answer is to be grasped in the question itself.

Regarding Master Kempo, the main figure in this koan, no details of his life are known except that he was a successor of Master Tozan Ryokai who was a founder of Soto Zen. As for the other important person in the koan, Master Unmon Bunen, since he appears in the fifteenth koan and on several earlier occasions, the details of his life are not given here.

One day a monk came to Master Kempo and asked, "It is written in a sutra that the Bhagavats of the ten directions have one way to Nirvana. Where is this one way?" "Bhagavat" is a Sanskrit word with complex meanings, but here it can be taken in the sense of "Buddha." The sentence therefore means "Buddhas pervading the universe have all entered into the paradise of satori by only one way."

The questioning monk was apparently philosophically minded, and his understanding of Buddha and Nirvana did not go beyond the conceptual interpretations of the terms. A monk in actual training will naturally try to open his spiritual eye to a completely new dimension. If Buddhas are in all the ten directions, can there then be any spot where Buddha is not? If one has truly cast himself away, everything, everywhere, is in the blessing of Buddha. There can be no place where Buddha light does not reach.

The "one way" is then the absolute, transcendental One Way for which there is no far and near, wide and narrow, coming and going. It is the ever unchanging One Way. It may be asking too much to expect a philosophically minded student to read into this sentence from the *Suramgama Sutra* the Zen significance implied in it. His eyes are wide open, but unfortunately he is unable to see. Standing in front of the White House, he is asking where the capital is. How foolish!

Master Kempo at once lifted up the stick he happened to have and drew a clear straight line and said, "Here it is!" Wonderful indeed is his working! Truly the answer is in the question itself. If it is true that "the Bhagavats of the ten directions have one way to Nirvana," how can there be any spot that is not "it"? What you see, what you hear, where you stand, where you sit, is nothing but "it," the One Way. I tell you, just open your spiritual eye. How regrettable that the questioning monk failed to grasp the essence of Master Kempo's supreme answer.

The koan here turns to the second scene. The monk who could not appreciate Master Kempo's reply later came to see Master Unmon. Telling the Master how the mondo had taken place between Master Kempo and himself, the monk asked for Unmon's elucidation, "I wonder where this one way is?" Master Unmon was an outstandingly capable Master who would never resort to a roundabout philosophical explanation. He immediately and most concretely presented the stark fact of "the one way." He held up the fan he had in his hand and said, "This fan has jumped up to the Thirty-third Heaven and hit the nose of the deity there. The carp of the Eastern Sea has leapt, and it has rained cats and dogs, as if a bucketful of water had been turned over." What big talk! What an eccentric remark! No common-sense interpretation is possible here. Let me warn you, however, don't stick to the superficial literal meanings! Listen once more to what Master Mumon sang when he was enlightened at the sound of the drumbeat:

> Everything under the sun has bowed at once.
> Mount Sumeru jumps up and dances.

The one who lives the fact of "the Bhagavats of the ten directions" knows no relativistic discrimination such as big and small, subject and object, wide and narrow. He is utterly free and nothing can ever restrict him. Everything before him is given a new life as the wonderful working of no-mind develops, and a completely new vista is opened up to him. Here I can only repeat that the answer is in the question itself. If I call this working "the wonderful working of no-mind," such naming has already marred "it." The One Way of Zen has to be grasped by each one of you as your own.

T E I S H O   O N   M U M O N ' S   C O M M E N T A R Y

"The one goes to the bottom of the deep sea and raises a cloud of sand and dust. The other stands on the top of a towering mountain and raises foaming waves to touch the sky. The one holds, the other lets go, and each, using only one hand, sustains the teachings of Zen. What they do is exactly like two children who come running from opposite directions and crash into each other. In the world there is hardly anyone who has truly awakened. From the absolute point of view, the two great Masters do not really know where the way is."

Master Mumon, commenting on Master Kempo's reply, says, "The one goes to the bottom of the deep sea and raises a cloud of sand and dust." On Master Unmon's answer he comments, "The other stands on the top of a towering mountain and raises foaming waves to touch the sky." When one reads these sentences literally, on the surface they sound absurd, completely wanting in common sense. One might suspect that they aim to make Zen unapproachable and impregnable for outsiders, but that is far from the truth. Master Mumon is only trying to show most concretely how to appreciate the fact of "the Bhagavats pervading the ten directions" in Zen. In other words, he is urging each of us to get in actual touch with the Truth of this saying and to cast away all of one's self. He wants us, by transcending all dualistic discriminations and attachments, to live a new life of another dimension with absolute freedom.

Some scholars explain that this saying of Master Mumon refers to the Kegon philosophy of "one is all." But Master Mumon used eccentric sounding expressions for no other purpose than to avoid such philosophically plausible interpretations.

He goes on to say, "The one holds, the other lets go, and each, using only one hand, sustains the teachings of Zen. What they do is exactly like two children who come running from opposite directions and crash into each other." Doubtless, "The one holds" is a comment on Master Kempo's answer, which may be described as the spirituality of equality only, or absolute negation. Philosophically it signifies Oneness, or the pure principle only, with no discrimination or intellection working at all. "The other lets go" refers to Master Unmon's answer, which may be explained as the spirituality of differentiation, or absolute affirmation. Philosophically stated, there is nothing to be negated in Dharma, and nothing can ever disturb this spirituality of absolute freedom. Let me remind you: "holding" and "letting go" are, fundamentally speaking, two provisional names given to a working aspect of "it," at one time and at one place. Master Mumon says of the two Masters, "The one works in absolute negation and holds, while the other works in absolute affirmation and lets go. Each develops incomparable Zen teaching in his own way, and it is just like two children who come running from both sides at full speed and crash into each other." Wonderful indeed is Mumon's comment, which beautifully transcends all discriminative argumentation about "holding" and "letting go."

Lastly, Master Mumon concludes with a severe statement, "In the world there is hardly anyone who has truly awakened. From the absolute point of view, the two great Masters do not really know where the way is." "Be that as it may, a truly enlightened one can hardly be found in this world of ours," says Master Mumon, seemingly approving and praising the two Masters. Then he changes his tone and boldly declares, "From this absolute Zen standpoint of mine, however, the two old Masters do not really know where the Way is." Thus he gives his finishing stroke. Viewed from the absolute standpoint, Bodhidharma and Rinzai, too, not to speak of Kempo and Unmon, all, including Mumon himself, do not really know where the Way is. In other words, the yardstick of knowing and not-knowing is of no avail here.

Do not be deluded by words. Grasp the real import of Master Mumon's superb commentary, by which he bluntly denounced the working of the two Masters.

TEISHO ON MUMON'S POEM

> Before taking a step you have already arrived.
> Before moving your tongue you have finished teaching.
> Even if at each step you may be ahead of him,
> Know there is still another way up.

If the Bhagavats pervade the ten directions, how can any place in the universe fail to be the absolute home of the Truth? Green mountains and blue waters, green willows and red flowers, each, as it is, is "it." How can it be otherwise? "Where else can you seek for Dharma? What else can you teach about Dharma?" asks Master Mumon. Actually you are right in "it." How foolish it is to argue about arriving and not-arriving, or teaching and not-teaching about "it"! From the absolute standpoint, Master Kempo's direct demonstration, and Master Unmon's outstanding working are both a lot of fuss about nothing. This is the meaning of the first two lines of Master Mumon's poem, "Before taking a step you have already arrived. Before moving your tongue you have finished teaching."

In the third and fourth lines, the terminology of the game of Go is used. The meaning is that even though you may be able to make an appropriate move at each stone to baffle the sharp movements of the two Masters, remember there is still another way up. This is Master Mumon's strong warning to his disciples. Now I ask you, what kind of way is this "other way up"? Etymologically, the Chinese word for way, here, can also mean "a hole." This is indeed an extraordinary hole in which all the forty-eight koan of the *Mumonkan* lose their light. It is again the incomparable hole that ever remains priceless in all ages and all countries. Is there anyone in the universe who does not lose his life in this hole? Is there anyone in the universe who is not given true life by this hole? Awful indeed is this hole; blessed indeed is this hole! Out of his irresistible compassion, Master Mumon gives his conclusive admonition: "Tear away the cobwebs of all the koan in this hole!"

Incidentally, the fourth line of Master Mumon's poem is quoted from Master Kempo's famous koan, "The Dharma Body has three kinds of diseases and two kinds of light. You must realize there is still another way up." We can see how considerate Master Mumon is in making his commentary poem.

Appendix

Originally the *Mumonkan* ended with the forty-eighth koan. The popular version circulating today, however, has the following appendices:

MUMON'S POSTSCRIPT

These sayings and doings of Buddhas and Patriarchs have all been correctly judged, as if they were crimes confessed by criminals. From the beginning there are no extra words; I have taken the lid off my skull and bulged out my eyeballs. I ask you to grasp "it" directly and do not seek for it outwardly. If you are a capable man of satori, you will immediately get the point as soon as you hear only a little of the presentation. Ultimately, there is no gate to enter and there are no steps to climb. Squaring your elbows, you pass through the barrier without asking the barrier-keeper. Have you not heard what Gensha said, "No-gate is the gate of emancipation; no-mind is the mind of the man of Tao"? Have you not also heard what Hakuin said, "Most clearly Tao is known. It is just 'it.' Why can't you pass?" These explanations are just like smearing milk on the red soil. If you have passed through the Gateless Barrier, you are then making a fool of Mumon. If you are unable to pass through the Gateless Barrier, you are making a mess of yourself. It may be easy to realize the so-called Nirvana mind, but wisdom in differentiation is difficult to attain. When wisdom in differentiation is clearly understood, the nation will automatically be at peace.

The first year of Jotei,
five days before the end of the summer session.
Respectfully written by Monk Mumon Ekai,
eighth in succession from Yogi.

MUMON'S ZEN WARNINGS

To observe the regulations and keep to the rules is tying oneself without a rope. To act freely and unrestrainedly just as one wishes is to do what heretics and demons would do. To recognize mind and purify it is the false Zen of silent sitting. To give rein to oneself and ignore interrelating conditions is to fall into the abyss. To be alert and never ambiguous is to wear chains and an iron yoke. To think of good and evil belongs to heaven and hell. To have a Buddha view and a Dharma view is to be confined in two iron mountains. He who realizes it as soon as a thought arises is one who exhausts his energy. To sit blankly in quietism is the practice of the dead. If one proceeds, he will go astray from the principle. If one retreats, he will be against the Truth. If one neither progresses nor retreats, he is a dead man breathing. Now tell me, what will you do? Work hard and be sure to attain "it" in this life, lest you have eternal regret.

MURYO SOJU'S POEMS
ON ORYO'S THREE BARRIERS

The "Three Barriers" is a koan that Master Oryo always used in questioning his disciples. Master Muryo Soju made a poem on each of Oryo's three barriers and added one of his own at the end, offering these poems as a way of thanking Master Mumon, who had been kind enough to come to give teisho on the forty-eight koan.

Why is my hand like Buddha's hand?
I could feel the pillow at my back,
And involuntarily I gave a great laugh;
In truth, the whole body is the hand.

Why is my leg like a donkey's leg?
Even before taking a step I have already arrived.
Freely I pass over the four seas just as I wish.
I ride backward on Yogi's three-legged donkey.

Everyone has his own cause of birth.
Each has realized his antecedent determinant.
Nata broke his bones and returned them to his father.
Did the Fifth Patriarch ever rely on any paternal relation?

Buddha's hand, donkey's leg, and the cause of birth:
They are neither Buddha, nor Tao, nor Zen.
Do not wonder why Gateless Barriers are so difficult.
They have aroused the monks' intense animosity.

Mumon was lately at Zuigan.
Settling down in the Zen seat, he criticized koan old and new.
He cut off the ways for both the wise and the ordinary.
A number of dragons in hiding may stir up a peal of thunder.

Master Mumon has been invited as the Leading Monk;
I thank him with this humble poem.

Late spring of the third year of Jotei [*1230*]
Written by Muryo Soju

TEISHO ON THE KOAN,
"ORYO'S THREE BARRIERS"

At a Zen monastery in Japan "Oryo's Three Barriers" is used as a koan in actual training, just as the forty-eight koan of the *Mumonkan* are. I will therefore take it up and give my teisho on it as a guidepost for students in training.

Master Oryo Enan (1002–1069) was a successor to Master Sekiso Soen and has been highly respected as the founder of the Oryo School of Zen. Together with his contemporaries Masters Seccho Juken and Goso Hoen, he greatly enhanced the Zen of his time. The following is taken from his biography: "In the sanzen room the Master always asked his monks, 'Everyone has his own cause of birth. What is the cause of your birth?' He squarely faced the student and exchanged mondo. He would also ask, holding out his hand, 'Why is my hand like Buddha's hand?' Thus he tested the attainment of the Zen man on his training journey. Again he would ask, showing his leg, 'Why is my leg like a donkey's leg?' For over thirty years he asked these three questions, and no one could ever satisfy him. Even though some tried to answer, the Master never said the answer was right or wrong. Monks called them 'Oryo's Three Barriers.' "

We can see from this account how Master Oryo guided monks by asking these three questions every day for over thirty years: "What is the cause of your birth?" Holding out his hand, "Why is my hand like Buddha's hand?" Showing his leg, "Why is my leg like a donkey's leg?" Master Oryo died in 1069 at the age of sixty-seven and is honored as one of the greatest Zen Masters of the Sung dynasty.

Another successor of Master Sekiso Soen and a contemporary of Master Oryo is Master Yogi Hoe, founder of the Yogi School of Zen. Rinzai Zen in Japan today belongs to this Yogi School. Master Yogi died in 1049, at what age is not known.

Master Muryo Soju was a grandson in the Dharma succession of Master Daie Shuko, belonging to the Yogi School of Rinzai Zen, and was contemporary with Master Mumon. No other details of his life are known.

Master Soju changed the order of Oryo's three barriers, making "Buddha's hand" first, "the donkey's leg" second, and "cause of birth" last; he made three poems using one of the barriers as the initial line of each.

His first poem is:

Why is my hand like Buddha's hand?
I could feel the pillow at my back,
And involuntarily I gave a great laugh;
In truth, the whole body is the hand.

What is fundamental in Zen is to cast oneself away completely. When there is no self at all, can there be anything in the whole universe that is not self? When you see, all of yourself is the eye. So it is not called "seeing" any longer. When you hear, all of yourself is the ear. So it is not called "hearing" any longer. When you hold, all of yourself is the hand. So it is not called "holding" any longer. When you walk, all of yourself is the foot. So it is not called "walking" any longer. If you fail to grasp this secret in your own experience, you are a stranger to Zen, however beautifully you may talk about Zen. This is exactly the reason Zen has so many varied koan to insist on the primary importance of actual training and experiential appreciation.

Master Oryo used to ask, holding out his hand, "Why is my hand like Buddha's hand?" A student whose spiritual eye is opened will immediately grasp the Truth as soon as Master Oryo holds out his hand, even before he has said a word. Otherwise he is not worthy of the name Zen man.

An ancient Zen Master said, commenting on it,

In the moonlight
He plays a lute.

This is a beautiful poem, but I am afraid that the Reality may have already been lost, and what there is is shadow only.

Master Soju adds his own lines to Oryo's "Why is my hand like Buddha's hand?"

I could feel the pillow at my back,
And involuntarily I gave a great laugh;
In truth, the whole body is the hand.

What he really wants to say must be the last line, "The whole body is the hand." I would say, if the whole body is the hand it is better not to call it "hand." Then, I ask you, how do you answer? Your concrete and live working has to be shown here.

The eighty-ninth koan in the *Hekigan-roku* has a mondo between Ungan and his teacher, Master Dogo. Ungan asked Master Dogo, "What does the Bodhisattva of Great Compassion do with his many eyes and hands?" Dogo said, "It is like a man feeling for the pillow at his back at midnight." Ungan said, "I have got it." Dogo asked, "How have you got it?" Ungan said, "The whole body is the eye and the hand."

Needless to say, the essence of Master Soju's poem is the same as the essence of this mondo.

The second poem is:

> *Why is my leg like a donkey's leg?*
> Even before taking a step I have already arrived.
> Freely I pass over the four seas just as I wish.
> I ride backward on Yogi's three-legged donkey.

Showing his leg, Master Oryo used to ask, "Why is my leg like a donkey's leg?" A student whose Zen eye is clearly opened will never be so stupid as to be deluded by such words as "Buddha's hand" or "a donkey's leg." He has to grasp the Truth firmly as soon as Master Oryo shows his leg. Otherwise, as in the case of "Buddha's hand," he is not worthy of the name of Zen man. An early Zen Master commented on this,

> Traces of clogs
> Clearly left on the green moss.

Rightly stated though it is, if you are concerned with the expression, alas, the Reality has already been lost and you are clinging to its shadow. When you truly transcend yourself, the whole universe is but the leg, isn't it?

To Master Oryo's "Why is my leg like a donkey's leg?" Master Soju adds his own lines.

> Even before taking a step I have already arrived.
> Freely I pass over the four seas just as I wish.
> I ride backward on Yogi's three-legged donkey.

The one who has truly transcended himself has no leg. How can there be any "taking a step" or "not taking a step"? Naturally, he can go over the four seas without moving his leg.

Once a monk asked Master Yogi, "What is Buddha?" "A three-legged donkey goes by clattering his hoofs," answered Master Yogi. "Three-legged donkey" is another name for the one who has transcended his leg; or it is another name for the True Self of no-form. Moreover, Master Soju says that he rides it "backward." He certainly must have been a veteran, firmly based on actual training in Zen. Vividly he presents here the Reality of which all expressions in words fall far short. No concept or philosophy can ever have even a glimpse of it.

The third poem is:

> *Everyone has his own cause of birth.*
> Each has realized his antecedent determinant.
> Nata broke his bones and returned them to his father.
> Did the Fifth Patriarch ever rely on any paternal relation?

Master Oryo made this the first of his three barriers. This is indeed the hardest nanto barrier of the three. It is an indisputable fact that every sentient being has its own cause. It has its direct determinant, and definite circumstances are responsible for its being born in the world. Concerning this, in India it has been traditionally believed that a life in this present world is the effect of karmic causation from one's past life, and that one's parents serve only as a subsidiary condition to help it. In this koan, the true cause of birth is to be grasped in the sphere even prior to past karmic cause, and students are urged to plunge into this absolute and fundamental Zen sphere. It is exactly at this point that the unique characteristic of Zen becomes apparent. In other words, Zen asks you to be awakened to "your True Self that is prior to the birth of your parents" and thus opens up for you a dimensionally different and new vista. It casts off the chain of transmigration and asks you to be born anew as the eternal True Self. For this, however, hard and assiduous training with your whole being is definitely required.

Commenting on "the cause of birth," an old Zen Master said:

> Early in the morning I ate rice gruel,
> Now I feel hungry again.

Though the comment is correct, I am afraid students may lose themselves in a cobweb of philosophical interpretations.

In training in a monastery the Master may suddenly ask you, "From where were you born?" If you hesitate even for a moment, the Master's severe slap will fall on you immediately.

Master Soju adds his words to Master Oryo's "Everyone has his own cause of birth":

> Each has realized his antecedent determinant.
> Nata broke his bones and returned them to his father.
> Did the Fifth Patriarch ever rely on any paternal relation?

To realize one's antecedent determinant is to awaken to "the True Self that is prior to the birth of one's parents." It is to be born anew as a person of Absolute Subjectivity.

The third line, "Nata broke his bones and returned them to his father," refers to a story in *Goto Egen*, volume 2: "Prince Nata tore off his flesh and returned it to his mother; he broke his bones and returned them to his father. Having done so, he revealed his true body, and making use of his supernatural power he taught the Dharma for the sake of his parents." This physical body of yours, given by your parents, is but a temporal form which is subject to coming and going. Only when you have transcended this temporal physical body can you attain the eternal, true body—that is, realize your antecedent determinant. This is what Prince Nata's story tries to illustrate.

The last line, "Did the Fifth Patriarch ever rely on any paternal relation?" is concerned with the following legendary story about the Fifth Patriarch, Master Gunin. In his previous life Master Gunin had been a hermit called Saisho Doja, who lived on Mount Hato. One day in that former life he happened to meet Doshin, the Fourth Patriarch, on a mountain and asked if he could study Zen under him. The Fourth Patriarch, however, told Saisho Doja that he was too old to start his study and that he should be reborn to study Zen. Thereupon Saisho Doja borrowed the womb of a daughter of the Shu family and was born again, without a father. Later when he grew up he met the Fourth Patriarch and finally became his successor.

In his last line Master Soju presents the true body, or True Self, which does not rely on the paternal relation, so that we may grasp the secret of the cause of birth that realizes our antecedent determinants.

Then Master Soju makes another poem to comment on all three barriers as a whole:

> Buddha's hand, donkey's leg, and the cause of birth:
> They are neither Buddha, nor Tao, nor Zen.
> Do not wonder why Gateless Barriers are so difficult.
> They have aroused the monks' intense animosity.

Oryo's Three Barriers, "Buddha hand," "a donkey's leg," and "cause of birth," are neither Buddha, nor Tao, nor Zen; they are those most impregnable barriers that are ever unnamable. As to the forty-eight barriers of the *Mumonkan*, it is no wonder that they are so rugged and unapproachable, resisting every possible effort to break through. They will certainly arouse the deep animosity of monks in the world and make them show the white feather.

What Master Soju really means is that it was very fortunate for the monks that they could face Mumon's barriers. In order to express the greatest joy, which can never be overemphasized, he uses such strong words as "intense animosity." Though superficially the words seem to mean just the opposite of what he says, this is again the usual favorite means of Zen Masters. Master Soju is encouraging his monks so that with this intense animosity they will create refreshing Zen winds in the world.

At the end Master Soju expresses his appreciation to Master Mumon in a poem.

> Mumon was lately at Zuigan.
> Settling down in the Zen seat, he criticized koan old and new.
> He cut off the ways for both the wise and the ordinary.
> A number of dragons in hiding may stir up a peal of thunder.

This poem expresses Master Soju's deep gratitude to Master Mumon, as well as his great expectation for his monks. Master Soju is saying, "Recently Master Mumon stayed at my temple, Zuiganji, and settling down in his Zen seat he criticized old and new koan without reserve, cut off the ways for both saints and ordinary men alike, and there was no holding him back. Inspired by Master Mumon's sharp and preeminent Zen working, it is expected that those Zen monks who are now quiet in their secluded life may muster up their courage for the sake of the Dharma, and stir up thunder in the Zen world."

At the end, Master Soju tells how his poem of appreciation came to be made:

> Master Mumon has been invited as the Leading Monk;
> I thank him with this humble poem.

The post of Leading Monk was important in a Zen monastery in the early days for guiding and instructing all the monks of the monastery. Master Soju invited Master Mumon to his temple as a special teacher, or Leading Monk, and asked him to give teisho on old and modern koan. Master Mumon in response greatly promoted the Dharma and encouraged the Zen world, which had been tending toward inactivity. This explains the historical background that produced this book, the *Mumonkan*, and the role it was expected to play in those days.

MOKYO'S EPILOGUE

Bodhidharma came from the West, and he did not rely on letters. He taught: pointing directly to one's mind, attainment of Buddhahood by seeing into one's Nature. To talk of "direct pointing" is already detouring. Further, to speak of "attainment of Buddhahood" is falling into one's dotage quite a little. It is gateless from the beginning. How can there be any barrier? He is grandmotherly kind and spreads his absurd teaching. Muan [Mokyo] by adding a few unnecessary words makes the forty-ninth talk. Read attentively, with your eyes wide open, and grasp the core of the complication.

In the summer of the fifth year of Junyu [1245]
the second edition was brought about.
Written by Mokyo

[Mokyo, who called himself "Muan," was a warrior who spent most of his life as a general on the battlefield. He was deeply interested in Buddhism. He died in 1246 in the southern Sung dynasty.]

AMBAN'S FORTY-NINTH TALK

Old Master Mumon made forty-eight talks and criticized the koan of the ancient Masters. He is like a fried-rice-cake seller who makes the buyer open his mouth, pushes the cake in, and then makes it impossible for him either to swallow the cake or to spit it out. Be that as it may, Amban wants to make another piece in his red-hot oven and to present it following these forty-eight examples; he thus adds an extra piece. I do not know where the Master will put his teeth into it. If he can eat it at one swallow, he will emit light and shake the earth. If he is unable to do so, the forty-eight pieces that have been presented will all be burnt away. Speak at once! Speak at once!

The sutra says, "Stop talking, stop explaining. This Dharma is wonderful and beyond speculation." Amban says, "Where does the Dharma come from? How can it be wonderful? How can it be explained?" Not only was Bukan a chatterbox, but Sakyamuni was talkative to begin with. The old man produced ghosts and drove the descendants of hundreds and thousands of generations into entanglements, in which they are so bound that they are unable to escape. As for the extraordinary talks given so far, you cannot spoon them up; they will never be cooked even though you may heat them in a steamer. There may be some outsider with mistaken understanding who asks, "Ultimately, what is the conclusion?" Amban, putting his ten fingers together, says, "Stop talking, stop explaining. This Dharma is wonderful and beyond speculation." Suddenly he draws a small circle to represent the essence of "beyond speculation" and shows it to the people. The five thousand volumes of the *Tripitaka* and Vimalakirti's "Gate of Nonduality" are all in it.

> If it is said that fire is a light,
> Do not answer, nodding your head.
> A burglar knows another burglar.
> At any question they at once agree.
>
> *Early summer of the sixth year of Junyu* [1246]
> *Written by Amban at a villa by Lake Seiko*

[Amban was the pen name used by Tei Seishi. He passed the state examination for government officials and was noted as a capable politician and a man of high literary talents. He died in 1251, in the southern Sung dynasty.

Master Bukan was abbot of Kokuseiji on Mount Tendai. Once, when he saw Kanzan and Jittoku come to the kitchen of his temple begging for food, Master Bukan worshiped them saying that they were Monju (Manjusri) and Fugen (Samantabhadra) come alive. When Kanzan and Jittoku heard that, they called him, "Bukan the chatterbox!" and ran off.]

Glossary

AMITABHA. Name of a Buddha in Pure Land Buddhism; Amida Buddha.

ANANDA. One of Sakyamuni Buddha's Ten Great Disciples, known as the disciple "of the best hearing and remembering." Ananda was Sakyamuni Buddha's attendant for twenty-five years and later became Maha Kasho's successor.

ARAYASHIKI. A transliteration of the Sanskrit *alayavijnana;* the basic consciousness from which everything in the universe takes its shape. The Vijnaptimatrata philosophy (Wei-shih) calls it the Eighth Consciousness and explains it as the deepest consciousness of man.

AVALOKITEŚVARA. A Bodhisattva of Great Compassion in Buddhist mythology, who saves all beings from their sufferings and troubles, assuming various forms. In Zen, Avalokiteśvara is often taken as a Bodhisattva representing free Zen working.

BHAGAVAT. Title usually explained as having six meanings, but in the forty-eighth koan it may be taken in the sense of Buddha. "Bhagavats of the ten directions" means "Buddhas everywhere pervade the universe."

BHIKKHU. An ordained Buddhist monk.

BODHI. Generally in Buddhism bodhi is taken as the True Wisdom of satori attained by Sakyamuni Buddha. In Zen, however, bodhi, the True Wisdom of satori, is to be attained by each individual as the actual fact of his experience.

BODHIDHARMA. Was born in India and came over to South China by sea around 520 A.D. He settled at Shorinji in North China, where he did zazen and taught Buddhism based on the realization experience of each individual, rejecting mere academic approaches with too much emphasis on sutra studies. Bodhidharma is regarded as the First Patriarch of Zen Buddhism in China, which greatly developed thereafter, and is one of the most important Patriarchs in the history of Zen. Few biographical details are known about him. Bodhidharma is a favorite subject of Zen paintings symbolizing the unique characteristics of Zen.

BODHISATTVA. Originally, a being one step below a Buddha; a Buddha-to-be. Hence a Bodhisattva is one who, out of compassion, stays in his Bodhisattvahood to save all beings, without becoming a Buddha. Sometimes a Buddhist in training who disciplines himself following Buddha's teachings is also called a Bodhisattva. In Zen the word is used as a title of respect for one who has outstanding Zen working based on deep experience.

BUDDHA. This word can be used in three different ways, depending on the context. (1) It may refer to Sakyamuni Buddha, who was a historical person. (2) It may mean an enlightened one; with this meaning the word can take a plural form. Or (3) it may refer to the Truth experienced by an individual and lived by him as actual fact, here and now, in his daily life.

BUDDHA DHARMA. The Truth taught by Sakyamuni Buddha.

BUDDHAHOOD. The Truth as fact actually attained by each individual.

BUDDHA NATURE. The True Nature all beings were originally born with. It is the Absolute Truth that everyone has, regardless of whether he is enlightened or not. This True Nature transcends all forms of dualism. The experience of awakening to this Buddha Nature is called satori in Zen.

CHAIN OF CAUSATION. Describes man's state as living subject to transmigration due to his good or evil karma. It is considered that one who lives in ignorance is unable to become free of causation. Zen, however, has its unique way of dealing with this problem: he who awakens to his Original Nature transcends causation and lives his free life, not at all bound by causality.

DAIBONTENNO MONBUTSU KETSUGI-KYO. A Chinese sutra which is well known as the origin of "Sakyamuni Holds Up a Flower." Its Sanskrit original has never been found, and it is the general opinion of specialists that this work must be a later fabrication by some Chinese writer.

DAIGAKU ("The Great Learning"). One of the most valued and famous of the Confucian classics.

DAITSU CHISHO BUDDHA. A Buddha who appears in a metaphorical story in *Hoke-kyo.* Zen takes up Daitsu Chisho Buddha in a koan based on its own unique standpoint and asks us to grasp the live Daitsu Chisho Buddha experientially ourselves as the Reality of no-form, no-definition. Needless to say, this has no connection at all with the metaphorical background or philosophical interpretations of the particular Buddha.

DHARMA. Has various meanings: the Truth, the principle of the universe, teachings left by Sakyamuni Buddha, existences in the objective world in their as-it-is-ness, or the essence of Zen experience which has been handed down in the teacher-disciple transmission of the untransmittable.

DHARMA SANCTION. Approval given by a Zen Master to his disciple as his Dharma successor qualified to guide monks in training. The approval can be verbal, written, or take any form, but the one who gives it has to be an authentic Dharma transmitter himself in the traditional Dharma genealogy in Zen. The disciple who is given the Dharma sanction has to be one who has deep Zen experience, outstanding ability, and a refined personality, not yielding even to his teacher. The mere fact of having broken through a Zen barrier, or having studied Zen for a long time, does not qualify him for Dharma sanction.

DHYANA. Traditionally translated as "meditation" or "concentration." In Zen dhyana is used to refer to the experience of satori, which transcends moving and nonmoving, activity and tranquility.

DOGEN. Founder of Japanese Soto Zen. Dogen went over to China in the Sung dynasty, studied Zen under Master Tendo Nyojo, whom he finally succeeded, and introduced Soto Zen to Japan. He advocated "only sitting," and his Zen is characteristically attentive, sincere, and precise. Throughout his life Dogen stayed away from powers and authorities of the world and worked exclusively to promote Zen teaching and to train his disciples. He is famous as the author of *Shobo Genzo* (ninety-five volumes), and died in 1253.

FOX-ZEN. Sham or false Zen. It is a popular legend in Japan that foxes bewitch and deceive people, hence this derogatory term.

FUGEN. A Bodhisattva of Great Compassion in Buddhist mythology. Often Fugen ("great compassion") and Manjusri ("great wisdom") are mentioned together to show the two major workings of Buddha.

GE-PERIOD. One *ge* consists of ninety days, usually from May 16 until August 15, corresponding to the rainy season in India. Because Indian monks could not go on their training pilgrimages during that season, they stayed in one place, carrying on their training there.

GO. A traditional indoor game in Japan involving intricate maneuvering, played by two people on a board, with small black and white stones to mark control of territory.

GOTAMA. Surname of the Sakya clan. In Zen writings, Sakyamuni (the Wise Man of the Sakyas) is often called Gotama in this familiar and rather informal way.

GOTO EGEN. Famous historical records of Chinese Zen Masters, comprising twenty-two volumes. (*Go* of "Goto" means five, and a *to* is a lamp.) Master Daisen Fusai compiled *Goto Egen,* combining and editing the five famous books recording Zen history in China: *Dento-roku, Koto-roku, Rento-roku, Zokuto-roku, Futo-roku.*

GRDHRAKUTA. Mountain near the capital of Magadha in ancient India. It is historically famous as the spot where Sakyamuni Buddha used to give his talks to his many disciples and followers. In Zen, Grdhrakuta is the place where the Truth is alive and shining, transcending time and space—where talk of the Truth is being given. It is therefore said, "The meeting at Mount Grdhrakuta is definitely present here, now."

GREAT DEATH. To be dead through and through—to transcend both life and death.

GREAT DOUBT. This is not our ordinary intellectual doubt, but the fundamental doubt, or quest, of man that drives him to the last extremity of his dualistic discriminating consciousness in order to break through it in the Great Death. It is the inner spiritual doubt that motivates the student's search for the fundamental meaning of his existence, and finally revives him as a new man of real freedom.

HAIKU. Traditional short Japanese poem, consisting of 5–7–5 syllables.

HAKUIN. Hakuin Ekaku was born in 1685, ordained as a monk of Rinzai Zen when he was fifteen years old, and after going through hard and assiduous training, succeeded Master Shoju. He stayed at Shorinji, Suruga, near Mount Fuji, and throughout his life never became abbot of any big temple. He trained many able disciples, was a good writer, and is famous for his calligraphy and his many Zen paintings. He died in 1768 in his eighty-fourth year. He was a Master with an outstandingly sharp Zen spirit and ability who insisted on the vital importance of religious experience in Zen. He established "Koan Zen" and greatly promoted true Zen training and satori experience when the inner life of Zen was dying out in

Japan. Hakuin is highly respected as one of the greatest Masters in the history of Zen in Japan.

HEKIGAN-ROKU. A collection of one hundred Zen koan. The book is full of deep and superb Zen spirit and refined poetical insight, and is highly valued as "The First Book in Zen." Master Seccho (980–1052), who was a Zen Master with great poetical genius, selected a hundred famous koan and wrote a commentary poem on each of them. Master Engo (1063–1135) added his own preliminary remarks, comments, and epigrams on each. The *Hekigan-roku* was completed in 1125.

HOKE-KYO *(Saddharmapundarika Sutra)*. A Mahayana sutra written around the beginning of the Christian era. In it various beautiful and interesting metaphors and symbolic expressions are used to praise Buddha as the eternally unchanging Truth. It is also valued as an outstanding literary work. Followers of Zen often refer to and appreciate the skillful and beautiful metaphors and symbolic expressions used.

HOSSU. A tuft of horse or ox hair tied to a short stick about thirty centimeters long. It was at first used to drive mosquitoes away, but today is often carried by Zen Masters in ceremonies or rituals.

IGYO SCHOOL. School of Zen founded by Master Isan Reiyu and his disciple, Master Gyozan Ejaku. Their Zen is kind and prudent, uncomplicated, reflecting the beautiful teacher-disciple accord of the two founders.

II! Exclamation implying various complicated feelings such as a strong warning, or admiration in a sarcastic tone, or strong encouragement; its meaning will change depending on how and where it is used.

INO. Title of the monk at a Zen monastery who is in charge of the registry and rituals.

"IT." the essence of Zen. In Zen the Truth, or Reality, is often called "it," because if any name or label is given at all, the Truth is already missed.

JITTOKU. Known only through legendary stories. He led an unconventional and extremely free life and was often with Kanzan. His poems are much appreciated as reflecting a deep and lofty Zen spirit. "Kanzan and Jittoku" has been a favorite subject of paintings in China and Japan. In China they are respected as incarnations of Manjusri and Samantabhadra. *See also* KANZAN.

JODO SHINSHU. *see* PURE LAND BUDDHISM.

KALPA. An extremely long period of time. There are various ways of illustrating how long one kalpa is, but all try to indicate the longest possible time, beyond human comprehension.

KANZAN. Figure about whom only legendary stories are known. He is said to have lived in the caves near Kanzanji, leading an almost lunatic existence with his hair untrimmed and wearing rags. Once in a while he would come to Kanzanji to ask for leftover food, and would laugh heartily, sing aloud, and write his uniquely free and beautiful poems on trees and rocks. *Kanzan-shi* is a collection of his wonderful poems. *See also* JITTOKU.

KARMA. In a narrow sense, good and evil deeds, but usually interpreted as a causal power which is the origin of transmigration. Zen teaches one to be the master, or Absolute Subjectivity, under any circumstances and to live Truth everywhere. A Zen man thus transcends the restriction of karma and freely develops his Zen life.

KASHO (KASYAPA). One of Sakyamuni Buddha's Ten Great Disciples, known as the disciple "of the best discipline." After Sakyamuni Buddha's death Kasho became the leader of the Buddhist organization; he is respected as the First Patriarch in Zen transmission.

KASHO BUDDHA. Buddhist legend has a genealogical table of transmission (different from the fact of Dharma transmission), according to which there have been seven Buddhas in the past. Kasho Buddha was the sixth and Sakyamuni Buddha the seventh. A reference to Kasho Buddha indicates the far distant past—time immemorial.

KEGON. Philosophy which teaches that "one is all, all is one," and "In one infinitesimal particle the whole universe is embraced; in one instant eternity is included." Expounded in the *Avatamsaka Sutra.*

KEGON-KYO (GANDAVYUHA SUTRA). In teaching Buddha Dharma, this sutra gives a philosophical explanation of the Kegon philosophy. There are three different Chinese translations of the *Kegon-kyo.* Ever since the T'ang dynasty, Zen Masters have frequently made use of Kegon philosophy and its expressions in commenting on their own realization experiences and Zen working.

KEITOKU DENTO-ROKU ("The Transmission of the Lamp"). Highly valued historical records of Zen which include the biographies and the sayings and doings of about 1,700 Indian and Chinese Masters (Zen transmitters). It is called *Keitoku Dento-roku* because all its volumes were compiled in the first year of Keitoku in the Sung dynasty (1004).

KENSHO. The same as satori; see SATORI.

KOAN. Sayings and doings of ancient Zen Masters which freely and creatively express their Zen spirituality. In Zen training today, a student will do zazen with the koan given to him by his teacher. The koan serves as a tool to deprive him of all his intellect and reasoning power, to make him realize how utterly incapable his discriminating knowledge is of solving the fundamental question of man, and finally to drive him to the abyss of despair, from which he will revive as a new man. It is completely different from an ordinary question or problem.

KONGO HANNYA-KYO (the DIAMOND PRAJNA SUTRA). Mahayana sutra which teaches that all existences are empty and have no-self. Zen asks a student to grasp the philosophical teachings of this sutra as his own experience and to make use of this Truth in his daily life. The *Diamond Prajna Sutra* has been highly valued in Zen, especially after the Sixth Patriarch Eno.

KWATZ! A forceful exclamation. The word itself has no meaning, but in Zen KWATZ! is uttered to show directly the Zen spirituality that can never be expressed or explained in words.

MAHAYANA BUDDHISM. There are two major branches of Buddhism: Mahayana and Theravada. Mahayana Buddhism teaches one to be awakened to Dharma so that he may save others, while in Theravada Buddhism the emphasis is on the emancipation of oneself. Mahayana means "great vehicle."

MAITREYA. The future Buddha who, it is said, will appear in this world 5,670,000,000 years after Sakyamuni Buddha's death, to save human beings. Often a reference to Maitreya indicates merely the far distant future.

MANJUSRI. A Bodhisattva of prajna wisdom in Buddhist mythology, known in Japan as Monju.

MANTRA. A syllable, word, or phrase supposed to bring about mysterious, occult, and supernatural effects. In some religions, including some Buddhist schools, a mantra plays an important role and is considered to have absolute power. Zen, however, asks each individual to awaken to his True Self, and as Absolute Subjectivity himself to live in the world with a completely new outlook. Zen naturally does not rely at all on any secret or occult rituals such as the chanting of mantras or sutras.

MONDO. Questions and answers freely exchanged by Zen monks, based on their Zen point of view. Mondo clearly show their Zen spirituality, and are totally different from ordinary dialogue.

MOUNT SUMERU. The mountain in the center of the universe in the mythological cosmology of ancient India. The Nine Mountains and the Eight Oceans (Scented Ocean) surround the foot of Mount Sumeru, and the Four Dhyana Heavens spread over them. Zen refers to the Eight Oceans and the Four Dhyana Heavens to indicate symbolically infinite space and infinite height. Mount Sumeru is also often mentioned as a symbol of the absoluteness of Truth.

"MU." The Truth that transcends both affirmation and negation, subject and object. Although *Mu* literally means No or nothingness, it is not a relativistic No standing over against Yes. It is the Truth experientially grasped by each individual by casting away all his discriminating consciousness. "Mu" is a temporary name given to the ever unnamable "it."

NANTO KOAN. A complicated koan given to a Zen student so that he may be free in developing his Zen working in differentiation. Unless one's Zen eye is clearly opened, he will be unable to grasp the real significance of a nanto koan.

NATA. A demon king in Indian mythology. He is four-faced, eight-armed, and has supernatural power.

NATIONAL TEACHER. Title of honor and respect given to a Zen Master who became the emperor's teacher.

NEMBUTSU. To recite aloud the name of Amitabha Buddha. Various philosophical explanations of Nembutsu are given in Pure Land Buddhism.

NII! Exclamation used to emphasize a strong demand or to stress the meaning.

NIRVANA. Satori of no-life, no-death. Ignorance is completely extinct, and the True Wisdom has been attained. Though taken from a Sanskrit word, its meaning in Zen is not the same as in Sanskrit.

NIRVANA HALL. A room for sick monks in a monastery. It is also called Enjudo, which means "life-prolonging hall."

NIRVANA SUTRA. This sutra records Sakyamuni Buddha's final teaching, prior to his death, that we should thoroughly extinguish the fire of our passions and ignorance and thus attain satori. Zen takes up this sutra from the experiential standpoint and maintains that each one of us must actually have the experience of dying in his small self full of passions and ignorance, and then revive as the True Self of satori personality.

NYOI. A stick about fifty centimeters long, usually carried by a Zen Master.

ORYO SCHOOL. School of Rinzai Zen founded by Master Oryo Enan in the Sung dynasty in China.

PARAMITAS. *Paramita* means literally, "to reach the other shore," that is, to attain Buddhahood. The Ten Paramitas are usually known as the ten virtues which a Bodhisattva practices to attain Buddhahood: offering (generosity), precepts (morality), endurance (patience), striving, dhyana (meditation), wisdom, skill in knowing the right means, vow (determination), will power, and prajna (wisdom) working. In Zen, however, the virtues would not be the means of attaining Buddhahood (although they might lessen distractions from zazen), but would be the consequences of that attainment.

PATRIARCH. Those Masters in the Zen tradition who have transmitted the true teaching of Sakyamuni Buddha as his Dharma successors. They are respected as true Zen men who lived Zen Truth themselves.

PRAJNA. In Buddhism generally translated as "True Wisdom." In Zen prajna means the experience of satori, in which Wisdom and its working are one. One can attain prajna when all of his dualistic discriminating consciousness has been cast away.

PRAJNA WISDOM. The True Wisdom that transcends all forms of dualism, such as subject and object, enlightenment and ignorance, good and evil, time and space. The Fundamental Wisdom from which the Truth develops its free working.

PRECEPTS. Commandments traditionally given to Buddhists so that they may train themselves and lead decent, orderly lives by observing them. Zen maintains, however, that no-precepts is the true Zen life, because precepts are the natural outcome of a Zen man's enlightened life. In other words, a Zen man creates precepts as he develops his free daily activities.

PURE LAND BUDDHISM. Branch of Japanese Buddhism founded by Saint Shinran. Its exact name is True Pure Land Buddhism. They believe in salvation by Amitabha and in their rebirth in the Pure Land after death.

RI-BI. Literally, *ri* means separateness and *bi* means subtle or mysterious. Ri refers to the Truth of the universe, Reality, the Self, or One, which is separate from all names, forms, and distinctions. This ri, or Truth, freely works and develops its activity in infinitely different ways, in accordance with varied circumstances of differentiation. This creatively free working is called bi.

RINZAI. One of the most famous Zen Masters in the T'ang dynasty in China (died in 867), founder of the Rinzai School of Zen. Master Rinzai developed his activities in northern China, but his Zen spread all over that country. His transcendentally free and superb Zen working, with deep experience and dynamically sharp spirit is unparalleled in the history of Zen. He upheld Zen of "great ability and great working," and is famous for his KWATZ! cry.

RINZAI-ROKU. A book containing Master Rinzai's sayings, doings, mondo, and biographical records. It is valued as "the foremost Zen book," compiled by his disciple Enen.

RINZAI ZEN. School of Zen founded by Master Rinzai Gigen during the T'ang dynasty in China. Rinzai Zen is noted for its creative and wonderful Zen working in differentiation, based on an incomparably free, lofty, and sharp spirituality which reflects the characteristics of the founder.

RYOGA-KYO (the LANKAVATARA SUTRA). A Mahayana sutra which represents Buddhist teaching in India; a rather indiscriminate collection of Mahayana thought. Zen takes up especially the "prajna wisdom of Self-realization" taught in this sutra. It is said that Bodhidharma handed down this sutra to Eka, the Second Patriarch.

SAH! Exclamation often used as a cry of encouragement or warning; the meaning differs according to circumstances.

SAKYAMUNI BUDDHA. Founder of Buddhism, respected as the Buddha. Etymologically, Sakyamuni means "the wise man of the Sakyas." He is a historical person who was born as a prince of the Sakya clan, ruler of a small kingdom in northern India. He left worldly life when he was twenty-nine years old, seeking the Truth, spent six years in ascetic discipline, and later attained Enlightenment while doing zazen under a bodhi tree near Gaya. For forty-five years after the attainment of satori he traveled extensively in India, taught Dharma, and developed his religious activities. He died in 486 B.C. His teaching has greatly influenced the religions and culture of India. Later Buddhism spread to China and then to Japan. Zen does not regard Sakyamuni Buddha as an omnipotent being, but respects him as the great ancestor, first in human history to attain satori.

SAMADHI. Originally a Sanskrit word meaning to concentrate one's mind on one point so that the mind remains still and quiet. In Zen, samadhi is used in a somewhat different sense, that is, it is the pure working of no-mind that has transcended both action and quietude.

SAMANTABHADRA. Known as Fugen in Japan. See FUGEN.

SANGHA. A harmonious gathering of Buddhists. In some cases sangha refers to the working aspect of the Truth.

SANZEN. Recurrent occasion on which the Zen student presents the result of his Zen training to his Master face to face, one to one, based on the absolute Zen point of view. In Rinzai Zen, to come to a Zen temple and do zazen, or listen to a Zen talk, or get advice from a Zen Master on various problems is not called sanzen, as is often misunderstood today.

SATORI. Zen experience of awakening to one's True Nature, in which all dualistic, discriminating consciousness has been cast away; the experience of dying to one's small, relativistic self and being reborn as a True Self, often translated Enlightenment. It is a fundamental change of the whole person and not a mere psychological insight, emotional ecstasy, or result of philosophical speculation.

SESSHIN. Intensive training period at a Zen monastery (literally, "training the mind"). Basically, every moment is sesshin for a Zen student. At a Zen monastery today, however, each month a sesshin period of a week is set apart for monks to devote themselves exclusively to carrying on their assiduous training.

SHIN BUDDHISM. True Pure Land Buddhism in Japan.

SHINRAN. Founder of Jodo Shin-shu (the True Pure Land School of Buddhism) in Japan. He became a Buddhist monk at an early age and studied Buddhist teachings extensively, but could not get peace of mind. Later he became a disciple of Honen and established his faith in "Other Power Nembutsu." He was exiled for years, during which he spread his teaching in remote provinces. At the age of sixty he returned to Kyoto, where he propagated the Pure Land teaching, and died there in 1262 at the age of ninety. Shinran says, "In one instant of faith, one's salvation is confirmed," and his genuine faith and direct attitude has a penetrating lucidity similar to that of Zen Masters.

SHIPPEI. Bamboo stick from about sixty to ninety centimeters long; usually carried or kept at hand by a Zen Master.

SHOBUTSU YOSHU-KYO ("Sutra of the Buddha Assembly"). A sutra in which extracts from various sutras are recorded. Except for the fact that the story of "A Woman Comes Out of Meditation" is taken from it as a Zen koan with its unique significance in Zen training, this sutra has no connection with Zen.

SHOTO-ROKU. Historical records consisting of biographies, sayings, doings, and poems of twenty-four Chinese and Japanese Masters of the Rinzai Zen School. Compiled by Master Eicho in 1501 in Japan.

SOTO ZEN. School of Zen founded by Master Tozan Ryokai during the T'ang dynasty in China. Its teaching is based on the oneness of satori and training. Soto Zen is known as Zen of deep and sincere spirituality, characterized by moderation and profundity.

SUMERU. See MOUNT SUMERU.

SUNYATA. Originally a Sanskrit term meaning emptiness: nothing in existence has entity of its own, therefore everything is empty. Later, sunyata became one of the principal teachings of Mahayana Buddhism, with a broader meaning. In Zen it is used to indicate the experiential fact of having transcended all forms of dualism.

SURAMGAMA SUTRA. Consists of answers given to the question as to what kind of samadhi practices may be needed for a Bodhisattva to attain satori. Practical instructions are set forth concerning the training to be followed. In Zen, the sutra is studied as a guide in "upward training"; also in "downward training" it is appreciated as showing the natural development of Zen life.

SUTRA. Usually a written teaching of Sakyamuni Buddha. Zen, however, insists on "transmission outside scriptures, not relying on letters." For Zen, the religious experience of each individual is the absolute requisite, and verbal or written teachings are of secondary importance. Zen does not depend on any particular sutra.

TAO. Name referring to the essence of Zen; the Truth experientially grasped by each individual. The meaning of Tao as used in Zen is not exactly the same as the Tao of Taoism.

TATHAGATA. One of the ten names for Sakyamuni Buddha; it means "the one who has come as the Truth."

TEISHO. Zen talk given by a Zen Master to the monks in training in a monastery. The Master directly and concretely presents his Zen spirituality and makes his comments on it. Teisho is not the occasion for philosophical explanations, scholastic lectures, or sectarian preaching.

TENJIN. A snack, refreshments. *Ten* means literally to "light up," and *jin (shin)* means "mind."

TEN PARAMITAS. See Paramitas.

TENZO. Title of the monk who is in charge of cooking and food supply at a Zen monastery.

THERAVADA. One of the two major branches of Buddhism, the other being Mahayana. Theravada Buddhism teaches the emancipation of oneself, abiding by precepts; the term means "the Way of the Elders."

TOSOTSU HEAVEN. Mythological abode of a Bodhisattva who is expected to become a Buddha in the future. It is said that the Bodhisattva Maitreya is living in Tosotsu (Tusita) Heaven now.

TRIPITAKA. The whole collection of all Buddhist writings, covering sutras, precepts, and commentaries. Zen insists on the vital importance of the realization experience, and although this can be expressed in infinitely different ways, such expressions in writing are all shadows of the Truth.

UNMON SCHOOL. School of Zen founded by Master Unmon Bunen. Unmon was a great

Master active from the end of the T'ang dynasty into the Five Dynasties; his school is noted for its strictness and loftiness, reflecting the founder's characteristics.

VIJNAPTIMATRATA. Philosophy teaching that all existences and phenomena assume their temporal appearances due to the work of consciousness, which is the basic source of mind. According to this philosophy, outside of consciousness there is no existence.

VIMALAKIRTI. In Buddhist mythology the hero figure in the *Vimalakirti Sutra*, a layman with great Zen ability.

VIMALAKIRTI SUTRA. Sutra of which Vimalakirti is hero: a rich, learned nobleman and lay Zen Buddhist who fully attained the real spirit of Mahayana Buddhism. The sutra consists of his mondo with Buddha's disciples, who were bound by various dogmatic interpretations and teachings and were not free at all. After Vimalakirti's warning to them, the story in the sutra develops to his final mondo with Manjusri on the subject of the Dharma of nonduality from the experiential standpoint. Zen maintains that each student should grasp the Dharma of nonduality as the fact of his experience, and live his life as Vimalakirti here, now.

VIPASYIN BUDDHA. First of the Seven Past Buddhas. Reference to Vipasyin Buddha often indicates infinitely distant past.

WAKA POEM. Traditional short Japanese poem, consisting of 5-7-5-7-7 syllables.

WORLD-HONORED ONE. Name of respect given to Sakyamuni Buddha, the founder of Buddhism.

ZAZEN. Can be traced back to the Sanskrit word *dhyana*, which means quiet meditation, but has quite a different significance in Zen. It refers to the Zen practice of assuming a full-lotus sitting posture, with straight back, and casting away all discriminating consciousness, thus ultimately awakening to one's True Self. Sometimes the word is used in the same sense as Zen.

ZAZEN WASAN. A song in Japanese consisting of forty-four versified lines, written by Master Hakuin. In it he taught what Mahayana Buddhism is, using simple and clear language so that the general populace could easily understand and recite it. The song describes how important it is for each individual to have the realization experience and to develop his Zen life.

ZEN. Truth experienced and testified to by each individual as the fundamental basis of one's personality, after sincere and assiduous search and training.

INDEX

Index